Shaky Palaces

THE COLUMBIA HISTORY OF URBAN LIFE
KENNETH T. JACKSON, GENERAL EDITOR

SHAKY PALACES

Homeownership and Social Mobility
in Boston's Surburbanization

MATTHEW EDEL,
ELLIOTT D. SCLAR,
and DANIEL LURIA

New York   Columbia University Press   *1984*

The authors and publisher wish to thank the following people and organizations for their kind permission to reproduce material in this book from the works cited:

Harvard University Press for the map of "Boston, Cambridge and Their Environs in the 17th Century," drawn by Erwin Raisz for Samuel Eliot Morison, *Harvard College in the 17th Century.* Copyright 1936 by the President and Fellows of Harvard College. Copyright © 1964 by Samuel Eliot Morison.

Harvard University Press for Sam B. Warner Jr., *Streetcar Suburbs: The Processes of Growth in Boston, 1870–1900.* Copyright © 1962 by the President and Fellows of Harvard College.

"Little Boxes," words and music by Malvina Reynolds. Copyright © 1962 Schroder Music Co. (ASCAP). Used by permission. All rights reserved.

The Print Department at Boston Public Library and the Bay State Society of Model Railroad Engineers were the sources for all the historic photos; Tetsuji Uchiyama drafted the maps and charts.

Funding for this project came from National Science Foundation Grant No. GS-36880 and National Institute of Mental Health Nos. 33379 and 22407

Library of Congress Cataloging in Publication Data

Edel, Matthew.
Shaky palaces.

(Columbia history of urban life)
Includes bibliographical references and index.
1. Housing—Massachusetts—Boston Metropolitan Area—
History.   2. Real estate development—Massachusetts—
Boston Metropolitan Area—History.   3. Home ownership—
Massachusetts—Boston Metropolitan Area—History.
4. Social mobility—Massachusetts—Boston Metropolitan
Area—History.   I. Sclar, Elliott.   II. Luria, Dan.
III. Title.   IV. Series.
HD7304.B7E34   1984   305.5′13′0974461   84-178
ISBN 0-231-05626-5
ISBN 0-231-05627-3 (pbk.)

Columbia University Press
New York   Guildford, Surrey
Copyright © 1984 Columbia University Press

Printed in the United States of America

*Clothbound editions of Columbia University Press Books are
Smyth-sewn and printed on permanent and durable acid-free paper*

This book is *"for the kids,"*
especially:
Corey, Gareth, Keir,
Jason, Jennifer, and Stephan.

2002

CONTENTS

TABLES

Appendix Tables

FIGURES

PREFACE

This book has a long history. When we first became concerned with the issues which are the substance of this study, it was not as scholars but as political activists in the Boston/Cambridge area of the late 1960s and early 1970s. That activism and "the Movement" of which we were a part met with astounding successes and dismal defeats. These mixed results suggested to us a greater need for understanding the economic and social forces which shape local politics. The conventional wisdom of the time, both mainstream and radical, provided inadequate explanations of the events which swirled around us. We realized that nothing less than a comprehensive study of the entire process of neighborhood formation in Metropolitan Boston would help us understand the complexity of the issues.

The decade of the 1970s was not kind to the neighborhoods of Boston. Communities were pitted against each other in a series of battles in which race was the dominant concern. Our research and analysis began to suggest that as intractable as was the question of race alone, the tensions in Boston had even more complex historic roots. We developed notions of how suburbanization, fiscal balkanization, and an ideology of perpetual social mobility had entrapped and to some extent controlled the people of Boston and, by extension, other American cities. We were led back into the history of how these forces had developed. They were, we discovered, neither the benign and automatic fruits of progress, as suggested by the analysis of mainstream social science, nor were they, despite their consequences, simply created for social control as a more radical analysis might suggest. Rather they emerged from a complex process of confrontation and compromise. This book is the result of our investigations and thinking.

In the Fall of 1983, as we were completing this book, Bostonians elected the first mayor in over three decades to have a base in neighborhood political action. The runner-up was also a product of neighborhood political struggle. The candidate of the city's financial elite finished a distant third. The Flynn-King contest was both a hopeful sign that local groups could produce a viable progressive leadership for a major American city and was also a warning that unity between diverse urban groups is hard to achieve, particularly where racial polarization is possible.

In the meantime, the gloss on the suburban lifestyle has begun to tarnish. Problems which had been seen as central city evils in the 1960s, and which we saw emerging in an inner ring of older suburbs when we were active politically around 1970, began to manifest themselves over a wider area. As one suburban planner told us, "Any problem you can name in the city we now have in the the suburbs." Actually, the suburbs, like the central city itself, presented a mixed picture. While the fastest population growth in the region was still in the newer suburbs at the metropolitan fringe and spilled over the New Hampshire border, some inner areas were being revitalized or gentrified. Other suburbs and inner city areas were doing worse. These areas are characterized by population loss, abandonment, crime, fiscal strain, and the like. A more intangible malaise or anger, sometimes expressing itself in radical forms and sometimes in conservative forms (both of which were tapped by tax reform movements in the 1970s) was also spreading. The particular campaigns in which we had been involved still seem today to be portents of the complexities of local movements which will continue into the forseeable future.

In seeking understanding, we have been led down complex paths of research and analysis; economic, historical and political. We have been fortunate to find both the support of many exciting collaborators, and a few dedicated funding sources. We also have been the beneficiaries of excellent critical comments wherever we presented our preliminary results. Our interpretations are of course our own, indeed sometimes representing compromise among our individual positions. But our research stands as a collective product.

Our first debt of gratitude is to the residents of metropolitan Boston who, in the 1960s, raised a practical critique of urban institutions, giving scholars like ourselves the crucial hints about where to seek understanding. Next, we thank those agencies which facilitated out particular research. The Center for the Study of Metropolitan Problems (Metro Center) of the National Institute of Mental Health, and the Economics

Program of the National Science Foundation, made generous grants to us, through the Center for the Study of Public Policy, Cambridge, Massachusetts, Brandeis University, and Queens College. The support of Dr. James Blackman at NSF is especially acknowledged. We also were able to carry out some of our researh as part of the Massachusetts Public Finance Project, funded by a grant from the Office of Economic Opportunity to Lynn Economic Opportunity Inc.

A very special debt of gratitude is owed to Dr. Elliot Liebow who directed the Metro Center at NIMH. Elliot Liebow gave us more than the financial means to carry out our research. He inspired us to do creative work. His agency challenged young scholars to march to the sound of their own drummers as they rode roughshod over the conventional boundaries of social research. Liebow never asked if it was history or sociology or economics. Rather he asked that the work be substantial and important. If American social science someday breaks out of its present confining boundaries, we have no doubt that it will owe some debt to both the intellectual and bureaucratic courage of Elliot Liebow. It never ceases to amaze us that such a vital and intellectually exciting enterprise as Liebow's could survive as long in a federal agency. Our thanks to Joan Schulman, Hal Vreeland, Lew Long, and Maury Lieberman, who all helped make the Metro Center such a special place in the 1970s.

Stephan Thernstrom generously shared the data from his study of fathers and sons in turn-of-the-century Boston with us. Without such generosity it would not have been possible for us to translate our economic findings into "people" terms. Richard Sennett and Jonathan Cobb shared early findings from their studies of working-class families in modern Boston. These findings were invaluable in helping us to formulate our ideas about the process which we were observing.

Robert Engle gave us access to his unpublished indices of property values and helped us with index methodology.

We also owe thank yous to Sam Bass Warner Jr. and Lloyd Rodwin. Although we didn't always see eye to eye with them on historical interpretation, we nonetheless are grateful for the paths they blazed and directions in which they pointed our work. They have both given personal support and encouragement to our "revisionist" enterprise. We are in debt to these world-class scholars.

We appreciate the assistance of the many busy people in county and town offices, libraries, historical commissions, and newspapers for giving us access to their information. In particular we would like to thank Greer Hardwicke of the Brookline Historical Commission for help in finding some truly rare old photos of Metropolitan Boston. We would also like to acknowledge R. Eugene Zepp of the Print Department of the Boston Public Library for the time and effort he gave us as we searched through the fine photo and print collection which he supervises.

The two senior authors of this book, Edel and Sclar, served as principal investors of the separate grants. Luria was one of the three senior research associates, and continued to work afterward on parts of the book. Barbara Sproat and Charles Levenstein, the other two senior research associates, performed mighty labors gathering and interpeting data, and helping us with our thinking. More important, they worked with us to help a large research staff coalesce into a group that, for the length of our grants, was a most exciting collaborative venture. Elaine Gordon was the administrator, executive secretary, and den mother for most of this period. Her contributions are beyond measure.

We thank the rest of our project staff, a truly remarkable group of people, whose enthusiasm always made our work a pleasure. Some of their contributions are drawn on for subsections of this work. Others contributed less quotable but just as important pieces of data, sometimes dredged from the dustiest of town records. Of this group, Lisa Dennen, William Mass, Tom Holzman, and Alan Matthews worked with us the longest and contributed valuable ideas and insights. Others served more briefly but with equal vigor and effect. The first summer, at the Center for the Study of Public Policy, the staff included Sandy Altman, Steve Karp, Minna Strumpf, Barbara Brickman, Sheldon Stein, Steve Allison, John Kryzwicki, Susan Adelman, Steve Glazier, and David Ashkenazi. At Brandeis, Paula Alberghini, Carol Dalpe, Mary Daly, Margery Davies, Celia Dunlap, Dolores Goode, Michael Harran, Sarah (Heubsch) Greenberg, Steven Kersten, Richard Krushnic, Peter Lemos, Donna Lind, Steven Miller, Kathy Schoen, Peter Skerry, Stephen Woods, and Libby Zimmerman, along with Herman Thomas, Jane Goldstein, and Jeffrey Bass from Queens College, all performed most notably. Nancy Lyons, who was an administrator for the Center for Study of Public Policy, continued to work with us editing parts of our manuscripts.

Staff from several other projects were also involved. At the time of the present project, Sclar was also co-principal investigator along with Raymond Torto of the Massachusetts Public Finance Project. Many of the ideas which shaped the present work were also tested in the research undertaken as part of that effort. We would like to thank the staff of that project for their contributions, too. Ted Behr and Jere Chapman as project directors defined much of the research effort. The highly competent work of Maralyn Edid, Timothy Greene, and Hub Stern of the full-time staff is also gratefully acknowledged. Research assistants at MIT including Takenore Inoki and Eugene Kroch assisted with calculations. Tetsuji Uchayama of Columbia University drew the fine maps and charts for this volume.

Although they were not on the project payroll, several other students of ours played an intellectual role in the project. Rosina Becerra's dissertation at Brandeis applied some of our ideas to the study of college admissions, giving us a major piece of evidence. An active student seminar at MIT debated some of these ideas, and carried out some of the original research under Edel's direction. Greg Palm, Robert Miller, Jay Jacobson, Charles Movit, Laurie Nisonoff, Geoffrey Handler, Stanley Smilack, and Alan Mathews were all actively involved. Undergraduate theses by Paul Brophy at MIT and Adam Goodfarb and Marc Draisen at Brandeis also contributed to this project.

Bernard Gronert, Executive Editor at Columbia University Press, gave us encouragement at times when we thought we would never pull it together. Even better, he gave us a good contract. In the final stages of work Leslie Bialler of Columbia University Press worked patiently with us to turn a very large amount of material into a finished product. We would like to thank him for an effort above and beyond the call of duty.

In addition to Elaine Gordon, we woulld also like to thank Barbara Isaacson at Brandeis University and Marga Walters, Nancy Situla and Anne Rosen at Columbia University for typing and retyping the many 'rafts of this manuscript.

Some of the most exciting input came from questions posed to us at meetings and informal conversations, where we had to subject our visions to scrutiny. The comments of K. H. (Nick) Schaeffer, Evan Stark, Robert Goodman, Steve Rose and Peter Marcuse were particularly important in pointing us in new directions, which are implicit in the way in which the second part of this book comments on the first half. And our ongoing dialogues with Candace Kim Edel and Nancy Aries have influenced our ideas and this book in uncountable ways.

Given all the support and collaboration which we enjoyed on this project, the only thing left to us is to take responsibility for all the errors which still remain.

Matthew Edel
Elliott D. Sclar
Daniel Luria

A Note to the Nontechnical Reader

This book contains several technical sections. These present numerical data analyzed using such formal statistical methods as regression and principal components analysis. We felt this material was necessary to test our new hypotheses about property value depreciation and entrapment. The reader who is interested in historical or political aspects of suburbanization may safely skip over the following sections and still follow the argument:

Part C of chapter 3.
Parts A, B, and C of chapter 4.
Parts B, C, and E of chapter 5.
Part B of chapter 8.
The appendices.

Shaky Palaces

PART ONE

Up the Down Escalator
The Worker as Homeowner

Introduction

A muse of many parts, the American dream is to get a good education, land a job with upward mobility, achieve success and, high on the list, to buy a home of one's own.[1]

AMERICA is a country of homeowners. Over 60 percent of American families own their houses.[2] A larger percentage are homeowners at some point in their lives.[3] Achieving this status takes up a large proportion of most families' expenditures. The typical American family traditionally spent about one-fourth of its income on shelter and related expenses; now that figure is rising.[4] Buying a house generally requires that a family invest more than half of its total assets, and go deeply into debt. Only for the wealthiest families does the equity in their homes fall to a small proportion of total assets.[5]

Many Americans feel these expenses are warranted by the economy, security, and comfort of a home of one's own. Economists comparing ownership and rental under current conditions recommend the former as less costly to most families.[6] But even more important, the home has been celebrated for more than a century both as an object of affection— "Home, Sweet Home"—and as a solution to problems:[7]

Owning a home is not merely a vehicle for better shelter. It is also supposed to increase one's wealth. "Relax! At least your home is worth more today than it was yesterday," claims a cigarette advertiser, urging us to enjoy our good fortune by smoking its product.[8] A planner writes that "the entry of millions of the depression poor into the middle class was aided by a rise in home values between the 1930s and 1950s."[9] A realtor cites "the ever-increasing value of your house due to inflation,"[10] and exhorts the reader to remember that

Images of City and Suburb: People buy a home to secure a better environment "for the kids."

Boston Elevated Railroad photo courtesy of
Bay State Society of Model Railroad Engineers.

Child on an Inner City Street at the Turn-of-the-Century (most probably Boston's West End).

Photo by Elliot Sclar.

Suburban Little League Game, Newton Mass., 1977.

> ever since the early American settlers bought land for two cents
> an acre, real estate has provided the largest single means to
> the accumulation of individual fortunes in this country. . . . .
> Accordingly, it would appear to be more than ordinary pru-
> dence for the individual investor to consider most seriously
> the many proven ways to build a fortune in real property.[11]

Homeownership is also supposed to bring other opportunities; many homeowner neighborhoods are favored because of "better" schools, and hence better career opportunities. People buy a home "for the kids" for this reason. It is not surprising that politicians and planners have sought to cope with the poor by making them homeowners. Former Vice President Hubert Humphrey urged legislation permitting those collecting welfare to own homes, saying "people could become property owners, which would provide them with equity and pride."[12] President Richard Nixon's advisors expressed similar thoughts in proposing "expanded" homeownership.[13]

Homeownership is considered in judging societies. One of the most frequently voiced defenses of American capitalism is the widespread ownership of housing. As *Time* comments: "Builders boast that the U.S. is the only nation in which a private house has been brought within the reach of the broad middle class. Quite true—and well worth keeping that way."[14]

American opinion even seems to *require* people to own homes. Home-buying is a "rite of passage" in the anthropological sense, according to Constance Perin. You must buy a house to be perceived as a full adult member of society. Thus, she writes, "In American society the form of tenure—whether a household owns or rents its place of residence—is used in categorizing and evaluating people, in much the same way that race, income, occupation and education are."[15]

The widespread attainment of homeownership in the United States might well indicate that Americans are realizing their dream. The current boom in home values would apparently confirm that the dream is in good shape, at least for the majority who already own homes. Yet there are signs that American homeowners are dissatisfied with their lot these days.

Specific complaints vary. Costs of housing repair and maintenance—even just the difficulty of getting a plumber—are common gripes. These problems are bitter, yet blackly humorous enough to be laughed at.

Property taxes are a more serious complaint—articulated not by Erma Bombeck but by Howard Jarvis.[16] Lack of services for home operation has led "stable citizens" to hurl snowballs at mayors and to deposit garbage on city hall steps. The fear of declining property values is important in the backlash against minority advancement.

The quality of homeowner life is also questioned. The suburban pattern of building, which accompanied the spread of single-family homeownership, leaves residents (especially housewives) isolated.[17] Associated commuter patterns are polluting, and wasteful of time and energy. More broadly, people seem to feel cheated because owning a home, supposedly the hard-won token of secure middle-class status, does not solve other problems.

The complaints of the American homeowners are often dismissed as the minor grumbling of the affluent. The extent of the property tax revolt was greatly underestimated until the passage of Proposition 13 in California in June of 1978. Up to that time, there was little criticism of Raymond Vernon's view that "the clear majority of Americans who live in urban areas look on their lifetime as one of progress and improvement . . . and confidently expect their children to do better still,"[18] or of his prediction that even problems of taxation could not bring the middle class "shouting into the streets."[19]

Even today, a typical academic response to homeowner discontent is Jencks' comment that

> The only significant group of individuals with long-term debts are homeowners, and they have been the biggest winners in the current round of inflation. Few homeowners are grateful for this inflation-induced windfall, however. Instead they spend their time whining about the fact that property taxes have gone up.[20]

This dismissal, however, is too glib. It is true that, even in the current recessionary period, American standards of living are among the highest in the world. But this does not mean that prosperity is either secure or universally generalizable. Nor does it mean that even the better-off homeowner is free from real and severe economic pressures.

In this book we consider some ways in which homeownership has failed to live up to its reputation. We conclude that the fear felt by the homeowner, particularly the moderate-income owner, has a basis in economic experience.

Our examination has focused on two aspects of the homeownership dream—property value increase, and the relationship of homeownership to social and economic mobility. These aspects are crucial because they link the housing market with the wider organization of American society. Wealth increase, and other possible contributions the home can make to mobility, affect the overall distribution of social rewards. Our focus allows us to examine whether homeownership has contributed to a widening of general economic opportunities and to a broadscale increase of equality; whether it has increased as a passive result of progress in other areas of society; or whether it has been a form of false mobility, *detracting* from progress in other areas, or at least *distracting* from its absence.

The results of our study can be summarized as follows. Homeownership proves to be an adequate vehicle for housing people, but it is a poor vehicle for upward mobility. A home represents an asset to its possessors. It gives them space in which they can live their lives with more autonomy and independence. But it is a costly asset. Buying a house is the single greatest investment made by most families. Though it is an asset, a house is a highly depreciable one. The value of the investment depends not only on how well the family cares for its home, but also on the amenities of neighborhood and the overall level of employment in the region in which the home is located. As a result, despite the high cost of the asset, there is little the individual family can do to protect its investment through independent action.

It requires collective action to keep the external environment hospitable for the family investment. Such action is difficult to muster in part because ownership *is* individual. As a result, American families frequently find themselves in the position of buying and selling homes not so much to achieve upward social mobility as to stave off downward mobility caused by changes in the larger environment. This attempt to run up a down escalator has been most characteristic of the suburbanization movement in this country.

We shall analyze homeownership as a facet of metropolitan growth. The American pattern of homeownership cannot be understood without also understanding the importance of where homes are located. At least within metropolitan areas, there is a clearly definable hierarchy of better and worse locations for homes. A continual process of creation of new, and generally prime, housing locations, is matched by the deterioration of some older residential areas. This deterioration often precedes, and accelerates, the deterioration of the homes as physical structures. In most

American cities, the expansion of housing has been a process of suburbanization. This has involved an extension of built-up areas, an increased range of commuting, private subdivision of hitherto unurban-
ized land, the creation of political jurisdictions outside earlier city borders,
and the social stratification of neighborhoods.

We shall study the experience of homeownership as an aspect of one
city's suburbanization. Boston was the city chosen for several reasons.
We knew the area and had lived and worked there. Our involvement in
community controversies over land use had alerted us to many of the
problems we shall study. But personal familiarity and convenience were
joined by several impersonal factors favoring Boston.

First, the area was one of the earliest in the United States to undergo
the process of suburbanization. As of the turn of the century, Boston had
more daily commuters entering its borders than New York and Chicago
combined.[21] Thus, a study of Boston affords us the opportunity to examine the process of metropolitan growth from its inception down to the
present. Many metropolitan areas in the United States did not follow in
this process until the advent of the truck in the 1920s, or even until cars
made possible the automobile suburb after World War II. Second, Boston has been the location of many major previous investigations of different aspects of the urbanization process. Thus our research had much
previous distinguished work to build upon.[22] Last, the New England states
in general and Massachusetts in particular have very detailed historical
sources of local-level data from which it is possible to infer a great deal
about social and economic change.[23]

The studies we report here cover the entire history of Boston, but they
focus on the period of most intensive suburban growth. The origin of
this movement is itself somewhat controversial. Sam Bass Warner dates
the origin of streetcar suburbs from the introduction of horsedrawn street
railways.[24] For some purposes, we have placed that beginning in the
horsecar era, with the 1870 census. However, for most purposes we find
it makes more sense to consider the era of mass suburbanization as beginning with 1890. This is the time of the mass introduction of the electric street railway or trolleycar. It is also the census year which fell in
the midst of a social struggle (chapter 9) which we argue led to the political acceptance of mass suburbanization. Most of our analyses run
through the 1970 census. We suspect that this census marks, like 1890,
a real turning point in the history of suburbanization. While suburbani-

zation and the spread of homeownership continued in the 1970s, they did so under more constraints in terms of energy and land availability, and in the face of more limited political acceptance than had previously obtained (chapter 11). Whether or not history proves us right in declaring 1970 the end of the era of mass suburbanization, our analysis of the 1890–1970 period at least allows examination of suburbanization through a long enough period (two major booms and an intervening depression, as well as World War II) that the main outlines and results of the process can be inferred.

The book has two main divisions. In part I, we consider the main outlines and results of Boston's suburbanization during the 1890–1970 period. Chapter 1 presents a theoretical overview of the process of metropolitan growth and the subsequent devaluing of older neighborhoods. We present this in the context of a discussion of a number of factors which in American society devalue the assets workers are able to accumulate. Much of what appears as social mobility is interpretable instead as the accumulation of devaluing assets: a process that leaves workers perpetually climbing a down escalator, and that may at times be an important concomitant of social control in a class society. Chapter 2 introduces the history of metropolitan Boston. Suburbanization in the streetcar and automobile eras is placed in the context of a longer history of development and localized property devaluation.

Chapters 3 and 4 present evidence on changes in house and land values over the past century. Chapter 3 traces values of samples of properties in specific neighborhoods and towns in the inner core of the metropolitan area; chapter 4 uses cross-sectional land and house value gradients, taken at different times in history, to estimate average rates of property value change for different parts of the metropolitan area. These chapters demonstrate that while there has been a wide range of gains and losses to homeownership in different times and places, relative asset depreciation has not been uncommon.

Chapter 5 takes a look at the same process from the perspective of people rather than property values. It draws upon and follows up on work pioneered by Stephan Thernstrom, using the sample of fathers and sons which he developed for *The Other Bostonians*.[25] Our research includes those fathers and sons lost to Thernstrom's study because they moved from Boston to its new suburbs. Our study shows that for the turn of the century period, homeownership did not add to career or overall class

mobility. Some evidence from other studies is presented for more recent periods, which tends to confirm the same finding.

Part II places the suburbanization process in a wider context. In a sense,
the analysis of part I takes the development of homeownership and suburbanization as a given phenomenon, and looks at its consequences; part
II attempts to explain the phenomenon in the context of a "materialist"
or "conflict" theory of historical change. Suburbanization is related to the
economic evolution of the society as a whole, and of class conflict in particular. We also consider the costs and benefits of the American pattern
of suburbanization, as it evolved at the turn of the century, from the
perspective of working class interests, and consider at least some of the
strategic options created for labor by the contradictions of the suburban
process.

Chapter 6 is a critique of existing explanations of suburbanization, both
orthodox and radical, emphasizing the extent to which their individual,
voluntarist perspective simply attributes whatever happens in metropolitan growth to individual desires. These explanations thus end up blaming homeowners for their own problems. The following two chapters examine the role of less atomistic actors who helped shape the process.
Chapter 7 analyzes three major land developers and their activities in
three distinct periods of Boston's history; chapter 8 considers the role of
government in the urban development process. Both chapters suggest
the importance of large-scale institutional factors in the suburbanization
process.

But what shapes the institutions that condition suburban growth and
devaluation? Chapter 9 suggests an explanatory and evaluative framework, based on theories of class conflict. It then reanalyzes the origins
of suburbanization in the light of this theory. We suggest that the American suburbanization process has been the result of a compromise solution to class differences, which was affected in the particular historical
circumstances of the late nineteenth century and reinforced in the 1930s
depression. Chapter 10 attempts to evaluate the outcome of that compromise from a working class perspective. Chapter 11 explores ways in
which contradictions in that process are now appearing, and examines
some of their implications for new political coalitions.[26]

ONE

Mobility and Entrapment in a
Market Metropolis

WHAT are the pressures and frustrations that affect the home-owner? A few years ago, we met a man whose experiences provide part of the answer. An engineer in his forties, he had grown up in a big-city neighborhood. Now he lived in one of the more distant suburbs. The move, he said, had been difficult. He spent little time discussing the break with his old neighborhood, apart from saying that it had been "an incredibly long trip." But the move both to the suburbs and into a profession beyond the dreams of his parents left him dissatisfied. As we talked, a welter of frustrations and complaints came tumbling out.

Since graduating from an engineering school, he had had at least twenty jobs. Most were in defense-related companies scattered around two states. Often he had a two-hour commute. Despite the promise of independence that came with his education, defense contracts determined where his work would be, what it would be, and even if he would have a job. There was, he said, no way out of that solution. "No one really beats that," he said. "If they think they do, they're crazy."

Nor was his life at home problem-free. Although he moved to the suburbs to give them opportunities, his two teenaged daughters refused to talk to him. And just as his mortgage was finally being paid off, he complained, the NAACP was demanding that low-income housing projects be put up in the meadows next to his house. His tax rate was rising. In short, he felt completely victimized.

He talked with wonder about a young woman who came to work in his office. She had been hired to type a manual to go with one of the company's products, some sort of military equipment. As she was typing, she realized what the product was, and asked, "Say, is this place part of the military/industrial complex?" After a moment of silence, someone finally said that yes, he supposed you could call it that. The woman turned off the typewriter, got up, said she was quitting, and left. Telling the story, the engineer turned and said, in a perplexed tone, "And you know, she didn't even pick up her pay for the three hours."

A. Mobility as Entrapment

This man had experienced what the sociologists call social mobility. He had "made it" in terms that he had set for himself in his youth. But his education, his professional job experience, and his suburban property did not give him enough independence to ponder long about whether he was right or wrong in his choice of jobs or in his fear of new neighbors. Although he knew that others might raise these issues, he could only try to survive as best he could.

The engineer, a man who has "made it" in the popular sense of the term, is at a different social level than "Rica Kartides," a maintenance man interviewed by Richard Sennett and Jonathan Cobb:

> When Kartides first began work as a maintenance man, he lived in an apartment where he received strict instructions to use the back door, and never let his children play on the empty lawn surrounding the building. He reacted to this by making heroic efforts of time, work, and personal sacrifice so that he could own a home of his own . . . a sanctuary, a living space where in being only with his immediate family, he could not find his place in society thrown in his face over the smallest matters. The home is therefore for him the center of freedom. The freedom is, however, quite restricted. He has bought property in a suburb of Boston in order to be free, yet must work fourteen houurs a day at two jobs in order to pay for his "freedom," leaving him scant time to enjoy his home. He bought property in order to create an independent sphere of living for himself and his family, yet, in the very process, finds himself sacrificing his social life to pay for this privilege. He makes repairs on his house, a modest one, to make it decent;

yet since he is taxed for his improvements, he must work even longer. Since his house, like many residences in or near American cities, lacks access to good public transportation, he must buy a car, and that, too, takes money. And more money, for a man who cleans or paints houses or sells shoes, comes only from longer hours spent on the job and away from home.[1]

Like our engineer, Sennett and Cobb's working class subjects see themselves as having achieved some mobility by hard work. They, too, are confused and threatened when the mobility does not bring them security. They resent welfare recipients, who are "getting away with something I never got away with." They resent their own children, who seem to learn only enough to look down on their parents' less educated status but not enough to achieve a status that will validate the parents' efforts.[2] These reactions are not so different from the engineer's attitude toward his children and toward the secretary who quit.

Similar feelings among American men have become the stock in trade of American dramatists over the last several decades, from Arthur Miller's salesman, Willy Loman, to Philip Hayes Dean's black auto workers.[3] Less has been written about working class women in this context, but Lillian Rubin's studies suggest their attitudes are similarly shaped.[4] Whether reported by the sociologist or the dramatist, the picture is the same. Each of these people, working at different economic levels and living in different neighborhoods, is in some sense "trapped." They are limited by economic pressures in what they feel they can accomplish, fearful of losing ground as real threats close in around them. Yet each has, in another sense, achieved some small place for himself and his family, and some measure of stability. Despite their anxieties, each can go on believing in the goodness of the system because it seems to allow personal mobility.

Enough in the experience of these people tells them it is at least plausible that society offers opportunities to those who will take them. The notion that they themselves are to blame for not having achieved more and that those who are below them in a social hierarchy are to be blamed even more can be derived from their suspicion that mobility works. The result is a divided and hardworking population.

Such an outcome is very convenient for those who employ these workers. They end up with a highly motivated, yet fragmented, labor force. The capitalist system, or any economic system for that matter, needs some sort of motivation to keep people working. Unless force is to be used (a costly method), people have to have some faith that they can accomplish something. Otherwise, more of them may follow the typist in the engineer's office and walk off their jobs. Worse yet for the employers, they may unite and walk off demanding higher pay for all or even more fundamental changes in the content of work. Providing some mobility can help prevent this. Giving people different rewards to defend from each other and some limited prizes they can win by hard work allows the owners to receive profits and to reinvest them undisturbed. But the outcome may be hell for those who are left to strive and to fight it out at the various levels within the workforce.

Two important works have made the argument that capitalism depends on a stratified workforce. David Gordon has examined divisions among employed workers while Frances Piven and Richard Cloward have discussed the usefulness to capitalism of maintaining a group of the very poor.[5] Gordon discusses "dualism" or the stratification of the laborforce into high wage (primary job security) and low wage (secondary security) sectors. Employers, he predicts, "will find it more and more in their interest to attempt to forge a highly stratified labor market, with at least several objectively defined economic classes, in order both to fill secondary jobs and to forestall the development of revolutionary class consciousness."[6]

Similarly, Piven and Cloward describe how defining a group of unemployed or underemployed welfare recipients, and regulating them through government policy, benefits employers as a class. In periods of social unrest, welfare can be used to cool the threat of discontent; once the immediate danger is past, it can be used to enforce low wage work.[7] Defining different groups of the poor as worthy and unworthy, and maintaining harsh conditions for welfare recipients, not only regulates the poor themselves, but also upholds incentives among the rest of the work force to avoid going on the welfare rolls. As a result of these conditions, the authors contend, the relief system "has made an important contribution towards overcoming the persistent weaknesses in the capacity of the market to direct and control people."[8]

These and other studies show how even partial barriers between different segments of the work force can be useful to the capitalist system, and why corporations or governments may wish to maintain these barriers.[9] But they do not fully describe how the inequality and control over the workforce are achieved. The existence of some mobility in the forms of movement to suburbs, acquisition of new consumer goods, attainment of higher educational levels, and entry into white-collar or higher skilled jobs, is not emphasized, and at first seems to argue against the applicability of these studies to American life. After all, to the many who achieve some mobility, or think they have, a rigid view of stratification will not ring true.

However, limited mobility is itself a useful complement to stratification. If some people are able to attain new assets—consumer goods, houses in the suburbs, educational degrees, and upgraded jobs—they will have additional incentives to work for the system. On the other hand, if these assets are not good enough to buy their owners' way out of the work force, if they are not widely enough distributed to wipe out stratification, and if they lose their value over time so that people must continually strive toward new goals just to keep their place within the stratified work force, then employers can reap all of the advantages of stratification plus the advantages of mobility incentives.

It is well known among both managers and among critics of the system that giving out some mobility rewards to those who try hardest, or appear to do so, secures incentives and hence keeps workers working.[10] It also makes those who receive some rewards fearful of losing them.

If mobility is widely believed to be the norm, failure of many people to advance may itself be useful to maintaining stability. Sennett and Cobb point out that those who do not advance are convinced that they have failed to do so because of their own weaknesses. But more are eligible than can possibly be rewarded. It is at this point that injured dignity serves a purpose: it maintains the legitimacy of a reward system that cannot deliver on its promises. By injuring human dignity society weakens people's ability to fight against class-imposed limits on their freedom.[11]

This outcome is also contingent on the fact that few workers are rewarded, although many seek the rewards. (If too many are rewarded, the class system must change; if too few strive, the incentives are not working.) The ideal situation requires either, as Berger found in looking at one factory, that 1500 workers strive for six foremen positions, or as Chinoy found in a plant he observed, that most of the workers aspire to become small businessmen themselves.[12]

B. Asset Devaluation and Partial Mobility

How can an economic system foster mobility and the work incentives that it requires, while at the same time it forces people to keep "in their place" in order to maintain an unequal distribution of income and power? The logical answer is that the system must with one hand give real resources that the recipients value, while with the other hand it devalues or neutralizes the gains, so as not to upset the existing stratification.

This devaluation or neutralization may be done in several ways. One method is to directly liquidate the asset. Another is to distribute the good so widely among the population (if it can be done cheaply enough) that no permanent status is achieved. The overall distribution of the good can raise overall standards of living, but could still benefit disproportionately the very top group if that group employs the others and if the main benefit of the good is to make people more efficient employees.

In the latter case, the ownership of new assets by persons in the middle and lower strata of the economy will mean *partial mobility* (the acquisition of specific goods), but not *class mobility* (the decrease in inequality between the different classes or strata) or even, in most cases, *total individual social mobility,* the movement of individuals from one class or strata to another. If the aim of mobility is to increase an individual's autonomy, or to free the individual of control by the system, then despite some improvements in the living standard, partial mobility will be only a false mobility, a pseudomobility. If partial mobility is seen as a substitute for other routes to individual social mobility or to class mobility, it becomes a trap.

Nonetheless, to the extent that partial mobility is necessary to prevent a fall in individual class position, and to the extent that it does improve the standard of living of some or all members of the lower or middle strata of society (even without changing relative positions of individuals), it is advantageous to the individuals who achieve it. In this sense, the gains of partial mobility are real. In describing partial mobility as pseudomobility, we do not mean to criticize those who have striven for it, or attained it. Our aim is to understand why and how opportunities are limited, not to blame the victims of limited opportunity for doing the best they can. Only if better alternatives are opened—the subject of our final chapter—can partial mobility cease to be the best option people face.

Four assets in particular have offered partial mobility to people, only to depreciate or fall short of offering class mobility or total individual social mobility; they are education, occupational position (white-collar status), consumer goods, and suburbs. We shall consider each of these briefly before examining how the growth of metropolitan areas has contributed to the devaluation of assets, particularly housing.

1. Education

It is by now commonplace to say that schooling has been one of the investments most sought by American working families. Although much of the pressure for the expansion of educational systems has come from the business elite, workers also have demanded more or better schooling, often at considerable economic cost. The result has been a continuing rise over the past century in the average number of years people have attended school.[13] The theme of parents sacrificing to invest in their children's schooling runs through many of the Sennett-Cobb interviews.[14]

A plethora of studies, many of them generated during the post-Sputnik era, have claimed that educational investments are considerable.[15] Higher lifetime earnings, they argue, justify the cost of more years of schooling. For the most part, studies look at one generation, comparing the incomes of those who have received varying levels of schooling. In effect, they ask what one individual gains, given the amount of schooling attained by other members of his (or occasionally her) generation, and given the structure of the labor market. They end up proving that an individual who fails to receive an education will suffer in terms of jobs or income.

What these studies do not ask, however, is this: if all members of a generation receive more education than their parents, will this improve the well-being of all? To be sure, some studies have attributed beneficial effects to the greater education of all by correlating general economic growth with increased years of average schooling.[16] However, this correlation in no way proves cause and effect. It is possible that the increase in the education of all will simply leave everybody in the same relative and absolute position they were in before the education. Or, a less extreme possibility, education may have positive effects on overall economic growth, but have little effect on *relative* social mobility.

The experience of some specific groups—aerospace engineers, for example—suggests that a skill or credential may yield good returns in job opportunities at first, but later become a ticket to unemployment as more people receive the same credential. Studies of the returns to higher education in general in the postwar period suggest that these returns were shrinking in the mid-1960s before prolonged recession led to widespread unemployment of college graduates in the 1970s.[17]

These studies and observations are, of course, limited to small groups within the population. A more general doubt about the contribution of educational investment to general social mobility has been raised by Jencks. He argues on the basis of a large statistical sample that if parents' status is taken into account, education adds little to the explanation of children's final social position. His study seems to imply that if one stratum of society educates its children more in order to advance their relative position, the strata above will maintain the difference by increasing the education of their children. Staying at any given level of education would thus imply a relative decline in one's position in the distribution of educational levels.[18]

Jencks raises some doubts as to whether education itself has an effect on the job attained (even assuming parental status controls educational levels). However, a study of educational levels required for and associated with specific jobs suggests that those who do not raise their educational levels above that of their parents may be forced to accept *lower* status jobs than their parents. Comparing the labor force in 1950 and 1960, Berg and his associates found that educational requirements for many jobs were being raised, although the jobs were unchanged, and that increasing numbers of people were educationally overqualified for their jobs.[19]

2. Occupations

Just as the value of education in terms of job potential is depreciating, so too is the value of some jobs in terms of status and relative income. The evidence here is less clear-cut, and some leading students of the occupational structure of the United States hold that the relative status of different occupations has remained relatively stable over time. Nonetheless, there are some signs that the increased proportion of the labor force in white-collar and service occupations has been accompanied by a decrease in the relative status of these occupational groupings. As a result, the attainment of white-collar status, like the attainment of primary, high school, and perhaps university diplomas, may well be an example of acquiring a depreciating asset.

The depreciation of certain occupations is not a new phenomenon. The declining position of the individual owner-operator of a small farm was an important factor in American politics of the late nineteenth century, and although in the twentieth century some larger farmers secured their positions through political support, many more farmers lost their land. The median income of farmers and farm managers was still declining relative to that of factory operatives in the postwar period. Similarly, the relative income and status of the small business proprietor has declined. In the early part of the twentieth century, several categories of workers (including clerical workers, gas and electric employees, postal and other Federal employees, and ministers) who began with above-average wages, had their real wages decline relative to the average for the population.[20]

A comparison of the median incomes of employed males in 1947 and 1965 showed that the incomes of several higher-income groups, including professional and technical workers, clerical workers, sales workers, and nonfarm proprietors, rose less rapidly than incomes of operatives. The incomes of craftsmen-foremen, independent professionals and technicians, and managers and officials rose even more rapidly, while farmers, farm laborers, nonfarm laborers, and service workers fell further behind.[21]

These changes were to some extent reflected in the public's notion of the status of different occupations. A comparison of the public's rankings of different occupations in 1947 and the late 1960s showed that, within the middle levels of occupations, such blue-collar crafts as electrician and plumbers had risen in status, while such white-collar positions as salesman had fallen.[22]

A study covering a longer time, although grouped by industry and not by occupational level, also supports the hypothesis of devaluation of white-collar occupations. Lebergott's series for annual earnings of full-time employees 1900–1960 shows lower rates of average earnings increase for trade employees, professional employees, and employees in finance, insurance, and real estate than for employees in construction, rail, and water transport, mining, manufacturing, or utilities.[23] The mix of white-collar staff and laborers in some of these fields may have changed over time, so that the wage increases shown for manufacturing, for example, may be inflated by an increase in the clerical staff of factories. Nonetheless, earnings comparisons at least suggest the plausibility of the depreciation hypothesis.

That depreciation of the relative position of at least some occupations (not all of them white-collar) occurs as new groups enter these occupations is implicit in Hiestand's study of minority employment opportunities: occupations showing the greatest relative increase in black share of employment were occupations that were diminishing in total employment.[24]

3. Consumer Durables.

Educational levels and occupations are obviously of considerable importance for any study of social mobility. But they are not the only assets people struggle to obtain, only to have them decline in value. A similar pattern exists in the distribution of consumer durables.[25] Many of these goods are luxury goods when they first come on the market. Thus they can be acquired only by a few favored families, and they provide their owners particular satisfactions and benefits: the mobility of the automobile, the communications access of television and telephone, the time-savings of some household appliances. Many more families begin to save so they can buy these goods and gain status by being among the first purchasers in the neighborhoods.

As these goods become widely distributed, of course, the status is lost. What is more, individual ownership of many of the goods comes to be a necessity. As more people acquire them, public services or businesses that had provided an alternative service lose customers, and go out of business. Thereafter, family survival without the durable good becomes extremely difficult. This process is most obvious in the case of the automobile, which was a luxury for some years after it was first on the market. The design of new neighborhoods on the assumption that residents would have automobiles and the decline or destruction of public transit systems in older areas have made the family automobile a necessity. Those without one in many areas face severe handicaps in access to jobs, shopping areas, and other facilities.

The process is not limited to the automobile. The refrigerator has eliminated both ice-delivery services and, in many areas, the neighborhood store that could be used for shopping for one meal at a time. The scope of communal laundry services is being circumscribed. More important, perhaps, the nation's wage structure is evolving toward a pattern that requires two earners in a nuclear family, in place of one wageearner and one house-worker, a practice made possible by some of the "labor-saving" appliances.

Thus, if one compares a family today with a family one or two generations earlier, the apparent increase in living standards implicit in the acquisition of a larger inventory of consumer durables may, at least in part, be illusory. A good portion of the investment in these durables may be buying the family only enough transportation and access to information, and enough household maintenance for it to subsist.

4. Neighborhoods and Housing.

The private home, our main concern in this book, is in one sense a consumer good, an alternative shelter to the apartment, the boarding house, or the communal dwelling. The private home is also an investment in the land on which it is located, and an admission ticket of sorts to a particular community and political jurisdiction. It is thus subject to depreciation of various kinds—not only to physical depreciation. It could decline in value if its property is affected by changes in economic activity or access; if the surrounding community deteriorates; or if public services decline and taxes rise in its political jurisdiction, or even if other communities duplicate its services. Although the values of houses can, and of course do, also rise, a number of forces in the economy tend to reduce their value.

Like the high school diploma, the white-collar job, and the automobile, the owner-occupied home and suburban community have over time become more widespread assets of working families. The proportion of families owning homes has risen from about one-third in 1900 to about two-thirds today. The proportion of the population living in the suburban jurisdictions of metropolitan areas has likewise risen, from a small minority to a population greater than that of central cities or of nonmetropolitan areas. But the increased availability of homeownership and of suburban communities has *not* fundamentally changed the distribution of wealth, income, or power in America. We argue that middle-income families were frustrated in part in their attempts to narrow the gap in distribution of wealth because their investments—houses in suburban communities—depreciated relative to the investments of the rich in stock or commercial properties.

C. The Question of Property Values

Because our argument hinges on the evolution of property values, the topic requires some additional explanation at the outset. Our results contradict a popular view that property values must always increase in real terms, a conventional wisdom particularly reinforced by the recent inflation. We argue in this section that the standard view is indeed not supported by either the historic record discussed in this book, or by current economic prognoses.

Faith in rising property values is an old American belief. Benjamin Franklin commented on a man who advised him not to open a printing house because "the expense would be lost; for Philadelphia was already a stinking place, the people already half-bankrupts."[26] In his autobiography, Franklin described his own business success, and poked fun at the cynic's advice, noting that the man "continued to live in this decaying place . . . refusing for many years to buy a house there, because all was going to destruction; and at last I had the pleasure of seeing him give five times as much for one as he might have bought it for when he first began his croaking."[27]

John Gardner, former Cabinet member and founder of the Urban Coalition and Common Cause, sees Franklin's faith as crucial to our national character and success. He cites Franklin's comments approvingly, noting that Franklin, "like generations of Americans after him . . . had extraordinary notions of what lay in store for his city, his nation, and himself."[28]

Benjamin Franklin's faith in increasing property values may well have been reinforced by his own career. In the area of real estate development, he ventured his investments often and successfully. However, he need have looked no further than the experience of his own faither, Josiah Franklin, to learn that increased building values were not the uni-

Selling the Dream.

Boston Elevated Railroad photo courtesy of
Bay State Society of Model Railroad Engineers.

Early Ad for homes, on the transit line to Everett. Housing in the early streetcar
suburbs was particularly subject to devaluation.

versal rule. The homeowning experience of the elder Franklin followed a pattern which, we shall argue, is more typical than that of his son.

Josiah Franklin lived in Boston's North End. In 1712, he bought a four-unit property, at what later became Union and Hanover Streets, for £320.[29] When his widow died in 1754, the property was advertised for sale by the executor, John Franklin, and by William Homes. After almost a year had passed without a buyer, Homes bought out Franklin for £188 13s 4d. Three years later, he sold the property for £266 13s 4d. Franklin's heirs, in other words, received a much smaller sum than Mr. Franklin and his widow had paid for it. Even the price paid by the eventual buyer to Mr. Homes was below the 1712 purchase price.[30]

This is not to say that Mr. Franklin necessarily made a bad purchase. He and his family lived in the home for several decades. The other houses on the site presumably brought in some rent. He may even have conducted his tallow-handler's business from the site. But the house itself did not bring fortune to him or to his heirs. Despite the growth that Boston had had and was to have as a city, the house did not increase in value while it was in the hands of the Franklin family. If hard work and good luck allowed at least one of Josiah's sons to prosper, the fate of Josiah's house was not part of that good fortune. Ben Franklin should have known that not all properties go up in value.

Many homeowners are, like Josiah Franklin, working people who cannot select their homes on the basis of speculative plans. They must buy on the basis of what they can afford, and in locations that are convenient to their work. For such homeowners, the experience of the elder Franklin may not be unusual.

Our data from the Boston metropolitan area from 1890 to 1970 bear this out. While total land value in the area has increased over time, in the already built-up areas it has not tended to increase in "real" terms, that is in terms of what its value will purchase. Rather its value has floated with the rate of inflation. While some developers and homeowners have received high returns on their real estate investments, the average homeowner has not. The majority of workers, building up equity over time, have kept the savings they made out of their earned incomes, but they have not made enough on their real estate to divert money from capital gains on their homes to other investments. A substantial number have actually lost money on their houses.

This historical record is worth remembering. Even in the 1970s bull market some neighborhoods' values declined, absolutely in some cases, and at least relative to the rate of inflation in others. There are areas of widespread abandonment in many major cities. And there is reason to suspect that, more generally, future gains for homeowners are being overestimated.

Housing depreciation has effects on the ability of low or moderate income Americans to defend themselves in other areas besides the housing market. While ownership of a home in the "right" areas may be an entry ticket to certain educational opportunities, the price of housing in these areas rations these tickets to the more affluent: it does not really promote mobility. And educational opportunities can depreciate along with the housing with which they are associated. Our empirical studies show that homeownership does not add to families' careers, wealth, or class mobility, and in some cases its effect may even be negative. Furthermore, the entire system of home-ownership and the associated focus on individual mobility may militate against other forms of progress for working or moderate income groups.

Over a century ago, Friedrich Engels warned working class organizations that homeownership schemes could prevent general gains for labor by dividing the working class, and entrapping the home buyer.[31] Engels' arguments are too narrow for direct application to modern suburban homeownership, but his general lesson holds. Homeownership itself can be a contradictory phenomenon, bringing both real gains and real problems to working class homeowners, in part cooling off discontent and disrupting organization, but in part creating new opportunities. Responding to this critique, we attempt to assess both the gains and the costs homeownership has led to for working Americans.

There is a problem, however, with the interpretation of homeownership as a simple form of social control. It is one thing to argue, as we have been suggesting, that suburbanization and the spread of owner occupancy have been useful to the capitalist class. But that does not prove *how* this "useful" system came into being. Government and large-scale land developers played major roles in the creation of Boston's suburbs. But there is no evidence that these groups, however powerful, ever "plotted" to entrap Boston's workers in threedeckers and tract homes. Rather, they acted out of expediency within an economic and political system. If one does not believe in some sort of "structural" analogue to the invisible hand that bends all actions to the ends of a ruling class,

then it is not enough to say that showing who benefits establishes pre-
sumptive cause (see chapter 6). Further, if suburbanization were only
the result of manipulation, it would probably not work for long. People
do not like to feel manipulated. We shall argue that suburban policy, to
a large extent, came as a compromise outcome to a conflict between capital and labor in the late 1800s. That may explain its origin. But even
then, its continued workings, at least until it came into crisis in the 1970s,
required something more for its effect. It had to operate more or less
automatically, once established, so that continued manipulation of a visible sort was not needed.

If depreciation of assets earned by workers—the "down escalator"—
facilitates capitalist accumulation and stability, it is particularly useful if
it occurs *automatically*, without the overt supervision that would anger
those whose assets are being devalued.[32] In the United States, both the
market, insofar as it operates on its own, and the Federal structure of
government, which creates a sort of market competition between governments at the state and local level, create the conditions for this devaluation to occur in a way which appears automatic—even "natural"—
if one does not enquire too closely as to the origins of the institutions
involved.

How, then, do these forces operate during what one might call the
normal processes of suburbanization? In the next section, we consider
the major forces at work in the growth and suburbanization of cities—
forces which have been analyzed at length in the field of urban economics. After a brief summary of these forces, we turn to some specific areas
in which government, particularly at the local level, has played a major
role in shaping the suburbanization process in the Boston area (and elsewhere). These are the acceleration of the "filtering" of housing, the provision and financing of commuter transportation systems and routes, and
the creation and financing of local public services within different local
jurisdictions of the metropolitan area.

D. Growth of the Urban Economy

In the last two centuries, cities have grown where capitalists have found
investment to be profitable. Their investments have provided the funds
for buildings and infrastructure; their demand for employees has pro-

vided the jobs that draw people to look for work. At times, the arrival or availability of low-wage laborers in a city has attracted investment; and in all cases, the actual work of construction and production has been done by working people (from hod carriers to architects) and not by their employers' money. Nonetheless, economists have considered a city's "economic base" to be not its working people but those sectors of investment that bring money from outside.[33]

The investments that fueled city growth have at times been directed toward industrial production, at times toward the establishment of commerce and financial institutions. In some cases, the so-called service sector, including everything from universities to military bases to recreational resorts, has been the key sector. (In the case of Boston, commerce and finance have been the most important elements in the economic base, but educational and industrial development have also been important.) Whatever the particular base may be in a given city at a given time, urban growth is likely to generate a number of advantages for those who can initiate businesses there. These advantages ("economies of agglomeration") include access to common public services—water, sewer, and power networks, intercity transport facilities, and social service facilities—and access to a growing diversity of business and labor skills within the metropolis. These advantages make the city more productive, attracting more investment and creating possibilities for further city growth, for more jobs, and for the advantages of location in the city to be reflected in rising rents or land values.

If the city is growing within a larger, evolving economy, the extent to which it will grow is determined not only by the productivity gains it may make on its own, but also by the overall economic system. The growth of capitalist economies has been marked by an increasing degree of centralization of capital. Over time, some cities have emerged as the headquarters for the successive waves of regional, national, or multinational corporations or financial institutions.[34]

The growth of metropolitan areas, in response to the continued accumulation and centralization of capital, can be seen as involving—and in some cases directly contributing to—a process by which new opportunities are opened to workers, allowing some partial forms of mobility, which, however, *then are devalued.*

First, the accumulation of capital, assisted by the economies of scale allowed by urbanization, permits production and cheapening of new consumer goods. But growth also turns some of these goods into necessities, forcing more people to work for wages.[35] Second, the concentration of capital requires greater paper work, thus increasing opportunities for white-collar work and allowing partial mobility of occupation. But the growth of these occupations eventually devalues the status, working conditions, and pay of clerks.[36] Third, the growth of white-collar and technological tasks requires more schooling, opening up educational opportunities. But the expansion of education devalues its relative import.[37] Finally, in a sense, the city itself (or at least parts of it) may be devalued by its own growth.

This last effect comes about partly because size and growth themselves create problems for a city. With more people and businesses located in an areas, public services and transport facilities may become congested; air and water may become polluted; rising rents force people to crowd into more densely packed residential areas. These sorts of costs are generally outweighed, from an accounting viewpoint, by the economies of agglomeration. Total land value, average wages, and average profits all tend to be greater in larger cities than in small ones. But the costs and benefits of growth may not be equally distributed. The higher wages of urban dwellers are matched, at least in part, by higher costs of living. The value of land in different neighborhoods of the city may not grow at the city's average rate. And therein lie still further reasons why the apparent opportunities for mobility opened up by city growth may turn out only to be opportunities to acquire depreciating assets.

E. Suburbanization

Suburbanization involves the development of new residential zones or "rings" around a central district where jobs are clustered. In general, construction in these new areas is designed initially for upper-middle income people. Lower income people are left to find housing in older areas of the city, vacated by those moving to the newer suburbs. In an ideal-type hierarchy of suburbs, newer and farther suburbs are those of highest status; those older and closer to the city are of intermediate and successively lower statuses; and the areas nearest to the central business district are of the lowest status, "inner city."

This suburban pattern is not inevitable even in a capitalist city. If there is no room geographically for new suburbs to be built within commuting range, or if land is so tightly monopolized at the periphery as to be priced out of the market, new construction must take the form of densification, not suburbanization. Or, if the upper income groups prefer central locations, and can repair or rebuild houses there to their specifications, the "American" pattern may be altered or reversed, and come to resemble the "Continental European" or "Latin American" pattern.[38] If centers of employment are decentralized rather than clustered, a much more complex pattern may emerge. If planning is not constrained by market prices, all sorts of patterns, logical or illogical, may emerge.

The suburban pattern can be sustained in the United States for a number of reasons described in the theoretical literature of economics and sociology. Most economists' models of city form are based on explorations of the tradeoff of more space for less access as real income rise and urban sites grew crowded.[39] The sociological study of suburbanization sees the value structure of the American upper or middle classes as compatible with the choice of spaciousness and newness over neighborhood density, maintenance of traditional homes, or easy access to city centers.[40]

These insights leave us dissatisfied. That the values of those with the most money to spend are compatible with the suburban pattern is a necessary condition for its existence, but not a sufficient explanation of how it came into being. Income and overall population growth *can* lead to new construction in both new and old suburbs, but it can also lead to rebuilding, or to the squeezing in of greater numbers of people in central city areas, so it is not in itself an explanation of why a metropolitan area can come to have a larger proportion of its population living in the suburbs.

Nonetheless, social scientists have generally suggested that rising incomes and transportation costs are the major market factors affecting suburbanization. Residence and property ownership in the suburban system are correlated with income, wealth, and other aspects of status.[41] Although the correlations are far from perfect, wealthier individuals are more likely than others to own homes in newer, more distant areas. However, as workers begin to accumulate any savings, homeownership is one of the first areas into which they direct their money. (Education of their children and saving through pension programs are the others.[42]) Although many workers can afford to buy only older homes, some have been able to afford smaller new homes in tract developments, at least in some historic periods. Meanwhile, middle class incomes, as they have grown, have also created a market for new suburban homes.

The aging of buildings and related facilities in the older areas, and the competition of newer construction in other areas, are at the heart of the models that have been developed by housing experts concerning a concept called "filtering." According to this concept, the capitalist market provides housing for low income people not by direct construction of low-cost homes, but by the sale or rental to them of older homes which have declined in value. Most of the literature presents this process as both normal and beneficial. It is said to come about because those with higher incomes prefer new, larger homes. As these homes are built, those moving to them leave older buildings available to those just below them in income. They, in turn, move out of somewhat older housing, and so on.[43]

Now it is clear that for this process to work, the housing in each age category must decline in value. As a group moves out into newer and better housing, the demand for its previous housing at its old price is reduced. Its price must therefore fall, and it is the fall in price that allows lower income groups to buy better or newer forms of housing. The filtering process is thus beneficial to each subsequent group as consumers, since it allows them to acquire better living space.

But it is a process that also penalizes each group of investors. Each homebuyer is investing in assets that will be devalued by the competition of newer homes. Thus the model that links income growth with suburban growth *also* shows how an asset devaluation process can occur automatically.[44]

A factor that may combine with filtering and transport to cause the decline of values of older, more centrally located neighborhoods is the presence of what economists call "local externalities," such as how the upkeep of one house affects the desirability of neighboring houses, how the presence of people with special skills (e.g., physicians with offices in their homes) in a neighborhood may make it a desirable residence area, and how noise or local pollution sources may make a neighborhood dirty and undesirable.[45]

Older neighborhoods with diverse land uses may provide many advantages. In general, the suburbanization and filtering process in the United States acts in many ways to remove the positive amenities and to create negative external influences on values. Filtering itself erodes incentives to keep properties in poorer areas in good repair because owners, particularly if they are not residents, know relative values will decline.[46] The spatial growth of cities in the United States also creates negative external effects on transportation. The construction of new radial highways or rail links not only creates competition for older neighborhoods, but also disrupts them directly by bisecting them with limited access freeways or rights-of-way. Older neighborhoods, with less affluent residents, cannot zone out noise, smog, and congestion, a failure that can have negative effects on property values. Thus can neighborhood externalities add to the depreciation of homeowners' assets.[47]

This devaluation of older neighborhoods is accelerated too by the actions of government and financial institutions. The U.S. government has deliberately relied on the filtering process as its principal program for lower income housing by focusing its incentives on the construction of new and particularly single-family housing, since the 1930s. A decision was made at that time to emphasize new home ownership over public housing. The programs set up for underwriting ownership through VA and FHA loan guarantees gave preference to single-family homes and suburban locations, while "urban renewal" was substituted after World War II for even the limited public housing program that had been begun before and during the war.[48]

In the Boston area, the urban renewal program was used by government to hasten the filtering down and removal of older buildings, often in quite deliberate ways. The West End of Boston, a predominantly Italo-American working class neighborhood, was torn down in the late 1950s. Subsequently, the threat of urban renewal (or the partial clearance of other areas through unfinished renewal projects) led many people to move out ahead of government eviction procedures. These cases have been well-documented, and were notorious enough to build a strong climate of public opinion against further urban renewal programs of the land-clearance variety. Nonetheless, until the very end of the 1960s, urban renewal-type programs were continuing to accelerate the deterioration of many neighborhoods. A similar effect stemmed from the decline in maintenance effort at government-run housing projects that began in the 1960s.[49]

A further acceleration of neighborhood deterioration may occur because of the actions of private financial institutions (banks and insurance companies). This factor generally becomes important after the others have set in. Banks and insurance companies come to perceive older neighborhoods as declining or high risk areas. They will generally direct their investment of mortgage funds, and their provision of insurance protection and business loans, away from those areas they see as risky. As a result, those thinking of purchasing land in these areas will not be able to receive financing or insurance protection. The consequent reduction in demand will reduce property values even further, in effect "justifying" the institutions' prophesies. Financial institutions may occasionally attack neighborhoods directly—denying them loans for reasons of racial prejudice or in order to drive out existing land uses preparatory to some major redevelopment scheme—but their more common disinvestment strategy, occurring through "ethical" business procedures, has the same effect.[50]

Finally, there is the effect of transportation. Imagine a city with jobs concentrated in a central business district. The differential advantages of equal-sized plots of land at different distances from that center depend, at least in part, on differences in commuting cost to the center. The land prices generated by differential access are shown in figure 1.1 by the solid line, a gradient indicating land values (or their annual rent equivalents) at different distances from the central business district. If transportation is improved so that the cost per mile falls, this curve becomes less steep—each mile makes less real price difference. More land comes within the feasible commuting range, and the total availability of housing sites forces the average value of land downward—unless more residents and business activity are drawn to the metropolitan area to increase housing demand. Assuming the total urban population is constant, the Rent Gradient after the transportation innovation is shown by the broken line in figure 1.1. Comparing the two curves, one can see a proportionate increase in land values that is greatest at distance m_2 from the center, and which is negative at distances below m_1. In the typical North American city (although not necessarily in all cities), the land closer to the center of the city has often been held by lower-income residents who thus find their houses to have continually eroding values.[51]

Even the owners who benefit from the rise in suburban land values may face similar losses if future transport innovations occur. (If transport is improved rapidly enough, even the *total* land value of the city may be reduced for a time, until the reduced costs attract new businesses and migrants.) Moreover, in practice, the suburban landowners who benefit may only be the land developers who can sell for a capital gain to those

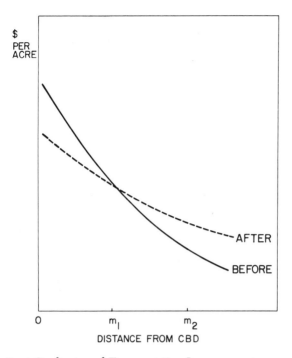

Figure 1.1   Rent Gradients and Transportation Improvement.

residents who will later feel the price effects of new land, new housing, and taxes. These effects may well lead to a lowered real rate of capital gain on already-built residential housing than on alternative invest-ments.

Most models which attribute suburban growth to improvements in commuter access take improved transport to be automatic, the result of the inexorable forward march of technology, independent of the mach-inations of government or land developers and of the conflict of contend-ing social groups. However, as we shall see, in the Boston area some of the key transportation investments—such as the building of the first toll bridges and the street railway systems—were in fact the self-interested work of specific developers. We shall argue that even the timing of transit research and development was crucially affected by urban social conflict.

The government, too, plays a major role in the provision of transport facilities; even if, in some sense, science proceeds autonomously, its ap-plication to urban development requires major investments that are generally made or regulated by government. Government also plays a crucial role in the financing of local transportation, either through subsidies or through rate-setting, and that affects the commuter's cost of using it.

In the Boston area, government played a critical role in the provision of transport, and the creation of more transport has favored the building of more suburbs. What is more, government subsidy and rate-setting policies have generally favored the suburban commuter at the expense of inner-city residents, thus increasing the incentives for people to move to suburbs and accelerating the devaluation of inner-city properties.

Differences in local tax burdens for transportation are only part of a broader pattern of tax differentials. As cities have developed in the United States, many of them have spilled over the limits of their political borders, creating metropolitan areas with fragmented political jurisidictions and tax bases that, in turn, created differences in the tax burden–benefit mix. Thus fragmentation is a historical result of jurisdictional conflict and, at times, deliberate creation of tax havens. There is a persistent tendency for these government services and taxes to benefit the newer, more suburban residential areas, the areas of still-incomplete development, and the nonresidential business core at the expense of older and poorer residential areas.

The older areas must, to begin with, bear a disproportionate share of the costs of social welfare and control. Assuming either that services are funded from fragmented tax bases, or that state, metropolitan, or large-city governments distribute tax resources in part on the basis of contributions to revenues, then the costs of maintaining the indigent, of paying for police to keep the poor under control, and of supporting fire and health departments will all be levied on the areas where these activities take place. Thus, the inner ring of residential areas, with lower average incomes, will have to bear higher tax burdens than affluent communities to pay for their poor and elderly residents and their health, police, and fire departments. They will have fewer funds available, if they are to keep their taxes in line at all, for school quality and other optional amenities. Different lower-income residential areas will adopt different mixes of service austerity and high tax rates, just as different suburbs may specialize in offering better schooling, other amenities, or even lower tax rates. But the choice of policies open to governments, and therefore the individual's choice of different public policies, will be more restricted in lower income areas and will be less favorable than that available where average resources are greater.

Those older areas which are also geographically the more central areas of a metropolitan region may also have to bear on their tax bases the costs of maintaining services that benefit the entire metropolitan area, as in the case of Boston's transport systems. The same central areas may have to pay directly for such public cultural facilities as zoos, libraries, or hospitals. Where such facilities (along with religious and educational institutions) are nonprofit, tax-exempt institutions, the inner-core communities may have to bear the costs of providing public services to these institutions without being able to charge them.

This latter problem may be offset in some metropolitan area whose downtown business districts provide a strong base for real estate or sales taxation. Cities like New York and San Francisco, with strong business districts, have their fiscal crises but are generally in stronger positions than their neighbors, like Oakland and Newark, where business taxes are lower, or than Boston and Cambridge, where the principal economic activities are concentrated in the nonprofit sector. In almost all metropolitan areas, however, the inner ring of towns just around the central city must bear many of the costs of coping with flow-through of commuters. And in all metropolitan areas, the problem of supporting services for the poor falls disproportionately on the less affluent communities.

This situation provides a strong incentive for more affluent people and for businesses vulnerable to local taxation to try to escape the older, more central, and poorer communities by fleeing to newer suburbs where tax–service mixes will be "capitalized" into higher land values, less favorable ones into lower land values. This is an additional source of depreciation of older residential areas.

TWO

The Uneven Development of
Metropolitan Boston, 1630–1980

THE growth and devaluation of consumer assets, described in chapter 1, exemplifies a more general development cycle that pervades American history. Perhaps some such cycles are inevitable in any civilization: Some are specific outcomes of competition in a capitalist economy; others may reflect an American habit of evading problems by rushing to "new frontiers." Whatever the ultimate causes (see part II), it is important to recognize that the effects run throughout American life.

Boston has the reputation (shared only, perhaps, by Philadelphia) as a stable community, still dominated by Puritan tradition and a set of Brahmin leaders who established the city more than three centuries ago. Yet the history of Boston, like other cities, is marked by the periodic growth and devaluation of towns and neighborhoods within the area, and by the rise and fall of economic activities within the region. We shall review here the history of the Boston metropolitan area, focusing on the rise and decline of economic activities, on the opening of new areas to urbanization through transportation, water, sewage, and other investments, and on the changing fortunes of older urbanized sections of the area.

A. THE ORIGINS OF BOSTON, 1630–1790

The emergence of Boston as the economic and political center of New England was marked by the differential ascent and decline of different communities within the region. The settlement which ultimately grew into modern Boston was just one of a large number of towns sponsored by the Massachusetts Bay Company in the early seventeenth century. Had it not been the seat of provincial government, little would have distinguished it from any of the other 28 towns designated by the provincial legislature by 1650.[1] The Boston settlement was not only one among many but it was an unintentional one at that.

In 1630, the Shawmut Peninsula, the land on which the present downtown Boston sits, was a very undesirable place on which to locate a settlement. It contained 783 acres of swampy land dominated by three craggy mountains and connected to the mainland by a very narrow isthmus which was under water at the highest tides (fig. 2.1).[2] It was so un-

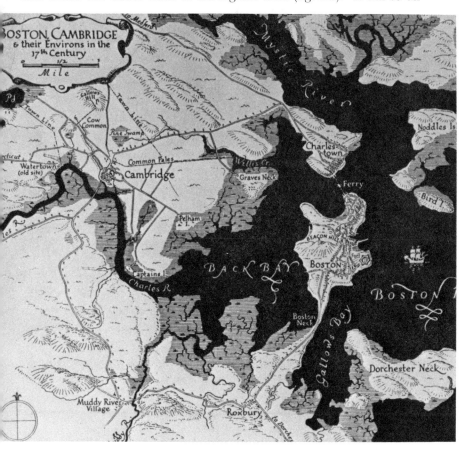

Figure 2.1   Map of Boston, Cambridge and Their Environs, Seventeenth Century.

desirable that Governor John Winthrop and his band of Puritans did not originally choose it as the point of settlement. Rather they chose a site across the harbor in what became the town of Charlestown. They remained there only a few days before relocating to the Shawmut Peninsula when the shallow spring water in the former area proved too brackish for drinking.

The decision to relocate on the peninsula would have far-reaching effects on the role of the new settlement. While the acreage was sufficient for a small city, most of the land was of poor quality and little but urban enterprises could occur there. At Charlestown, the city could have grown inward as well as seaward. Administrators might have had to share some local power with at least some of the more wealthy farmers. From the Shawmut Peninsula, Boston could *only* grow as a seaport and trading center. And that it did. By the early 1770s, Boston was not only the leading commercial port of the eastern seaboard, but also the hub of trade with the Caribbean, Europe and Africa.

Boston's growth meant the eventual economic subordination of rival mercantile towns. In particular, Salem sought to compete as a seaport. Throughout much of the colonial period, it rivaled Boston in size, and its merchants extended Massachusetts' trading influence throughout the world. But it could not compete indefinitely with a port that was also the site of Colonial administration. By the end of the 1700s, Salem was declining as a trading center. Eventually it would become a secondary industrial and residential suburb within the metropolitan area. Several of the major Salem trading families relocated to Boston during the period of decline, and became leaders in Boston commerce. But for those less mobile than the Cabots, the loss of power was real enough. Other mercantile towns, like Marblehead and Newburyport, as well as agricultural and market centers like Roxbury and Quincy, also lost power to Boston around the time of the Revolutionary War. Quincy's leading families played an important role in independence, in opposition to the British administration at Boston. With victory, the Adams, Otis, and Quincy families, like their Salem colleagues, relocated to the growing new center.

B. Post-Revolutionary Boston, 1790–1850

Boston's commercial expansion, interrupted by the war, resumed with the winning of independence. In 1765, the city's population had been

Spatial shifts in Boston's economic base. The harbor was the key to the vitality of nineteenth-century Boston. "High Tech" industries cluster along today's suburban highways.

Boston Harbor, 1841.

The Polaroid Company, Route 128 Waltham, Mass.

15,520.[3] By 1790, the population was 18,320.[4] The post-Revolution decision to make Boston the capital of the newly independent state accentuated the effects of postwar prosperity. By 1800, the population had grown to 24,937. In annual terms, the growth rate in the 25-year period from 1765 to 1790 was 0.6 percent per year; between 1790 and 1800, it quintupled to just over 3 percent per year and continued at this rate until 1830.

Population growth created pressure to expand business, public, and residential areas. The flat and dry regions of the Shawmut Peninsula could not accommodate this growth and the settlement began to spread into areas more difficult to develop. The opening of these areas, in turn, started a cycle of neighborhood growth and decline within the built-up area of Boston. As new areas were developed, some of them became new centers of power and affluence. Older areas were left behind, sometimes achieving a modicum of stable prosperity, but sometimes decaying into slums.

The initial expansion of Boston took several forms. The first response was to create more land by leveling the hills to fill the coves and marshes. In 1795, the new State House was erected on Beacon Hill. The adjacent hill, Mount Vernon, was purchased by a syndicate of real estate speculators led by Harrison Gray Otis (see chapter 7). The syndicate removed 60 feet of soil from the top of the hill, and used the earth to fill other of its properties in the marshes along Charles Street. This land was then sold, at eye-opening profits, to merchants looking for new home sites away from the din of the older harbor areas, yet close enough to walk to work.[5]

Faced with a continuing problem of Boston development, and the paucity of buildable land, the Otis syndicate had simply moved earth from the top of a hill to make it buildable and placed it in a marsh at the bottom, making the marsh similarly developable. While this solution worked when hills abutted marshes, its application was limited. Long-distance landfill was not a viable option until after the 1830s, by which time steam railroads connected the city with distant sources of landfill.

An alternative method of expansion was the construction of bridges to Cambridge and other land-rich areas close to the center of Boston. Thus in 1786, 1793, and 1809, bridges were built across the Charles River to provide access to East Cambridge. In 1804, the Otis Syndicate acquired property across South Bay on Dorchester Neck, to the southeast of Bos-

ton (see Fig. 2.1). They then arranged to have their newly acquired land
annexed to Boston over the strenuous objections of the Dorchester town
fathers. As soon as this was accomplished, they promptly threw up a toll
bridge between central Boston and what is today South Boston. The
proposition proved to be a money losing venture. While the Charles River
bridges were successful at stimulating East Cambridge development, the
toll on the South Boston Bridge was an impediment to the use of the
land in that area by those willing to trade a long walk for cheap
land.

In 1828 a second bridge was built to South Boston. This time, though,
the bridge was toll-free and city-built, and businesses and their employees poured in. Meanwhile, between 1812 and 1824, the top third of
Beacon Hill was razed, the earth used to fill in the Mill Pond at its base.

Although the population growth was high in the four decades between
1790 and 1830, it did not match the growth of the next two decades.
Population more than doubled between 1830 and 1850, growing at an
annual rate of 4 percent, from 61,392 to 136,881 souls.

This rapid growth was accompanied by, and interacted with, a change
in the city's economic base. Although Boston had bested its immediate
neighbors as a commercial center, it began to fall behind such rivals as
Philadelphia, Baltimore, and especially New York. New York's advantages of scale and better inland access apparently outweighed the fact
that Boston is closer to Europe, Africa, and the east coast of South
America.

The slow growth of the port of Boston in the early nineteenth century
led the city's capitalists to seek other investment opportunities. They found
these in manufacturing. The rivers around Boston and generally
throughout New England are not suitable for navigation, but their many
rapids and falls make them an excellent source of cheap and reliable water
power. With the coming of railroads, manufacturing plants could locate
wherever there was water power, with less concern about locally available raw materials and local markets for the manufactured goods. By 1850,
a whole string of such manufacturing towns had sprung up within a
hundred miles of Boston. To the west there were Waltham, Fitchburg,
Worcester, Chicopee, and Pittsfield; to the south, Fall River and Brockton. To the northwest along the Merrimac River there were Lowell and
Lawrence in Massachusetts, and Nashua and Manchester in New Hamp-

shire. These towns had populations from 5,000 to 30,000 and were growing at a rate even faster than the City of Boston.

Until about 1850, the smaller industrial cities were able to staff their burgeoning mill operations by drawing population from the surrounding farm country. This countryside, too, was suffering from the effects of competitive devaluation. As canals and then railroads opened flatter and more fertile lands to the West, competition in agricultural markets cut in to the value of New England farm produce. The New England farmers responded valiently, turning everything from ashes from their fireplaces to ice from their winter-frozen ponds into export commodities. But bit by bit, New England agriculture fell into a century-long decline, and farmers' daughters and sons began to leave for the new industrial towns and for Boston itself.

The initial industrial advantage of the smaller cities did not last for long. New technologies offered alternative sources of power to the waterfall sites. Industrial unrest began to spread, raising the spectre of increased labor costs. And, perhaps more important, Boston found a new source of labor in Irish immigrants. Beginning in the 1830s and accelerating in the 1840s during the potato famine, massive numbers of Irish began migrating to Boston. By 1855, there were 46,237 Irish-born residents of Boston (29% of the population). By creating a source of cheap labor for the city, they enabled it to overcome its locational disadvantages in commerce vis-à-vis New York and other eastern seaboard cities and its water power disadvantages vis-à-vis the rest of its region. In the words of Oscar Handlin's classic study, *Boston's Immigrants:*

> Therein lay the significance of the Irish in the city's economic life. Before their arrival, the rigid labor supply had made industrialization impossible. It was the vital function of the Irish to thaw out the rigidity of the system. Their labor achieved the transition from earlier commercial to the later industrial organization of the city.[6]

The growth of Boston as a manfacturing center, as well as some continuing expansion of trade and business services, required more land. This time around eyes turned across the harbor to East Boston. In 1830, East Boston was called Noddle's Island (see Fig. 2.1) and was almost wholly owned by the Sumner family. In 1833, the Sumners set up the East Boston Company, and began operating a ferry to the mainland's

North End. This ferry charter was timed to coincide with the start of service by the Eastern Railroad, which brought, over a new causeway, passengers and freight from the coastal towns northeast of Boston to the island. With ferry service to Boston and rail service to the north shore, East Boston and its port facilities prospered. By 1857, its population was 16,600, almost a tenth of the total Boston population. The assessed taxable valuation of the area had grown from $60,000 in 1833 to $606,000 in 1835 and to $8 million in 1856.[7]

The impact of the ferries on the extension of Boston was, however, minor compared to that of the railroads. In Boston, as elsewhere, the era of the early railroads occured simultaneously with a surge in industrialization and the migration of large population groups to the cities. Since these trends interact it is difficult to tell which comes first—the railroads, the industrialization, or the population influx. The railroads, though they may not have started the growth cycle in Boston, were a necessary spark for accelerated growth.

In the summer of 1835, three other systems joined the Eastern Railroad: the Boston and Lowell, the Boston and Worcester, and the Boston and Providence. Unlike the Eastern, these three lines all entered the Shawmut Peninsula directly, and established terminals at the periphery of the built-up area. Four more railroads built lines into Boston during the 1840s and 1850s. All these, save one, also established their terminals at the periphery of the built-up area. The exception was the Boston and Maine, which entered Boston from the north over a bridge across the Charles River.

The railroads greatly facilitated landfill operations, for they permitted the inexpensive hauling of fill from outside the area. Boston could now fill its tidal flats on a grandiose scale. During the next half century, all coves were filled, the Back Bay was transformed from a tidal swamp to the city's best residential area, and the South Bay, between the Shawmut Peninsula and Dorchester Neck—South Boston—saw its tidal flats turned into ship and rail yards, wharves and warehouses. Through these land-recovery operations, Boston more than doubled its inner city land area from 783 acres in 1804, to 1,929 acres by the end of the century. In the process the narrow Shawmut Peninsula became a rounded piece of level, well-drained land surrounded on three sides by water without a neck or isthmus.[8] Aided by the railroads, Boston, which once did not have enough usable land for a medium-sized walking city, created suffi-

The first railroad suburbs. Note the difference between the housing at Walnut Park and Washington Park. Both are located near the old Boston and Worcester line. Walnut Park is one stop closer and was designed for a more affluent resident than the later Washington Park, with its smaller building lots.

Boston Public Library, Print Department.

Railroads Enter Boston, 1849.

Photo by Elliott Sclar.

Walnut Park, Newton Corner, Mass., 1984.

Photo by Elliott Sclar.

Washington Park, Newtonville, Mass., 1984.

cient access to the mainland to expand henceforth like any other land-rich city.

At the same time that the railroads expanded the possibilities for the physical growth of Boston, they also created the possibilities for its first suburbanization and social stratification. An example is the history of Newton, today an affluent community adjacent to Boston's western border. Its transformation into its present shape can be traced to the opening of service on the Boston and Worcester Railroad in 1834.

The original plan for the Boston and Worcester called for the line to move west through the towns of Watertown and Waltham. Local opposition was so strenuous that the railroad sought another route. William Jackson, a descendant of the first settler in Newton, interceded in the dispute and secured a right-of-way through open acreage on the northern edge of the town.[9] Service from West Newton to Boston was begun in 1834. The running time was 39 minutes, with stops at Newtonville and Newton Corner. Fortuitously for Mr. Jackson, he owned a sizable amount of the open acreage through which the railroad ran.

The Irish influx into Boston in the 1840s created a demand by the upper classes for housing space farther away from the chaos and poverty of the new arrivals. Newton, with its short rail commute and pastoral setting, became ideal. During the 1840s, Jackson's land and other parcels became prime home sites for these first "commuters." It was in this era that lots were sold by the square foot for the first time in the town's history (at Walnut Park in Newton Corner, in the early 1840s). This upper class influx became the basis for subsequent migrations and played a major role in shaping the character of modern Newton. Such railroad suburbanization was typical along other lines as well.[10]

Aside from such affluent suburban enclaves, by 1850 metropolitan Boston was an area stretching about two miles from Boston City Hall, comprising Boston and the communities of Charlestown and Cambridge to the north, and Roxbury to the south. The area had a population of about 190,000. But its growth and expansion did not amount to mass suburbanization, as we now use that term. Some new areas—like East Boston, with its shipyards, and Upper Roxbury—were factory districts as well as residential areas. Many workers walked to their jobs. The older dockside areas of the North End were filled with crowded tenements, while shanties covered one of the remaining hills just south of downtown. The mill towns and farms of the surrounding countryside were still remote, though the railroads were making them less so.

C. The Horsecar Era: 1850–1890

By 1850, Boston had been an area of continual European settlement for more than 220 years. Much of its character had been determined by the spatial relations and physical forms characteristic of a preindustrial walking city. The United States in the mid-nineteenth century was a society on the cutting edge of technological advancement. Its great eastern cities, New York, Philadelphia, and Boston, were very much the center of that change.

Though the industrial revolution had been born in England almost a century earlier, its mechanical muscle power did not transform America's leading cities until the mid-nineteenth century. But when it did come, it led to a powerful change in the relationship between town and countryside. Before industrialization, the countryside was at least potentially independent of the city. Residents of rural areas not only possessed the wherewithal to feed themselves but also could locally manufacture virtually every artifact they used in their daily lives.[11] Those items not produceable on the farm were produceable at the local blacksmith, grist mill, or saw mill. The contribution of cities to that social order was limited to trade and commerce, and to governmental and religious administration. Simply put, the country folk could materially survive without their urban brethren, but the opposite was not true.

The new mechanical production methods changed all that. Because they could produce textiles and other manufactured goods of better quality more cheaply and quickly than the older hand methods, they altered the town–countryside relationship. By 1850, cities had become the locus of manufacturing production on which both town and country depended and rural folk were able to devote themselves to the production of food. This new specialization of tasks worked out better for the living standard of both urban and rural dwellers, but it removed the one-sided material dependency of city on countryside forever. It also left the rural areas dependent on cash income for more necessities, leaving them vulnerable to competition and subject to more extensive devaluation as agriculture developed in the West.

The new methods also brought new pressures to bear on the city. These new productive techniques had a logic of their own which required a major reorganization of the spatial relationship between home and work. The introduction of machine production represented an enormous investment of capital in a set of highly fixed assets (plant and equipment).

In order for such large fixed investments to be profitable, they require use as intensive and continuous as is possible. Because they are only one part of a continuous production process, the other parts have to be altered to ensure that the requirements of the machine for economic functioning are met. In practical terms this means that the major production problem is to ensure a reliable and continuous stream of raw material and labor inputs into production. The distribution problem is to identify and service all the markets which can absorb the output of the process. If any part of this system does not function, the entire system does not function. As a result, much of the economic history since the middle nineteenth century has been a story of concern with the fits and starts of maintaining this socially complex input–output mechanism.

Cities became important as a solution to some of these problems. They became the locus of productive activity because they were terminal points for transportation, which meant access both to raw materials and to markets. They also had the ability to provide the large pools of wage-dependent laborers. A major difficulty with the solution was that the demands of industry for labor far exceeded the existing supply. As a consequence, the era from 1850 to 1890 is one in which metropolitan Boston attempted to provide housing and services for the burgeoning labor force required by the newly industrialized urban economy.

Because the Boston area is a balkanized region of cities and towns, the era in question was one in which the home-to-work trip began to take increasing numbers of people across municipal borders. In that sense it was the forerunner of suburbanization as we now know it. Consider table 2.1. It contains information on the growth rates of the metropolitan area from 1790 to 1890. The towns of the region are divided into contiguous rings around Boston. In the early part of the nineteenth century, the city itself had the most rapid population growth, but by the 1840s, it was the first ring of suburban towns which were undergoing most rapid growth. That rapid growth trend has continued to move outward down to the present, as we shall see below. To the extent that industry did not move out at the same pace as population, the area became subjected to increasing intercommunity travel as part of daily life.

While such travel was beginning to take place, overland travel was still very expensive and time-consuming. Consequently, only the most affluent were capable of traveling any significant distance on a daily basis. For the rest of the population, it was still a matter of going only as far

Table 2.1
Intercensal Growth Rates in Boston and Surrounding Rings 1790–1890

Decade	Boston	First Ring	Second Ring	Third Ring	Fourth Ring
1790–1800	36.1[a]	27.0	10.3	9.9	10.5
1800–1810	35.5[a]	7.4	13.4	21.8	8.8
1810–1820	28.2[a]	17.3	17.9	6.6	6.5
1820–1830	41.8[a]	34.9	17.9	9.5	7.3
1830–1840	52.1[a]	35.8	25.3	19.7	14.4
1840–1850	46.6	81.3[a]	42.0	38.1	31.4
1850–1860	29.9	67.6[a]	32.4	27.7	18.2
1860–1870	40.9	44.7[a]	23.8	19.9	11.3
1870–1880	44.8[b]	33.1	24.3	29.3	18.4
1880–1890	23.6	41.3	46.6[a]	26.0	17.5

SOURCE: Adapted from L. Schnore, and P. Knights, "Residence and Social Structure: Boston in the Ante-Bellum Period," in Thernstrom and Sennett, eds. *Nineteenth-Century Cities: Essays in the New Urban History* (New Haven: Yale University Press, 1969), p. 250.
[a] Denotes the Highest value for each decade (except the 1870s).
[b] Boston annexed three towns in 1874. These towns, together with their 1870 populations, were Brighton (4,967), Charlestown (28,323), and West Roxbury (8,683). Subtracting their 1870 total population (41,973) from recorded 1880 Boston total (362,839), and recomputing the Boston growth between 1870 and 1880, yields an adjusted growth rate over the decade of 28.1%. This would leave the first ring as the area of most rapid growth. And even it assumes all Boston Growth was in the nonannexed area, and thus is an overestimate.

as one's feet could comfortably transport one's body; generally less than two miles from the urban center. During the period in question, population growth occurred in the area within two miles of Boston's City Hall.

Given that limitation, the period in question was a time when living densities were significantly increased in cities. The result was that the original city of Boston, the "North End" and "West End," was transformed into slums. The North End was infamous for its crowded and unsanitary tenements.[12] By 1860, squalor had spread to the South End too, an area opened in the 1840s with high hopes of housing the city's upper classes. The settlement house studies of the South End, which seemed to many to show the worst of urban degradation, were clearly labeled by the author as depicting a neighborhood one step up from the bottom. Yet even these studies showed that, by 1892, rent was "a staggering burden," and often, too, one-third of workers' limited incomes. And this for a neighborhood where single rooms, rather than full apartments, dominated, and where the underlying landfill was unsanitary, and the streets dirty (particularly until electric trolleys replaced horse-drawn vehicles).

The houses are often damp owing to the water in the cellars
and to insufficient heat. The great amount of landfill in the
main streets, and the macadam pavements in the side streets
produce so much dirt and dust that it is impossible to keep a
room free from it. It blows through streets and alleys, swirls
up the sides of buildings, and settles in attic windows as much
as in parlors and basements.[13]

Stephan Thernstrom reports that in 1870, only 11 percent of Boston
working-class families were homeowners. In 1880, 56 percent of the fathers in his sample had no taxable property at all. Another 10 percent
had taxable property worth less than $2,500, but it is not known how
many of them owned homes.[14] In a subsample of families from the
Thernstrom sample, which was checked more carefully for types of
property owned, only 6.7 percent were homeowners in 1880. However,
the sample includes sons who were not yet living away from their parents in 1880, and this underestimates home ownership by family heads.[15]

There were a number of responses on the part of the region and its
citizens to this growing density of population. It was in this period that
the last major landfill within the limits of the original city of Boston was
completed. Between 1850 and 1880 the Back Bay, below Beacon Hill
and adjacent to the public garden, was completely filled and turned into
housing for the city's elite. Elegant brick row houses and well-designed
streets are still the hallmarks of this area's enduring charm.

The landfill of the Back Bay aborted the attempt to develop the South
End into an elite area, and to ensure its decline (see chapter 3). A major
long-term result of the development of the Back Bay as an area of upper-
income housing was to stimulate a corridor of luxury housing west of the
old city. This westerly corridor ran through the Back Bay into Brookline,
Newton, and out to Weston. The implications of this for the eventual
decline of affluent areas in *other* corridors will be explored in later chapters.

A second response of the city to crowding was the attempt to expand
its borders through annexation. Boston annexed Dorchester in 1869,
Roxbury in 1873, and three towns (Brighton, Charlestown, and West
Roxbury) in 1874. But later other surrounding towns resisted annexation, and the movement died out (see chapter 8). Annexation did not
ensure the spread of the built-up area (which required adequate transportation technology), nor did the end of annexations end that spread,

since once adequate commuting technology was available, suburbanization could cross town lines. But the result of annexation's failure was to create a balkanized metropolis, in which some jurisdictions could grow at the expense of the tax base of others.

Although overland transportation was not sufficient to expand the radius of the metropolitan area, horsecars did begin to bring some new order to its land use patterns in the second half of the nineteenth century. Horse-drawn street railways began operating in the Boston area as early as 1852, and were the region's main public transit system until the early 1890s.[16] But the horsecar line had little effect on extending the outer periphery of the built-up area. During the forty years of the horsecar lines, the built-up area grew in most directions by only a little over a mile, and in no direction by more than two miles, although the population nearly tripled. To absorb such a population influx, the Boston area needed to extend its urban fringe less than other urban centers, since the city, as well as Cambridge and Charlestown, gained acreage from landfill operations.

Although the horsecars were not a very effective means of extending the city, they were a major force in reorganizing the area.[17] Lines were constructed in the built-up areas and operated at an effective speed of five to six miles an hour, slightly faster than a person could walk. Over the short distances the time differentials between the two modes were inconsequential. Thus, at first the horsecars did not attract commuters. Most people still lived within easy walking distance of work and could save on fare and get to work in about the same time by walking. The horsecars primarily attracted passengers with bundles and parcels, and people on special errands to a distant part of the urban area.

As the city grew, the car lines began to attract commuters of three types. First there were those who, under the influence of the horsecar, moved to the urban fringe and had to commute more than two miles to work. Secondly, there were the railroad commuters, who lived in the countrified towns, came to the city by railroad, and used the horsecars for crosstown commuting from the stations. These latter were usually from the upper-income groups. Both groups were rather small and had only marginal impact on the urban structure. Not so the third group. These were the workers who, since the coming of the horsecar, had accepted new jobs in other parts of the urban area and chose to commute by horsecar rather than move their families. To this group must be added

Horsecars and Landfill. The horsecars allowed a slight spreading out of the older urban core prior to 1890.

Boston Public Library, Print Dept.

Bowdoin Square, Boston, Mass., ca. 1856.

Boston Public Library, Print Dept.

Commonwealth Avenue in the Back Bay during its development, 1872.

Boston Public Library, Print Dept.

Worcester Square in the South End, ca. 1890.

new settlers, who first located in a congenial neighborhood and then scoured the whole urban area in search of jobs. The horsecars thus facilitated the growth of large areas with uniform working class and ethnic residential populations, even in the face of dispersed worksites. The spatially undifferentiated walking city passed into oblivion.

D. The First Surburban Wave, 1890–1940

The era that began in 1890 was the first in which a self-consciously metropolitan region, with an urban core and suburban ring, began to take shape in the Boston area. It was the time when the urbanizing forces set loose by the industrial revolution were married to appropriate infrastructure in order to permit effective long-distance urban–suburban commutation and work styles.

Suburbanization is frequently considered a result of economic prosperity and growth. Boston's first suburban expansion was in part a concomitant of regional population growth; average incomes in the area were considerably higher on the eve of the 1930s depression than they had been at the preceding cyclical peaks before the 1873 and 1893 "panics." But economic development in the region in this period was hardly an "even" process. For some industrial sectors, and for some towns and neighborhoods, the picture was one of decline.

The years of first suburban growth in Boston were not good ones for the long-term stability of the Massachusetts economy. The rise of the midwestern heavy industries, commercial and financial dominance by New York, and the beginnings of outmigration of the textile and shoe industries were already beginning to weaken the state's industrial base as the region entered the twentieth century. The 1873 and 1884 depressions had undermined industry in many small towns as the larger, national firms which survived these downturns were able to drive smaller competitors in more localized markets into bankruptcy or merger. By 1895 the proportion of the state's population engaged in industrial activity had fallen significantly.[18]

The impact of this decline was felt most strongly in some of the textile and shoe making towns further from Boston. Fall River suffered from the loss of local ownership, and the subsequent shrinkage of employment, in its textile mills. Never having fully recovered from its losses in the 1873 depression, it was the first town in the state to be forced into bankruptcy in the 1930s, when the major new industry it had attracted, a tire factory, also shut down.[19] Lowell, Chicopee, and other mill towns were also devastated, although new industries, like electrical equipment in Lynn, took up some of the slack in a few places.

Nor did Boston itself escape some of the effects of decline. Industry was hard hit. The 1893 depression left 37 percent of the membership of three dozen Boston craft unions out of work.[20] Port activities fell sharply, too. Even banking, the Boston business staple, fell from a high of sixty banks with a total capitalization of $53.8 million in 1869 to twenty-eight institutions with a capitalization of $28.4 million in 1905.[21] Thereafter, when activities began to expand, investment was limited to a degree by the unwillingness of investors/capitalists to risk an environment dominated by an unfriendly "Irish" political machine.[22]

While industry and economic activity did contract, it did not disappear. Until the 1920s, the Boston region was able to retain a significant proportion of the many industries which had their start in that area. Their location within the metropolis, however, did shift in response to the new transportation technologies and population pressures of the early twentieth century. The key to this shift was the truck.

Before the truck, industry had to locate in the urban core or at railroad sidings. Since these sites were limited, good industrial land was scarce. With truck transport, any area with serviceable roads and not too far from the core could become an acceptable site. Trucks became generally available by 1909 and their impact on the metropolitan area was immediate. Between 1909 and 1919 manufacturing employment in the inner-ring communities, two to six miles from the city center, grew dramatically faster than those either closer in or farther out from the center.[23]

The shift to the inner-ring communities did not occur equally among all industries, but was concentrated in the "high-value-added" industries. These industries, which use relatively greater amounts of machinery, or capital, per worker, found it to their particular economic advantage to substitute truck shipment costs for high land prices. From 1914 on, the inner-ring communities outstripped the core in value added per production worker. The data suggest that some of the high value-added plants may have relocated from the outer ring communities and the rest of Eastern Massachusetts, where they had rail access to Boston, to the inner-ring communities, where they depended on truck access.

The 1920s, the second decade of the truck, were declining years for manufacturing employment in the Boston area. But this decline affected the inner-ring communities less than the core or those further from the center. The expansion of inner-ring manufacturing fostered the growth of working class suburbs in those locations in two ways. First, it created a base of working-class jobs that could be reached without commutation. Second, pollution, noise, and a general sense of working-class activity made these areas less attractive for upper income groups, and preserved inexpensive land for working-class housing.

Though the advent of the truck spread industry and working-class communities beyond the core, it did not do so in a random fashion. Rather, the spread followed patterns which reflected the shape of the existing urbanized region and its industrial location along with the possibilities built into the new transport and production technology. In general the major areas of inner-ring industrial suburbanization were found directly north of the city and southeast along the shore. A small working-class enclave also spread to the west into parts of Watertown, Waltham, and Newton. The primary north–southeast orientation of this move reflected the fact that industry was still tied to the railroad. Because the development of the railroad came after the initial settlement of the city, the depots were never permitted to be constricted at the heart of the built-up area. As a result, they located at what was then the periphery. In the case of Boston, the closest one could get to the center but still remain on the periphery was to the north and south of the city. Consequently, given the presence of rail facilities in these areas, it followed that they would be the first to experience the newly suburbanized industrialization the truck permitted. Some growth of industrial enclaves to the west reflected the fact that there was also rail access in that direction and that previous industrial activity had located there to take advantage of the water power of the Charles River, which circles around Newton before heading past Waltham and Watertown on its way between Boston and Cambridge and out into the Massachusetts Bay. In general, however, the west remained the location of affluent residential suburbs. To the southwest and northeast of Boston (except for an industrial enclave in Lynn) development was also primarily residential and largely for the middle and upper-middle classes.

These classes were themselves growing because of a shift in the area's economic base. With industrial growth retarded, economic development in the region had come to depend more on the financial sector, which recovered by the 1920s from the temporary decline of banking. It must be remembered that because New England was a major locus of the initial industrialization of the nation, capital to industrialize the country further would come from that region. As a result, economic activity of a new type began to grow in Boston. This was the office-based activity associated with banking, insurance, and investment. This activity in turn created more demand for office workers in a centralized location. But many of these workers demanded better housing than the crowded core provided. Thus, the further spatial expansion of metropolitan Boston was vital to continued growth.

Desire alone would not have been adequate to the task of converting the region to its new role. Several other factors were required. One was a transportation technology which was capable of making the land area comprised of Boston and its suburbs into an effective unified economic region. Until 1890 the dilemma which faced the region was that all existing forms of transport technology were inadequate to the task of housing populations which lived at increasingly further distances from the locus of work in the core area. The result was, as we have seen, that in certain quarters of Boston the living densities had become so high that public health difficulties and social unrest threatened to bring an abrupt end to the newly found prosperity of the late nineteenth century.

The solution to the problem took the form of electrified mass transit. In its initial and most popular form it was the electric street railway or trolley. The trolley was the first system which permitted the movement of people at effective speeds of six to ten miles per hour. The result was that the effective radius of the city was extended beyond that of the old walking city. Thus it was in 1890 that the urbanized region began to grow from its two- to five-mile range to a region which extended eight to ten miles beyond the center. There were four characteristics of the trolley which allowed this transformation to occur. First the electric motor was able to propel the vehicle at higher speeds than was possible for a horse to pull a load of people. Secondly, unlike the earlier steam systems, electric travel was clean and safe. As a result, it was possible to locate lines in dense core areas and not worry about air pollution and fire. Thirdly, because they did not need to build up a head of steam to roll, they were ideal for the frequent stop and go required by the transport system as it moved through the core. Finally they could rather cheaply be put in place merely by laying rails along existing street level rights of

way. When additional speed was needed, it was not that much more difficult to construct exclusive rights of way in tunnels or on elevated platforms.

Massachusetts was one of the major centers of trolley use. By 1902,
the state had 2,378 miles of electric street railways. On an area basis,
that was 287.64 miles for every 1,000 square miles of area. The comparable New York ratio at the time was 54.26.[24]

Boston was also the first major U.S. city to have a subway system. On
September 1, 1897, the first underground transit system in North Amer-
ica opened for service under Tremont Street between Park Street and
Boyleston Street adjacent to Boston Common.

This development followed the consolidation of the several operating
street railways into a single monopoly during the late 1880s. The West
End Street Railway Company, under the leadership of Henry Whitney
of Brookline, had become the effective provider of street railway service
in metropolitan Boston on the eve of electrification. The impetus that
permitted this traction monopoly to exist was the streets of downtown
Boston, which were too narrow to handle the tracks of several different
companies. The creation of a monopoly was an effective way to handle
the complex problems of coordination. Despite this monopolization of
service, the problems of movement in the downtown area were becoming increasingly severe. A rival group of capitalists formed the Boston
Elevated Street Railway Company and leased the lines of the West End
Street Railway Company in 1897. The very name of the new company
suggests something about the problem facing the area by the middle 1890s.
Simply put, that problem was street congestion. It was virtually impossible for the street railways to move people through the downtown core
because of all the competition for street space from horsedrawn wagons,
hand-drawn carts, and people on foot. Some method had to be found to
get the streetcars off the streets and onto exclusive rights of way so that
they could serve to sustain effective population circulation in the dense
core and move people in a timely fashion to the new suburbs which were
springing into existence during this era.

In addition to the erection of elevated lines, a tunnel was constructed
in the downtown core area. This was the beginning of publicly sponsored, publicly financed, and privately operated mass transit. Given the
built-up character of the downtown, there was no speculative real estate
incentive for private developers to take on the considerable capital costs

of tunnel construction. Furthermore, the benefits of cheap rapid transit cannot by definition be captured at the fare box. Rather they are diffuse social and economic externalities.[25] Therefore the costs of tunnel construction were undertaken by the City of Boston through the creation of a Boston Transit Authority. The tunnel and lines were then leased to the operator, the Boston Elevated Street Railway Company.

Though the system was successful as a transportation system, it was not profitable as a business venture even with the government underwriting the capital construction costs. In 1918 the state legislature was forced to pass a Public Control Act assigning operating authority for the system to the Boston Transit Authority. The Authority was empowered to assess the fourteen cities and towns served by the system for the cost of the deficit between revenues and costs. At the time, this was viewed as a temporary measure to get the system over a rough period. Stockholders in the defaulted company were promised an approximate 5 percent return on their investment for use of their rolling stock and other equipment. The arrangement proved to be permanent. However, it was not until after World War II that the the permanence was recognized and formal ownership was vested in the Metropolitan Transit Authority (MTA), which, in 1964, became the Massachusetts Bay Transportation Authority (MBTA) and extended its service to the greater metropolitan region. At present it covers 79 cities and towns.

It was in the 1920s that the first automobile-based suburbanization occurred, but this suburbanization was still quite different from the one that followed World War II. Though the suburbanization of the interwar years made allowances for auto access, it was still fundamentally public-transport based. All houses had driveways and frequently garages to provide off-street parking, and one-family homes became the rule rather than duplexes and triplexes; still the suburbanization occurred only where there was good access to Boston by public transit. The developers generally kept the lots sufficiently small to generate a traffic density that could support public transit—if everybody used it. The communities that experienced the greatest interwar residential growth were the suburbs along the streetcar and rapid transit lines.

During the 1920s, population growth ranged from approximately 50 percent in such southern and southwestern communities as Quincy and Needham, to over 80 percent in the western community of Wellesley, and over 90 percent in the northwestern towns of Arlington and Belmont. Before the 1920s, suburban real estate had to locate within easy walking distance of either the railroad or the public transit facilities. In the 1920s, the automobile allowed the developer to move further away from the terminals. This brought additional land into the housing market and dropped accessible land prices sufficiently to expand the market for suburban living. But it also increased social differentiation among suburbs, with most of the older streetcar zones "filtering down" to the working class, and only a few older towns, notably Brookline, Belmont, Milton, and Newton, along with university enclaves in Cambridge and Medford, remaining affluent.

A second set of investments, besides those in mass transit, was also necessary to massive suburban growth. These involved water supply and sewage. Before the 1890s, those had been provided locally by cities or towns. Boston, which had built a reservoir and aqueduct system beyond its borders, made the water available only to its residents. This, indeed, had been an inducement to other towns to accept annexation.

The dilemma which faced the emerging Boston region in the late nineteenth century was that if annexation of surrounding communities in the central city were to cease, it would have been impossible to construct the necessary infrastructure for a viable region. It must be remembered that county government was merely a shadow government in the Massachusetts frame of reference. The city or the town was the effective unit of local government. Between the local community and the state, therefore, a great vacuum existed. Spatially, each of the cities and towns around Boston was quite small and financially unable to construct all the water and sewer facilities necessary for their growing population. Furthermore, unless methods of moving people between these communities quickly and cheaply could be put in place, it was impossible for metropolitan Boston to become a major center in the burgeoning American economy. The solution was in the development of metropolitan districts which could provide the service in question. These districts could in turn assess their constituent communities for costs. The solution was, in effect, a stone which killed four birds at once. By establishing a metropolitan-area-wide service district, the suburban communities could maintain their independence of the mistrusted central city administration. The direct service need could be addressed at the proper scale to solve the problem, i.e., metropolitan-area-wide agency. The fiscal resources of Boston could be put, at least partially, in the service of suburban expansion. Finally the state legislature, by regulating the service district, could gain further indirect control over Boston without undermining the basis of local independence elsewhere.

The first of the metropolitan districts was the Metropolitan Sewer Commission. It was established in 1889. Its roots extend back to an 1872 report by the State Board of Health that warned of the dangers posed by untreated sewage. The State therefore undertook to construct a sewage system,[26] which was completed by 1885. While this new system did much to lessen the problem, it was not capable of addressing the problems in those cities and towns which surrounded it. The major rivers of the area were at that point serving as an open sewage system. The Charles, Mystic, and Neponset Rivers were carrying dangerous effluents past Boston on their way to polluting the Massachusetts Bay. The sewer problem was sufficiently severe that it was attributed as a cause of the city's high death rate relative to other major cities of the time. Given that the problem could be exported downstream and that it was expensive to solve, the suburban communities were reluctant to undertake a commitment to changing their ways. The Metropolitan Sewage District was the solution to the problem. It was established by the legislature and required to be self-financing through assessments upon the constituent communities of the district. The exact method of assessment was left to an assessment commission appointed by the supreme judicial court on the assumption that justices would be less political or, ideally, a bit more high-minded than the rest.

The second district established was the Parks District. Unlike the Metropolitan Sewage Commission which preceded it and the Metropolitan Water Board which followed it into existence, the Parks District, established in 1893, was not born of infrastructural necessity. Rather it was the child of the late-nineteenth-century desire to help cure the ills of urbanization and its debilitating effect upon the poorest classes by providing open green spaces in which they might find recreation. In that respect, this district might be thought of as an element of reform social policy rather than urban development *per se*.

The third district, established on the heels of the other two in 1895, was the Metropolitan Water Board. The rationale for its creation was quite similar to the rationale behind the creation of the sewage district. An 1893 State Board of Health report documented that it was only through a regional approach that the entire Boston area would be able to enjoy

Building the Streetcar Suburbs. Trolley lines and triple deckers of varying quality expanded the metropolis.

Boston Elevated Railroad courtesy of the
Bay State Society of Model Railroad Engineers.

Streetcar tracks and substantial tripledeckers being put in place together. (Location Unknown)

Boston Public Library, Print Dept.

Bennington Street at Day Square, East Boston, 1918.

Boston Public Library, Print Dept.

View from East Boston toward Chelsea and Orient Heights, 1921.

an adequate supply of water for its growing population. As with the other two districts, it solved the problem of delivering a service without changing the existing political alignment of cities and towns *vis-à-vis* the state while at the same time removing local autonomy from Boston.

A major initial controversy which surrounded the creation of the three districts pertained to the need to devise a formula for assessing the costs of operation against the constituent communities. During the post-World War II years, there was a drastic change in the formulae, placing a heavier burden on the older cities and towns of the metropolitan core. At the beginning, however, the assessment commissioners made a diligent effort to ensure that ability to pay was always a major part of the assessment formula.[27] Thus, while the impetus for the establishment of the districts was an attempt to foist costs for regional development onto the core, it was nonetheless carried forward with a good deal of reformist principle and concern for social equity. In 1901 the water and sewer boards were combined and in 1919 the Parks District was added. The three agencies are today the component parts of the Metropolitan District Commission. The shift in assessment procedures and the growth of the Parks District into a major supplier of regional highways after World War II would effect the shape of postwar suburbanization.

The changes in transportation and utility supply, which occurred in and after the 1890s, appear to be simple, rational responses to a need for expansion. In practice, their development required a complex resolution to a wide variety of conflicts—between workers and their employers, between both of those groups in general and the interests of specific land and transit monopolists, and between competing Irish and Yankee factions in state politics. That story we reserve for the latter part of this book. For the moment, we need only to summarize the effect of the new shape of the metropolitan area, in terms of population movements that led to rapid growth for some towns, and stagnation for others.

The demographic shift which took place between 1890 and 1940 can be seen by a perusal of tables 2.2, 2.3, and 2.4. Table 2.2 contains the population figures for all the cities and towns of the Boston region that were within 10 miles of the core. From 1890 to 1940, the population of that region grew by just over one million people (from 868,311 to 1,888,369)—a fifty-year growth of 117.48 percent. On an annual basis, that amounted to 1.57%. While that rate is sufficiently healthy to demonstrate that the area was economically viable, of more interest to us are the differential growth rates for the various rings within that region. It

Table 2.2
Population of Municipalities Within 10 Miles of Boston

Municipality	1890	1900	1910	1920	1930	1940
Boston[a]	458,670	574,136	686,092	748,060	781,188[b]	770,816
3 MILES						
Brookline	12,103	19,935	27,792	37,748	47,490[b]	49,786[b]
Cambridge	70,028	91,886	104,839	109,684	113,643[b]	110,879[b]
Chelsea	27,909	34,072	32,452	43,184	45,816[b]	41,259
Everett	11,068	24,336	33,484	40,120	48,424[b]	46,784
Somerville	40,152	61,643	77,236	93,091	103,908[b]	102,177
4 MILES						
Medford	11,079	18,244	23,150	39,038	59,714	63,083[b]
Winthrop	2,726	6,058	10,132	15,455	16,852[b]	16,768
5 MILES						
Malden	23,031	33,664	44,404	49,103	58,036[b]	58,010
Revere	5,668	10,395	18,219	28,823	35,680[b]	34,405
6 MILES						
Arlington	5,629	8,603	11,187	18,665	36,094	40,013[b]
Belmont	2,098	3,999	5,542	10,749	21,748	26,867[b]
Melrose	8,519	12,962	15,715	18,204	23,170	25,333[b]
Newton	24,379	33,587	39,806	46,054	65,276	69,873[b]
Quincy	16,723	23,809	32,642	47,876	71,983	75,810[b]
Watertown	7,073	9,706	12,875	21,457	34,913	35,427[b]
7 MILES						
Milton	4,278	6,578	7,924	9,382	16,434	18,708[b]
10 MILES						
Braintree	4,848	5,981	8,068	10,580	15,712	16,378[b]
Dedham	7,123	7,457	9,248	10,792	15,136	15,508[b]
Lexington	3,197	3,831	4,918	6,350	9,467	13,187[b]
Lynn	55,727	68,513	89,336	99,148	102,320[b]	98,123
Nahant	880	1,152	1,184	1,318	1,654	1,835[b]
Needham	3,035	4,016	5,026	7,012	10,845	12,455[b]
Saugus	3,673	5,084	8,047	10,874	14,700	14,825[b]
Wakefield	6,982	9,290	11,025	13,025	16,318[b]	16,223[b]
Waltham	18,707	23,481	27,834	30,915	39,247	40,020[b]
Wellesley	3,600	5,072	5,413	6,224	11,439	15,127[b]
Weymouth	10,866	11,324	12,895	15,057	20,882	23,868[b]
Winchester	4,861	7,248	9,309	10,485	12,719	15,081[b]
Woburn	13,499	14,254	15,308	16,574	19,434	19,751[b]

[a] Includes Hyde Park for years before annexation (1890, 1900, 1910).
[b] Peak Year of Population.
SOURCE: U.S. Censuses of Population.

is these differential rates which tell us something about the redistribution of the population. In 1890 the city of Boston contained the majority
of the area's population (52.81%). By 1940, its share had dropped to just
over two-fifths (40.8%). The area in which the largest growth occurred

Table 2.3
Population Distribution Within 10 Miles of Boston 1890–1940

Location	1890 Pop.	%Tot.	1900 Pop.	%Tot.	1910 Pop.	%Tot.	1920 Pop.	%Tot.	1930 Pop.	%Tot.	1940 Pop.	%Tot.
Center	458,670	52.8	574,136	50.4	686,092	49.3	748,060	46.3	781,188	41.8	770,816	40.8
3 Miles	161,260	18.6	231,872	20.3	275,803	19.8	323,827	20.0	359,281	19.2	350,885	18.6
4–5 Mil.	42,504	4.9	68,361	6.0	95,905	6.9	132,419	8.2	170,282	9.1	172,266	9.1
6–9 Mil.	68,699	7.9	99,174	8.7	125,691	9.0	172,387	10.7	269,618	14.5	292,031	15.5
10 Mil.	136,998	15.8	166,703	14.6	207,647	14.9	238,347	14.8	289,873	15.5	302,371	16.0
TOTALS	868,131	100.0	1,140,246	100.0	1,391,138	100.0[a]	1,615,040	100.0	1,870,242	100.0[a]	1,888,369	100.0

SOURCE: Table 2.2.
[a] Due to rounding.

Table 2.4
Annual Population Growth Rates, 1890–1940

Location	1890/1900	1900/1910	1910/1920	1920/1930	1930/1940	1890/1940
Center	2.27	1.80	.87	.43	(.13)	1.04
3 Miles	3.70	1.75	1.62	1.04	(.24)	1.57
4–5 Miles	4.87	3.44	3.28	2.55	.12	2.84
6–9 Miles	3.74	2.39	3.21	4.57	.80	2.95
10 Miles	1.98	2.22	1.39	1.98	.42	1.60
TOTAL	2.76	2.01	1.50	1.48	.10	1.57

SOURCE: Table 2.2.

was the area from four to nine miles from the core. In 1890 this area contained just under 13% of the population (12.81%). By 1940, almost one-quarter of the population resided in this ring (24.6%). This shift is also seen in a perusal of the annual growth rates contained in Table 2.4. In the four to nine mile ring, annual growth rates always exceed growth at either the center or the periphery.

Either the data by rings or the data on individual towns indicate that in 1930, total population had peaked in Boston and most of the towns in the rings up to five miles out. While declining population in these towns in the 1930s seemed at the time to be a temporary result of the Depression, it would become clear with time that the change was a permanent one. For some, there would be a brief postwar recovery, for others not even that. Growth of total population in the urban core had ceased, and in some towns, as well as in some parts of Boston, a long-term decline was underway. Decline would also continue in the outer industrial enclave of Lynn. In most, but not all, of these communities, the decline also involved economic activity as well as simply population size.

E. Massive Suburbanization, 1940–1980

In the forty years between 1940 and 1980, Boston experienced the most rapid physical growth in the size of the metropolitan region. In 1940, the effective metropolitan region was located within a ring approximately 10 to 12 miles from Boston City Hall. By 1980 the effective metropolitan boundary extended approximately 25 miles beyond the center (fig. 2.2). This growth, which represents a more than fourfold increase in

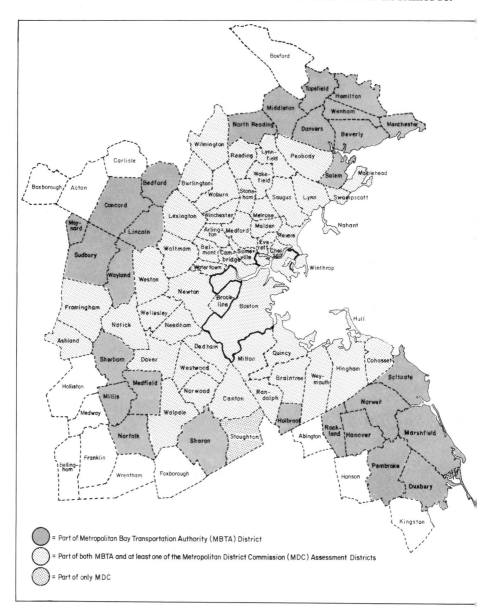

Figure 2.2 Metropolitan Boston.

urbanized space, is reflected in the Census Bureau's treatment of Boston. The Boston Standard Metropolitan Statistical Area (SMSA) was defined in 1950 as containing 78 municipalities. The 1980 SMSA is larger by fourteen communities. This is a reflection of the degree to which the spatial range of metropolitan activity had increased in the region. The majority of the new communities (seven) are in the area to the southwest of Boston City Hall. There was also some expansion to the northwest (three) and north (one) and south (four) at the same distance.

This spatial growth was accompanied by population growth. But the pace of population expansion has been slower than that of the urbanized area. Metropolitan area population grew, from 2,264,759 in 1940, to 2,763,357 in 1980. However, the older cities and towns of the area saw their population level off or decline. The population of Boston itself peaked in 1950, and by 1980 had fallen below its 1900 level. In 1940, one in three metropolitan area residents lived in Boston. By 1980 the figure had dropped to one in five, one of the smallest proportions for a major city anywhere in the country.

This growth of suburban population was necessarily matched by a wave of suburban homebuilding. Although very few homes were added to the housing stock during the Depression or during the War, construction began immediately with the return of peace. Between 1940 and 1959, roughly 200,000 units were added to the housing market in metropolitan Boston. Of these new housing units, only 16 percent were built in the city of Boston and an additional 20 percent in the other thirteen cities and towns of the old metropolitan transit district. The other 64 percent—more than 125,000 units—were built in the suburbs outside the transit district, primarily in communities which had no major highway or rail connection to Boston. Despite urban renewal efforts, this trend has persisted to date. During the 1960s, Boston accounted for only 11 percent of all new housing units, while the suburbs beyond the old transit district built 72 percent of the new housing. This percentage is really an understatement, for the most active building in Eastern Massachusetts during the 1960s occurred generally in communities beyond the area then in the designated Boston SMSA. Most of the new construction took the form of single-family homes, a marked contrast to the first wave of suburbanization in which the triple decker had predominated. Thus the postwar period also became an era of greatly expanded homeownership.

Three contextual factors contributed to the suburban expansion: national prosperity, federal subsidies to homeownership, and subsidies to highway development. As the only nation with its economic plant intact after World War II, the United States became the center of the world economy. In addition, the War had imposed a high incidence of forced savings and postponed consumption which burst forth immediately after the cessation of hostilities. The era from 1945 until approximately 1970 was perhaps the greatest period of sustained economic expansion and prosperity in the history of the nation. This prosperity provided the underpinnings for the expansion of home and automobile ownership, which characterized the period.

The combination of Depression-era programs to bolster confidence in the banking system and a number of specific programs to make home mortgage money readily available together created an era of extremely low-cost home financing. These programs included Federal Housing Administration (FHA) and Veterans Administration (VA) mortgage guarantees to encourage banks to loan mortgage money to young families, and the creation of the Federal National Mortgage Association (FNMA) and the Federal Deposit Insurance Corporation (FDIC) to insure that an abundant supply of savings bank deposits was continually available for mortgage loans.

In addition, income tax deductions for interest costs and property taxes led to lower effective rates in both categories of homeowning expenses than otherwise would have been the case. These deductions are not available to renters.

The postwar era also witnessed the creation of an enormous federal effort to construct highways to the exclusion of virtually every other means of travel. The federal highway trust fund, established in 1956, which was empowered to receive all federal highway and motor vehicle tax receipts, was limited to spending these funds only on highway construction and maintenance. The interstate highway system was a 90 percent federally funded endeavor. In addition, the federal government paid half the cost of certain designated urban highways. The combination of depletion allowances and other favorable treatment of the petroleum industry helped to finance the lowest cost gasoline in the world. This contributed in no small way to the rapid growth of the American automobile and truck fleet.

In the Boston area, access to suburban land did not have to await the coming of the interstate highway program after 1956. During the

Depression, Boston had constructed a system of "parkways," landscaped roads restricted to "pleasure vehicles." To combat this Depression, local and federal funds were made available for public works projects, especially those that could be planned quickly and required many workers. Highways met this bill, if they could be planned quickly. The Metropolitan District Commission (MDC) already owned park land in 36 member cities and towns of the Greater Boston area. Since the MDC already owned its land, it could start construction quickly. The MDC built a major portion of the roads in the Boston area during the 1930s. By taking full advantage of all the available resources to combat the Depression, the MDC built a network of roads and parkways that interconnected park and recreational areas with the population centers of the region. Because most of the new parkways were radial connections, linking Boston with what was then the outer fringes of the built-up area, the open spaces that the MDC connected to the city because it had some parks there became prime sites for new housing.

The postwar Master Highway Plan, issued in 1948,[28] built upon this existing radial network. It added additional radial highways and a series of planned circumferential routes, opened more land to housing with commuter access to Boston, and allowed the development of commuter networks among different suburbs, thus favoring the growth of suburban industrial and commercial activities. Some of these were built by the State or the MDC, others became part of the federal interstate highway program. Once built, they became a major impetus to the relocation of population out of the city and away from public transit or commuter rail access to work and shopping locations. New suburbs first followed existing MDC routes, and then filled in the interstices. Continuing earlier patterns, upper income areas continued to proliferate to the west of the city, while smaller tract homes tended to cluster to the north and south.

Highways and ready mortgage money would not have been enough to create a suburban boom, however, if the regional economy of the Boston area had not undergone a period of growth during and after the War. Economically, the region had been declining during the half century up to World War II. Lack of good local energy sources, distance from the midwestern centers of gravity of industry and population, and the competition of the larger New York port complex had weakened Eastern Massachusetts' shipping and manufacturing. The traditional industries of the area—textiles, shoes, and shipbuilding—all declined drastically, and

Autos extended the city's commuting range. Automobile suburbs featured
single-family houses of varying sizes and quality.

Boston Elevated Railroad courtesy of the
Bay State Society of Model Railroad Engineers.

Auto commuters pass a trolley stop in Allston, ca. 1925.

Photo by Elliott Sclar.

Modest Cape Style house in West Newton Mass., 1984.

Photo by Elliott Sclar.

Large center entrance Colonial house in Weston, Mass., 1984.

apart from a few centers of the electrical equipment industry, manufacturing areas had stagnated even before the Depression.

While such an industrial decline obviously affects everyone in a region, Boston's capitalist elite, the "Brahmins," had been shielded from its major consequences. By the time the decline became serious, much of their investment was already diversified, into equities in midwestern manufacturing, western mining, Latin American plantations, and railroad and gas companies in a variety of states and nations. Financial institutions—bank and trust companies and insurance companies—were another major field for investment. While the latter were, to some extent, still located in Boston and provided some jobs there, they did not invest much money in the region, and particularly avoided Boston city itself. Indeed, it has been claimed that the city was effectively redlined, as a result of political antagonism to the city's Irish political machine.[29]

Even during the period of greatest capital export, however, the Brahmins did direct some of their wealth into building up one sector of the Boston economy: a network of nonprofit institutions. Harvard, MIT, and a number of smaller colleges, as well as institutions in the arts, sciences, and medicine, all were beneficiaries of the Brahmin bank account. The scientific and educational establishments created over the years became the infrastructure for a new wave of local private investment by Boston capital after World War II.

During World War II, numerous defense research contracts, radar in particular, were granted to Harvard and MIT. The postwar growth of an ever more technologically oriented military kept the connection alive. Boston businessmen set up venture capital investment firms to back the development of private business in the universities' orbit. A large complex of research and manufacturing businesses, in electronics and related fields, grew from this base. By the late 1950s, the universities, hospitals, and other nonprofit institutions themselves began to expand as a major part of the region's economic base, stimulated by rising university enrollments and federal funds for social programs as well as continuing military procurement. Finally, in the 1960s, employment in the city of Boston itself, which had been falling for some time despite regional recovery, began to rise. Thus, up to the end of the 1960s, suburbanization and a continuing spread of homeownership were supported by incomes from a generally expansive local economy.

There were always some countertrends. First, the older industries of the region continued to stagnate. The smaller industrial cities on the edges of the Boston area often failed to capture the new firms. Thus the suburbs found themselves growing toward a ring of depressed industrial centers. But through the end of the 1960s, most of these towns were still separated from the newer suburbs by unbuilt areas. Within the metropolitan area itself, industrial depression in the traditional sectors was reflected more in the low incomes of blue collar workers than in an abandonment of large industrial areas.

Second, because the new employment base, both in electronics and in services, was so closely tied to the universities, many jobs were filled by recent graduates. Many of the high incomes in the area were thus obtained by persons not yet ready to "settle in" to home ownership. A high demand for apartments in the inner core was thus generated. As rents drove large families out, and some apartments were subdivided, Cambridge and parts of Boston found that the number of units rented was rising despite a fall in total population.

To some extent, blue collar families were attracted by, or at least compelled to remain in, the inner core neighborhoods by the prevalence of work for women in the new nontechnical jobs. The decline of blue-collar employment meant that families needed women's wages to ensure steady incomes. Thus they were less able to afford the commuting time and costs of distant suburbs. And conflict between working-class families and the new university population occurred over the use of several neighborhoods. Thus, particularly later in the 1970s, certain core areas became rivals to the suburbs for the attention of housing developers.

The movement of population to the suburbs was also favored by the location of many new industries in the urban fringe. When the new companies that grew up around MIT needed land to build their facilities, they searched out the first open acreage with good access to Cambridge. This open land was in several communities: Waltham, Lincoln, Bedford, Lexington, Burlington, and Wilmington. Electronics firms sprang up on properties in all these communities within 10 to 15 miles of one another. These plants became known as the Route 128 industries, because of their pxoximity to the middle-ring highway, built under the 1948 master plan, that goes through these towns. It is worth noting that route was probably not a major factor in their location there. Had Route 128 truly been the attraction, Boston's electronics firms would have located much closer to it than they did. Many plants, and especially the older

Table 2.5
Population of 1980 Boston SMSA by Distance 1940–1980

Municipality[a]	1940	1950	1960	1970	1980
Boston	770,816	810,444	697,197	641,071	562,994
Inner Ring (to 10 miles)					
Arlington (50)	40,013	44,353	49,953	53,524	48,219
Belmont (50)	26,867	27,381	28,715	28,285	26,100
Brookline (50)	49,786	57,589	54,044	58,886	55,062
Cambridge (50)	110,879	120,740	107,716	100,361	95,322
Chelsea (50)	41,259	38,912	33,749	30,625	25,431
Dedham (50)	15,508	18,487	23,869	26,938	25,298
Everett (50)	46,784	45,982	43,544	42,485	37,195
Hull (50)	2,167	3,379	7,055	9,961	9,714
Malden (50)	58,010	59,804	57,676	56,127	53,386
Medford (50)	63,083	66,113	64,971	64,397	58,076
Melrose (50)	25,333	26,988	29,619	33,180	30,055
Milton (50)	18,708	22,395	26,375	27,190	25,860
Newton (50)	69,873	81,994	92,384	91,066	83,622
Quincy (50)	75,810	83,835	87,409	87,966	84,743
Revere (50)	34,405	36,763	40,080	43,159	42,423
Saugus (50)	14,825	17,162	20,666	25,110	24,746
Somerville (50)	102,177	102,351	94,697	88,779	77,372
Stoneham (50)	10,765	13,229	17,821	20,725	21,424
Waltham (50)	40,020	47,187	55,413	61,582	58,200
Watertown (50)	35,427	37,329	39,092	39,307	34,384
Winchester (50)	15,081	15,509	19,376	22,269	20,701
Winthrop (50)	16,768	19,496	20,303	20,335	19,294
TOTALS	913,548	986,978	1,014,527	1,032,257	956,627
Middle Ring (to 15 miles)					
Braintree (50)	16,378	23,161	31,069	35,050	36,337
Burlington (50)	2,275	3,250	12,852	21,980	23,486
Canton (50)	6,581	7,465	12,771	17,100	18,182
Dover (50)	1,374	1,722	2,846	4,529	4,703
Hingham (50)	8,003	10,665	15,378	18,845	20,339
Holbrook (60)	3,330	4,004	10,104	11,775	11,140
Lexington (50)	13,187	17,335	27,691	31,886	29,479
Lincoln (50)	1,783	2,427	5,613	7,567	7,098
Lynn (50)	98,123	99,738	94,478	90,294	78,471
Lynfield (50)	2,287	3,927	8,398	10,826	11,267
Marblehead (50)	10,856	13,765	18,521	21,295	20,126
Nahant (50)	1,835	2,679	3,960	4,119	3,947
Needham (50)	12,445	16,313	25,793	29,748	27,901
Norwood (50)	15,383	16,636	24,898	30,815	29,711
Peabody (50)	21,711	22,645	32,302	48,080	45,976
Randolph (50)	7,634	9,982	18,900	27,035	28,218
Reading (50)	10,866	14,006	19,259	22,539	22,678
Salem (50)	41,213	41,880	39,211	40,556	38,220
Swampscott (50)	10,761	11,580	13,294	13,578	13,839
Wakefield (50)	16,223	19,633	24,295	25,402	24,895
Wellesley (50)	15,127	20,549	26,071	28,051	27,209
Weston (50)	3,590	5,026	8,261	10,870	11,169
Westwood (50)	3,376	5,837	10,354	12,750	13,212
Weymouth (50)	23,868	32,690	48,177	54,610	55,601
Woburn (50)	19,751	20,492	31,214	37,406	36,626
TOTALS	367,960	427,407	565,710	656,706	639,830

Municipality[a]	1940	1950	1960	1970	1980
Outer Ring (to 20 miles)					
Abingdon (80)	5,708	7,152	10,607	12,334	13,517
Bedford (50)	3,807	5,234	10,969	13,513	13,067
Beverly (50)	25,537	28,884	36,108	38,348	37,655
Cohasset (50)	3,111	3,731	5,840	6,954	7,174
Concord (50)	7,972	8,623	12,517	16,148	16,293
Davers (50)	14,179	15,720	21,926	26,151	24,100
Hanover (60)	2,875	3,389	5,923	10,107	11,358
Medfield (50)	4,384	4,549	6,021	9,821	10,220
Middleton (50)	2,348	2,916	3,718	4,044	4,135
Natick (50)	13,851	19,838	28,831	31,057	29,461
North Reading (50)	2,886	4,402	8,331	11,264	11,455
Norwell (60)	1,871	2,515	5,207	7,796	9,182
Rockland (60)	8,087	8,960	13,119	15,674	15,695
Scituate (60)	4,130	5,993	11,214	16,973	17,317
Sharon (50)	3,737	4,847	10,070	12,367	13,601
Sherborn (70)	1,022	1,245	1,806	3,309	4,049
Stoughton (80)	8,632	11,146	16,328	23,459	26,710
Walpole (50)	7,443	9,109	14,068	18,149	18,859
Wayland (50)	3,505	4,407	10,444	13,461	12,170
Wilmington (50)	4,645	7,039	12,475	17,102	17,471
TOTALS	129,730	159,699	245,522	308,031	313,489
Exurbs (beyond 20 miles)					
Acton (80)	2,701	3,510	7,238	14,770	17,544
Ashland (50)	2,479	3,500	7,779	8,882	9,165
Bellingham (80)	2,979	4,100	6,774	13,967	14,300
Boxborough (80)	376	439	744	1,451	3,126
Boxford (80)	778	926	2,010	4,032	5,374
Carlisle (80)	747	876	1,488	2,871	3,306
Duxbury (60)	2,359	3,167	4,727	7,636	11,807
Foxborough (80)	6,303	7,030	10,136	14,218	14,148
Framingham (50)	23,214	28,086	44,526	64,048	65,113
Franklin (80)	7,303	8,037	10,530	17,830	18,217
Hamilton (50)	2,037	2,764	5,488	6,373	6,960
Hanson (80)	2,570	3,264	4,370	7,148	8,617
Holliston (80)	3,000	3,753	6,222	12,069	12,622
Kingston (80)	2,783	3,461	4,302	5,999	7,362
Manchester (50)	2,472	2,868	3,932	5,151	5,424
Marshfield (60)	2,419	3,267	6,748	15,223	20,916
Medway (80)	3,297	3,744	5,168	7,938	8,447
Millis (70)	2,278	2,551	4,374	5,686	6,908
Norfolk (60)	2,294	2,704	3,471	4,656	6,363
Pembroke (60)	1,718	2,579	4,919	11,193	13,487
Sudbury (60)	1,754	2,596	7,447	13,506	14,027
Topsfield (60)	1,150	1,412	3,351	5,225	5,709
Wenham (50)	1,220	1,644	2,798	3,849	3,897
Wrentham (80)	4,674	5,341	6,685	7,315	7,580
TOTALS	82,905	101,619	165,227	261,036	290,419

[a] Figures in parenthesis denotes year municipality classified as in SMSA.

ones, are three to five miles from the highway. Had management truly thought in terms of the bypass rather than access to Cambridge, the industry would have arisen all along Route 128, to the north and to the south of Boston, rather than in the one narrow northwest sector that is bound by the old highways and commuter railroads that lead out from Boston through Cambridge. The industry which Route 128 actually did attract was not the glamorous electronics firms, but the more mundane warehouses which moved there from the inner city. By having their trucks and shippers use the circumferential highway, these operators in effect could cut their distribution costs in the Boston metropolitan area.

As new middle and upper income suburbs were built, and as industry and commerce also found new suburban locations, older neighborhoods lost population to them. The communities that had been built up in the streetcar era were particularly affected: their housing stock was now old, and threedeckers were not favored by FHA regulations and lenders' practices as a prime vehicle for homeownership. These neighborhoods were not, as a rule, abandoned. (Only in the 1970s did that problem appear on a significant scale in a few of the poorest areas.) Some of the neighborhoods were torn down, by urban renewal, highway construction, or, occasionally, private redevelopment. But most remained in existence as a residential "inner ring."

This was possible because population grew. Even apart from the new professional immigration, an influx of blacks from the South and French and English speaking Canadians from the North were filling the traditional channels for working-class immigrants. Thus, occasionally being upgraded for use by the professionals, but more generally filtering down

Table 2.6
Distribution of SMSA Population 1940–1980

Location	1940 Proportion	1950 Proportion	1960 Proportion	1970 Proportion	1980 Proportion
Center City	34.04%	32.35%	25.94%	22.11%	20.37%
Inner Ring	40.34	39.84	37.74	35.61	34.62
Middle Ring	16.24	17.25	21.04	22.65	23.15
Outer Ring	5.74	6.45	9.13	10.63	11.34
Exurbs	3.66	4.10	6.15	9.00	10.51
SMSA TOTALS[a]	100.00%	100.00%	100.00%	100.00%	100.00%

[a] May not total to 100% due to rounding.

Table 2.7
Intercensal and Annual Population Growth Rates for Rings of Metropolitan
Boston 1940–1980

| | Intercensal Growth Rates | | | | |
	1940/50	1950/60	1960/70	1970/80	1940/80
Center City	4.06%	(13.01%)	(8.05%)	(12.18%)	(26.96%)
Inner Ring	8.04	2.80	1.38	(6.99)	4.72
Middle Ring	16.22	32.34	16.11	(2.57)	73.98
Outer Ring	23.10	53.74	25.46	1.77	141.65
Exurbs	22.57	62.59	57.99	11.26	250.30
SMSA TOTAL	9.41%	8.52%	7.85%	(4.68%)	22.02%

| | Annual Growth Rates | | | | |
	1940/50	1950/60	1960/70	1970/80	1940/80
Center City	.39%	(1.38%)[a]	(.84%)	(1.29%)	(.78%)
Inner Ring	.78	.27	.17	(.75)	.11
Middle Ring	1.51	2.84	1.50	(.26)	1.39
Outer Ring	2.10	4.39	2.29	.18	2.23
Exurbs	2.06	4.98	4.68	1.07	3.18
SMSA TOTAL	.90	.82	.76	(.48)	.50

[a] Parentheses denote negative growth rate.

to the poor, the older streetcar suburbs found new uses. Nor did all of the working-class families that had survived the 1930s move; many stayed, out of choice or necessity, to face the rising costs that taxes and aging buildings imposed, along with the new confusions of neighborhood change.

The story of uneven development within the Boston metropolitan area can be read in part from census figures on population in the region's different towns and cities. Tables 2.5, 2.6 and 2.7 detail these population shifts.

Table 2.5 contains demographic information on all the 92 cities and towns which comprise the 1980 Boston SMSA. The data are for each federal census from 1940 to 1980. The area is divided into five subgroups: center city, inner ring (within 10 miles of Boston City Hall), middle ring (10 to 15 miles of City Hall), outer ring (15 to 20 miles of City Hall) and exurbs (beyond 20 miles of City Hall). The subsequent tables analyze population dispersion over the last forty years. Population in the center city has been declining steadily since its 1950 peak. The population peak for the inner and middle ring of communities was reached in 1970. The outer rings have demonstrated continuous growth over the entire period.

Despite the evidence provided by the 1980 census, we think it would be wrong to view the present period as a mere continuation of the past. While the data do contain evidence that further suburbanization is in the offing, there are also several factors which indicate that the situation through the end of the century may be very different. The combination of increasing time and money costs for metropolitan transportation, rising costs of single family homeownership, changing demographics of household composition and increased demand for highly skilled and highly paid workers in the central business district suggest that a new pattern may be unfolding. This pattern would be one in which higher income groups begin to demand residential space in areas which are closer to the downtown in neighborhoods and communities which previously saw the outmigration of such people. We leave it until the end of the book to speculate about this future. For now we can begin to look at the development of Boston's suburbs and their impact on the people who created them.

THREE

Real Estate Values:
Boston and Three Inner Suburbs

"HOW will it affect property values?" is a question raised again and again in debates on urban policy. Neighborhoods can be mobilized over supposed threats to the values of houses, caused by the inflow of new residents, by the siting of potentially intrusive commercial and public facilities, or by threats to the environment. The potential for property value increase is often claimed by real estate salespeople. Implicit in these fears and hopes is a belief that rising property values are normal, and that falling values may be explained by specific intrusions.

Suppose, however, that rising property values are not the norm. Suppose that values tend to remain constant in real terms, or to move up and down cyclically, in response to nonlocal forces. In that case, many of the assumptions of local politics and policy-making need reconsideration. Our model of asset devaluation, sketched in chapter 1, and implicit in the history of Boston outlined in chapter 2, suggests that this reevaluation may be needed.

In this chapter and the next, we present empirical evidence on the evolution of property values in the Boston area over the past century. This chapter examines land and housing values in the city of Boston and in three other municipalities of the urban core: Brookline, Somerville, and Cambridge. Evidence for Boston is drawn from a variety of reports and statistical sources. Data on housing values in Brookline and Somerville, on the other hand, was assembled directly from a sample of property records. Finally, the more limited examination of Cambridge, also assembled from town records, focuses on changes in house values during a process of neighborhood "upgrading" which began in the 1960s. Taken together, the town studies show that property values tend, in the long run, to follow the rate of inflation. They show marked cyclical patterns in some cases. They also show that there may be striking differences between the value changes of different properties, or of properties in different communities. Even in a revitalizing community during a boom period, not all properties will provide high capital gains to their owners.

The community studies in the present chapter are complimented in chapter 4 by a statistical analysis of town averages for real estate and housing values throughout the metropolitan area, over the 1890–1970 time period. Taken together, the two chapters present considerable evidence that value stagnation, or devaluation, is a common, rather than exceptional, feature of the urban scene.

A. Real Estate Values in Boston City

One of the oldest ex-suburbs in American cities is Boston's South End.[1] Originally the tideswept strip of land connecting Boston to Roxbury and Dorchester on the mainland, the "neck" was widened by landfill in the first half of the nineteenth century. Development of the land was mostly the work of private investors.[2] They tore down hills and widened the upper part of the neck for railway terminals and yards, a warehouse and business district, and a residential area which, because of its location near these jobsites, was quickly subdivided for tenements. The land farther south on the peninsula, toward the mainland, was filled by the city. It was in this area that residential suburbs developed in the 1850s.

As early as 1801, Boston had appointed a committee to manage and lease the semi-submerged lands along the South End shores. After Boston received its charter as a city in 1822, the local government took a more active role in land development, extending Tremont Avenue down the neck to the mainland and filling land along it. Of the land created, some was sold in large lots for individual homes and, by the 1850s, the development of elegant squares off the main avenue was begun. The city auctioned off the land for Worcester Square and Union Park in 1851. The Metropolitan Railroad, built in 1853, provided transit to downtown.[3]

After the Civil War, the new South End began to decline as a residential district for the affluent. In part, public policy brought about the change as state government entered into partnership with private companies to fill the Back Bay for a new upper-class residential district more closely connected to Beacon Hill. The new district, which came on the market in the 1870s, was also more closely planned than the South End and afforded it much competition. Although the South End developers had attempted to create a uniform environment, the fiscal crisis which accompanied the panic of 1873 led the city to withdraw support for controlled development in the area. Lots along the main avenues were acquired by tenement developers renting to immigrant shanty-dwellers recently evicted from Fort Hill, which was demolished in 1866. The problems of the area were further exacerbated by the very development of the neck itself. Since the widened neck was able to carry increased traffic loads between Boston and the mainland, it became increasingly difficult for the South End to maintain the character of a quiet residential neighborhood.

The South End ceased to be an attractive neighborhood for the affluent. But this did not lead to its depopulation. Other groups moved in, first as renters but, by the early twentieth century, increasingly as owners. Irish and Jewish names appear regularly on the tax rolls for the early part of the century. Later, individual blocks became concentrations of homes owned by black, Levantine, and Chinese immigrants. Absentee ownership, sometimes by immigrants who had lived in the area and made enough money to leave, also grew more frequent by the mid-twentieth century.

Changes on land and building values in the area cannot be deduced from those changes in occupancy alone. Sometimes a slum may be an area of high land values, sustained by the crowding of many people into a small area. Lack of housing elsewhere may force people to pay a high proportion of their salary in rent. This was true of the South End residents encountered by the settlement house workers who entered the area at the turn of the century. High percentages of enough small incomes can at times sustain high land values. In those older portions of the South End, where land was used more and more for commercial uses, high land prices were in fact sustained, despite the poverty of the residents. However, in much of the residential South End, high values were not sustained.

In 1906, as part of a study of the lodging house district, Albert Benedict Wolfe traced assessed values and sales prices for Union Park, one of the squares developed in the early 1850s.[4] Wolfe found that assessed values had fallen by 42 percent between 1869 and 1905. Where sales prices were available, they showed an even greater decline, since houses had been assessed at 10–20 percent below value around 1870, but often above value by the late 1880s. In figure 3.1, a continued trace of values for the same houses shows that values continued to fall well after Wolfe's study. Except for a modest gain during the boom of the 1920s, assessed values continued to fall into the late 1950s. Only in the 1960s did they start to rise. Since assessment/sales price ratios were dropping throughout the postwar period, and particularly in the 1960s, the market value of houses probably rose slightly between 1940 and 1960, though not as rapidly as the general price index.

After 1960, price increases were much more rapid than assessments indicate. With the expansion of the downtown business district into the area between the Back Bay and the South End through the Prudential Center development, and with the rehabilitation of many of the old squares of the South End, prices moved upward steeply. Yet many of the previous residents of the area did not benefit from the boom. After

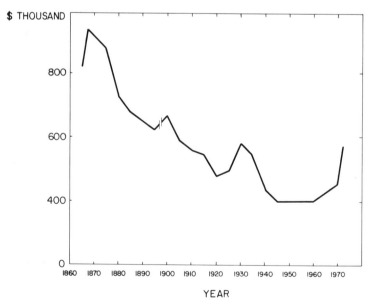

Figure 3.1   Assessed Values for Two-Block area, Union Park (South End).

Housing on the "Escalator." The South End was devalued but later gentrified. Further down Harrison Avenue, abandonment has begun.

Tremont Street Near Rutland Street in the South End, ca. 1890.

The Corner of Harrison Avenue and Eustis Street.

generations of immigrants had bought into the area, over more than half a century, only to ride the escalator of land values downward before selling out to the next group, much of the area had passed into the hands of outside landowners before becoming "ripe" for revitalization. Even among *resident* owners of the 1950s, gains on selling were probably modest. A study of the effects of the Prudential Center on the South End shows that the land value increases which swept through the area were *preceded* by a wave of sales to *new* owners.[5] Only persons with access to architectural skills and to credit or cash could undertake the rehabilitation necessary to restore middle class occupancy. At best, the previous owners might pick up a portion of the value increase by selling to the redeveloper. The redevelopers bragged about the bargains in old housing in the South End; the previous owners barely escaped the capital losses that had burdened their predecessors in the district.

The South End is a clear example of how a neighborhood's homeowners, for more than three-quarters of a century, follow the example of Josiah Franklin, rather than that of his illustrious son. It is obviously an extreme case: a neighborhood planned as a center of opulence fails as that and soon becomes just a well-known slum. For us to argue that housing has *generally* been a depreciating asset for the working homeowner, *in the sense of chapter 1*, we must demonstrate the relative downward pattern of real estate values in many more residential areas.

Alexander S. Porter traced the assessed values and sale prices of a number of downtown Boston properties in 1886. He found that many of the properties within what had become the business district (which had been residential in 1800) had risen to 15–22 times their original values. But Porter's sample was not random. In some cases, his figures were based just on land value, in some on land plus buildings. He concluded that

> Real estate has always been a sure and safe investment in the long run. The old families of Boston owe much of their wealth of today to the steady, and in some cases enormous rise in the value of their houses and stores. To be sure there have been, and will be, periods of depression, when it would seem that the more real estate one has, the worse it is for him; but during all these depressions there is an undercurrent of growth that is quietly going on, which is sure to make itself felt when the tide turns and the clouds pass away.[6]

On the other hand, writing in 1941, John C. Kiley showed that, for many properties in the downtown area, prices per foot in 1930–40 were comparable to or even below the level of the 1870s, though they had at times risen much higher, particularly in the 1910s and 1920s. Kiley attributed part of the fall to the Depression, but found other factors at work as well:

> The study of real estate values in the 1930–40 period may be divided into two parts. The first half, like other periods of real estate depression, ran parallel to the depression in securities and business. The second half seems to have had no parallel or yardstick in the history of Boston. It is within this period that the greatest recession in realty values has taken place.[7]

Kiley attributed this decline to the impact of the automobile, which made available suburban land that had been selling at prices of 15¢ to $2.00 per square foot, compared to prices of $25.00 to $50.00 downtown, and to the effects of high taxes and vacancy rates following the construction boom of the 1920s.

"I am of the opinion," Kiley concluded, "that, if the present wearing down taxing conditions are allowed to continue, much of the real estate in our older cities, which was once a great contributor to national prosperity, will have so little value that it will be given back to the cities from which it was purchased in the early years of the settlement of the country."[8] But although this prediction might seem to have been borne out by the well-publicized abandonments of buildings in many cities— including Boston—in recent years, land values in the business districts of the city were caught up in a new boom by the late sixties.

Where Porter and Kiley spoke of the city as a whole, and used evidence only from the business district, other studies have shown considerable differences in the pattern of land value changes between neighborhoods. Henry Whitmore calculated in 1896 that land value assessments in the city had grown less rapidly than population. Whitmore believed these assessments to have been made at relatively constant ratios to the market values. Broken down by districts of the city, the changes showed considerable variation. For the "city proper," including the downtown area, land values increased 41.7 percent over the period 1875–1895, and in the newly urbanizing Brighton district, 62.2 percent. However, in the older East Boston and Charlestown areas, the increases ran 7.8 percent and 11.1 percent, and in South Boston assessed land values actually fell. In all, Whitmore concluded, capital gains were below returns on alternative investments.[9]

These figures are suggestive, if not statistically conclusive. A well-constructed series on Boston house values, based on a carefully drawn sample of properties, is available only for the postwar period. This is a series of housing-price indices for different neighborhoods of the city prepared by Robert Engle and John Avault.[10] The index is based on property sale price information taken from title-deed tax stamps. Only houses which were transferred in two or more arms-length sales during the period are included in the index. It is thus based on changes in price for specific properties and is not biased, as a comparison of *average* sale prices in specific years might be, by differing qualities of houses sold at different times. The index is discussed in Appendix B. The results that Engle and Avault report for different Boston neighborhoods located on the map in figure 3.2, are presented in table 3.1.

During the postwar period as a whole, the indices increased in all neighborhoods of the city. This sustains the general view of rising rather than depreciating house values. There are considerable differences, though, between the neighborhoods sampled. While on average values more than tripled, the 1970–72 index was at 217 percent of its 1946 level in the Washington Park ghetto, but 618 percent in Charlestown. These figures exceed the rise in the cost of living index over the quarter century, so that the real change is at least marginally positive in all neighborhoods. But the timing of the increases varies among the different neighborhoods. In a number of cases, real values declined or grew at a very slow pace.

For the South End, the increase in values is concentrated entirely in the immediate postwar inflation years and in the 1960s. Values did not rise at all during the 1950s, and the 1960 index is lower than the same year's consumer price index, taking either 1946 or 1950 as the base. Values more than tripled in the 1960s. Charlestown shows a somewhat similar pattern. Its values barely outpace the average price index up to 1960, then almost quadruple in the 1960s. Both communities were subject to upper-income entry and rehabilitation in that decade, after earlier decades as low-income areas.

Neighborhoods farther from the center of the city show slower rates of value growth after 1960. Real values for Washington Park (Roxbury)

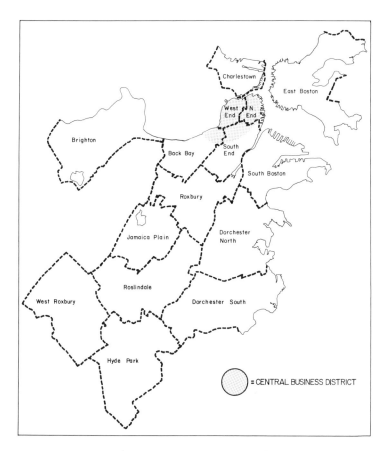

Figure 3.2   Map of Boston's Neighborhoods. Central Business District is also known as "Boston Proper."

and Dorchester decline in the 1960s; market values in Jamaica Plain, Roslindale, Hyde Park, West Roxbury, and Allston-Brighton outpace the CPI, but grow more slowly than in areas closer to the center. The indices thus show that, despite the increases in average house values for Boston in the postwar period, some neighborhoods suffered declining values in real terms. In others, real values did increase, but only in small amounts, and certainly by less than values of competing assets. Other neighborhoods show extremely rapid gains. Either the fate of Josiah Franklin or that of Ben seems possible in this period. The South End may be an extreme case, but declining values are not unique to it.

Table 3.1
Price Indices for Twice-Sold Houses (1946 = 100)

Neighborhood	1950	1960	1970	1970–72
ENTIRE CITY	138	190	348	357.1
East Boston	133	170	351	382.5
Charlestown	113	185	659	618.0
South Boston	127	169	313	347.0
Central/N.End	158	215	611	554.5
Back Bay/Beacon Hill	140	230	527	498.3
South End	149	141	485	490.9
Fenway/Kenmore	131	215	455	532.2
Allston/Brighton	143	198	342	350.7
Jamaica Plain	149	194	317	296.6
Washington Park	145	162	207	217.4
Dorchester/Mattapan	136	210	247	257.1
Roslindale	131	215	320	328.5
West Roxbury	126	194	313	317.5
Cost of Living	123	152	199	207

SOURCES: Robert F. Engle and John Avault, *Residential Property Market Values in Boston* (Boston: Boston Redevelopment Authority Research Department, 1973); Robert F. Engle, "De Facto Discrimination in Residential Assessments: Boston," *National Tax Journal* XXVII:4 (December 1975), 445–451; Cost of Living is U.S. Bureau of Labor Statistics consumer price index for urban wage earners and clerical workers, with base changed from 1967 to 1946 for comparability.

Even the rapid increases in central Boston in the postwar period are, however, somewhat misleading if seen in isolation: 1946 marks the relaxation of wartime controls, the first beginnings of civilian prosperity following depression and war; 1970–1972 mark the approximate end of the quarter-century postwar boom. The Engle indices, therefore, cover only the upswing of a long business cycle. If one looks not just at the postwar years, but at the entire twentieth century, value increases after 1946 amount to a period of "catching up" after two decades of falling values beginning in 1925.

The figures in table 3.2 show the land value per square mile in different neighborhoods of Boston, computed by applying the assessment ratio to land value assessments in the area as a whole, published by the city. They indicate that postwar value increases for the city as a whole did not quite restore the values prevailing in 1925. The value per-square-mile figure returns to $40.7 million in 1970 after being only $20.7 million in 1945, but the 1925 figure was $42.5. These figures may be somewhat underestimated, as assessment ratios are based on comparison of the sales price of *whole* properties (including land and buildings) with assessements which often exclude buildings. As buildings age, even if assessments move with changes in total values, Gaffney has argued that assessors may assign too high a portion of the value to the aged building and not enough to its location.[11] Such understatement is suggested by the fact that land value assessments rose more slowly in the postwar period than Engle's index. For the city, on average, values at the peak of the 1960s boom probably did exceed land values on the eve of the 1929 crash, but by less than the 107 percent by which the cost of living had increased nationally between 1925 and 1970.

The period 1900–1925 was, according to the table, also one of generally rising values. On average, land values rose from $25.4 million per square mile to $42.5 million. Before 1900, figures on land values and building values were not separated by assessors, so the table cannot be continued backward. However, the studies by Porter and Whitmore suggest rising average values in the area.

The existing assessment figures that include both land and buildings show a distinct increase.[12] They undoubtedly overstate the increase, as

Table 3.2
Estimated Land Values Per Square Mile
$Millions
(Estimated from assessments as corrected for
assessment/sales-price ratios)

	1900	1925	1945	1970
TOTAL CITY	25.4	42.5	20.7	40.7
Boston Proper[a]	363.0	291.5	148.9	324.1
Charlestown	29.4	30.3	25.1	53.1
East Boston	10.7	6.0	9.7	14.0
Dorchester	4.6	17.0	13.3	32.6
Roxbury	24.9	91.5	13.4	22.8
South Boston	21.3	62.6	22.3	44.5
Allston-Brighton	7.2	7.3	12.0	29.8
West Roxbury and Jamaica Plain	4.0	4.0	5.7	13.9
Hyde Park	—	1.1	3.2	10.0

[a]Boston Proper includes original city borders (Downtown, North End, South End, West End and Back Bay).
Assessed land values and areas by wards from City of Boston Assessing Department *Reports*.
Assessment ratios for 1900 and 1925 from calculations for this study by Barbara Sproat. Ratios for 1945 and 1970 are closest dates available from Robert F. Engle's calculations. Changes in ward definitions may bias 1900–1924 comparisons.

they include the areas annexed to Boston, particularly in the early 1870s. But the overestimate cannot account for much of the overall increase.

The Depression may be unique in having led to a *general* decrease in property values throughout the area and for a prolonged period of time. Yet, for specific areas of the city, long periods of value stagnation and decline have not been exceptional. In the late nineteenth century, values declined in the South End, South Boston, and perhaps the North End. In the first quarter of the century, values fell within the original city limits ("Boston Proper," including the North, South and West Ends, downtown and the Back Bay) as well as in East Boston; in Charlestown they were stagnant. Growth at that time was concentrated in the new "streetcar suburbs" of South Boston, Dorchester, and Roxbury. The still semirural outer areas of the city (West Roxbury, Jamaica Plain, Hyde Park, and Allston-Brighton) also had stagnant property values during this period, but then became areas of growth between 1925 and 1945. During this time the city continued to lose values in all of its inner areas (except East Boston, the site of the new airport and much landfill), as well as in the older streetcar suburbs. After the war, value increases continued rapidly in the new districts (slowing down in the 1960s), while the inner areas recovered values of the pre-Depression era only in the late 1960s—pulling ahead in some of the inner areas, but not in the streetcar suburb areas of white South Boston and black Roxbury.

Taking the entire area and the past century as a whole, cyclical and locational considerations clearly undercut the conclusion of ever-increasing property values that appears in the studies by Carter, Whitmore, or Engle, or in the total assessments for the whole city. What appears instead is a pattern in which land value increases occur first in the center of Boston, then spread out to the streetcar suburbs and finally to the outer neighborhoods. In each area, after an initial period of growth, values stagnate and may actually drop, particularly in an economic depression.

In the late 1960s, a new boom at the center became the first deviation from this pattern. It represented a redevelopment of old areas to new uses; whether it represents the start of a new outward-moving wave of value increases remains unclear. The evidence to date is mixed. Neighborhoods go through a cycle of rising and falling values, driven both by local factors such as neighborhood aging and by the overall business cycle. This is the main lesson from the Boston city data.

B. Brookline and Somerville[13]

Outside of the City of Boston, few areas have had property values actually fall, except in the Depression. However, rates of value increase have sometimes fallen behind rates of inflation or (more often) returns on alternate investments. In addition, losses occur on individual properties, even when average values increase. This section studies the phenomena by considering samples of properties in two inner-ring towns.

The two towns are, in many ways, contrasting cases. Brookline was an early upper-income suburb in the favored western sector of the metropolitan area. The development of part of the district by Henry Whitney and the West End Street Railway Company will be discussed in chapter 7. The area has remained, to this day, one known for its good schools and public services. It is at least a middle-class bastion, if no longer a town of estates and mansions. Somerville, on the other hand, declined in reputation very quickly, despite some initial fashionable development on Winter Hill. It became part of the group of working-class towns making up the northern sector of the inner ring. Its schools and other public services have an unfavorable reputation. In average income and average house values, it is reported by the Census to be much less affluent than Brookline.

Yet there are similarities in the development of the two towns. Both lie about four miles from Boston. Both initially developed as streetcar suburbs. Both were close enough to Boston for annexation to the city to be discussed seriously at the end of the nineteenth century; both, however, avoided annexation—Brookline by its own vote in a referendum and Somerville after political debate found the town divided on the issue. Both have suffered somewhat from the competition of newer automobile suburbs—Brookline losing in fashionability to towns like Wellesley, Somerville afflicted by a severe traffic problem caused by commuter flow-through from newer suburbs to the north. Both have undergone ethnic succession after beginning as largely Protestant communities. Somerville became mostly Catholic; Brookline has a large Jewish community as well as a Catholic population. Finally, both Brookline and Somerville were affected in the late 1960s and 1970s by the large influx of students and young technicians into the Boston area, which resulted in shortages of apartments and rising rents: both enacted rent controls in the early 1970s.

To analyze the real estate history of the towns, small samples of houses were drawn for each, representing houses from the different neighborhoods of each municipality. For Brookline, a sample of 36 houses was used; for Somerville, 43 houses. Ten of the Somerville houses had been built before 1870; six of the Brookline houses between 1930 and 1954. All others had been built between 1870 and 1930, the main era of growth for both towns. For Brookline, eight were built 1870–1889; nine were built 1890–1909, and thirteen built 1910–1929. For Somerville, the figures are eleven built 1870–1889; fourteen built 1890–1909; eight built 1910–1929. All were structures still in use in the early 1970s. Ownership records for the properties were traced through the files of their respective county deeds registry, and checked against assessors' records. Properties which had been sold more than once were used to analyze price increases or decreases for houses. For Brookline, 160 pairs of transactions involving the purchase and later sale of the same already-built structure were found for which price information was available from the deeds; for Somerville, 298 were found.

This information was first used to construct housing price indices for the two communities. The indices, like those computed by Engle and referred to in the previous sections, use ratios between sale prices in two years as the basic units. The series of price ratios can be combined, by regression analysis, to form an index of house values which reflects the price changes over the whole period. This technique, as Engle has argued, has the advantage over the comparison of averages of prices from different periods, because it is not biased by differences in the composition of the samples averaged in different years. Individual years in the index may still be biased if very few transactions take place in those years and if they are for buildings that differ greatly from the rest of the sample. Such a phenomenon may account for the few severe deviations from the general trend which the indices show (especially that for Somerville in the Depression years 1935–39). But over the long period covered by the sample, the regressions do indicate the general trend in values facing the owner-revendor of an existing property.

Indices were constructed for Somerville for the period 1870–1973 and for Brookline for 1890–1972 (see Appendix B). The two indices are graphed and compared with each other in figure 3.3. The details of index construction, and the calculation of the indices including their margins of error, are left for the appendix. As figure 3.3 shows, the general trend

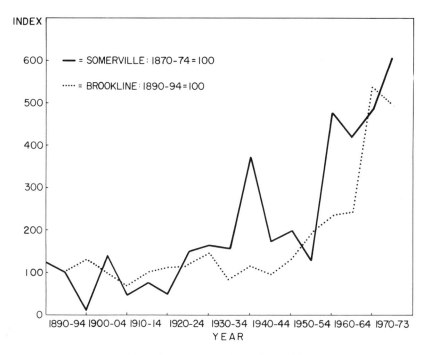

Figure 3.3   House Value Indices, Somerville and Brookline.
SOURCE: Appendix B.

of values over the period is similar in both municipalities, though Somerville's shows greater short-period fluctuations. The indices vary around
an only slightly increasing trend from as far back as 1870. The increase
that occurs in average house prices between 1910 and the end of World
War II does not exceed the rise in the national wholesale price index
over this period, so that, on average, home owners in the two towns did
not make capital gains in real terms. On the other hand, the period between the early 1950s and the early 1970s is one of rapidly rising prices
far exceeding the increase in the national price indices.

The similarity in trend between values in Somerville and Brookline
indicates that differences in value appreciation have not been great during the past eighty years between the more affluent suburbs in Boston's
west and the older working-class areas to the north. This does not mean,
of course, that the areas are similar in absolute levels. Rather, the relative *differences* tend to be preserved. The median value for homes sold
in Somerville in the 1890s was less than $1,000, while in Brookline it

was $7,000. The median sales value in Somerville was $2,500 during the 1920–24 period, and $8,000 for 1925–29. For Brookline the figures were $10,000 and $15,000. In the second half of the 1960s, the median value for Somerville was $22,000, for Brookline, $51,000.

There is another difference between the two towns, which involves the risk of loss on sales. Despite average price increases, some owners have had to sell for less than they paid, and others' gains have not kept up with inflation. Over the 80-plus years for which values were traced, 36 of 112 sales in Somerville were for less than owners originally paid, and another 13 were at gains of less than 2 percent a year. Thus 43 percent of sales in Somerville were at a gain of less than 2 percent per year; 31½ percent actually lost money. For Brookline, losses are less frequent: 15 of 76 sales (20 percent). But another 19 sales were at gains of less than 2 percent per year, so that 45 percent of all sales were at losses or at annual gains of less than 2 percent. (see Appendix B, tables B.1 and B.2).

Some of these losses, of course, occurred during periods of deflation. If only houses purchased after 1940 are considered, the proportion of houses showing substantial gains in value is higher for both towns. In the case of Brookline, only one of 27 sales shows a loss and just two a gain of less than 2 percent. In Somerville, however, 10 of 39 sales show an absolute loss, and another three a gain of less than 2 percent a year; 31 percent of resales in Somerville as opposed to 10 percent in Brookline, that is, took place either at an absolute loss or at a gain less than the average rate of postwar inflation. This is a main difference in investment outcomes between owning a home in a working-class community to the north of Boston and one in an upper-middle-class town to the west.

C. The Upgrading of Cambridge[14]

If the South End of Boston in the early 1900s was an extreme case of value decline, the redevelopment of Cambridge since the late 1950s has been the archetype of neighborhood "upgrading" in the urban core.

A study of Cambridge's housing market in the 1960s gives some insight into the distribution of land and housing value changes in a period of shortage. Although value decline and filtering give way to apparent value increase, returns are still distributed unequally among property owners, with long-term owner-occupants receiving the lowest returns. Cambridge, across the Charles River from downtown Boston, is the home of Harvard University, the Massachusetts Institute of Technology, and a variety of research-oriented corporations. These institutions grew rapidly in the 1950s and 1960s. Meanwhile, Cambridge's traditional industrial base declined, as several large manufacturing plants including Lever Brothers, the Dagett Company, Simplex Wire, and the Riverside Press moved out. While total employment in Cambridge remained constant, the number of blue-collar jobs declined from over half of the jobs in Cambridge in 1950, to a third in 1970. Thus the economic position of the city's older blue-collar population was weakened, while the new technical and white-collar jobs attracted educated young people to the area. These people often were single, or had small families. The result was that although total population declined from 121,000 in 1950 to 100,000 in 1970, the number of households rose from 33,000 in 1950 to 36,000 in 1970.[15]

One result was tremendous pressure of new demand on a housing market which included old working-class districts as well as long-established upper-and middle-class areas of private homes and apartments closer to Harvard.

The Cambridge "housing shortage" has been often analyzed with respect to the effects it had on tenants. Rents rose rapidly in the 1960s. The census estimate of median contract rents rose from $37.10 in 1950 to $63.00 in 1960 (a 5.4 percent annual increase), and then to $119.00 in 1970 (6.6 percent annually). Rents for vacant apartments advertised in the Boston Globe rose 10 percent a year between 1960 and 1969, rising most rapidly after 1965.[16]

Large apartments were at a premium because many had been removed from the market for subdivision.[17] One would expect that rising real estate prices could only benefit the homeowner, as his property rose in value also. Furthermore, the market forces which raised rents were also making it profitable to convert homes into apartments through subdivision or demolition for new construction. Therefore, homeowners should have been in a very advantageous position. They could either have converted their property and reaped the profits, or they could have sold their houses to other entrepreneurs at the high prices which prevailed in the market. However, these opportunities were not equally open to all.

According to Matthews' analysis of activity in the Cambridge housing market from 1960 to 1969, there were 2,230 new apartments constructed, in 119 new buildings. Meanwhile, 300 buildings, with 684 housing units, were demolished. Thus net new construction was 1,546 new units (mostly in large apartment houses, which mostly replaced one, two, or three family buildings). This was not the only new source of apartments, however: 416 new apartments were added to the housing stock by the subdivision of homes or apartments (in 123 buildings). Only 28 apartments were lost through the conversion of 19 buildings, which had had smaller apartments, into larger units. Most of the subdivision took place in the early part of the decade, while new construction was greatest in 1965 and 1968.[18]

The changes in housing were accomplished via the market mechanism. That is, the people who desired housing got it by paying other people, who either owned it or produced it. The changes in the population living in Cambridge had major effect on prices.

The census estimate of the median value of owner-occupied homes rose from $9,980 in 1950 to $13,800 in 1960 and $24,200 in 1970. The annual increases come to 3.3 percent in the 1950s and 5.8 percent in the 1960s, slightly less than the increases for rents. These figures, and the corresponding rent changes fail, however, to indicate price changes for individual homes or apartments, since the stock of houses and apartments for which these averages is taken changed so greatly.

An alternate estimate, similar to that used for Brookline and Somerville, is a yearly price index of housing for the period 1946–1970, constructed by Robert Engle and shown in figure 3.4. The index was constructed from a random sample of properties which were sold in Cambridge. Since houses sold more than once are included, the index excludes some of the effects of changes in the proportion of different housing types in the housing stock.[19] The index may, however, underrepresent the price of houses in stable neighborhoods, which are less likely to have changed hands over the past 25 years. This indicator showed Cambridge housing prices as rising 6.1 percent in the 1950s and 6.7 percent in the 1960s, a faster increase than shown by the census medians.

To investigate the distribution of housing price changes, two additional indices were computed, for two subsamples of buildings (see table 3.3). The first is a biennial index of housing prices covering the period 1946–1972. The index is based on a random sample of 47 properties which

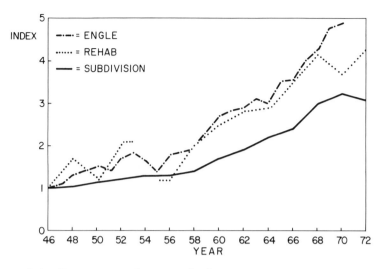

Figure 3.4.   House Price Indices, Cambridge.

underwent some kind of rehabilitation in the sixties, but which were not subdivided. The prices from which the index was computed were obtained from the deeds of sale, and therefore are market prices as in the Engle index. The index was constructed in a manner similar to the Engle index. The price effects of renovations on the properties were separated from the pure time trends of the market price, so that the index has corrected for the quality changes resulting from renovations. This index, which will be referred to as the rehabilitation index, was constructed from relatively few observations. The result is that it fluctuates substantially in the fifties, and shows a perhaps larger than actual decline for 1970–71. On the whole, though, the rehabilitation index moves closely with the Engle index.

The final price series is another biennial index of housing from 1946 to 1972. This index, to be referred to as the subdivision index, is based on the sale prices of properties which were subdivided in the sixties. Prices were obtained and the index computed as for the rehabilitation index; the effects of quality changes have been controlled for. These two indices are also shown in figure 3.4.

The differences in the population on which the various price measures are based pose a question of whether a price exists which is representative of all housing in the city. Neoclassical price theory suggests that if

Table 3.3
Increase in Value of Several Real Property Measures, Cambridge

| | YEARLY PERCENTAGE RATE OF INCREASE | | | |
	1950–60	*1960–70*	*1946–58*	*1958–70*
Engle Index (1)	6.1	6.7	5.5	8.3
Monthly Median				
Contract Rent (2)	5.4	6.6		
Median Value of				
Dwellings (2)	3.3	5.8		
Rehab Index (3)	7.9	4.4*	5.5	5.8**
Subdivision Index (3)	4.0	6.8	2.5	7.6

* 1960–1972.
** 1958–1972.
SOURCES: 1) Robert F. Engle and Robert Richter, Unpublished Property value indices, M.I.T 1971.
2) U.S. Censuses.
3) Alan Mathews, tabulation from Middlesex County property deeds and City of Cambridge building permits. See Appendix B.

two commodities are (gross) substitutes in demand then if the price of one rises, *ceteris paribus*, the quantity demanded of that commodity falls and the quantity demanded of the other commodity rises, thus inflating the price of the latter.

This theory implies that price changes in one type of housing are closely related to price changes in another type. Price should also move together because buildings can be altered. To the extent that a one or two family house can be subdivided, it is a potential multi-family dwelling.

Consider the properties used to make the subdivision index. These properties were ones which actually did get subdivided. They were, needless to say, potential apartment houses. Also, they were located in those sections of the city into which the new entrants were moving. Because location was an important dimension of the housing service which the new entrants were seeking, they viewed one and two family houses as close substitutes for apartment buildings. Speculators, of course, realized this, and that explains why the properties were subdivided in the first place. The implication is that prices of the properties which were subdivided should be expected to rise in value at nearly the same pace as the prices of other buildings.

The evidence, however, is only partly consistent with the expectations (See table 3.3). The Engle index of Cambridge real estate values and the census data on rents grew at about the same rate during the 1950s and

1960s. The index for rehabilitated unsubdivided houses also rose at the same rate in the 1950s, but then fell behind in the 1960s. (This discrepancy suggests that much of the rehabilitation involved was done to fit houses to the needs of specific families, and that the costs of such rehabilitation were not fully recovered when houses were resold later.) Another discrepancy is that the census estimate of the observed appreciation of owner-occupied one-family homes was much lower than those of rents during the 1950s, and slightly lower in the 1960s. This difference may simply represent erroneous subjective valuation by census respondents. If the data has value it suggests that those owners left out of the Engle index (because they never sold their homes) had homes that were not appreciating as rapidly as homes that were sold. This possibility is suggested also by the greater similarity of the census index to the appreciation of homes that were later subdivided.

In the sixties, when the property was subdivided, the price of subdivided properties grew at the same rate as housing in the city as a whole. The rise of real estate values during this time was very rapid. During the period in which the housing market took off, between 1958 and 1970, the Engle index grew at a rate of 8.3 percent per year while the subdivision index grew at a rate of 7.6 percent per year. At this pace, prices were doubling in 9 to 10 years. Before this period of speculation, between World War II and 1958, the story is different. In Cambridge, real estate values were increasing at the moderate pace of 5.5 percent per year. At that rate the value of a property would double in 13 years. The properties which would later be subdivided, however, were appreciating at the much slower rate of 2.5 percent. At this rate, it would take more than 28 years for a typical house to double in value.

A possible explanation for the discrepancy lies in what classes of people owned those properties which were subdivided, and how ownership by classes changes hands when the properties became profitable to own. There were speculative profits to be made in converting houses into apartments, but access to these entrepreneurial opportunities was not equal for everyone. The pattern of ownership by class and property type for all the properties which were subdivided suggests this is so. Ownership of the 109 properties which were subdivided in the period 1960–1969 is examined in table 3.4. Ownership of each property was traced by title search for the period 1950–1972. The owners were then divided into two groups, according to whether or not they owned 10 or more

Table 3.4
Ownership of Residential Properties, by Occupational Category, Subdivided
in Cambridge During 1960–1969

| | Ownership[a] as of | | | Owners who |
	1950	1960	1972	subdivided
SINGLE UNIT DWELLINGS				
% ELITE[b]	25.0	25.4	23.6	30.0
% WHITE COLLAR	8.9	9.1	9.1	5.5
% BLUE COLLAR	30.4	25.5	12.7	16.4
% OTHER	14.3	10.9	12.7	10.9
% N.A.	8.9	12.7	9.1	10.1
% PROF. LANDLORDS	12.5	16.4	32.7	25.5
N:-	(56)	(55)	(55)	(55)
2–4 UNIT BUILDINGS				
ELITE	8	7	4	0
WHITE COLLAR	3	4	3	0
BLUE COLLAR	5	7	4	0
OTHER	5	5	5	0
N.A.	5	2	0	0
PROF. LANDLORDS	6	7	16	16
N =	32	32	32	16
5 UNITS OR LARGER				
ELITE	2	2	2	2
WHITE COLLAR	1	1	1	1
BLUE COLLAR				0
OTHER				0
N.A.	1	1	0	0
PROF. LANDLORDS	17	18	19	19
N =	21	22	22	22

[a] SOURCE: City of Cambridge and Middlesex County records, *Cambridge City Directory*, Price & Lee, New Haven CT., 1972.
[b] For definitions of occupational categories, see Alan Mathews, "A Study of Rehabilitated Homes in Cambridge." Unpublished BA Thesis, MIT, 1973.

units simultaneously in Cambridge during the period of the study (1950–1972). The purpose of this grouping was to identify those people who made a living, at least to a major extent, by being landlords. In order to further identify those people who owned less than ten units, their occupations were determined by referring to the Cambridge City Directory. The occupations were then coded into classes similar to those which the Bureau of the Census uses.

Ownership patterns did not change much between 1950 and 1960, before these buildings were subdivided. The big change in ownership came just prior to subdivision. Professional landlords (owners of ten or more units of housing) increased their share of the ownership of what had been single family houses from 16 percent in 1950 to 32.7 percent in 1972. Their share of what had been two to four unit buildings rose from 22 percent to 50 percent. Members of "elite" occupations (professionals, proprietors, and managers) apart from professional landlords decreased their share of ownership slightly, but many of their sales came after subdivision. At the time of subdivision, they owned 30 percent of single-unit buildings, although they owned only 25.4 percent as of 1960 and 23.6 percent as of 1972. Professional landlords and members of elite occupations accounted for more than half of the ownership of buildings in all categories at the time of subdivision.

In contrast, the blue-collar share of ownership declined considerably. Blue-collar workers were the largest group among homeowners in the sample in 1950. They owned 17 of the single-family houses in 1950 and 14 in 1960. But only 9 houses were subdivided by them. By 1972 they owned only 7 of the properties. This loss of blue-collar ownership is not due merely to "attrition"—that is, the rate at which this class was migrating out of Cambridge because of the loss of blue-collar jobs. While from 1950 to 1970, the number of blue-collar jobs fell by 36.6 percent, the number of houses owned by blue collars in this sample fell by 52.5 percent. The share owned by white-collar workers (sales, clerical, and semiprofessional) also fell.

The process by which these properties were subdivided was characterized by "speculation," if this is defined as the rapid buying and selling of the properties.[20] In the absence of speculation, properties would change hands with the usual frequency from time to time. Owners would carry out investment decisions on their properties. Such was the case with those owners who rehabbed their property during the 1960s without subdividing it. The median length of time between when these owners acquired their property and when they rehabbed it was ten years. But for those properties which were subdivided, the median length of time between when these owners acquired their property and when they subdivided it was only three years.

For example, 27 one and two family houses changed hands less than one year before they were subdivided. Table 3.5 gives an indication of who the speculators were, and who they bought from. Less than a year before subdivision, the landlord class owned only one of these houses.

Table 3.5
Buyers and Sellers of Subdivision Properties
(For 1 & 2 family units, transfers in which the subdividers acquired the
property less than a year before subdivision)

| | Owners Who Subdivided | | | | |
Previous Owners	Blue Collars	Other	Elite	Landlords[a]	Total
BLUE COLLARS	1	2	1	4	8
OTHERS		6	3	3	12
ELITE			3	3	6
LANDLORDS			1		1
TOTAL	1	8	8	10	27

SOURCE: Same as Table 3.3.
[a] Owners of 10 or more units.

One landlord sold to a member of the elite who then subdivided. But 10 landlords bought up properties from other classes for the purpose of subdivision.

While the landlord class was the speculator, the blue-collar class was the speculatee. Eight properties were purchased from blue collars less than a year before subdivision, yet only one of the buyers was another blue collar. Four were landlords, one was a member of the elite, one was a student, and one was not a resident of Cambridge.

The elite were also speculators, although not to the extent that landlords were. Six of the properties were sold by this class, and eight were purchased by this class for the purpose of subdivision.

Nine of the single-family houses *were* subdivided by blue collar owners. But, with one exception, they did not buy the properties with the intention of subdivision. Five of them owned the houses 10 years or longer before they subdivided (four of them more than 18 years), and only two owned their property fewer than five years before subdividing. This does not mean that workers did not desire to be entrepreneurs, or that they were unaware of the profits to be made. Most of them had boarders living in their "single family homes" before subdivision, as did the majority of the owners who sold for subdivision. What they lacked was not the motivation but the means, the access to capital with which to invest. The length of time these blue-collar workers owned the property before they subdivided it is an indication of this. Banks may have been unwilling to lend them the money to invest until they had built up enough equity in their property to make them a good risk.

Subdivision was profitable. An analysis of the costs of subdivision and the prices of properties which were subdivided show that, *ceteris paribus*, for every dollar invested in subdivision, the value of the property was increased by $1.27.[21] But this does not mean that the rate of profit for speculators who bought property, then subdivided it, and then sold it, was 27 percent. The capital invested includes not only the money spent in subdividing but also the money spent in purchasing the property. Take the case of a typical single-unit dwelling. The speculator would purchase it for $23,855 and spend $8,625 converting it into apartments. If there were not a price rise reflecting the trend of prices in the overall housing market, the speculator could sell the property for $34,804. His "profit" is $2,324 ($34,804 − $23,855 − $8,625), or *only 7 percent* of the money he invested. However, if his property value was also appreciating at the normal rate of 7.6%, he could sell it after a year for $37,449. His profit would then be $4,969 or 15.3% of his capital invested. If one considers also the rents collected from tenants, the landlord's profits (actually a capital gain on the sale of property, and profits on the net rent collected) could be about 25 percent of his capital invested. If one further considers that the speculator leveraged the sale with typically less than 20 percent of the purchase price of his own capital, using bank finances for the rest, the return on invested capital is far higher. It can easily exceed 100 percent!

Although a few blue-collar workers did manage to subdivide their homes, it is clear that most had little access to the profits available from quick resale. Recall that only two were able to subdivide within five years after purchase. Even returns to long-term ownership of homes is unevenly divided. If the cases are examined in which buying and selling prices of the same house are available, there appear to be class differences in yearly rates of appreciation. The median rate of appreciation for blue-collar owners was 4.1 percent while for the professional landlords it was 7.1 percent and for professionals and managers it was 9.35 percent, and for non-landlord proprietors even higher. Within any class, there was wide variation. Even so, the maximum annual gain for blue-collar workers was below the median for the higher status groups. (See table 3.6.)

Table 3.6
Yearly Rates of Property Appreciation

Group	Median Rate of Appreciation	Max	Min	No. of Observations
ALL	6.60	758.6	9.30	61
SUBDIVISIONS	8.00	758.6	4.50	13
Blue Collar				
(skilled; semi-skilled laborer)	4.10	8.7	0.07	9
White Collar				
(semi-professional; clerical; sales)	8.80	4.5	31.1	4
Petty Proprietor	28.70	11.9	45.5	2
Elite				
(Professionals; Managers)	9.35	758.6	0.0	8
Other				
(Includes Students)	3.40	126.4	3.1	8
Landlord	7.10	585.2	9.3	23
Unknown	7.00	15.7	0.9	7

SOURCE: Same as Table 3.3.

Thus, even in the case of a buoyant housing market, where rehabilitation and subdivision of homes were possible, it appears that not all homeowners benefited equally, and that blue-collar workers, while they were generally able to make some capital gains beyond the average inflation rate on their homes, were those who received the lowest returns.

FOUR

Real Estate Value Changes:
Metropolitan Patterns, 1870–1970

THE previous chapter considered the evolution of property values in Boston and its older residential suburbs from the 1870s to the early 1970s. Although values rose in general over that century, there were periods of general value decline, like the 1930s, and more frequent periods for which values in specific neighborhoods fell or were stagnant. The loss of money on reselling one's home was not an experience suffered by a majority of the population but, particularly in Somerville and in some of the neighborhoods of Boston, it was far from unknown. Returns that individual home owners received, among those who did make some gain, also varied widely, with the average capital gain more or less following the general rule of inflation.

The present chapter extends the analysis of land value changes to encompass a wider sample of communities, and to compare observed value changes with returns to other economic assets, between 1870 and 1970. (Changes in the 1970s will be discussion in Chapter 11.) The analysis presented here allows us to conclude that, on the average, real estate investments by individual homeowners were not as remunerative as those investments open to larger-scale investors. Among homeowners, some differences in average returns are also discernible. Persons able to invest in more expensive housing were able to obtain slightly higher average capital gains than their less affluent fellows.

The Urban Mosaic. High-quality apartments and houses have long been found particularly to the west of Boston. Tripledeckers and smaller one and two family homes generally followed the transport routes north and south. But even to

Luxury Apartments west of downtown along Commonwealth Avenue, ca. 1920.

Two Family Housing along the transit line, ca. 1920.

the west, one finds old milltown enclaves of worker housing, as well as some tripledeckers (see next page).

Photo by Elliott Sclar.

Washington Park, Newtonville, Mass., 1984.

Photo by Elliott Sclar.

Tripledeckers in Brookline, Mass., 1984.

Photo by Elliott Sclar.

Mill worker housing, Waltham, Mass., 1984.

Photo by Elliott Sclar.

Mill worker housing, Waltham, Mass., 1984.

A. Studying Metropolitan Patterns

Since the late nineteenth century, Boston has been a commuter metropolis, with a large proportion of its population living beyond the city
limits in the surrounding towns and cities. Using the definition of the
Standard Metropolitan Statistical Area (SMSA) of the 1960 and 1970 censuses, the city of Boston contained only 42.0 percent of the area's population in 1895 and 23.6 percent in 1965. To be sure, at the turn of the
century, the outer portion of what became the SMSA did not yet consist
entirely of suburbs. But it was no empty void. Apart from streetcar suburbs just outside of Boston, there were farming communities and several
self-contained manufacturing centers, including Quincy to the south,
Waltham to the west, and Lynn and Salem to the north. Like Boston,
they exerted some influence on the price of land. However, over the
past century, the principal influence on real estate in the metropolitan
area has been the growth of a unified metropolitan area linked by commuting and centered on downtown Boston and, to a lesser extent, the
neighboring city of Cambridge. In studying housing values, therefore, it
is necessary to study the entire area to which people moved upon leaving Boston.

Our task is facilitated by the fact that Massachusetts has no unincorporated areas: all land is assigned to one or another town or city. Thus,
municipal statistics on assessed land and building values give a full accounting of real estate in the metropolitan area, so long as the ratio of
each town's assessments to market values can be known. Such ratios have
been computed by the state government since 1960. We have computed
them for 1900 and 1925. A state study in the early 1940s indicated close
to accurate valuation at that time (a result of value decline and consequent pressure on assessors during the depression), so we take 1940 assessments to represent true values. Thus, assessment ratios are available
for four separate periods. The census of population has, beginning in 1930,
also reported median house values for the different towns, which provide us with an additional set of prices to consider.

The Balkanization of the metropolitan area into 78 separate municipalities gives us a large enough sample of different observations for formal statistical analysis to be applied, and we present such an analysis in
this chapter. We base it on the relation of real estate values to distance
from Boston and other measurable characteristics of towns since 1870.

We relate values to distance and to the other factors by using regression analysis to fit the "best" straight line or other simple mathematical function to a scatter of points. The resulting function or bid-rent curve will serve as the basis for the analysis presented here.

While the regression technique is subject to a great many subtle problems and complexities, the reader who is not an economist or statistician can still get some sense of what is being done in this section by considering the relationship between distance from downtown and land values in a hypothetical metropolis (see figure 4.1). The different points indicate per-acre land values and the distances from downtown of the metropolitan area's different towns. (For each town, the distance is represented by how far to the right of the vertical axis the point is, land value by how high above the horizontal axis.) The point P_j, representing land values and distance in "J-ville" (a hypothetical suburb) is marked by an arrow. Regression analysis is a technique for plotting through the scatter of points that line which is "best" in the sense that it misses the different points by "less" than other possible lines do. In figure 4.1, the unbroken line would be the best fitting straight line. It would indicate that, on average, land values at the center of the metropolitan area were $14,000

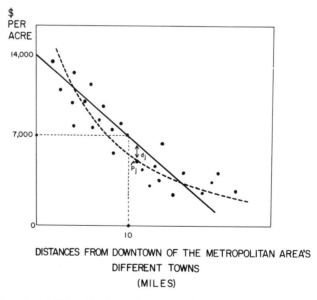

Figure 4.1 Land Value Gradient for a Hypothetical Metropolis.

per acre, and fell on average by $700 for each mile of additional distance from downtown. Of course, not all towns have exactly the average land value for their distance from downtown. In the case of "J-ville," the difference is the deviation d_j. The regression technique minimizes the sum of the squares of these deviations, but many individual deviations remain. The statistical expression R^2 is a measure of how well the regression line fits the points: the closer R^2 is to 1, the better the possible fit.

It is possible to extend the use of the regression technique. Additional variables besides distance can be added to the analysis; the regression analysis would then calculate to what extent the value of these other variables would give towns land values above or below the average for their distance. (For example, values for towns with high air pollution might be below the line by an average amount, reflecting the average effect of pollution.) Also, besides a straight line, the analysis can be used to select some other simple mathematical function. In figure 4.1, the broken line is a representation of the best parabola fitted to the points. Choosing which curve to use can be a problem. The parabola comes closer to the value for "J-ville's" land than does the straight line, but the straight line comes closer than the parabola for some other towns. The choice makes a difference, between the two curves suggest different average relationships because values and distance. The parabola indicates values drop off more rapidly in the first 10 miles out than does the straight line, but at further distances it shows values dropping less rapidly. The choice among different curves, as well as the choice of what additional variables to include in the analysis, is thus very important. Measures of the "statistical significance" and the "explanatory power" of individual variables or entire regressions can help in selecting among curves, but discretion and hence a possibility of errors in choice cannot be avoided.

In the case of the Boston metropolitan area, we have investigated the use of quadratic functions (parabolas) and cubic functions (curves which can change direction twice) as well as straight lines in finding the best relationship between distance and property values. In general, we used the cubic regressions, which we found to give the most accurate fit. We also had to consider the use of additional variables. For example, one problem is that the simple inverse relation between land values and distances from the center of Boston, of the classic sort indicated by figure 4.1, does not exist. Rather, instead of a simple pattern of rings of different land uses and values around the city, or a continuous and monotonic gradient that is uniform in all directions, there is a pronounced sectoral effect. For the past century, the western suburbs of Boston and a few towns located on peninsulas to the east have been the higher-income suburbs, while the lower-income and industrial suburbs have, in more cases, been located directly to the north and south.

To take account of this effect, we have run two separate sets of regressions. One used regressions with "latitudinal" distances north or south and "longitudinal" distances east or west of downtown Boston as separate variables (table 4.1, below). This technique showed clearly that values did fall more rapidly to the north or south than to the east or west during several census years, and gave reasonable shapes for the value gradients. But it was highly inaccurate for estimating average values in the far northwest and southwest corners of the metropolitan area. So, in a separate set of regressions, we measured distance as straight-line miles from Boston City Hall. We then added separate variables, one favoring towns to the west, and a second indicating location near an industrial subcenter. Table 4.2, below, shows that the subcenters had some effect on real estate values up to 1950, while the zone effect has slowly gained in importance, being highly significant in 1960 and 1970. Additional variables were entered when using house values rather than land values to take account of the differences between housing ages in different towns.

B. Assessed Property and Land Values

The statistics available over the longest period are those for real estate assessments. However, these assessments include both the value of land and that of the buildings on the land. Nor are they corrected for assessment biases. Different towns' assessors estimates also vary. As a result, the estimated assessed value gradients cannot be taken as representing true land values.[1] Their changes will not show the actual value gains an investor receives. Nonetheless, their evolution over a century does show a filling-in of the outer parts of the metropolitan area over time, confirming the pattern of an outward movement of growth, and increasing stagnation at the center of the metropolitan area.

Tables 4.1 and 4.2 present regression estimates of the geographical pattern of assessed real estate values, including buildings and land, for each census year since 1870. North–south and east–west distances are entered separately in table 4.1, while table 4.2 uses straight-line dis-

Table 4.1
Regression Estimates of Assessed Real Estate Value Gradients 1870–1970 (A)

Year	Regression Intercept (value at Boston) (A)	North or South Change Per Mile (b₁)	East or West Change Per Mile (b₂)	R²
1870	3,003.6	− 138.6	− 113.2	.176
1880	3,103.6	− 143.5	− 110.4	.257
1890	5,767.8	− 261.5	− 208.4	.311
1900	7,804.8	− 354.7	− 286.7	.315
1910	9,357.9	− 423.5	− 335.6	.333
1920	10,437.4	− 472.0	− 360.7	.387
1930	16,394.4	− 738.6	− 556.1	.449
1940	14,974.4	− 669.4	− 497.9	.481
1950	16,658.8	− 739.9	− 547.1	.495
1960	19,799.6	− 853.4	− 606.7	.536
1970	32,375.5	− 1,280.5	− 709.3	.342

Figures are in thousands of current dollars per square mile, based on a regression on town averages, of the form

$$VAL = A + b_1 DNS + b_2 DEW + e$$

where DNS is the number of miles north or south of Boston and DEW is the number of miles east or west of Boston. All values of b_1 and b_2 were significant at the .05 level.

Table 4.2
Regression Estimates of Assessed Real Estate Value Gradients 1870–1970 (B)
(Assessed values in $1,000 per square mile)

Year	regression coefficients for dependent variables						
	C	D	D²	D³	Sub	Zone	R²
1870	6,400††	− 1,300††	+ 80††	− 1.5††	+ 0.8	− 0.98	.700
1880	7,800††	− 1,500††	+ 94††	− 1.8††	+ 0.9	+ 0.34	.676
1890	13,500††	− 2,600††	+ 154††	− 2.9††	+ 1.5†	+ 1.27	.780
1900	17,300††	− 3,300††	+ 193††	− 3.6††	+ 1.6	+ 2.59	.819
1910	21,300††	− 4,000††	+ 236††	− 4.4††	+ 2.1†	+ 5.44	.837
1920	27,800††	− 5,100††	+ 292††	− 5.3††	+ 3.0††	+ 10.90	.853
1930	38,900††	− 6,100††	+ 360††	− 6.3††	+ 4.7	+ 21.10	.880
1940	32,100††	− 5,100††	+ 260††	− 4.3††	+ 3.7††	+ 23.72†	.870
1950	34,600††	− 5,300††	+ 269††	− 4.4††	+ 3.8††	+ 26.81†	.866
1960	34,700††	− 4,600††	+ 204††	− 2.5††	+ 3.1	+ 40.15††	.846
1970	34,400††	− 1,900	− 32	+ 1.9	− 5.5	+ 146.41††	.521

NOTE: C = constant; D = distance from Boston City Hall to center of town, in miles; ZONE = degrees off north/south axis (max. value is 90° due west or east of Boston); SUB = access to industrial subcenter (1/distance²). Dependent value is assessment for land plus buildings from State data.
† t-statistic greater than 1.67 (10% significant level).
†† t-statistic greater than 1.96 (5% significance level).

tances and a zone variable. The figures show, first, that locations farther from downtown Boston have been "catching up" in value with the central city over time. Values one mile from the center are 78 percent of the estimated value in the center in 1870 (using the straight-line estimate). They rise to 94 percent of the central value in 1970. At ten miles out, values are less than 5 percent of the central figure through 1920, increase to 20 percent in 1930 and get up to 41 percent of the central figure in 1970. While the overall gradient was flattening, values at the center at first increased by at least 20 percent, and sometimes as much as 73 percent per decade, up to 1930. They fell in the Depression and never fully recovered. Since the end of the Depression, however, values have been rising faster at the 10-mile distance or beyond than they had been nearer the center of the SMSA in the earlier period.

The figures also show an increasing advantage of properties in the suburban zones west of the city and on the eastern peninsula over those north or south of downtown. The zonal variable is negative at the outset, but becomes increasingly positive and significant over time, so that by 1970 a town due west of Boston would have assessed values $146,000 per square mile greater than those at an equivalent distance due north. Gradients based on separate north–south and east–west regressions show similar results. The effect of proximity to subcenters has been less important. Even when correctly estimated, assessed-value changes include the value of new construction, and are not directly applicable to estimating the gains to ownership of existing housing or land, although there is some reason, in theory, to expect land values to follow the evolution of total real estate prices. A more direct test of value changes can be made, however, from assessments of land values alone.

Land and building components of town real estate assessments have been reported separately in Massachusetts state documents since 1890, though the separation of land from building values has been sporadic and often arbitrary since World War II. Ratios of assessments to sale prices, however, were not available until the late 1890s, when the practice of putting a stamp tax on title transfers was instituted. Thus the periods for which estimates of land values are available are limited. Calculated ratios have been applied to assessments to estimate corrected land values per square mile for 1900, 1925, and 1970, while 1940 figures are based on state assessments.

Relationships of land values to straight-line distances from downtown,

Table 4.3
Regression Estimates of Land Value Gradients
(Assessed or corrected values, $1,000 per square mile)

	C	D	D²	D³	SUB	ZONE	R²
	Regression coefficients for independent variables and year						
			Assessed Land Values				
1890	7,070††	−1,390††	+85††	−1.6††	−804†	+1.42	.788
1900	8,870††	−1,750††	+106††	−2.0†	+861†	+2.16	.803
1910	10,910††	−2,160††	+132††	−2.5††	+1,135†	+2.53	.802
1920	12,780††	−2,540††	+155††	−3.0††	+1,702††	+3.47	.793
1930	14,430††	−2,810††	169††	−3.2††	+2,271††	+5.94	.813
1940	12,240††	−2,230††	+126††	−2.3††	+1,428	+11.69†	.757
1970	6,710	+310	−63	+1.5	+804	+34.82	.228
			Corrected Land Value Estimate				
1900	11,180††	−2,240††	+137††	−2.6††	+1,048	+5.10	.788
1925	19,980††	−4,000††	+245††	−4.6††	+3,269††	+8.57	.756
1940	12,240††	−2,230††	+126††	−2.3††	+1,428	+11.69	.757
1970	11,950	+1,010	−49	+2.1	−501	+38.63	.151

NOTE: Independent variables defined as in Table 4.2. Corrected value estimates for 1900 and 1925 based on our estimates of assessment/sale-price ratios; 1970 value based on state published estimate of assessment/sale-price ratios for real estate; 1940 assumes assessments were correct.
†t-statistic greater than 1.67.
††t-statistic greater than 1.96.

and to subcenter and zone variables, are estimated in table 4.3. The distance relationships, holding zone effects constant, are graphed in figure 4.2, which shows a loss of the central city's advantage in land values between 1925 and 1970. The figure suggests land values at the center of the metropolitan area have shown little net change over nearly three-quarters of a century, although shorter-term changes have been significant. Value increases have continued at greater distances, so that even in inner-ring areas two to seven miles out, values were higher in 1970 than in 1925 or 1900. Beyond eight or nine miles out, estimated value increases are small between 1900 and 1925, or 1940, but have been great since then, as the suburbs have filled in.

Thus, calculated values at the center of Boston rose 79 percent between 1900 and 1925, but fell 40 percent between 1925 and 1970, to return to close to their 1900 level. However, at four miles north or south of the city, there are increases of 86 percent from 1900 to 1925, and 92 percent from 1925 to 1970. Four miles west, increases are at a similar 84 percent between 1900 and 1925, but from 1925 to 1970 values there

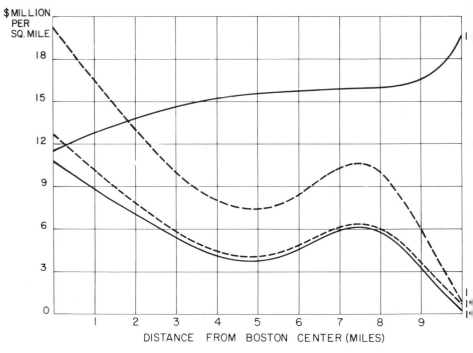

Figure 4.2   Estimated Cubic Land Value Gradients.

increase by 156 percent, outstripping those to the north or south. Ten miles west, increases are greater yet: 120 percent from 1900 to 1925, more than 1,000 percent from then until 1970.

These estimates are first approximations. The 1970 figures are suspect, inasmuch as assessors may attribute too large a share of value to buildings and not enough to land, while the State assessment-to-sales-prices ratios are for total property values, not for land alone, although we have applied them to land values. The cubic form of the regression used may exaggerate effects at the extreme distance values: the very center and the farthest suburban regions. Finally, the substitution of separate latitude and longitude variables for straight-line distance and a zonal term reduces the estimated value gains for the farthest suburbs (fig. 4.3). The value increase at ten miles west from 1925 to 1970 is little above 100 percent in this variant. This alternate form of the regression also reduces the land value decline estimated at the center after 1925, leaving central values for 1950 slightly above the 1900 level. Neither of the separate

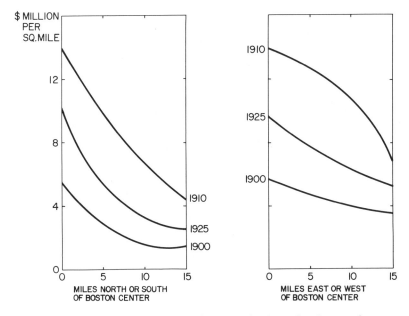

Figure 4.3 Estimated Latitudinal and Longitudinal Land Value Gradients.

north–south and east–west gradients from the center estimated by this procedure are left flat or upward-sloping in 1970, as is the gradient in figure 4.2, although the 1970 slope is much reduced from that of 1900 or 1925. However, the revised procedure also reduces the proportion of variance explained (R^2), so its importance is doubtful.

Given the statistical difficulties besetting the overall equations for the metropolitan area, it is important to examine the considerable variations among individual towns. In particular, among the rural towns becoming suburbs and among middle-ring towns, there is a greater variation than among the towns nearest to Boston. These variations suggest the estimated equations may suffer from statistical problems of heteroskedasticity, but their examination also confirms, at an informal level, the general pattern of value changes posited in chapter 1.

In the 1900–1925 period, for example, five towns (Duxbury, Marshfield, Norwood, Swampscott, and Topsfield) all had values which more than quadrupled. All are rather distant suburbs. Eleven other towns more than tripled their land value—but only one of the sixteen (Belmont) lay within five miles of Boston, and it was an upper-income enclave. (see chapter 8) The combination of these individual town results with the overall gradients confirms that value increases were smallest in the older residential areas near the center of Boston and greatest at points of new suburbanization and in high-income residential areas.

Between 1925 and 1970, the majority of towns sampled (29 of 50), including some, but not all, of the towns at the fringes of the metropolitan area, quadrupled in value. Some older upper-income towns, including Belmont and Wellesley, also had values quadruple in this period; others (Newton and Brookline) showed only small increases. Not all groups of towns show such variation, however. Among the older, working-class residential communities close to the core of the area, only one (Everett, which was successful in attracting industry), had land value quadruple; in most such communities values failed even to double, though the overall price index rose 109 percent. (See table 4.7.)

C. Changes in House Values

Land value estimates are only as reliable as the data that underlies them. Since the Depression, assessors' estimates of the division between land values and total real estate values have become less reliable. Fortunately, since 1930 census estimates of the value of houses provide an alternative source of data to assessors' figures. The census figures, of course, have some obvious limitations. In the first place, the two most recent censuses undercount the poor. House values, however, are estimated from responses given by owner-occupiers, a group much less likely to be undercounted than tenants. Second, the census figures at best give house values, not true land values. A change in values between censuses may reflect a change in the type of housing in a town, rather than changes in values of existing property.

Statistical comparisons of census house values and market prices do, however, show a good correspondence.[2] The discrepancy between house values and land values (or the lack of a constant ratio between them, based either on different structural costs at different building densities or on different lot sizes) is reduced somewhat by multiple regressions including other variables besides distance in the explanation of house values.

Finding an adequate set of variables to use to correct house prices is,

of course, a different matter. Studies in the United States and England
which use house prices to estimate land value gradients have used a wide
variety of characteristics both of dwellings and of their residents as additional variables, attempting to net out their effect and thus show the
effect of location alone on values.[3] Much controversy among econome-
tricians has attended the choice of variables, and with some reason. If
house or lot sizes or other variables of importance in the determination
of house values are omitted, and if these variables are concentrated at
certain distances from the downtown area, the estimated land value gradient may be seriously distorted.

Comparing value gradients over several census periods makes this
problem unavoidable, since the same characteristics are not available from
all the relevant censuses: since the 1930 Census is less detailed than more
recent ones and omits data for smaller towns, a thoroughly acceptable
set of control variables cannot be used if all towns are to be included in
the sample. In the absence of a fully adequate data base, therefore, we
rely on two quantities available for all periods to represent building quality
for Boston-area towns. One is location of the community in the zone to
the east or west of Boston rather than to the north or south: such location is correlated to more opulent construction and availability of local
services. The impact of zone location on value is controlled for by an
independent variable in the regressions for each period that use straight
line distances from Boston (table 4.4). The effects are then standardized
in drawing the gradients. We also estimated separate equations using
distinct variables for latitudinal (north–south) and longitudinal (east–west)
distance from the central city (table 4.5). We standardize the age of
housing. This variable was not available for most towns for the 1930 census, but could be estimated on the basis of house ages reported in the
1940 census by subtracting out those houses reported as less than ten
years old in 1940. Variables for the proportion of housing in each town
estimated as new (less than ten years old) or old (more than thirty years
old) on each census are used as controls in the regressions.

Gradients drawn from these equations appear in figures 4.4 and 4.5.
The first of these shows the gradients drawn using straight-line distances, controlling for house age and zone. The results seem surprising.
Unlike the land-value gradients of figures 4.2 and 4.3, the house-value
gradient of figure 4.4 is relatively flat; if anything, it peaks a few miles
out. Clearly, if this gradient is correct, houses farther out from Boston,

Table 4.4
Regression Estimates of House Value Gradients
(in dollars)

Year		Regression coefficients for dependent variables:							
	C	D	D^2	D^3	ZONE	OLD	NEW	DENS	R^2
1930	7,580††	158	-1.39	+.033	+27††	-2,048	+4,131	—	.474
1940	3,622††	+76	-13.79	+.265	+13††	-277	+10,241	—	-.440
1950	12,977††	-23	-4.46	+.179	+15†	-5,252††	-1,756	—	.200
1960	34,977††	+768	-87.98††	+2.341	+32††	-25,279††	-23,161††	—	.434
1970	24,974††	+1,038	-80.75	+1.325	+133††	-12,486†	-5,432	—	.375
1930	6,724††	+184	-32.60	+.793	+34	—	—	—	.411
1940	2,866	+433††	-36.53††	+.729	+19	—	—	—	.281
1950	7,802	+414	-36.36	+.873†	+22	—	—	—	.116
1960	8,722	+1,820††	-151.51	+3.75††	+47	—	—	—	.292
1970	13,070	+1,516†	-86.40	+1.14	+135	—	—	—	.336
1930	8,747	-131	-17.30	+.544	+33††	—	—	-.084	.423
1940	5,689	+16	-16.00	+.400	+19††	—	—	-.122	.330
1950	11,942	-188	-7.00	+.415	+23††	—	—	-.177	.177
1960	17,245	+699	-102.00††	+2.842††	+51††	—	—	-.417	.378
1970	29,246	-470	-3.76	-.003	-142††	—	—	-.853	.419

NOTE: House values used as dependent variables are census medians by town. OLD is proportion of units less than 10 years old. DENS is population density per square mile of town area. Other variables and symbols as defined in Table 4.2.

† t-statistic greater than 1.67.

†† t-statistic greater than 1.96.

Table 4.5
Regression Estimates of Latitudinal and Longitudinal House Value Gradients

Year	R^2	Constant	DN	DN^2	DN^3	DW	DW^2	DW^3	Old	New
				Independent Variables						
1930	.409	7,368	+83	−32	+1.1	+395	−43	+1.1	−25	+37.0
1940	.421	3,172	•+227	−36	+1.0	+278	−33	+0.9	−1	+106.0
1950	.367	9,318	+138	−42	+1.2	+73	+27	−1.5	+5	+138.0
1960	.279	13,084	+787	−149	+5.6	+366	−21	+0.3	+77.9	+59.2
1970	.373	43,230	−1,373	+550	−1.1	+561	−4	−1.0	−195	−170.0

Dependent variable is median house value for each town in dollars. DN is absolute value of distance north or south of latitude of Boston Common in miles. DW is absolute value of distance east or west of longitude of Boston Common. OLD is percentage of housing units more than 30 years old; NEW is percent less than ten years old.

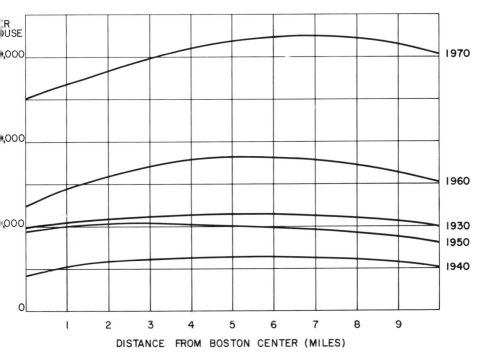

Figure 4.4   Estimated Cubic House Value Gradients.

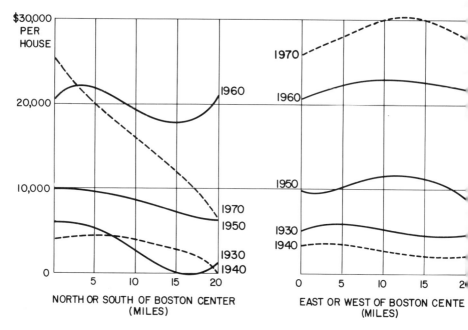

Figure 4.5   Estimated Latitudinal and Longitudinal House Value Gradients.

because they are built on larger lots and are better in quality, sell at prices equivalent to those closer in despite less-costly land.

More intuitive results are obtained if separate longitudinal and latitudinal distance variables are used instead of straight-line distances and a zone variable. Gradients estimated from such a procedure are graphed in figure 4.5. They show only slight downward slopes to the west for 1930 and 1940; after that, values are higher in the western suburbs than in the center, as in the straight-line distance estimates. However, to the north and south a downward slope is maintained, except perhaps in the 1960 regression. The statistical significance of these differences is unclear, because the presence of towns in the far northwestern and northeastern corners of the metropolitan area means that variance is not uncorrelated with distance terms, but the differences do make sense in terms of the specific geography of the Boston area. The northern and southern suburbs are less affluent than those to the west, and also have less rapid highway access. As a result the flatter curve toward the west may reflect both larger or more opulently built homes, and a smaller offsetting land value decline due to travel time and distance, than do the curves for the north and south. While the shape of the value gradient may be distorted by differences in house size or quality, this should not affect the estimate of value changes as long as size and quality effects remain the same over time. Some evidence that this is the case comes from a comparison of estimated changes in census house prices to the price indices for twice-sold houses in the postwar period prepared by Engle and Richter (Table 4.6).[4] Like Engle's indices on Boston neighborhoods discussed in chapter 3, these indices are more accurate than the change in census house values within a town. They cannot, however, be used as a check on our value gradients, because they do not allow for comparison of value *levels* between houses or towns, but only in rates of change.

Unfortunately, the Engle-Richter index covers only 28 of the 78 towns for which census data are available. Few of these are in the outer suburban ring. Changes in house values from the census (uncorrected by the addition of other variables to the regression) and from the Engle-Richter index are estimated for the 1950s and 1960s in Table 4.6. The two are similar, although the regressions from the smaller sample are less significant statistically and indicate less variation between towns than do the census figures.

Table 4.6
Changes in House Value by Distance: Comparison of
Census and Sample Results

Change in Median House Value (U.S. Census of Housing)
1960/50 = 1.633 − .0161DNS + .0069DEW $(R^2 = .108)$
1970/60 = 1.241 + .0313DNS + .0081DEW $(R^2 = .208)$

Change in Index of Value of Twice-Sold Houses (Engle/Richter)
1960/50 = 1.71 − .0218DNS − .0111DEW $(R^2 = .179)$
1970/60 = 1.638 + .0018DNS − .0060DEW $(R^2 = .044)$

NOTES: Dependent Variables are [2]Index Ratios (last year divided by first).
D = absolute value of distance north or south of downtown latitude
W = absolute value of distance west (or east) or downtown longitude.
_____ (underlined): t-statistic significant at .05 level for sample size.
Number of observations: Census median value 78; index of value 28.
SOURCE: Engle and Richter Data.

D. Social Distribution of the Changes

The preceding section has shown that the relative appreciation to investment in housing has varied with location in the Boston region. If the very center of the metropolitan area (only partially characterized by owner-occupied housing) is excluded, then the areas with higher income residents (the suburban fringes) showed the highest rates of increase in house values in most decades between 1930 and 1970. The analysis of suburban land value assessments suggests that a similar pattern of land value change distributions may have occurred earlier, in the period 1900–1925. Within the Boston area, there is evidence from the house value-regressions for slightly faster appreciation in western than in northern or southern suburbs, as well as for a general flattening of gradients regardless of direction. The land-value gradients of figures 4.3 and 4.5 suggest a greater flattening toward the north and south than toward the east and west in the period under consideration; however, the regressions using direct ratios of end to beginning year values for specific towns support the evidence of house values in pointing toward slightly lower rates of appreciation for towns in the core area around the center and extending

Table 4.7
Property Value Changes for Various Locations 1900–1970

Location and Method of Estimation	Time				
	1900–25	1925–40	1940–70	1925–70	1900–70
Brookline Index[a]	+ 24%	− 30%	+ 397%	+ 247%	+ 332%
Somerville Index[a]	+ 13	+ 7	+ 260	+ 286	+ 334
Land Value Index[b]					
Center	+ 78.8	− 38.7	− 2.4	− 40.2	+ 5.0
1 mi. N,S	+ 80.3	+ 37.9	+ 25.1	− 22.3	+ 41.0
1 mi. West	+ 79.6	− 35.3	+ 44.2	− 5.6	+ 70.0
4 mi. N,S	+ 85.7	− 45.4	+ 253.0	+ 92.7	+ 258.0
4 mi. West	+ 83.9	− 38.1	+ 248.6	+ 156.1	+ 371.0
7 mi. N,S	+ 82.2	− 41.1	+ 166.4	+ 56.8	186.0
7 mi. West	+ 81.0	− 35.6	+ 176.1	+ 77.8	+ 222.0
Wholesale Price Index	+ 84.4%	(− 24.0%)	+ 171%	+ 107.1%	+ 282.0%

[a] See Chapter 3. Rates of Change Calculated comparing five-year period beginning with end year with five-year period beginning with base year.
[b] See Table 4.3, bottom portion, for estimating equations. Figures compiled setting SUB = P and letting ZONE-0 for North-South calculations, ZONE-90 for West.

a few miles toward the north and south than obtained in other towns. The geographic pattern of value changes is demonstrated further in tables 4.7 and 4.8. The importance of these geographical patterns lies in the relationship of residence to class in the Boston area. In general, the highest incomes in the area are to be found in the outer suburbs to the west of Boston. Northern and southern suburbs, and the inner Boston areas, present a mix of incomes; but with a lower average than the farther western towns.

Table 4.8
House Value Changes for Various Locations, 1930–1970

A. Using Straight Line Distance and Zone Variables

	Time		
	1930–1950	1950–1970	1930–1970
OLD HOUSING			
Center	+40.0%	+62.0%	+126.0%
1 mile north	+36.0	+73.4	135.8
1 mile west	+12.1	+179.2	213.0
5 miles north	+19.5	+110.4	151.0
5 miles west	+1.7	+213.3	219.0
10 miles north	+2.2	+123.0	130.0
10 miles west	−9.1	+216.6	+188.0
NEW HOUSING			
Center	−.04%	+.74	+.67
1 mile north	−5.2	+82.3	73.0
1 mile west	−11.9	+157.7	127.0
5 miles north	−11.7	+107.7	83.0
5 miles west	−17.0	+181.8	134.0
10 miles north	−18.7	+118.1	76.0
10 miles west	−22.7	+191.1	125.0

B. Using separate longitudinal and latitudinal distance variables

	Time		
	1930–1950	1950–1970	1930–1970
OLD HOUSING			
Center	+31.0%	+140.0%	+214.0%
5 miles north	+109.0	+85.0	+287.0
5 miles west	+39.0	+291.0	+443.0
10 miles north	+127.0	+61.0	+265.0
10 miles west	+51.0	+137.0	+258.0
Change in (Wholesale) Prices[a]	+83.4%	+34.9%	+147.5%

[a]SOURCE: 1972 Economic Report of the President.

The sectors, to be sure, are not tightly segregated. Thus, for example, in 1960, median family income by town was related to location by the following regression:

$$INCOME = 6907 - 34.4DNS + 44.3DEW \ (R^2 = .095)$$

where DNS is distance north or south of a latitudinal line through the same center. Less than 10 percent of variance is "explained." Nonetheless, both distance coefficients are significantly different from zero at the .05 level, with incomes falling to the north or south and rising to the east–west. Thus, the presence of the highest appreciation rates in the western suburbs does mean that the more affluent homeowners were reaping higher capital gains than their fellows.

The conclusion that land value increases vary inversely with residents' affluence is strengthened if real estate value changes are related to the residence patterns of different ethnic groups. The principal streams, numerically, of working class and poor migrants to Boston have historically been from outside of the United States, and thus leave records in the form of census estimates of foreign stock and foreign born proportions of the population in each town. To relate land value changes by community to the proportion of immigrants is a possible shortcut for relating land value changes to class.

Regression of changes in house values by towns on immigrant percentages in the population demonstrates that it was in the immigrant communities in which the lowest increments to house values can be found. When house value ratios (CHV) between two years are stated as functions of foreign-born proportions in the population at beginning years (IMM), the results are:

$$CHV \ (50/30) = 2.29 - 2.97 \ IMM(30) \ (R^2 = .095)$$
$$CHV \ (70/50) = 4.54 - 4.73 \ IMM(50) \ (R^2 = .113)$$

Despite the relatively low coefficients of determination (R^2), both the F-statistics and the t-statistics are significant at the .05 level. There is, as with the land-value estimates, indication of a tendency for the low status (in this case, high-immigrant) communities to have lower rates of land value increase, although there is much random variation around the trend.

This is not to argue that ethnicity had an independent effect on house values. The immigrant proportion is included along with other explanatory variables such as population density and distance from Boston: it has no significant effect on value. Rather the significant reverse relation between ethnicity alone and real estate appreciation shows that immigrants in some sense had lower opportunity to purchase the best housing assets in terms of future appreciation or had to trade off future appreciation for other characteristics of the housing purchased. Yet to compare the appreciation of house values received by different groups is to tell only half the story. When housing is compared with other investments, even the housing investments of the most affluent suburbanites do not necessarily compare well.

Taking the land value estimates of table 4.7 and comparing them to the increase in the wholesale price index, 1900–1970, suggests that over that period, the value of land in the inner seven miles of the metropolitan area failed to keep up with prices (except a few miles west of downtown). There are major differences over time. Someone selling in 1925 would earn a considerably better return than someone selling in 1940. But even then, if the increase of the general price level is taken into account, the average annual increase is quite modest at best.

Land value assessments yield a lower appreciation estimate than do our other figures. The Brookline and Somerville house value indices do exceed inflation over the 1900–1970 period. Nonetheless, *real* price increases there amount to less than 1 percent per year; hardly equivalent to profits in the corporate sector or even to real interest rates over most of the period.

House value increases from the census tell a similar story from 1930 to 1970. Those with mortgages outstanding on their homes sometimes lost their investment through foreclosure during the thirties. Those not foreclosed, however, retained possession of an asset which appreciated faster than the *New York Times* stock exchange index for the period 1930–1950, although falling more rapidly during the 1930s alone. Compared with the price index over the twenty-year period, the price of housing does *not* do well in many areas. Estimates vary with the assumptions used, but in many cases, house prices rise less than the inflation rate.

From 1950 to 1970, house prices in many areas did outperform the consumer price index. But they did not outperform many other competitive assets available to large investors.

Comparing the value in 1970 of $1,000 invested in competing assets yields the results shown in table 4.9. There is variation in results de-

Table 4.9
Comparison of Capital Gains to Housing and Other Assets
(Estimated value in 1970 of $1,000 invested in 1950)

Housing investments by distance	Est. from Table 4.4 regression[a]	Est. from used house sample[b]
center of Boston	2,315	2,760
5 miles North-South	1,869	2,600
5 miles East-West	2,465	2,960
10 miles North-South	1,622	2,390
10 miles East-West	2,378	2,600
20 miles North-South	*loss*	*loss*
20 miles East-West	2,515	2,670
Other investments and Indices	*Est. from national figures[c]*	
5% compounded annually	2,786	
Consumer Price Index	1,620	
Prime Rate of Interest, Cumulated	2,000	
FHA Mortgage Rate of Interest, Cumulative	2,920	
Dow-Jones 30 Industrials	4,017	
Mutual Funds Average	7,861	
Maximum Growth Mutual Fund Average	8,062	
Corporate Profit/Equity Ratio, Cumulated	8,450	

[a] From cubic regressions, using assumption of houses over 30 years old in each of the two time periods compared. (table 4.4, top section.)

[b] From index for sample of twice-sold used houses, regressing index change by town on distance terms (cubic form). (Engel and Richter.)

[c] From President's Economic Report, except for Dow Jones Average and Mutual Funds Averages (from trade associations). For the two Interest Rates and for the Corporate Profit ratio, each year's rate used to compute that year's gain. For loans made in different years on long-term basis, actual figures would vary.

pending on the assumptions used in estimation, but the results suggest that housing values increased at slightly less than 5 percent annual rate at the center of the metropolitan area, and perhaps slightly above that rate in some northern or southern suburbs over the twenty years. Some of the far north or far south areas (tract home districts without good transit access) did not gain value at all, however.

In the postwar period, then, the appreciation of house values did exceed the increase in consumer prices by a substantial margin in most districts. Housing was, at least, a hedge against inflation, and it often yielded real capital gains. But even in the areas more than 10 miles west of Boston, in the affluent suburbs, the appreciation of housing did not keep pace with the Dow Jones average for stock investment. In Boston, appreciation rates were lower than the rate of accumulation on Federal

Housing Administration (FHA) mortgages. A home buyer purchasing his house at this relatively favorable interest rate would, in these neighborhoods, not accumulate equity from the difference between home value appreciation and the interest rate paid on the loan. Only part of his actual savings from current income would be added to his equity. Those buyers a few miles west of Boston would have made some capital gain on the mortgage-financed portion of their investment, but not as much as from investment in stocks.

There are, of course, limits to what can be inferred from this comparison. First, the rates of value change indicated for housing are capital gains figures, not cumulations of true economic rates of return. The owner of a privately occupied house will receive a benefit from use of the house, which may be considered equivalent to a stream of income. This benefit will at least be equal to the difference between homeowner costs of maintenance and taxes and the normally higher amount that would be paid to rent a similar dwelling which include a markup for management costs and profit. The benefits may be increased further by the tax advantages of home ownership in the United States. The owner of a rental property will, similarly, receive a rent which may exceed annual costs. Thus, the rates of capital gain presented in Table 4.9 are understatements of full rates of return to investment, while some of the rates compared in that table (though not the Dow Jones Index, which omits dividends) are rates of return.

Second, even if a house is held vacant, or yields an annual flow of rents or services which merely cover upkeep and taxes, the figures of table 4.9 may not present the rate of return to the owner's equity, if a portion of the purchase price is covered by a mortgage. In this case, the owner's capital gain on equity will be at a higher rate than the rate of appreciation of the property if the rate of interest on the mortgage is lower than the rate of property value appreciation. If, however, the mortgage interest rate exceeds the rate of appreciation on the house (as is the case for inner core residential areas shown in the table), the latter rate will be an overestimate of the rate of growth of the owner's capital.

These considerations do not alter the conclusion that returns are unequally distributed among homeowners. Tax advantages work primarily to the interest of those with higher incomes. The discrepancy between mortgage rates and appreciation rates lowers individual returns on mortgaged property in the inner ring and raises it in the outer rings. This is

strong evidence of unequal returns. While one must make careful qualifications before stating that "returns to housing investment" are below
"returns to other assets," we nonetheless infer that this is frequently true,
and that this helps explain the stability of inequality.

First, there is some evidence that real rates of return to ownership of
residential properties, at least in the inner portions of metropolitan areas,
may be below those available to top wealth-holders or nonhousing corporations. Housing is a sector of the economy from which capital is
draining. New investment in many urban neighborhoods fails to keep up
with depreciation, even if no massive flight of capital is apparent, because capital is tied up in long-lived, immobile assets. More careful studies
of returns to investment by commercial residence-owners in inner cities,
such as Sternlieb's study of Newark, show low returns. It may thus be
(Hypothesis I) that the measured differences in capital gains are accompanied by real (although smaller) differences in true rates of return.[5]

This would confirm and explain Lampman's findings for the period up
to the early 1950s that top wealth-holders, who held a smaller proportion of their assets in housing than did others, received greater capital
gains than other investors. Lampman found that except during the 1930s,
this differential offset the decline of wealth-disparities, because of the
fractioning of properties in inheritance and to the similarity of savings
rates out of lifetime or "permanent" personal income among different income groups.[6] If savings rates out of income are equal, the group with a
higher income–wealth ratio, the small wealth-holders for whom wages
are the main income source, will have a higher savings–wealth ratio. This
will tend to equalize wealth. It must, then, be the case that moderate-
income families invested primarily in low-yield assets (housing). The
principles of improper foreknowledge (unexpected capital gains), market
imperfections limiting freedom of investment (need to invest in housing
to have housing services for consumption), and risk averseness (trading
lower rates of return for the security of ownership) might explain some
of the differences in returns. The overall conclusion would be that a systematic pattern exists which limits lower-wealth households to low-re-
turn investments, and thus acts so as to increase wealth inequality.

It is possible that nonmonetary returns may be such as to equate returns to different investments (Hypothesis II). However, this does not
change the picture of the dynamics of wealth inequality. If returns to
housing investment are understated by our capital gains figures, then

nonmonetary housing benefits must be significant enough that reported incomes of homeowners are understated. This would indicate that the annual flow of real incomes is less unequal (comparing the very wealthy with the rest of the homeowning majority) than is usually estimated. However, it would also indicate that the savings rate and wealth/income ratio for small wealth-holders are inflated by the exclusion of the same nonmonetary income. Thus the persistence of wealth disparities would be explained not by differential returns offsetting inheritance, but by important wealth/income ratio and savings rate.

The principal implication is that there is an important difference between housing and other investments. An investment portfolio largely tied up in an occupied home may provide the owner with the best shelter he can afford, but it will not grow as fast as a larger portfolio that includes primarily nonhousing investments (including, perhaps, other forms of real estate). Under either possible assumption about true rates of return, investment in housing is not an offset to the concentration of wealth. This is true, first, because wealthier households tend to reap greater capital gains from land than those whose lesser wealth restricts them to investment in inner-ring land, and, second, because there is a difference between housing and other investments. The housing investment either yields lower returns than other investments, or, if it yields equivalent returns, these returns include nonreinvestable, nonmonetary benefits—a form of consumption to which the homeowner is committed by being a homeowner and which is associated with a lowered savings rate if income is defined to include the benefits. Thus, both among different strata of the labor force and between them and top wealth-holders, the distribution of real estate values changes helps to maintain relative wealth disparities.

These estimates and conclusions are all based on data from the turn of the century to 1970. During the 1970s, there was a rapid increase in housing prices, as indeed there had been in the 1920s. Whether the recent rapid increase was a phenomenon which is likely to continue, and to invalidate the conclusions of this chapter, or whether, like the increase of the 1920s, it is likely to prove a transitory result of the business cycle, will be considered in chapter 11.

FIVE

The Reality of Suburban Entrapment

A. The Conventional Wisdom

I N the late 1960s, three architects set out to examine how physical urban dwelling environments affected people over their lifetimes. Caminos, Turner, and Steffian chose two hypothetical families, one in Lima, Peru, the other in Boston. The two families, constructed to be "representative of characteristic patterns of life in Boston and Lima," were described as follows: "A third generation of a European immigrant family from the "upper-lower" or "skilled blue-collar" class . . . [for] Boston; and a first-generation immigrant family . . . [for] Lima."[1] The Boston family was envisioned as moving through several localities, represented by (1) the North End, an inner city neighborhood; (2) Cambridgeport, an old community just outside the political limits of Boston; and (3) Lincoln, a suburb some 13 miles from downtown.

In this migratory process, the authors saw the family's income slowly rising from $7,000 to $10,000 in 1960 prices. This fairly moderate growth in income was paralleled in the Caminos-Turner-Steffian view by a much more substantial increase in access to the amenities of life associated with suburban location and homeownership. Moreover, the family's income and geographic mobility would also be paralleled by significant property mobility:

> The Boston family . . . uses its property investments as equity and maintains a high degree of geographic as well as social mobility. . . . [In fact,] the Boston family . . . achieves or maintains upward mobility by means of its geographic [mobility].[2]

This view of American life as a series of parallel upward moves in income, property, and location still sits comfortably with many people. This "typical family" construct, in fact, conforms nicely to "scientific" notions about social existence in the United States. First, it assumes widespread mobility from inner-city, working-class life situations to suburban, "middle-class" ones. Second, it assumes that real estate acquisition, in common with such other factors as education, facilitates upward social movement. Third, it assumes that, even in slower-growing metropolitan areas such as Boston, overall living standards are constantly improving; hence, the achievements of suburbanizers are not costs to those who remain in the city. In a word, there is nothing in the structure of the metropolis which traps families in particular locations, jobs, or social classes.

A similar view permeates much of the writing done on suburbanization and homeownership. This is true particularly of hypothetical arguments that property ownership *should* increase other aspects of mobility. Let us consider a typical version of this argument.

Consider two families with $10,000 annual before-tax incomes (in 1960s prices). Both begin, let us say, with $6,000 in liquid wealth. One family uses its $6,000 as the down payment on a $26,000 home with a ten-year, $20,000 mortgage.[3] The other rents, placing its savings in short-term certificates of deposit earning an effective annual return of 7 percent. A 1960–61 survey conducted by the Bureau of Labor Statistics reported that homeowners on average spent 15.8 percent of their before-tax-and-deduction income on shelter; tenants spent just under 14 percent.[4] We make the assumption that all of the homeowning family's saving is home-related,[5] and that both families save all of their interest. The homeowning family's property is assumed to appreciate at 4.1 percent annually, with tax deductions and partial capital gains tax immunity raising the true rate of return to 5 to 8 percent.[6]

Table 5.1 is based on these assumptions. It compares the two families at the start and finish of a 10-year period. It suggests that the homeowning family accumulates nearly three times as much over the decade as its tenant counterpart. Homeownership appears to lead to real accumulation.

There are, however, good reasons to dispute the relevance of table 5.1 and the conclusion it supports. First, assumptions about returns underlying the computation of the several entries in the table may be overoptimistic, as we suggested in chapters 3 and 4. Second, if home-

Table 5.1
Owning, Renting, and Accumulation

	Homeowning Family	Renting Family
Beginning wealth	$ 6,000	$ 6,000
Annual income	10,000	10,000
Income over decade	100,000	111,802
From wages	100,000	100,000
From interest	0	11,802[a]
Non-shelter consumption expenditures over decade	84,200[b]	84,200[b]
Non-housing savings at End of Decade	0	2,661[c]
Wealth at end of decade	45,760[d]	20,464[e]
Decade Accumulation	39,760[f]	14,464[f]

[a] $6,000 $(1 + 0.07)^{10} = \$11,802$.
[b] $100,000 $(1 - 0.158) = \$84,200$.
[c] 10
Σ $(0.158 - 0.14)$ $(\$100,000)$ $(1 + 0.07)^t = \$2,661$; $t = 1$.
[d] $26,000 $(1 + 0.058)^{10} = \$45,760$.
[e] $6,000 + \$11,802 + \$2,661 = \$20,464$.
[f] $45,760 - \$6,000$ and $\$20,464 - \$6,000$.
SOURCE: Daniel Luria, *Suburbanization, Homeownership and Working-Class Consciousness*, Ph.D. Dissertation, University of Massachusetts, Amherst, 1976.

ownership represents such a sound investment from the standpoint of pecuniary returns, the fact that top wealth-holders shy away from making real estate a large portion of their asset portfolios[7] is most puzzling. Third, an analysis which treats all real estate as identical misses the highly uneven pattern of value appreciation in different geographic locations which we have documented in previous chapters. Fourth, the assumptions ignore possible effects of the investment in homeownership on other investments, including children's education. These effects may be positive *or* negative.

Similarly, the "typical family" pictured by Caminos, Turner, and Steffian is *not* typical. Very few families have ever made it from the North Ends or even the Cambridgeports to the Lincolns. In fact, Caminos et al. offer no support for their inclusion of real estate acquisition among the steps of the mobility ladder. In their depiction of the "typical family," real estate is not purchased until the family is settled in its final destination.[8] Perhaps this is because, had the family been saddled with homeownership at its intermediate spatial situation—Cambridgeport—it might never have made it to suburban Lincoln.

It is our contention that mobility in American cities, either between economic classes or between neighborhoods of significantly different levels of amenities, is very limited. While many families do move to more suburban locations than those from which they started out, and do acquire higher levels of education and income than their parents, the neighborhoods, schooling, and jobs into which they move are themselves declining in worth. In our view, these non-upper-class assets— homes, education, and white-collar jobs—are double-edged swords. Because these hard-earned assets tend to depreciate in social and economic value, they limit the very mobility that they appear to promote. A great deal of energy is diverted into defending these depreciating assets from the competition of other families. Thus, instead of providing real mobility, these assets may lead to conservative efforts aimed at defending relative status levels, effectively blocking the formation of coalitions of low- and middle-income working families which could exercise great power in determining the very distribution of key economic assets and hence the very direction of the economy. Subsequent chapters discuss the extent to which this possibility has been realized.

In this chapter, we set ourselves the task of evaluating these rival views about mobility in American cities. Our emphasis will be on the part played by real estate acquisition in the overall process of social mobility, or, as we see it, of social *entrapment*. We present a direct test of the rival claims concerning the role of suburban residence and homeownership on upward mobility for the first suburbanization period (1890–1910). We then review some indirect tests for the post-World War II era.

B. Ownership, Suburbanization and Mobility 1880–1910

In a well-known study of Newburyport, Massachusetts, Stephan Thernstrom suggested that home ownership might reduce intergenerational career mobility for working-class families. Analyzing mid-nineteenth-century data, he found that families who accumulated property did so "at the expense of their children," giving them less education while using the children's labor incomes for home purchase.[9]

In his later study of Boston, Thernstrom retreats from his earlier finding of a tradeoff between parental home ownership and sons' achievements. In Boston, he argues:

The ownership of a modest working-class dwelling simply made
no difference either way. . . . . Fully 83 percent of the children coming from propertyless households themselves obtained no property in the city; only 8 percent accumulated
holdings as large as $5,000. The sons of men owning homes
. . . were not in a dramatically different position. The large
majority of them—two-thirds did not become homeowners
. . . [and a] mere 12 percent of them, little more than the 9
percent figure for the sons as propertyless men, succeeded in
accumulating $5,000 or more.[10]

We find that Thernstrom may have been too quick to dismiss the
tradeoff as holding for Boston. His finding of an apparent discrepancy is
due in part to differences in data base. The Boston study covers families
from the whole range of occupations while the Newburyport study examined only the families of laborers. This should have made for a richer
study, but if different social levels are not clearly distinguished, a study
may fail to address whether homeowning had differential effects for families of different social-class position. Also, Thernstrom's Boston findings
do not differentiate between wealth-holding in the form of homes and
other types of asset ownership. As a result, it may be that it was the
non-home wealth of homeowners which aided their children's prospects,
masking a positive intergenerational disadvantage to homeowning per se.
Finally, and perhaps most damning, Thernstrom restricts his inquiry to
the city of Boston proper: his study, therefore, is of mobility for those
who were geographically immobile. As our analysis of his data will show,
an extension of the research into Boston's suburbs would have convinced
Thernstrom of a very different dynamic: property mobility in Boston led
to homeownership in the suburbs, leading in turn to geographic, occupational, and property immobility in the new suburban location.

In this section, we document this less optimistic dynamic by examining the wealth-holding and mobility in a 9 percent subsample ($n = 358$)
of Thernstrom's 2 percent random sample of 1880 census listings of Boston fathers and sons. Thernstrom's information on the units in the subsample was expanded by additional traces of residence, occupation, and
property holding. This restored to the sample some individuals who were
lost to Thernstrom's sample for years after 1880 because they had moved
across county lines. Also, all of the variables which Thernstrom expressed in dollar terms were recomputed into "constant" 1880 dollars so

as to be comparable over time. In addition to this, two entirely new traces
were undertaken:

1. A land- and home-ownership trace: Grantee indices for each of
   the SMSA's five counties, from 1860 to 1930, were used to determine which of the sample units had purchased land and/or
   housing. When a purchase was uncovered, the relevant
   deed(s) were studied, and the location and price recorded, the
   latter then being deflated.

2. A city and town data trace: Data were collected for all of the
   SMSA's cities and towns on property tax rates, population
   density, per pupil education expenditure, and average commuting time to Boston. This was done on the theory that the
   structural meaning of "residence" is that the resident takes on
   and is subject to the distribution of characteristics exhibited by
   his town of residence. For instance, owning a home means different things to those living in towns where owning is the rule
   than to those living in towns composed primarily of tenants.[11]

The sample study documents ample geographical mobility. Although all of the people sampled lived in Boston in 1880, over half of
those traced to 1910 had left the city (table 5.2).[12]

Table 5.2
Population Distribution by Residence, 1890–1910 (%)

Residence[a]	1890 (n = 202)	1900 (n = 177)	1910 (n = 115)
Pedestrian City	80.4	63.1%	45.6%
Old Suburbs	11.4	16.6	19.0
Streetcar Suburbs	4.6	10.6	14.4
New Suburbs	2.1	6.0	13.9
Far Suburbs	1.4	3.7	7.1

[a] Residence has been divided, following Sam Bass Warner, Jr., *Streetcar Suburbs* (New
York: Atheneum, 1971), p. 179, into:

(1) The "Pedestrian City," comprising those districts within 2 miles of Boston City Hall,
    which include Boston (center city), East Boston, South Boston, Charlestown, Rox-
    bury, Allston-Brighton, and parts of Cambridge.
(2) The "Old Suburbs," very much connected to the city of Boston, at distances of 2 to
    3 miles, which include Dorchester, Brookline, Chelsea, and most of Somerville and
    Cambridge.
(3) The "Streetcar Suburbs" of West Roxbury, Everett, southern Lynn, Medford, Quincy,
    Revere, and Winthrop.
(4) The new suburbs of Arlington, Belmont, northern Braintree, Malden, Melrose, Na-
    hant, Needham, Newton, Waltham, Wellesley, and northern Weymouth.
(5) The far suburbs of Framingham, Hingham, Hull, Norwood, Reading, Salem, Sci-
    tuate, Wakefield, Weyland, and Woburn.

SOURCE: Same as Table 5.1.

This suburbanization affected all occupational levels. While semi-professionals and clerical/sales workers were somewhat more likely to suburbanize than manual workers, the differences were not significant, and the pattern of migration was approximately the same for all occupational groups (table 5.3).

Suburbanization was well-nigh synonymous with greatly expanded homeownership. In Boston, homeownership grew from 13.6 percent to 18 percent among the sample. In the suburbs the rates were much higher. (See table 5.4). Over the SMSA, the proportion of sample members owning homes grew from less than 14 percent in 1880 to 20.8 percent in 1890 and 40.4 percent in 1910.

Table 5.3
Occupational Distribution by Residence, 1910

Occupation in 1890	Residence in 1910					
	Pedestrian City	Old Subs.	Streetcar Subs.	New Subs.	Far Subs.	Total
Professional	5	2	0	3	1	11
	(45%)	(19%)	(0%)	(27%)	(9%)	(6.1%)[a]
Managerial	7	3	1	3	1	15
	(46%)	(20%)	(7%)	(20%)	(7%)	(8.3%)[a]
Semi Professional	3	2	1	1	1	8
	(37%)	(24%)	(13%)	(13%)	(13%)	(4.4%)[a]
Sales/ Clerical	18	11	11	13	2	55
	(32%)	(20%)	(20%)	(24%)	(4%)	(30.6%)[a]
Petty Proprietor	3	2	1	1	1	8
	(37%)	(24%)	(13%)	(13%)	(13%)	(4.4%)[a]
Skilled Labor	22	7	9	1	4	43
	(51%)	(16%)	(21%)	(2%)	(10%)	(23.8%)[a]
Semi-skilled Labor	16	2	2	2	2	24
	(75%)	(6%)	(6%)	(6%)	(6%)	(13.3%)[a]
Unskilled Labor	7	3	1	1	1	13
	(54%)	(22%)	(8%)	(8%)	(8%)	(7.2%)[a]
Unemployed	1	2	0	0	0	3
	(33%)	(67%)	(0%)	(0%)	(0%)	(1.7%)[a]
Totals:	82	34	26	25	13	180
	(45.6%)	(18.9%)	(14.4%)	(13.9%)	(7.2%)	(100%)

[a] Percent of column total; other percentages are shares of row total.
Chi-Square 30.221, significant at 46%, with 32° of freedom.
SOURCE: Same as Table 5.1.

Table 5.4
Homeownership by Area of Residence, 1890–1910 (%)

Residence	1890	1900	1910
Pedestrian City	13.6	16.0	18.0
Old Suburbs	39.7	41.1	40.3
Streetcar Suburbs	61.0	66.6	66.4
New Suburbs	59.2	65.7	70.1
Far Suburbs	65.6	69.4	75.9

SOURCE: Same as Table 5.1.

One apparent result of the spread of homeownership by working families was an increase in wealth equality. By using the Assessor's Valuation Books for Boston and tax and assessor's records for suburban towns, table 5.5 was constructed. It seems to indicate a significant leveling in wealth-holding disparities between 1890 and 1910.

Results such as those summarized in table 5.5 provide much of the basis for the inclusion of homeowning as among the positive causes of upward mobility. Further analysis, however, shows that such an inference cannot be drawn.

The key to the analysis is to separate home equities from other forms of wealth. In our society, not all forms of wealth-holding are equivalent.[13] Assets may be rated by whether the returns associated with their ownership is of an amount and of a form which could be accumulated over time in such a way as to raise their owners' position in the society's wealth distribution. We have argued above that the rate of return to homeownership was low relative to yields on alternative assets. This suggests that for purposes of analysis, homeownership might best be separated analytically from other forms of wealth.

The empirical aspect of this view is contained in the construction of

Table 5.5
Distribution of Total Wealth, 1890–1910 (%)

Category	1890	1900	1910
Bottom 30%	0.22	0.26	0.69
Low Mid 30%	4.50	5.64	10.69
Mid-Upper 30%	17.40	19.21	24.38
Top 10%	77.88	74.89	64.24

SOURCE: Same as Table 5.1.

two variables from our data. First, we made a separation of total wealth into home equity and non-home wealth.[14] Second, a variable called class was constructed as a measure of relative class status. We interpret class as reflecting relative opportunity to transform wealth into new investments. The "class" variable can also be termed "capital access." This variable was created by a principal component analysis of fourteen characteristics of individual members of the random sample of the 1880 male population of Boston, as described in Appendix D.

Figures 5.1 and 5.2 show the frequency distribution of the new variable. In both cases, the distribution is skewed, with one small group standing out from the rest as an "upper class" with more "capital access."

These new variables prove to be more unequally distributed than is total wealth. Table 5.6 shows non-home wealth became more unequally distributed in the period 1890–1910, in contrast to total wealth (table 5.5), which became more equal because of the spread of homeownership. As figures 5.1 and 5.2 show, "capital access" remained relatively unchanged.

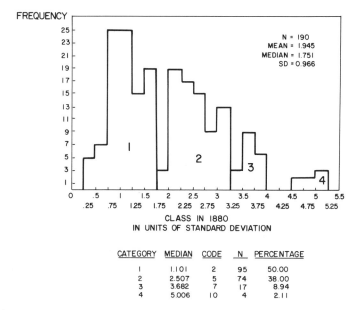

Figure 5.1   Class (Capital Access), 1880.
(*Source:* Luria, Subsample)

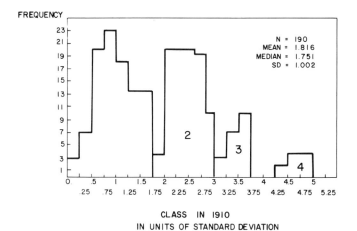

CLASS IN 1910
IN UNITS OF STANDARD DEVIATION

CATEGORY	MEDIAN	CODE	N	PERCENTAGE
1	0.942	2	96	50.53
2	2.390	5	72	37.90
3	3.505	7	17	8.94
4	4.699	10	5	2.63

Figure 5.2   Class (Capital Access), 1910.
(*Source:* Luria, Subsample)

These new variables allow some observation on the relationship between different kinds of mobility. Tables 5.7 and 5.8 present the results
of an analysis of variance between total property-holding and different
job categories, for two types of wealth. Table 5.7, on total wealth holding, shows three distinct groups. First, there is a "wealth-positive" group,
composed of managers and professionals, who hold significantly more total property than average. Second, there is a "wealth-negative" group,

Table 5.6
The Distribution of Non-Home Wealth,[a] 1890–1910 (%)

Category	1890	1900	1910
Bottom 30%	0.19	0.18	0.16
Low-Mid 30%	6.07	5.40	5.22
Mid-Upper 30%	21.58	19.54	18.61
Top 10%	72.16	74.88	76.01

[a]"Non-home wealth" is computed as total property-holding less estimated owner's equity in owner-occupied real estate.
SOURCE: Same as Table 5.1.

Table 5.7
Analysis of Variance: Total Wealth by Occupation, 1890

Occupational Group	Coefficient	t – Statistic	Simple r
Professionals	19.013	3.01	0.195
Managers	40.270	7.31	0.466
Semi-professionals	– 2.786	– 0.36	– 0.009
Sales/Clerical	– 6.003	– 1.76	– 0.098
Petty Proprietors	– 6.096	– 0.74	– 0.032
Skilled Laborers	– 11.120	– 2.93	– 0.175
Semi-skilled Laborers	– 11.477	– 2.70	– 0.154
Unskilled Laborers	– 13.738	– 2.24	– 0.120

Dependent variable: 1890 total property.
R-squared = 0.561, F = 12.448 (significant at 1% with 194° of freedom)
SOURCE: Same as Table 5.1.

composed of manual laborers, who hold significantly less than average total property. Third, there is a group that might be called "wealth-average," composed of semiprofessionals, clerks, secretaries, salesmen, and small merchants and retailers, and characterized by average levels of total ownership.

For non-home wealth, there is less of a gap between white-collar and blue-collar groups. What appears as a three-class system in the data on total wealth now seems more like a two-class system, with only professionals in an intermediate position. This suggests that, while suburban-

Table 5.8
Analysis of Variance: Non-Home Wealth by Occupation, 1890

Occupational Group	Coefficient	t – Statistic	Simple r
Managers	56.074	11.40	0.058
Professionals	13.665	1.89	0.160
Petty Proprietors	– 9.891	– 1.96	– 0.105
Semi-professionals	– 9.333	– 2.09	– 0.118
Sales/Clerical	– 7.093	– 1.99	– 0.110
Skilled Laborers	– 9.950	– 2.84	– 0.166
Semi-skilled Laborers	– 10.031	– 2.90	– 0.146
Unskilled Laborers	– 10.773	– 2.35	– 0.119

Dependent variables: 1890 non-home property.
R-squared = 0.624, f = 12.910 (significant at 1% with 192° of freedom)
SOURCE: Same as Table 5.1.

ization was a process involving people in different job categories in closely similar proportions, the effect of suburban homeownership on the future net worth of those in different occupations was far from uniform. Table 5.8 confirms this assertion. While not all of the decade-to-decade changes are statistically significant, it is worth noting that only those in managerial posts were able on average to increase their non-home net worth significantly over the period. And, since homes have been shown, in chapter 4, to yield a rate of return below that yielded by most other types of assets, homeownership must have increased the size of the gap between workers and capitalist managers.

These are inferences about wealth. A more direct test of the effect of homeownership may be made using our subsample. First, we consider the simple correlation between the homeownership share of a person's total wealth, and his observed occupational and property mobility. Table 5.10 presents partial correlations between changes in occupation and wealth and the ratio Home Wealth–Total Wealth, holding initial occupation and wealth constant. Equity in homes[15] would be shown to aid correlations if they are positive; homeownership *impedes* mobility if they are negative.

The table suggests the correlations between homeowning and mobility are negative, but they became increasingly so over time. It appears, then, that homeownership—as it became (or, perhaps, *because* it became) more widespread—acted as a drag on owners' career prospects. Clearly, the *ceteris paribus* assumptions underlying the construction of table 5.1, which compared renters and owners, are not justified; this in

Table 5.9
Probability That Non-Home Wealth ÷ Total Wealth Exceeds 0.10, by Occupational Category

Occupational Category	1880	1890	1900	1910	1920
Managerial	.92	.92	.87	.92	1.00
Professional	.60	.54	.51	.51	.43
Semi-professional	.45	.39	.40	.36	.31
Pretty proprietorial	.82	.70	.53	.50	.33
Sales/Clerical	.33	.37	.28	.19	.17
Skilled Laborers	.42	.38	.32	.25	.17
Semi-skilled Laborers	.29	.29	.23	.18	.15
Unskilled Laborers	.32	.26	.20	.13	.13

SOURCE: Same as Table 5.1.

Table 5.10
Effects of Homeownership on Occupational and Property Mobility

Correlation Between Homeownership, Share of Wealth, and:	Holding Constant	r =
Change in Occupation, 1890–1900	Occupation in 1890	−0.047
Change in Occupation, 1900–1910	Occupation in 1900	−0.068
Change in Property, 1890–1900	Property in 1890	−0.074
Change in Property, 1900–1910	Property in 1900	−0.101

SOURCE: Same as Table 5.1.

itself seriously questions the Caminos-Turner-Steffian view of the role of homeownership in the mobility process.

The possibility remains, however, that homeownership led to improvements in career experiences, but that its positive impact was delayed by the countervailing effects of ethnic background: immigrant homeowners, for example, may have been at a disadvantage in the job market. This job access problem would, of course, have led to property accumulation disadvantages as well. These possibilities lead us to attempt to estimate an intergenerational model of the effects of parental homeownership on sons' mobility experiences, so as to allow for the probability that the salutory impact of homes often took time to manifest itself. In the model we use as the measure of overall social class position, the index of class is depicted in figures 5.1 and 5.2.

In this section, a four-equation econometric model is presented, the estimation of which suggests that parental homeownership adversely affected the occupational, property, and overall social class position of sons. In our estimates, father's and son's occupations were measured using an eight-category ordinal scale. Wealth variables were in units of one per $250 of dollars of 1880. Father's nativity was coded zero for foreign-born and one for U.S.-born. See Appendix D.

Figure 5.3 provides a path diagram of the hypothesis. Attributes of fathers, including homeownership, affect the social class position of sons by their impact on sons' occupational and wealth-holding attainments. Father's occupation affects son's occupational group. Paternal wealth-holding and homeownership affects son's class through both his occupational and his property positions. Father's nativity operates through son's property-holding but, interestingly, not through his occupation. Finally, a son's occupation also affects his overall class position through the wealth-holding made possible by holding a high-paying job.

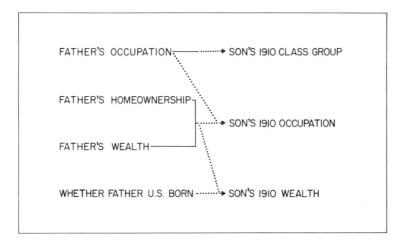

Figure 5.3 PATH DIAGRAM: Determinants of Son's Relative Social Class Position.

Equation (1) (table 5.11) reports that high filial class position in 1910 was positively predicted by having had an American-born father with a good job and significant wealth-holding. Most intriguing, son's class was *negatively* predicted by paternal homeownership. A homeowning father, the equation shows, "robbed" his son of 0.1819 units of class score, equivalent to approximately one decile. But the entrapment hypothesis does not maintain that parental homeownership had a *direct* adverse effect on children's social position.

Equations (2) and (3) provide tests of the more plausible contention that parental homeownership impeded children's mobility indirectly, through reduced occupational, and hence property, mobility. Having a rich father gave sons a certain advantage in the labor market, as did previous family job success. Paternal homeowning, though, was a significant negative predictor of son's occupational attainment. In fact, homeowning fathers on average denied their sons 0.96 units of occupation—about one on a scale of one to eight—or the difference between a craftsman and a machine operator or between a clerk and a street peddlar.

In equation (3), high filial wealth-holding, like occupation, is positively predicted by father's property, and negatively (at the 6% level) by paternal homeownership. In addition, son's property-holding is significantly predicted by son's occupational category and by having a native-born father. According to this equation, a native-born father bestowed,

Table 5.11
Regression Results for Homeownership and Mobility 1880–1910

equation number	(1)	(2)	(3)	(4)
Dependent variables	son's 1910 class group	son's 1910 occupation	son's 1910 wealth	son's 1910 class group
Independent variables		coefficient (t-statistic)		
constant	—	2.966 (4.70)††	16.18 (4.01)††	1.390 (5.90)††
Father's occupation	0.1337 (6.11)††	0.32 (3.81)††	—	0.238 (7.89)††
Father's wealth	0.01135 (6.84)††	0.0089 (1.91)†	0.58 (12.40)††	—
Father's Homeownership	−0.1819 (−2.10)††	−0.958 (−2.73)††	−3.602 (−1.87)†	−0.0030 (0.22)
Father U.S.-born	0.417 (2.13)††	(†††)	3.899 (1.95)†	—
Son's 1910 Occupation	—	—	2.39 (3.62)††	0.065 (1.97)††
Son's Wealth	—	—	—	0.0099 (3.41)††
R^2	.529	.244	.638	.576

Units: Class group: See Appendix D.
  Wealth: Units of 1 per $250.
  Occupation: 8 category scale.
  Homeownership: value of home/wealth.
  U.S.-born: 0 = no, 1 = yes.
†Variable significant at 10% level.
††Variable significant at 5% level.
†††Equation 2 was also estimated with "whether father U.S.-born" as a predictor, but its effect was insignificant even at the 10% level.
SOURCE: See Table 5.1.

on average, 3.899 times $250, or $975 of "additional" wealth on his son—no paltry sum in a time when two dollars a day was a living wage. Significantly, paternal homeownership was nearly as disadvantageous as U.S. birth was helpful: a homeowning father "took" 3.602 times $250, or $900, from his son's wealth-holding.

Since father's home ownership affects son's wealth and occupation, and these in turn affect son's class position, it is necessary to check on whether homeownership can affect son's occupation on its own, apart from its influence through wealth and occupation. This is done in equation (4), which is technically the structural equation corresponding to the reduced form of equation (1).

The most important, and illuminating, finding of equation (4) is that the inclusion of son's 1910 job and wealth captured most of the effect of father's homeownership on son's class position.[16] Thus, the effect of father's homeowning is shown to work not in any direct but mysterious way, but in the obvious direct way of competing with job mobility (perhaps via education as Thernstrom initially suggested) and by diverting wealth away from more lucrative assets.

The results of this section are at odds with the belief that homeownership accumulation has an overall mobility advantage for homeowners. Clearly, the *ceteris paribus* assumption covering income and beginning wealth in table 5.1 was unrealistic. In fact, homeowners' sons tended to have lower-income jobs, and hence lower net worth, than tenants' sons from the same father's job and wealth categories.

C. Mobility of Somerville Residents

How much of the finding that homeownership led to reduced social mobility applies only to the first wave of suburbanization? Data that would be needed to duplicate our 1890–1910 model for more recent periods were not available: information on individuals requires access to census manuscript schedules, unavailable after 1910 at the time of our study; and changes in tax laws mean that the non-home wealth of individuals is no longer computed by local assessors.

Still, a number of imaginative studies cast considerable light on individual mobility experiences in the post-World War II period. The most relevant is Charles Levenstein's trace of the families and progeny of 273 residents of Somerville, Massachusetts.[17] Levenstein used local newspaper obituaries to construct a sample of decedents. Using information provided in the obituaries and in birth records and city directories, he was able to trace a fair number of members of decedents' families and the families of the decedents' children. Levenstein's data allow us to infer information relating to the effect of residential tenure—a good proxy for homeownership—on geographic and occupational mobility.

Somerville is a blue-collar, inner-ring suburb of Boston. Into its scant four square miles are packed some 77,000 people; most commute to jobs outside Somerville, and virtually none are professionals. Between September 1971 and September 1972, Levenstein chose 273 random obit-

uaries from the weekly *Somerville Journal.* Since the town has few fa-
mous or rich residents, the local plumber, teacher, and waitress receive
the sort of listings that the *New York Times* reserves for the wealthy and
the powerful. The data collected included name, address, occupation,
age, sex, place of birth, religion, years of residence, and organizational
membership, as well as maiden names of female decedents, spouses,
parents, and children, plus names and addresses of siblings and children.

The average decedent was 70 years old, and had lived in Somerville
for just over four decades: the SMSA average is closer to a single decade. Stability, if not entrapment, is hence already indicated. The 273
obituaries yielded 676 reported children, with addresses recorded for all
but 93 of them. Of the 583 children of known residence, 431 lived in
the Boston SMSA, and 69 lived elsewhere within Massachusetts. The
obituary listings also provided the names and sexes of 541 siblings, of
whom most remained within the Boston area.

Levenstein first tested for whether residents of Somerville and their
children had been able to move to more suburban locations. In other
words, he was concerned with whether moves such as the one from
Cambridgeport to Lincoln used by Caminos, Turner, and Steffian were
at all typical. Using the index of town suburbanization which is described in Appendix A, Levenstein constructed frequency distributions
for the degree of suburbanization of where the decedents themselves lived
when they died, and where their children were living at the time. One
entry was entered for each family, with the location of the decedent and
his or her siblings averaged in the older generation, and the residences
of the different children in the family averaged in their generation. Results are shown in table 5.12. Levenstein's data show some very strong
results. In the generation of the decedents and their siblings, over half
of the families had average suburbanization scores at Somerville's level
or lower. No families had average values over zero, the mean of the index for the Boston area.

In the children's generation, somewhat more suburbanization was observed. Slightly less than one-third of the families had degrees of suburbanization at or equal to the Somerville level. Some families had sur-
passed the median level for the SMSA, but the number was small (only
4.4%).

Levenstein also tested the effects on suburban migration of a number

Table 5.12
Suburbanization of Somerville Families

Example	Suburbanization Index	Decedents' Generation		Children's Generation	
		Absolute Frequency	Relative Frequency	Absolute Frequency	Relative Frequency
Chelsea	−3.06	0	0	0	0
Boston	−2.66	0	0	3	1.5%
	−2.65 to −2.46	9	3.3%	10	4.9
Somerville	−2.45	130	47.6	54	26.3
	−2.44 to 2.00	19	7.0	8	3.9
Cambridge	−1.99	3	1.1	1	0.5
	−1.98 to −1.78	12	4.4	7	3.4
Everett	−1.77	1	0.3	0	0
	−1.76 to −1.75	2	0.8	2	1.0
Malden	−1.74	1	0.3	3	1.5
	−1.73 to −1.56	12	4.4	9	4.4
Winthrop	−1.55	0	0	1	0.5
	−1.54 to −1.33	13	4.8	8	3.9
Medford	−1.32	2	0.7	6	2.9
	−1.31 to −1.08	17	6.3	18	8.8
Arlington	−1.07	1	0.3	3	1.5
	−1.06 to −0.97	2	0.8	2	1.0
Revere	−0.96	0	0	1	0.5
	−0.95 to −0.74	16	5.8	12	5.9
Melrose	−0.73	0	0	0	0
	−0.72 to −0.54	6	2.2	2	1.0
Nahant	−0.53	0	0	2	1.0
	−0.52 to −0.29	15	5.5	2	1.0
Woburn	−0.28	1	0.4	1	0.5
	−0.27 to −0.14	2	0.7	1	0.5
Winchester	−0.13	1	0.4	1	0.5
	−0.12 to 0.0	8	2.9	39	19.0
Over	0.0	0	0	9	4.4
TOTALS		273	100.0%	205	100.0%

SOURCE: Charles Levenstein, *Class, Assimilation and Suburbanization* (Boston: Studies in Urban Political Economy).

of characteristics of his sample, including the length of time they had lived in Somerville, which he suggested might be a proxy for homeownership. (In a related study, he found that the average length of time homeowners lived in Somerville exceeded the average for homeowners and nonhomeowners in his sample of decedents.)[18] Other variables used included age, an occupational scale, and an "assimilation" measure, based on the degree of inter-ethnic marriage in the parents' or the children's generation.

The correlations between these variables, for families where the decedent was over fifty years old, are shown in table 5.13. The simple correlation coefficients suggest that years in Somerville had no effect on the degree of suburbanization of either generation, but had another, slightly negative, effect on the degree of assimilation (which might prove to be another partial measure of mobility). A regression equation was estimated with the following results:

Suburbanization (children) = $-1.23 + .48$ Surbanization (Parents) +
                                              (2.53)
.14 Age $-$ .11 Assimilation (children) $+$ .06 Assimilation (Parents) $-$
(1.0)   (0.37)   (0.14)
.01 Occupation $-$ .01 Years in Somerville
(0.14)   (0.14)
   ($R^2 =$ .15)

Table 5.13
Correlation Coefficients of Variables, Somerville

	Occ.	Age	Years in Som.	AFAMP	AFAMC	SFAMP	SFAMC
Occ.	1.00						
Age	.03	1.00					
Years in Som.	$-.14$	.18	1.00				
AFAMP	$-.22$	$-.37$	$-.05$	1.00			
AFAMC	.10	$-.05$	$-.10$	.02	1.00		
SFAMP	$-.18$	$-.20$	$-.01$	.02	.10	1.00	
SFAMC	$-.09$	.08	$-.01$	$-.02$	$-.10$	.35	1.00

A = Assimilation Index.
S = Suburbanization Index.
FAMP = Parental generation.
FAMC = Children's generation.
SOURCE: See Table 5.12.

The equation suggests that we can explain 15 percent of the variance in the average degree of suburbanization of children's residences. The average degree of suburbanization of the parents' generation and the age of the decedent are the significant variables. The greater the degree of suburbanization of the parents' generation, the greater the suburbanization of the children. The older the decedent parent, the greater the average degree of suburbanization of the children.

Later regressions for "assimilation" showed parental occupation and parental age to be the significant predictors of intermarriage. Parents with higher occupational status, and those born later, were more likely to have "assimilating" families.[19]

The regression, like that for suburbanization, shows length of residence in Somerville having a negative effect on mobility, but at a statistically insignificant level. Because a direct measure of homeownership was not made, little can be said as to whether homeownership itself had any negative effect, and, if so, what its strength was. That stability of residence did not have any significant positive effect is, however, itself interesting: at least, giving this finding and the overall low rate of mobility for Somerville residents, it can be concluded that "buying into" the inner ring does not appear to increase mobility.

Years of residence do appear to have a negative relationship with decedents' occupation. When Levenstein uses years in Somerville as one of the "predictors" of occupation, it is significant with a negative sign.

$$(1) \quad \text{Occupation} = 4.79 + 1.51 \text{ Catholic} - 0.485 \text{ Suburbanization (Parents)}$$
$$(2.29) \quad \quad (1.71)$$
$$- 0.20 \text{ Years of Residence} - 1.06 \text{ Assimilation (Parents)} - 0.77 \text{ Italian}$$
$$(1.81) \quad \quad (1.74) \quad \quad (1.14)$$
$$- 0.20 \text{ Irish} + 0.02 \text{ Age}$$
$$(0.34) \quad \quad (0.13)$$
$$(R^2 = \quad .15)$$

Since occupation is measured in such a way that increasing levels have lower values, the negative sign on years of residence means that those who lived in Somerville longer had higher occupations. This is consistent with the suggestion that longer-term residents stayed because they had been able to become homeowners, not because they were otherwise trapped by occupational immobility. But it also suggests that the insignificant impact of length of stay on later homeownership or suburbanization or assimilation cannot be attributed to occupational failure. Reversing the order of causality in the regression, we get:

Years of Residence = 2.03 + 0.49 Age + 0.38 Irish − 0.20 Occ. +
                              (3.45)   (0.64)   (1.81)
        0.75 Catholic − 0.58 Italian − 0.19 Suburbanization (Parents)
      −(1.12)   (0.86)   (0.67)
        0.3 Assimilation (Parents)
      −(0.52)
R^2 =   .23

The equation explains 23 percent of the variance in Years of Residence. Only three of the variables, however, have acceptable t-statistics: age, occupation and the dummy variable "Catholic." What this equation suggests is that, given age, the higher the level of occupation, the longer the decedent resided in Somerville. It also indicates that Catholics remained in Somerville longer than other religious groups. The positive correlation with age, of course, is not startling, but the occupation/years of residence relationship is indeed surprising.

In order to see if generational differences among the decedents were affecting our results, another regression equation was constructed, restricting the cases to those decedents 50 years of age or older. This eliminated those decedents who were at lower levels of occupation because of their age. This time R-squared falls from .23 to .12. The significant variables are age and occupation. The sign of occupation's coefficient remains the same.

Taking the different correlations and regressions together thus suggests that if you did well occupationally as a Somerville resident, you were more likely to stay there. If you did, your children were not likely to be very mobile.

D. Schooling in Brookline and Somerville

A comparison of Brookline and Somerville suggests some of the reasons for the limited mobility of the children of the latter town.[20] From the beginnings of the period of streetcar suburbanization, Somerville had very little in the way of school system resources. This in part reflected the condition of the two muncipalities even before suburbanization. Brookline was one of the oldest towns in Massachusetts. It had a functioning educational plant and an innovative tradition. By the mid-1800s, the town had supported the educational reforms of Horace Mann, who as a member of the first Massachusetts State Board of Education aided the growth of the school system. As the town grew, expansion of the schools was supported by strong public sentiment in favor of schooling, which was reflected in a policy of noninterference by town government in the decisions of the school committee.[21]

On the other hand, Somerville entered the suburban era with an inadequate educational plant. The town, then mainly rural, had separated itself from Charlestown in 1842 largely because its taxes were going to pay for services in the latter, while Somerville requests for more schools were not met. Several schools were built over the next four decades, but several fires also destroyed some of the buildings. By 1890, when horse-drawn street railways had led to the development of a heavily populated residential area in East Somerville, the high school had only ten teachers for 487 students, a 1:49 ratio. The ratio for the elementary schools was 1:60, and the school committee stated, "It is impossible to do satisfactory work or justice to these children."[22] Nonetheless, expansion of buildings and staff proceeded only slowly. The school committee, perceived as dominated by the middle class, was at odds with a broader-based board of aldermen, who continually rejected its requests to expand. Except for five years (1900–1905), Somerville gave the mayor and chairman of the aldermen seats on the school board.[23]

The different town attitudes toward schools were seen in the early 1900s in policies concerning vocational schools. In the 1890s, Brookline's high school curriculum included music, calisthenics, sewing, adult education, and manual training as integral to academic education. In 1902, with some class distinctions developing in the town, Brookline built a separate manual high school. This allowed tracking in the system. Between 1913 and 1916, for example, 160 students were refused admission to the high school and sent instead to the School of Practical Arts. But most students maintained academic goals. A 1917 educational survey of 823 elementary students showed that only 14 students did not expect to finish ninth grade, 127 expected to finish ninth grade but not go on to high school, 277 to finish high school but not go on to college, and 405 to go on to college.[24]

In Somerville, tracking was inhibited by the refusal, in 1912, of the City Council to fund even a two-year business course. A new high school, either as a vocational school or for the newly built up West Somerville area, was also refused, although the high school was operating at over one and a half times its planned student enrollment. By 1920, tracking within the school was expanding. In that year, 334 students were enrolled in the college course, 260 in the general course, 262 in the science course, 39 in the normal course, and the largest number, 772, in the commercial course. The academic had become the underemphasized program.[25]

The orientation of the entire Somerville school system away from college preparation, and the limited funding even of construction to relieve overcrowding, may have reflected the interests of a growing working-class population of the city. These residents could not in any event have afforded college for their children. In many cases, they used the resources they had for parochial school education. Somerville became increasingly important as a manufacturing center in the early part of the twentieth century, and its population became increasingly blue-collar. If the industrial base proved stable enough to buffer the town from some of the worst unemployment in the 1930s, nonetheless, no new schools could be afforded from 1935 to 1950. By that year, fourteen of twenty-four schools dated from the nineteenth century, and one had just been condemned as unsafe. Only five of the schools were considered adequate to be included in the town's plan for rebuilding the system.[26]

In Brookline, which had no industries locally, the Depression also temporarily reduced resources. But it also removed most of the town's non-middle-class population.

> Middle class people got rid of servants which they could no longer afford, and other blue-collar people, who had benefitted from prosperity and had moved into Brookline, also moved out because they could no longer afford it. The depression saved Brookline from loss of status.[27]

A rising number of professionals can be seen in street list samplings. Many of these people moved in when land became available at the end of the War, owing to the breakup of the estates area. Large acreage lots in these new developments insured a continual rise in land prices and an affluent population. However, as Brookline was too expensive for many young families and had a very high proportion of elderly, demands for school expansion could be focused on *better*, rather than just *more*, classrooms.

During the 1940s and 1950s, the Brookline schools continued to develop as an excellent college-oriented system which also provided major remedial programs for its slower students.[28] During the 1950s and early 1960s, the pendulum swung toward promoting the education of advanced and gifted students. Advanced Placements, an advanced fifth grade, early admissions according to test scores, and an emphasis on honors and awards suggest the schools were college and achievement oriented. At this point, the classes were tracked.

However, by the late 1960s and early 1970s, the school system had again expanded its interests. Tracking had been abandoned in favor of heterogeneous grouping, and an elective system established in the high school from which students can choose among 380 course offerings. The *1972 Evaluation by the New England Association of Colleges and Secondary Schools* stated that "Brookline has been on the forefront of educational innovations during the past ten years," and "The breadth and diversity of the curriculum was indeed impressive . . . [as was] a flexible multi-faceted program in occupational education." The report commended Brookline for blending the needs of both college-bound and vocationally oriented students, while providing much opportunity for the development of creativity, individual interests, and the ability to cope with responsibility and decision-making. However, Brookline was criticized for a "lack of overall coordination of curriculum . . . and lack of on-going evaluation of . . . curriculum," the need to view problems with long-range thought, interracial conflict, and noticeably few minority teachers.[29]

In Somerville, on the other hand, resources remained limited as the industrial base of the city, now faced with regional and suburban competition, began to shrink. The school budget had to be devoted largely to physical rebuilding. It was not until the 1960s that the system turned to curricular upgrading, for which federal assistance was available. Somerville began many federally funded programs, including BLAST, SMILE, STAR, SMART, and ADVENTURE. In addition, Somerville received Federal funding under the MDTA program, Public Law 874, Title III, Title L, Title II, Title VIB, the Federal Highway Safety Act, and the Occupational Education Act.

The school system itself lengthened the school day, added midyear and final examinations to its program, intensified its guidance and testing programs, offered civic education, and began a work-study program and a cooperative training program. By 1971, Somerville had a modified open campus and mini-courses, had completely revised the junior high school curriculum, and had added a machine transcription lab, a chef's food course, a journalism course, and health education to its high school curriculum.

Although this would give one the impression of a well-balanced school system, the New England Association of Colleges and Secondary Schools viewed the system more critically. They reported, in 1970, that Somerville's schools suffered from a restricted curricular and extracurricular program, that the students had little voice in school policy and a small degree of participation, that the guidance department lacked leadership, and that the system was characterized by fragmentation and heavy student loads. The school buildings were in deplorable condition, as were the library and audiovisual departments. Classes were still tracked.[30]

Altman, et al. conclude:

> Because of limited funding and the remnants of an archaic administration and faculty the schools are not providing the education which its students need. However, the improvements which have been made do seem to be oriented towards creativity nor high power intellectualism, but towards the acquiring of skills, pre-school development of basic skills, and practical Adult Education courses. . . .

> Thus we find that Somerville is, to a large degree, perpetuating its own kind. The improvements in the schools which have been mentioned might be expected of a blue-collar school system. There are little if any improvements in the direction of orienting students towards college entrance or towards entering high white-collar professions. Is Somerville holding back the potential which its students possess? Or is it serving a community which cannot afford to send its students to college, and thus wishes to provide them with blue-collar skills

which will eventually result in the perpetuation of the status quo?[31]

E. Statistical Comparisons: Education in the Postwar Period

The differences in schooling between Brookline and Somerville are typical of a wider set of differences that appear in statistical analyses of Massachusetts towns. These differences in schooling have been well documented. In part they parallel town incomes, but the correlation is not perfect. Among the more affluent older suburbs, for example, there are those like Belmont which have the reputation for underemphasizing public schooling, attracting families that wish to use private or parochial schools to their more affluent districts. These towns contrast sharply with Brookline, or with some of the newer education-oriented suburbs like Lexington.[32]

We have made several attempts to "explain" town schooling expenditures by other town characteristics. These typically gave a better "fit" for 1950 and 1960 data than for 1970. That is, they predicted expenditures more clearly, on the basis either of income or proportions of professionals or of high school educated in the adult population (for periods when schooling was still considered scarce and attractive) than for the period after the increase in federal aid for compensatory programs and after the postwar notion that education could solve all problems had begun to fade.[33]

One of our exploratory analyses also is interesting in that it gives partial evidence for a continuing tradeoff between schooling and homeownership. We tried regressions relating per-pupil school expenditures to a number of town characteristics. (See table 5.14.) If a large number of background characteristics are controlled for—including distance from Boston, town population and population and manufacturing density, the age of housing, town debt, and the proportions of high school educated, immigrant, black, over-65 and under-21 in the population—the proportion of homeowners appears negatively related to per-pupil school expenditures. The effect is significantly negative for 1950, and remains negative but becomes statistically insignificant for 1960. (Of the other variables, the proportion high school educated has the clearest positive effect in both years.) These are not strong findings, given problems of

Table 5.14
Regression Estimates of Town Per-Pupil School Expenditures

Independent Variable	regression 1940	coefficients 1950	(and t-value) . 1960
Constant	274.4	395.2	120.89
	(3.75)	(3.73)	(1.39)
NS Distance	−2.11	−0.72	−1.41
	(2.39)	(0.53)	(1.70)
EW Distance	−0.49	−1.18	−0.61
	(0.60)	(1.06)	(0.89)
Log. of Population	−15.6	−11.84	−3.73
	(−3.03)	(−1.67)	(.75)
Population Density	−.0012	−.0033	+.0013
	(1.02)	(1.59)	(−0.95)
Immigrant Population	−60.03	6.03	+1.96
	(1.43)	(.08)	(1.51)
Under 21 Proportion	−131.9	−28.0	−1.12
	(2.11)	(0.39)	(0.95)
Over 65 Proportion	62.13	−204.0	6.24
	(0.88)	(0.52)	(3.45)
Black Proportion	348.5	312.0	3.90
	(0.63)	(0.78)	(1.51)
Manufacturing Density	13.84	5.63	8.45
	(1.02)	(.33)	(1.08)
Proportion Owner Occupant	0.37	−2.32	−48.73
	(0.38)	(3.45)	(1.25)
Proportion Old Houses	−8.26	−37615.0	95123.0
	(0.21)	(0.90)	(2.14)
Proportion New Houses	17.17	−63.0	−125.3
	(0.17)	(0.40)	(2.26)
Manufacturing Density	13.84	5163.0	8.45
	(13.50)	(0.33)	(1.06)
Per Capita Debt	.013	.143	−.0063
	(0.12)	(1.64)	(1.29)
Proportion High School	—	2.53	1.11
Educated	—	(4.97)	(3.31)
R^2	.2915	.5104	.8366
F	1.99	4.095	21.2119
(df)	(13.63)	(14.55)	(14.58)

SOURCE: Mathew Edel, "Property Taxes and Local Expenditures: A Hundred Year View." *Massachusetts Public Finance Project*, Report #34 (Lynn, 1974).

multicollinearity among the explanatory variables. But they do suggest that the effect first noted by Thernstrom for Newburyport may have some contemporary relevance.

Per-pupil expenditures are not, however, the best measure of the quality and effectiveness of schooling. The same cost per pupil may be generated by greater expenditure on enrichment programs, by more costly school security forces and truant officers, by buildings that are more costly to heat, or by higher administrative costs. An alternative approach focuses on an output measure—students' eventual success—rather than on schooling inputs. Of course, this approach also is subject to certain ambiguities. Success, as Jencks has pointed out, may be correlated with parents' economic level, with schooling variables reflecting the latter and not adding much, statistically, to the eventual outcomes.[34] Nonetheless, such an approach is worth exploring if one is trying to link parental residence to children's mobility.

One interesting attempt to test our hypothesis that parental residence in certain inner ring or other towns might "entrap" the next generation was made by Rosina Becerra.[35] Her study related the types of colleges attended by residents of different towns to characteristics of the towns and their schools. Her findings clearly establish that where one lives in Massachusetts greatly affects one's chances for attending a prestigious college.

Becerra argues that these levels are important:

In our class-conscious society, we attribute to people particular characteristics based on perceived social status. For example, most people would perceive a student attending Harvard to be very intelligent, from a professional family which is financially comfortable—variables commonly associated with the upper class. Conversely, people might perceive a student attending Salem State College to be of average intelligence, from a median income working-class family of high-school graduates—variables commonly associated with the middle class. The mere designation of a particular college places one in a different perceived status which may enhance or obstruct one's ability to gain access to other resources or, more simply, to "open doors." Thus, the power and influence of social class perceived in a student can depend greatly on the particular college attended.

Also, educational quality is assumed to be better at one college than another; occupational opportunity available to a Harvard student is not necessarily available to a Salem State College student. Furthermore, some colleges provide better job possibilities for their students by attracting recruiters from large firms who actively seek out their graduates. Even if one postpones employment and seeks to continue his higher education, graduate schools also tend to choose their students from well-known colleges. Therefore, the undergraduate college attended does have built-in consequences for later opportunities.

Another consequence of the choice of college is the mix of students one encounters. Prestigious colleges tend to attract students from socially prominent, professional and affluent families who have social contacts in business. To attend a college with students who come from these backgrounds allows a person to meet people from whom he may gain access to the business world. It further allows him to learn the speech, dress, and life styles of other classes. Without contact with people who have access to a wide range of choices, a person finds his occupational entry ability severely limited. If he attends a college where everyone is from the same social stratum, then undoubtedly few persons will have social contacts significantly different from his own.[36]

Becerra classified Massachusetts colleges into a number of groups (Table 5.15) based on characteristics such as faculty salaries, endowments, general expenditures, enrollment, and quality measures, including library holdings, SAT math and verbal scores, student–faculty ratios, and percent of faculty holding PhDs. A factor analysis was combined with a program to group the colleges based on their scores on the different factors. The results were roughly parallel to schools' general reputations. For example, public community colleges were grouped at the opposite extreme on the scores from a group including only Harvard and MIT.[37]

For 68 collegiate institutions (of 80 in the state), Becerra also had data on the town of residence of full-time students. She also had data, from the census and state sources, on the characteristics of the 257 towns and cities in Massachusetts with populations of 2500 or more in 1970. Thus, she could analyze the relationship of town characteristics to the number of students from each town attending each of the groups of colleges.[38]

Table 5.15
Grouping of Colleges

Group 1		Group 2
(Community Colleges)	A. (Low Expend, Private)	B. (State Colleges)
Berkshire	American International	Framingham
Bristol	Assumption	Westfield
Cape Cod	Atlantic Union	
Greenfield	College of Our Lady of	C. (Low Expend, 2-yr.)
Holyoke	the Elms	
Massasoit	Emmanuel	Bay Path
Mass. Bay	Hebrew College	Bradford
Middlesex	Lesley College	Dean
Mt. Wachussett	Merrimack	Endicott
North Essex	Newton College of the	Mt. Ida
North Shore	Sacred Heart	Pine Manor
Quinsagamond	Nichols College	Wentworth
Springfield	Suffolk	
	Weaton	
	Wheelock	

Group 3	Group 4	Group 5
A. (State Colleges)	A. (U-Mass.)	A. (High Expend, 2-yr.)
Boston State	U-Mass. Amherst	Garland
Bridgewater		Lasell
Lowell Institute	B. (BU-NE)	Leicester
North Adams		
Salem State	Boston University	B. (High Expend, 4-yr.)
Southeastern Mass. U.	Northeastern	
U-Mass. Boston		Anna Maria
Worcester State		Eastern Nazarene
		Regis
B. (Business Schools)		Stonehill
Babson		
Bentley		

Group 6	Group 7	Group 8
(Elite Liberal Arts)	(Private Universities)	(Harvard-MIT)
Amherst	Boston College	Harvard
Brandeis	Clark University	MIT
Mt. Holyoke	Holy Cross	
Smith	Tufts University	
Wellesley	Worcester Polytech	
Williams		

SOURCE: Rosina Becerra, *Does Equal Opportunity Mean Equal Access?* (Brandeis University Ph.D dissertation, 1975).

Her regression analyses for the state as a whole are presented in table 5.16.

Not surprisingly, they show that community college attendance was higher for towns of lower incomes. For all other colleges, higher town incomes were reflected in *more* students going to colleges, but the positive effect of income was most significant for elite private institutions.

The proportion of foreign born and nonwhite population affected some, but not all, groups of colleges. So did median education, the proportion of high school educated in the young adult population. Towns with higher per-pupil expenditure were more likely to send students to some of the highest prestige categories, controlling for income. But they proved to have little effect (once income was controlled for) on attendance at most of the groups of colleges.

Becerra also analyzed access separately for five regional groupings of towns. This was done because the distance to different types of colleges was different for students from different areas, and because she hypothesized that some of the tracking mechanisms might be different in metropolitan and rural areas. Her findings, for Metropolitan Boston, are summarized in Table 5.17.

The "Boston metro" area used here encompassed only the inner portions of the SMSA. Becerra finds that students tended to come from higher-income areas.

> A resident of the Metro-Boston area is the most likely to remain in his own region. He will probably attend one of the private four-year colleges in the region: most likely BU, NE, BC, or Tufts. This resident has probably come from a family whose home is in one of the suburban towns around the city of Boston. This resident's family income is probably higher than average; the median educational level of the town is high, the number of high-school graduates in the youth population is high, and the proportion of private secondary-school attendants is high. This cluster of variables tends to characterize the majority of college students who reside in the Metro-Boston region.[39]

Although high income is a predictor of attendance at the private colleges, it is not as strong for the Boston area as it is elsewhere in the state. This is so because public colleges, which might elsewhere take up the lower income college attendees, are scarce in the Boston region. As

Table 5.16
College Attendance: Regression Results for Massachusetts
(N = 257)

College Group	Regression Constant	Income	Expend. Stdnt.	Median Educ.	HS Grads	Stnt/ Tchr.	Pub/ Pvt.	Prop. in School	Foreign Born	Prop. Nonwhite	R^2
1 Comm. College	.042	−.0143††	—	—	.324	—	—	—	−.0489†	−.2079††	.096
2a Low Expend. (4 yr.)	−.009	.0148	—	—	.0194†		0	—	—	—	.238
2b Low Expend. (State)	.004	.0035	—	—	—		—	—	—	−.0684	.240
2c Low Expend (2 yr.)	−.006	.0086††	.0002	—	.0103†		—	—	—	—	.192
3a State Colls.	.154	.0275††	—	−.0135††	.0587††		—	—	−.0176	—	.141
3b Business Schls.	−.008	.0071††	—	—	.0104††		—	−.0020†	.0101††	.0118	.444
3a U Mass	−.024	.0086	.0013	.0050†	—				−.0382	.1926††	.068
4b BU−NE	−.036	.0242††	—		.0581						.191
5a High Expend. (2 yr.)	−.004	.0024††	.0002			.000					.195
5b High Expend. (4 yr.)	.002	.0053††		−.0005	.0069†						.115
											.464
5 Elite	−.011	.0078††	.0004		.0066†	000					.001
7 Private Univ.	−.007	.028††		−.0015	.0231†				.0069		.333
8 Harvard-MIT	−.014	.0099††	.0005								.389

† Significant at .05 level.
†† Significant at .01 level.
SOURCE: See Table 5.15.

Table 5.17
College Attendance: Regression Results for Metro Boston

	College Group					
Community Colleges	Private LE 4-Yr.	State College	Private LE 2-Yr.	State College	Business Colleges	U-Mass Amherst
− foreign †††	+ HS grads †††	+ HS grads †††	+ HS grads †††	− income ††	+ HS grads †††	+ HS grads †††
− income ††	− stud/teach	− pub/priv †	+ income ††	− foreign	+ foreign ††	+ pub/priv †††
+ pub/priv †	+ pub/priv †	(65.9)	+ nonwhite †	− tax rate	+ income ††	+ income †
(51.5)	(44.9)		(63.8)	(25.6)	+ pub/priv	(82.2)
					(72.2)	

	College Group				
BU-NE	Private HE 2-Yr.	Private HE 4-Yr.	Elite	University Priv. 4-Yr.	Harvard-MIT
+ income †	+ income †††	+ income ††	+ income †††	+ HS grads †††	+ income ††
+ HS grads	+ HS grads †††	− foreign †	+ HS grads †††	+ income †††	+ HS grads
pub/priv	+ foreign †††	− pub/priv	− pub/priv †††	+ foreign ††	− pub/priv
(31.6)	+ nonwhite ††	− HS grads	+ foreign †††	− pub/priv †	(39.0)
	(87.6)	(54.5)	+ nonwhite ††	+ nonwhite	
			(86.2)	(71.8)	

a result, "the Metro-Boston area exhibits a curious reversal: the less affluent are having to travel greater distances for a less expensive education than the more affluent who remain in the area and pay high tuitions at private colleges."[40] As a result, some go to private institutions despite their higher cost, but others do not go to college at all.

All in all, Becerra concludes,

> Town of residency is a major determinant of the college one will be most likely to attend because associated with residency is socioeconomic status, instrumental in determining the probability of access to any particular college. This appears most clearly in western and southeastern Massachusetts, both low-income areas whose residents predominantly attend low-tuition public institutions. On the other hand, private college attendance is greatest in the northeastern and metro-Boston regions where incomes are significantly higher than the rest of the Commonwealth.
>
> Therefore, a person's socioeconomic status greatly determines his probability of access. The probability of attending high-resource colleges is greater among students who reside in high-resource towns. For example, two students who have the same high school grades and the same SAT scores but are from different towns have different probabilities of access to elite colleges (Amherst, Brandeis, Mt. Holyoke, Smith, Wellesley, Williams). In real terms, a Chelsea resident has 12.8 percent probability of attending an elite college while a Weston resident has 33.5 percent probability of attending an elite college. Thus, all things being equal, the Weston resident has almost three times the access that a Chelsea resident has, based only on town of residency.[41]

F. Conclusion

The evidence in the Becerra and Levenstein studies suggests that residence in low-income towns was associated with limited educational and spatial mobility of Boston area residents in the postwar period. True, no test as direct as that presented for the first wave of suburbanization is possible. Nonetheless, the suggestion is strong that entrapment, rather than mobility, has continued to characterize the experience of Boston's inner-ring suburbanites. Together with the previous chapters' findings with respect to the spatial pattern of property value appreciation, the present chapter suggests that we should question whether worker home-ownership has led to accelerated mobility into other forms of wealth, better education, or better careers.

PART TWO

Lawns for Pawns?
The Homeowner as Worker

Introduction

WE have shown that housing, the major asset of workers, did not appreciate as rapidly as the assets held by major capitalist institutions during the century from 1870 to 1970. Housing, though it was a valuable consumer good, was not "capital": a ticket to income from wealthholding, an escape from the need to hold a job. The working homeowner did not gain additional mobility either in terms of jobs or social power from homeownership. In Boston, a slowly growing metropolitan area, many workers ended up just about where they started on a scale of relative wealth and power. There is evidence some workers sacrificed other aspects of mobility for homeownership. For most families, homeownership neither added to nor subtracted from possibilities for advancement.

Now we shall consider why homeownership has not proved a more advantageous asset. Was the suburbanization process simply a reflection of workers' desires for a piece of land, or a voluntary trading off of mobility for security? Was it the work primarily of real estate developers, intent only on selling off properties? Were working-class suburbs built, and then devalued, as a result of government policies? And if so, what role did workers and capitalists have in the formation of those policies?

This section considers some of those questions. In particular, we wish to question two interpretations, each of which is as erroneous as the view that suburbanization has meant affluence for all. The first is a view that suburbanization, as it occurred in the United States, was an inevitable or natural process, and hence a best possible outcome, even if it fell short of its advertised perfection. The other is the view that homeownership and suburbanization were a mistake, or a trap for workers, as individuals and as a class.

We discuss these two views in chapter 6. Chapters 7 and 8 scrutinize the roles of the government and of developers. Finally, we turn to an alternative perspective, which sees suburban homeownership as a sort of compromise, resulting from an impasse in the economy and in labor–capital confrontation. Suburbanization has always been an uneasy compromise, worked out in a particular historical situation which, if it was able to survive for a century, is today increasingly under strain. Our final chapter considers just how far its bases may be falling apart.

SIX

Blaming the Victim for
Homeowner Discontent

THE problems of homeownership are underplayed by most celebra-
tions of American society, but they have not been unnoticed completely. This chapter discusses both orthodox and radical critiques of
suburbanization and homeownership. We discuss an orthodox or liberal
view that suburbs developed problems because workers overreached their
means in buying homes, and a radical view that workers were manipulated into homeownership simply for purposes of social control. We argue that both of these views are too simplistic for historical explanation.
Perhaps a worse sin is that they end up throwing the blame for the discontents of suburban homeownership directly on the homebuying worker.
By seeing the worker either as overambitious or as a naïve dupe, they
blame the victims for their problems.[1]

A. The Homeownership Debate

In 1912, the National Housing Association sponsored a symposium on
whether workers should be encouraged to own homes.[2] The issue was
not new. The first streetcar suburbs had appeared half a century earlier.
The electric trolley had been in use for over two decades. The automobile was already a working vehicle, although not yet priced for a mass
market. Each of these innovations had allowed some relatively advantaged workers to move to their own homes in new suburbs and had provoked controversy over whether or not this was a good thing.

The 1912 panel was an unusual airing of different viewpoints. Although most speakers favored the trend of spreading ownership, two objections to a national policy of encouraging homebuying arose. One was that homeownership was economically inefficient; the other, that it might be politically harmful to workers.

The economic case against extending homeownership was a simple one. Given their wages and other expenses, the argument went, workers might not have the funds to maintain their homes adequately. They would lose their homes through foreclosure, or allow them to decay into slums. In either case, the result would be the waste of the initial investment both by the worker and by society.

Most speakers countered this objection with suggestions for still-cheaper housing, and with accounts of individual workers who owned homes and who maintained them well. Implicitly at least, this argument casts blame on those workers who could not manage this feat on their low salaries. This was pointed out by the one speaker who identified himself as "a member of a labor union for nearly twenty-five years." Henry Sterling declared:

> Some members of this conference . . . are striving to bring the home down in cost, down to where the ten dollar-a-week man can afford it. They have not yet succeeded in bringing that about. There is another great body of citizens, 3,000,000 strong, who insist in this country that the right way is to bring wages up to where the man can afford to have a decent home.[3]

Sterling's response was both a proposal for action, through wage demands, and a refusal to accept that low wages and resulting bad housing were individual faults. Yet Sterling did not address a possible flaw in the homeownership program he advocated, As another speaker suggested, home ownership might undercut wage goals:

> A workingman owning his home, which is purchased after many years of saving, puts himself to some extent in the hands of such employers as are most convenient for him to get to for employment. In some cases that may not be good for him.[4]

Further, a worker

> must remember that if he buys his home and gets it half paid for, it is likely, as in the case of a strike, pressure may be brought to bear which will prevent him from getting a raise in wages or betterment of conditions.[5]

No one at the symposium disputed this objection. Indeed, it was pointed out that no less important an employer than the Pennsylvania Railroad was not afraid of strikes because its employees "live in Philadelphia and own their homes, and therefore, cannot afford to strike."[6] Most speakers, representing Chambers of Commerce and other elite organizations, felt that an incentive not to strike was a good thing, that homeownership led to "social responsibility," "good citizenship," "stability and responsibility," and "economy and thrift." For most participants it was no drawback to homeownership that it might be a means of social control.

These objections have been argued again and again, from Frederick Engels' disputes with Emil Sax and A. Mulberger in the early 1870s, through debates over homeownership vs. public housing between the World Wars, to poverty program discussions in the late 1960s and more recent discussions of effects of inflation. Essentially, homeownership, and particularly suburban homeownership, is defended as an economical way to provide the housing that people need, and as a means to bring the less advantaged "into the system" on better terms. Its critics claim that individual ownership—involving suburban location, nonprofessional maintenance, cheap construction, and often costly transportation and utility services—is economically unjustified. What is more, they say, homeownership locks workers into a system at a permanent disadvantage, divides them from each other, and weakens both their individual job mobility and their ability to strike.[7]

Engels suggested in 1872 that homeownership programs threatened "to stifle all revolutionary spirit in the workers by selling them small dwellings to be paid for in annual installments," which would have the effect of "chaining the workers by this property to the factory in which they work."[8] And Herbert Marcuse, nearly a century later, suggested that these monetary chains could be tightened by psychological dependence on the home, as workers came to define themselves through the commodities they bought:

> They find their soul in their automobile, hi-fi set, split level home, kitchen equipment. The very mechanism which ties the individual to his society has changed, and social control is anchored in the needs which it has produced.[9]

Homeownership, in the view of its critics, then, simply amounts to providing lawns for the pawns, tying people down with properties that, in the end, are not even that economically sound.[10]

Our analysis of homeownership in a sense fits in with the critics' position that it is detrimental to the worker, both economically and politically. The pattern of homeownership that has emerged over the course of American suburbanization has yielded at best very limited capital gains to most residents. Homes have been depreciating assets, sometimes absolutely and almost always relative to business and financial investments. People keep working, and they practice the "thrift and economy" and the compliant "social responsibility" preached at the 1912 conference in order to achieve the limited mobility that is open to them. But then they find themselves back where they started in terms of relative (and perhaps absolute) wealth and status. Meanwhile, options of collective action to change society may be left unexplored.

In other ways, however, it is dangerous to swallow whole the theory that homeownership has been simply a gross economic mistake or, worse, the manipulation of the worker by the elite. From the viewpoint of the individual, the purchase of a home is still frequently a better alternative than renting from a private landlord or a city housing authority.[11] Similarly, the working class was not simply manipulated by a Machiavellian elite to sell its birthright for a mess of cottages. Its options—as a class—have been limited. While many of Engels' arguments do hold up in our analysis, they are not the whole truth.

It is true that housing reform often was designed to keep workers controlled and contented at low cost and to buy off their more radical aspirations. Business leaders and a generally pro-business government guided the transportation and the financial systems that shaped the development of working-class suburbs, and business did benefit from this process, both in terms of current profits and of long-term stability. But a picture of "lawns for the pawns" is inaccurate simply because workers have not been mere pawns. At times their actions provoked the limited changes that business and government did grant. And the winning of lawns did not leave the workers as docile as the social-control view would have it. Offering workers homes to buy off discontent won time for capitalism, but it also created new problems that are becoming the basis for further conflict. To deny the active role that the working class sometimes played, and the validity of some of their gains, is also to blame the victim.

We stress these dangers of blaming the victim because we too have fallen prey to them. We sang along with Malvina Reynolds' teasing song about "Little Boxes," "all made out of ticky-tacky and they all look just the same," enjoying the architectural critique. Only later did we realize the inaccuracy of depicting those in the houses as "doctors and lawyers and business executives" whose "children go to summer camps and then to the university" to be processed into more ticky-tacky.[12] The rows of houses south of San Francisco that inspired the song are not the homes of professionals and executives but of clerks, public employees and union laborers whose children are more apt to end up in junior colleges than in the university. Tracked schools and tract homes are not the environment of the executives against whom we thought we were rebelling in the 1960s.

We sometimes share the feelings of Paul Cowan, who, despite having written some of the most sympathetic analyses of working-class homeowner discontent, could angrily describe his fellow Peace Corps volunteers as insensitive because they came

> from the much larger middle class to whom democracy and freedom mean the sacred right to buy a second car or build a new home: for whom America is the sterile paradise, and Richard Nixon its perfect leader.[13]

Cowan's later realization that this criticism could reinforce a radical intellectual's "comfortable disdain for the citizens of Nixonia"—and thus mask the intellectual's own prejudice—is a worthwhile warning to any social analyst. We had to be reminded of this on occasion.[14]

Similarly in our intellectual training we had been exposed first to a series of liberal positions that traced the rise of both urban reforms and urban problems to "American values" or "consumers' choice," and then to a revisionist historiography and a radical economics that offered a "social-control interpretation" of government economic and social policies. This book and the research that led to it were conceived at a time when we had broken with the "liberal" view: yet many of the historical studies on which we relied came out of the liberal tradition. While attempting to read critically the works of Oscar Handlin, Sam Bass Warner and Lloyd Rodwin on the development of Boston, we undoubtedly were influenced by their views as well as their data.[15] The social-control view was more important in our thinking. The work of Frances Fox Piven and Richard Cloward on welfare, of Samuel Bowles and Herbert Gintis on education, of Herbert Marcuse and of many others who interpret economic and political institutions as fulfilling a capitalist need to control labor provided fruitful parallels for what we were discovering about housing.[16] But we cannot accept a one-sided social-control hypothesis either.

When we stress the role of depreciating assets, particularly suburban homes, in maintaining the work incentives and inequality that benefit capitalism, our point is that social institutions constrain the options of workers. Many workers do accept views or act in ways that stabilize the system. But we do not mean that all institutions are deliberately designed by the capitalist class to manipulate workers and thus to ensure perfect docility. The elite may, of course, consciously seek control. But institutions are shaped by historical forces, the episodes of a continuing class struggle. Compromises buy some control for the rulers, but only at the cost of concessions to the ruled. Nor do institutions necessarily work to stifle all of the aspirations of the workers or the poor. Their interests and aspirations also affect the form institutions take, whatever the elites may have planned.

From the elite viewpoint, an attempt at social control has worked only in part. Housing costs have risen to impede the orderly collection and reinvestment of profits, and rebellion, though scattered and disorganized, has not been quashed. Of course, many options are closed to working people, and many potential areas of rebellion are defused by the way housing is provided. But to ignore either the limits to individual options, or the limits to social control, is to accept too narrow a view of reality.

B. The Orthodox View

The conventional wisdom is that working-class homeownership in the United States represents a triumph of American society. The U.S. government, the media, and most mainstream social scientists point out that a majority of Americans own their own homes. The housing shortages of the Soviet Union, Japan, and Western Europe are cited to argue that not only "Communism" but even competing brands of "welfare state" capitalism are inferior to the American system. The ability of American workers to buy homes symbolizes their ability to get ahead in society. For example, an article in a suburban California newspaper states,

> More American families enjoy "pride of ownership" in their own homes today than ever before. Proportionately, they own

more homes—and larger, more luxurious homes—than is the
case in any other country in the world. . . . To really appreciate our fortunate position as owners of our own castles, we
need only consider the situation in other countries.[17]

Many Americans agree. Automobile workers in Chinoy's interviews saw
the possibility of homeownership as an important opportunity open to
them.[18]

The ability to buy a house (although not a new one) is still open to the
majority of Americans, although the recent inflation has begun to limit
this option. But the question of how these homes benefit workers is more
complex. Homeowners, for instance, gripe about costs of upkeep, taxes,
and lack of space. Complaints of being "chained to a mortgage" abound.

Even scholars who admit that problems exist generally do not challenge the notion that, in general, American society "works" well. Instead of tracing relationships between the structure of American capitalism and the specific housing problems people face, most social scientists
have either attributed the problems directly to the homeowners or tenants, or have indirectly suggested "we are all to blame," by accepting as
the cause a general social ethos of "urbanism" or "privatism."

The direct casting of blame crops up most blatantly in studies of housing conditions of the poor. The "rediscovery" of poverty by the non-poor
in the 1960s led, after the first disclosures of slum conditions, to attempts to explain why slums existed. Academics, the press, and common citizens alike emphasized that cultural disabilities kept tenants from
maintaining well-ordered apartments. The notion that the poor deserved
to live in slums because they would turn any housing they inhabited into
slums was bandied about after a few major housing projects failed. Then
came more sophisticated arguments about "class culture" or the failure
of minority families to avoid a "tangle of pathology." At best, these arguments are the misapplications of anthropological theory or overesti-
mates of the alternatives the poor have to slums under the prevailing
conditions of segregation and underemployment. At worst, they are the
special pleading of slumlords or the means to vent racist feelings. But,
whatever the intentions, these arguments blame slum dwellers for the
conditions in which they live.[19]

A related set of arguments holds that the poor, or at least those be-
longing to ethnic minorities, choose to live in slums. This is wrapped in
the cloak of the philosophy or economics of choice in a free market: slum

dwellers opt for center-city life, with its crowding and lack of sanitation, over rural or peripheral locations where land is cheaper, where conditions are less crowded but not necessarily more sanitary, and where job opportunities or social contacts are harder to come by. Or black and other ethnic groups may just choose to live among their peers. This intellectual process performs a sort of vanishing act on the problems: everyone is assumed to be choosing whatever fate the social scientist has observed. If the language of this approach is more neutral than that of the "tangle of pathology" school, its placing of blame on the victim is, if anything, greater. The life the victim is said to have chosen is not even dignified by a recognition of the hardship endured.

Other positions acknowledge that a problem exists, but ascribe it to natural forces that arise either through the workings of an unquestioned economic system or an unquestioned law of city formation. Thus economists theorize that poverty is due to a lack of "human capital" or poor housing to a lack of incentives to invest in upgrading, or they simply spin out mathematical representations of a market in which those with less wealth get fewer goods. These theories are, in an important sense, completely circular, and explain only the surface workings of a system. The basic ground rules are not questioned.[20] Similarly, the "ecological" sociologists who define the causes of slum formation by using concepts such as succession of land uses, or zones of transition, equate phenomena they observe in cities with the laws of natural ecology. They ignore a basic difference between the systems studied by natural ecology and the systems studied by social science. Only the latter systems

> reflect directly the consequences of deliberate human decisions—both in the determination of actions within the systems and in the choice of the basic institutions of the systems themselves.[21]

Attributing inadequate housing for the poor merely to the workings of "the housing market" of "the urban environment" is, in a sense, to set up as omnipotent deity what is in fact a human artifact. Karl Marx equated such fatalism about the economy as a whole to the "fetishism" of those who would submit themselves to graven images that they themselves had made.[22] To blame the inevitable workings of urban society for problems is to commit the same sacrilege to the possibility of human freedom.

Social critics have pointed all of this out in considering the lot of the

Making the best of adversity. A tripledecker at the corner of Blue Hill Avenue and Seaver Street in Roxbury is adapted as a liquor store. Such adaptive reuse is at times seen as the cause rather than the effect of the decay; "blaming the victim."

Photo by Elliott Sclar.

poor in the housing market or the experiences of working people on the job. But we have have found a similar tendency to blame either the victims or a common ethos for the problems of the homeowning worker. When we turn our attention from the ghetto to the surrounding neighborhoods of moderate or middle-income homeowners, we find a variety of problems besetting them: deteriorating structures, high maintenance costs, mounting taxes, blinding mortgage debt, inadequate transportation and public services, and fears of further deterioration or loss of homes. Homeowners are angry. The social scientists tell them that they are getting what they paid for, that they wanted what they got, or that, perhaps, they are being overambitious in their desires and irresponsible in their fears.

This is the framework in which Sam Bass Warner Jr., and Lloyd Rodwin studied the process of low-income suburban development around Boston in the late nineteenth and early twentieth centuries.[23] In a similar vein, John Kain, an economist, examined relations between housing demand and other economic factors in neighborhoods of the Boston area, looking only at current densities and prices, and not at historical data. All three scholars seem to argue that the residents who today complain of problems got what they wanted.

For Kain, the demand for housing is simply a matter of income. As affluence increases, families want to have more space and to drive more. Thus they move further into the suburbs. The intermediate position of older, more dense communities fits the needs of their less-affluent residents. Occupied older housing, like new tract homes or high-income dwellings, is simply a response to demand by a well-functioning private market.[24]

In much the same way, Warner finds that houses were built in the past by "a partnership between large institutions and individual investors" who created "a weave of small patterns," an unplanned, market response to individual needs.[25] Rodwin is less certain that it is just a matter of consumer desires and incomes. He feels that the housebuilding industry's lack of response to needs may have created problems:

> Rising income and rising standards of demand, coupled with inadequate adjustments on housing supply in response to such rises in income and standards, are the sources of most of our vexatious problems of housing and neighborhood development.[26]

But his primary focus is on suburbanization as a response to individual demand.

The type of residence the "market" provided in Boston, and continues to resell in these neighborhoods, is the "tripledecker," a three-story wooden frame house originally built for occupancy by three families including that of the owner's. Warner, who first celebrated the uncoordinated building of houses by many small investors, describes these buildings and their builders as the cause of later problems. "Not only was the pattern of lower middle class building destructive of nature, it was destructive of itself," he writes in his historical account of the development process.[27] In an essay prepared for Boston's anti-poverty agency, he calls the deterioration of the tripledecker neighborhoods

> an integral part of their creation. Though the story varied from place to place, the habit of discarding was an old tradition in American society and its works could be seen everywhere. The farmer burned the forest, planted his wheat until the soil turned sand, and then moved on. Almost all the houses . . . have been discarded both by the descendents of their builders and the class that built them. . . .
>
> When these cheap buildings were built, men of the day regarded such construction below their standards too, but they accepted it as the best compromise of the moment. Such houses were thought to be better than the city tenement, but not what middle class builders and buyers would have wanted . . . What was built was so tied to the compromise of the moment that any rise in the standards of housing made these standards undesirable.[28]

Rodwin, while arguing that the prevention of further tripledecker construction by zoning after World War I made housing conditions worse by reducing construction of dwellings, presents a similar analysis of the houses themselves.

> All sorts of objections, relevant and irrelevant, were leveled against the three-deckers. . . . the three-deckers were clearly a fire hazard, dangerous to both occupants and surrounding properties. . . . Three-deckers were also costly to the individual and society. As a long-run investment, they were presumably more expensive for the owner, if not the builder. Higher insurance, maintenance, and especially depreciation charges were supposed to wipe out any apparent advantages from lower initial costs or tax payments. Their impact on surrounding property values was notorious. . . . Moreover, few slum types, including even the cheaper varieties, flaunted their sheer ugliness more brazenly.[29]

And Kain presents a similar, if not as graphic, conclusion by arguing that high-density, multiple-unit construction raises public service costs.[30]

These arguments seem to blame the original middle-income residents of the working-class suburbs, and the later buyers of their houses, for not building or maintaining homes better than they could afford. But a further argument places even more blame on the low-income homeowners for their eventual dissatisfactions. The possibility is raised that the workers who streamed into the three-decker neighborhoods, when they were "zones of emergence" for various immigrant groups, set their aspirations too high and therefore lost out economically. Homer Hoyt suggests that immigrants were so eager to escape from the status of tenement renter that they bought inferior houses that rapidly declined in value:

> The foreign-born in general were more eager than native Americans to attain the prestige of land-ownership, which was frequently impossible for them in Europe. Prior to the shutting-off of the main current of immigration, there was a steady business in the older sections of the city in selling the poorer grade of houses to the newest immigrants.[31]

Stephan Thernstrom, in his study of Newburyport, Massachusetts, goes even further, arguing that property acquisition was more highly valued than education. Families sacrificed mobility for security by putting their children to work at an early age in order to accumulate money for houses, and in so doing they restricted their children's opportunities. Their sons advanced less in occupational terms than the children of non-homeowners.[32]

Proponents of neoclassical economics, which recognizes the possibility of different returns to different forms of investment if the risk varies inversely, argue for a similar conclusion. Faced with evidence that the working-class or low-income homeowner earned less, proportionately, from the investment in homeownership than other landholders or financial investors, this theory automatically argues that the low-income investors were evading risk. A "peasant conservatism" or a short-sighted familism, attributed to immigrants by their sociological detractors, is implicitly assigned to them by this theory as well.[33] The circle is closed: working homeowners have trouble with housing because of their low incomes, but they have low incomes because of their housing. In both cases, their desires are somehow at the root of the troubles.

If the homeowner is not at fault, then the problem may be laid at the feet of a general urban ethos. Robert Park, the founder of ecological sociology, saw the city as reflecting the "moral order" of society; Warner

attributes the problem to an "American tradition of privatism."[34] One
version of this view sees problems arising from inevitable (but still generally beneficial) progress, which in itself is the desire of all citizens. Louis
Wirth speaks of the fragmentation of the experience and the weakening
of the family as consequences of city size. He attributes other problems
to the same root:

> On the whole, the city discourages an economic life in which
> the individual in time of crisis has a basis of subsistence to
> fall back upon, and it discourages self-employment. While in-
> comes of city people are on the average higher than those of
> country people, the cost of living seems to be higher in the
> larger cities.
>
> Homeownership involves greater burdens and is rarer. Rents
> are higher and absorb a large proportion of the income. Al-
> though the urban-dweller has the benefit of many communal
> services, he spends a large proportion of his income for such
> items as recreation and advancement and a smaller propor-
> tion for food. What the communal services do not furnish the
> urbanite must purchase, and there is virtually no human need
> which has remained unexploited by commercialism.[35]

Since these theorists see city growth implicitly as progress, they consider the problems to be just a side effect of an otherwise desirable phenomenon.

Implied in the view that city growth signals progress, but inevitably
brings problems as well, is an argument about increased social mobility:
the city provides more chances than some presumed "nonurban" society
for people to get ahead. These chances are bought not only at the cost
of a direct psychological suffering that affects people who have no fixed
place in the world. The urban society, in this view, also presents people
with a "double bind" situation in which dissatisfaction is inevitable. If
one gets ahead in wealth and occupation, any problems that arise are
simply a byproduct of advancement. On the other hand, if one does not
succeed and has problems, then the lack of advancement, which is seen
as an individual fault, must be the cause of the problems.

Thus, Richard Sennett attempts to blame the city (in this case, Chicago) for the frustrations and for the anger against immigrants felt by
residents of the homeowning neighborhood of Union Park in the late
nineteenth century:

the idea of seizing opportunities, the idea of instability of job tenure for the sake of rising higher and higher, constituted the commonly agreed-upon notion of how sure success could be achieved at this time among respectable people; in the same way, this chance-taking path was presented, in the Horatio Alger novels and the like, as the road into the middle class itself. One should have been mobile in work, then, for this was the meaning of "opportunity" and "free enterprise," but in fact the overwhelming dissolutions of the giant cities seem to have urged many men to retreat into the circle of their own families, to try simply to hold onto what they knew they could perform as tasks to support themselves, in the midst of the upheaval of urban expansion.[36]

As a result, Sennett speculates, they "invested" their emotional energy into the home and kept the family secluded. And their children did not have the gumption to go after further mobility the society promised to the daring. They turned instead (in frustration at their drop in status relative to their parents) to a panicked attack on immigrants moving into the area whom they perceived as intruders if not dangerous rivals.

These arguments can help illuminate some of the immediate causes of discontent. Lack of resources, fear of dangers in the city, difficult choices between risk-taking and family life, or between education and the purchase of property, all forced compromises on working families. These compromises left them with depreciating houses in deteriorating neighborhoods, or with jobs that fell short of their aspirations. And the conditions that placed these restrictions on them were in fact related to the growth of cities as economic and social systems.

Yet there is also something incomplete about the arguments. They assume that there were tremendous opportunities for advancement in the cities and that the problems somehow stemmed from these opportunities, either because individuals did not take adequate advantage of them, or because they tried to take too much advantage of them. The structure of opportunities themselves is never really scrutinized.

Another interpretation, however, is that neither the problems confronting working homeowners nor the very limited set of opportunities available to them may have stemmed from their personal choices. Instead, the problems may be byproducts of a social and economic system that distributed its rewards principally to a small class of major investors and, as a consequence, offered only limited opportunities and repeated frustrations to the many. Further, the system, at times out of inertia but at times because it was manipulated by the few, may have offered opportunities in a form that pushed the many into channels that benefited the few.

C. The Social-Control View

In recent years, a number of studies in such areas as welfare reform, criminology, and education have presented a view of history that stresses social control by a ruling class instead of individual attainment or social consensus. William Muraskin has summarized this position as follows:

> Since social-control historians see conflict as basic and believe history shows that groups are not equal in their resources and power, they postulate the existence of ruling and subordinate groups. In this unequal environment, those with power, status and wealth will fight to use their assets to maintain themselves. They will try to control their subordinates by manipulation or brute force. The social-control historians have been especially interested in the past use of nonviolent means for controlling the population—especially the use of apparently "progressive," "humanitarian" reforms.[37]

This viewpoint can easily be adapted to homeownership policy. For over a century, business leaders and entrepreneurs have been promoting homeownership as a means of social control. A century after Engels criticized such a view, the liberal-Republican Sabre Foundation claimed that if "every man [sic] could have a fair chance to acquire and enjoy the ownership of some form of property" (including homes) the beneficial results could include respect for law and order, responsible democracy, and individual opportunity.[38]

The authors of the report claimed to criticize corporate ownership because it restricts opportunities for personal ownership. Nonetheless, the benefits they claimed for property ownership would benefit corporations: the house, which is the principal form of investment they would make available to individuals, does not compete with corporate investments and would not remove individuals from the workforce.

As the authors argue it,

The opportunity to acquire the ownership of property will motivate an individual to employ his best efforts to increase his productive skills. It will give him an incentive to industry, thrift and foresight. . . . Those who own property are least likely to condone the destruction of property and other lawless behavior. . . . Those who own property, and are thus subject to taxation by government, are more likely to be active and responsible citizens than those who have nothing. They are most likely to resist the demagogic appeals for political redistributions of the wealth of others.[39]

In other words, people who own property will work harder and will not rebel or seek redistribution of wealth. But if people are working as employees of others, and if the only property they own is their home, the result of their better productivity and discipline will be higher business profits.

The ownership argument is not limited to Republicans. In 1972, for example, Senator Hubert Humphrey urged passage of legislation permitting those collecting welfare to own homes, inasmuch as "people could thus become property owners, which would provide them with equity and, more important, with pride."[40] This statement echoes themes raised in the 1912 National Housing Association debate.

Even earlier William Philips, first president of the Provident Institution for Savings in Boston argued that savings and homeownership would make workers feel integrated into the economy, and thus not "regard the whole structure of society . . . as an inhabitant of a conquered territory looks upon a citadel of the conquerors."[41] Without a stake in society," in this view, the worker would be "an enemy of the government claiming his allegiance," but "Give him hope, give him the chance of providing for his family, of laying up a store for his old age, of commanding some cheap comfort or luxury, upon which he sets his heart; and he will then voluntarily and cheerfully submit to privations and hardship."[42]

On similar grounds, Boston's mayor, Josiah Quincy (grandson of the mayor of the 1820s) proposed in 1871 that housing be provided in suburbs for at least some workers. In the 1890s Edward Atkinson's slogan was "every man his own landlord," and his ideas were accepted by many political leaders among the Mugwumps and, later, the Progressives.[43] F. B. Sanborn praised building association methods of spreading homeownership. Borrowing, which he normally considered an evil for the poor, was different for the homebuyer:

> It is here an incentive to industry; for he must earn and save money to keep up his investment. . . . the return he gets in relief from renting is itself a profit, which also appears in his imagination to be greater than it commonly is. . . . the pleasure of house building, the companionship and competition which he finds in belonging to such a society, all lure him forward in the way of economy.[44]

Sanborn's theme, that the rewards to homebuyers as they appear in the workers' imagination are great enough to tie workers into the system, has been iterated recently by Lipset and Bendix, who claim that improvements in style of life help to preserve a belief in opportunity: "A man who can buy his own house . . . will feel that he has moved up in the world even if he has not changed his . . . occupational position."[45]

Radical analyses of homeownership sometimes simply echo the conservative view: homeownership is a means to entrap workers in an investment their imaginations will inflate, which will keep them loyal and hardworking employees and thus avoid class unrest. Only the moral is reversed. Harvey Wasserman's radical history of the United States suggests that an aristocracy of laborer homeowners was deliberately created to split the working class. Stanley Aronowitz, in his pessimistic summing up of trade unionism's "False Promises" draws upon his experiences as an organizer to argue that, at times, payment on a home may be an important factor in decisions not to strike. Herbert Marcuse, in the analysis quoted above, argues that identification with consumer goods, including the home, ensures the docility of the American working class. Thomas Angotti similarly presents the suburban home as an illusory gain.[46]

Eli Zaretsky suggests that, under capitalism, the separation of work from the household or community allowed the bourgeoisie to foster an individualist ideology, in which the family is "the retrograde preserve of private wealth," and where "the property owner and his authoritarian family . . . are the center of a well-ordered society." The combination of this domestic life with property ownership in the form of a home gives society the appearance of being classless, since families and homes, unlike productive assets, are not limited to capitalists. Home life is left as "the only space that proletarians owned;" a sphere that allows retreat from identification with the "vast army of labor that, every morning, goes to work, and evenings and weekends, recovers from it." The result is a tendency to divert workers from identification with their workplace and with the working class as a whole.[47]

This view of homeownership's effects usually claims that the workers have been manipulated into wanting homes in the first place. Thus the novelist Doris Lessing asks rhetorically, "Why should we spend all the capital we are ever likely to have tying ourselves down to a place we detest?"[48] And John Kenneth Galbraith and Vance Packard among the liberals, and Paul Baran and Paul Sweezy and Herbert Marcuse among the radicals, respond with accounts of the ideological and advertising blitz with which capitalist society accomplishes the task.[49]

Our analysis of pseudomobility and diminishing assets could be seen as a simple extension of the social control view. We show that individuals are blocked by a set of limited opportunities; that their attempts to advance just leave them frustrated and more or less back at the same point from which they started in a social and economic system that mainly benefits others. We reject the orthodox view that they are victims of their own excessive aspirations. We might conclude, therefore, that the system as a whole was designed to ensnare them, through a class of social controllers or hidden pursuaders. But this view, while common to much of the social-control literature, assumes too easily that the existing housing pattern was the first and the best choice of capitalists, an entire defeat for the working class, and evidence therefore of how easily the former can manipulate the latter.

Indeed, we only partially accept the social-control view. The social-control studies have helped to discredit the tendency of American historians to attribute events to vague goals that "society" or "the Americans" wanted, just as a similar set of radical studies has challenged the view that economic results occur simply because "consumers choose them." Social control studies have also elucidated some of the mechanisms that shape reforms and keep people in line—the stratification of labor, the growth of bureaucracies of regulators with their own goals, the occasional direct intervention of big business into policy formation, and the spread of systematic propaganda. But they also oversimplify both the ease with which control has been maintained and the processes of regulation.

Thus William Muraskin criticizes social-control historians, arguing that they both "reduce middle-class ideology to the concept of propaganda: conscious manipulation and lies," and see people as more manipulable than they are. He argues that "the social-control historians have asked the right questions and revealed part of the truth. But their conceptual scheme, imputing conscious manipulation of ideas for purposes of social control, is too primitive and simplistic to be adequate."[50]

Muraskin contends that the analysis can have an unintended conservative influence by making the elite appear omnipotent. The social-control interpretation, he writes, "reflects and supports the alienation and cynicism that characterize the 1970s and as a result holds widespread appeal."[51] A similar criticism has been made of social-control views within the radical camp.[52]

D. Control or Compromise?

These criticisms of the simple social-control position match our interpretation. We want to understand both the causes of homeowner discontents and why it is difficult to link the struggles of homeowner and other communities to other anti-establishment struggles. But we do not see the discontented simply as pawns of the ruling class. That not only puts the blame on the victims but also leads to a pessimism about any possible change. So we must analyze how homeownership has limited the options for workers, but we must also account for the reasons—which may be very good ones—why individuals get boxed into positions of limited options and what strategies might widen the options.

The difficulties and possibilities of this undertaking are perhaps best seen through a critical analysis of the work on housing that is, in many ways, a precursor of the social-control view—but one that was written with faith that change was possible and with a sensitivity toward the victims of capitalist development. Frederich Engels' *The Housing Question*, written as a set of articles in 1872, criticized the proposals for expanded homeownership that flourished in the wake of the Paris uprising of 1871. Engels revised it as a pamphlet in 1886–1887, a time when urban unrest, particularly over housing conditions, was again rife in Britain and the United States. Proposals to sell cheap housing to workers were designed to solve other problems as well—health problems, high rents even for the middle class, and capitalists needs to cut costs because of international competition. Engels argued that such proposals, whether deliberately designed by big business interests or proposed by his rivals in the workers' movement, could lead only to greater control of the workers by business, and to a worsening of the workers' living standards.[53]

Engels argued his point on both economic and psychological grounds. First and foremost, he said, homeownership would tie workers down and would force a reduction in wages at least to match the lowering of costs and perhaps more. He cited the immobile cottage-owning workers in rural Germany who worked for exceedingly low wages, while

> For our workers in the big cities freedom of movement is the first condition of their existence, and landownership could only be a hindrance to them. Give them their own houses, chain them once again to the soil and you break their power of resistance to the wage cutting of the factory owners.[54]

Engels presents this argument both in a discussion of the place of rent in Marx's value theory, and by a number of examples. In rural Germany, he argues, ownership of housing leaves rural wage-workers chained "in semi-feudal fashion" to their own separate capitalists, and as a result they were paid lower wages than workers elsewhere in Europe.[55] In discussing the United States, he cites a letter, describing "miserable little wooden huts, containing about three rooms each, still in the wilds" in a muddy desert an hour away from Kansas City. Engels comments that

> the workers must shoulder heavy mortgage debts in order to obtain even these houses and thus they become completely the slaves of their employers; they are bound to their houses, they cannot go away, and they are compelled to put up with whatever working conditions are offered to them.[56]

Engels is less specific in pointing out the psychological drawbacks of homeownership for workers. He writes:

> In order to create the modern revolutionary class of the proletarian it was absolutely necessary to cut the umbilical cord which still bound the worker of the past to the land. The hand weaver who had his little house, garden and field along with his loom, was a quiet, contented man in all godliness and respectability despite all misery and despite all political pres-

sure; he doffed his cap to the rich, to the priests and to the officials of the state; and inwardly was altogether a slave.[57]

This, says Engels, is what the homeownership reformers wish to restore. Engels also argues that capitalists will use homeownership to make workers docile. He cites Emil Sax's claim that

> society as a whole has the greatest interest in seeing as many of its members as possible bound to the land. . . . All the secret forces which set on fire the volcano called the social question which glows under our feet, the proletarian bitterness, the hatred . . . the dangerous confusion of ideas . . . must disappear like mist before the morning sun when . . . the workers themselves enter in this fashion into the ranks of the property owners.[58]

Engels comments that Sax hopes that through homeownership "the workers would also lose their proletarian character and become once again obedient toadies like their forefathers who were also house owners." He also cites approvingly the comments of the Spanish newspaper *La Emancipacion* that French businessmen and officials were trying to create an urban class of small property owners as an army to use against revolution.[59]

Yet, it is not entirely clear that Engels believed homeownership would seriously affect the revolutionary potential of workers. Their objective status in production, as he states, would remain that of wage workers no matter how often they were told that homeownership had made them "capitalists." And he basically believed that that status was the prime determinant of consciousness.

Indeed, Engels never directly says that homeownership will alter the consciousness of the workers, but only that the capitalists hope it will. That hope means homeownership schemes are reactionary as well as economically self-defeating. Engels is eager to discredit what he considers mistaken reforms clothed in the rhetoric of proletarian advancement. But this is *not* the same as saying that homeownership itself will have adverse psychological effects on workers' views of their class position; that it will enhance, as well as follow from, a false consciousnes; and that it must therefore always be fought.

While it is fruitless to debate what Engels "really meant" on any particular subject, we find it more useful to accept an interpretation that does not rely so heavily on a theory of false consciousness. We would hold that Engels was primarily raising economic arguments against homeownership, arguments that can be evaluated in the context of the particular era (1872–1887) in which he wrote on housing. Homeownership programs, he concluded, would not be advantageous to the workers in a direct economic way. Secondarily, he argued, homeownership could prevent workers from giving full support to the working class movement. Mortgage obligations, like tenure terminable at the option of one's employer, would be a strong incentive not to strike. Isolated homesteads would limit a worker's exposure to new ideas being spread by the workers' movements.

Nonetheless, Engels wrote before the introduction of the trolley car, and the growth of cities in which many varied jobs might lie within commuting distance. He wrote before modern mortgage markets had reduced borrowing costs. In Engels' day, housing production required either that workers' homes be encumbered by very high mortgage obligations because of the high cost of urban land, or that the homes be isolated in rural areas. Thus he could not envision homeownership without one or the other of these problems arising.

One need not hold that homeownership *per se* deludes its owner in some mysterious sense in order to accept Engels' arguments. He presented a case, based on the state of the economy and the technology of his time, against programs claiming that homeownership would greatly improve the workers' lot. He thought pursuit of these programs would be a strategic error for the working class, and that his arguments would carry weight. This is a far cry from assuming an easily manipulable class of workers.

The development that made homeownership available to a large proportion of the American working class without upsetting basic capitalist institutions was suburbanization. The linking of large hinterland areas to cities by cheap commuter transport allowed individual homes to be built more cheaply. Continuing expansion also provided a "filtering down" of older homes for lower-income workers. It assured that homeownership would not become a source of capital gains that would allow many people to escape from the working class.

Although analysts have portrayed suburbanization simply as a result of transportation improvements, its prerequisites were sociopolitical as well. Not only did suburbanization require research and development efforts into appropriate ways to transport people from urban jobs to suburban homes, it also required substantial changes in land and railway ownership patterns that had previously restricted investments in suburban development. Both the institutional and the technologcal changes came about because class struggles in the cities in the 1880s and 1890s directed the focus of private research and development, and public policy, toward suburban possibilities.

The development of suburbs allowed American cities to expand as centers of capitalist employment without increasing urban social tensions. Indeed, even with rapid immigration, population densities in the central cities declined. Thus, the availability of new neighborhoods enhanced the standard of living for at least some strata of the working class in the 75 years after the introduction of the electric street railway.

Engels had not foreseen this possibility, but not because his theory logically precluded such a development—neither Marx nor Engels ever doubted that working class action could win immediate and mediumterm gains in living standards.[60] What Engels did not foresee, however, was capitalism's ability to develop metropolitan areas, with labor markets large enough to allow workers mobility among jobs and residential areas designed to give enough small homes access to the jobs through massive transit systems. Engels took the position in *The Housing Question* that the technical possibilities open under capitalism allowed individual housing only when homes were so dispersed that their owners would be isolated from the urban labor market. He thought that this rural-urban separation would not be overcome until the development of a future socialist order and that even in the early states of socialism, the housing question would have to be tackled by subdividing the mansions of the ruling class.

Nonetheless, Engels was right in some respects. American workers found suburbanization and the spread of homeownership to be a mixed blessing: suburbanization caused many frustrations, and divided the working class into strata that identified with distinct local interests. It isolated many individual workers from close contact with their peers and thus furthered the conservatism that Engels had feared. But homeownership was able to do so only because Engels was wrong when he predicted its economic failure. Suburbia could work for a time as an agent of social control only because it was an economic success. If workers accepted conservative views, it was because they had some concrete evidence of progress in their lives.

Judged by its effects, suburbanization was a compromise for the American working class. Sam Bass Warner speaks of a "suburban compromise" in the sense of an adjustment of aspirations to limited opportunities on the part of individual workers.[61] But, as we shall argue in chapter 9, suburbanization was also a political and a class compromise between workers and capitalists. The working class did not receive suburbanization, with its benefits and costs, as an automatic spinoff of general technical progress. It was not tricked or forced into suburbanization by a ruling-class conspiracy. Instead, at least part of the working class, conscious of at least some of the costs, chose suburbanization as the best option it could win in the context of the American political economy of the late nineteenth century. By the same token, suburbanization was a system that was beneficial to capitalists over many decades, but which also had its costs, both initially and in the long run.

Viewed in this light, suburbanization is neither simply "the people's choice" nor a "ruling-class plot." Rather it is a complex phenomenon, which must be understood both in terms of how individual choices are constrained by the institutions of society, and in terms of how those institutions themselves are formed historically. In the next three chapters, we consider how the interplay of government action and market forces have induced individuals to suburbanize, and how both the influence and decisions of major real estate developers, and the compromise solutions to conflicts between capital and labor have shaped government and market responses.

CHAPTER SEVEN

Land Developers
Channelers and Beneficiaries

THE position that suburbanization reflected the desires and efforts of residents has never been stated more clearly than in Sam Bass Warner's description of suburban growth as "a weave of small patterns."[1] According to Warner, the design and specific characteristics of suburbs varied from place to place, within the ring of new housing being developed at any particular time. Underlying the architectural variation was the diverse nature of the area's developers. Despite uniformities imposed by economic necessities—"regulation without laws"—growth was the unplanned work of individuals working on a small scale. Warner writes:

> The Boston metropolis is the product of hundreds of thousands of separate decisions. Looking back . . . one can make out a kind of partnership which constructed the new industrial and suburban metropolis. It was a partnership between large institutions and individual investors and homeowners. No organization, however, tied together the two groups. . . . The building of the new divided metropolis was a popular movement, a movement executed by hundreds of thousands of middle-class citizens.[2]

As we argued in chapter 6, Warner's view may amount to a simple claim that suburbanization gave people what they wanted. If some failed to benefit, by implication they are to blame for missing out on this "popular movement," or for overreaching themselves in picking their level of participation. We shall look next at the evidence for Warner's view. We contrast the view of suburbanization as the result of hundreds of thousands of separate decisions with a view that stresses the role of certain major developers.

In support of his interpretation that suburbanization was a mass movement, Warner presents evidence that, of more than 23,000 building permits taken out in Roxbury, West Roxbury, and Dorchester from 1872 to
1901, only 23 percent were obtained by the 122 builders who built twenty
or more buildings over the period. In all, 9,030 separate individuals took
out building permits, the majority only building one structure (see table
7.1).[3]

This general pattern can still be found in some suburbs. Paul David
Brophy analyzed building permits taken out during the 1960s in three
of the suburbs, Middleton, North Reading, and Wilmington, then developing in the outer ring around Boston. The results, presented in table 7.2, show that while in all cases the majority of developers built only
one structure, in two of the three towns the majority of dwellings were
constructed by developers who build 20 or more units over the decade,
and who on the average built more than eighty units. (In the third town,

Table 7.1
**Builders Classified by the Size of Their Operations, Roxbury, West Roxbury,
and Dorchester, 1872–1901**

Type of builder	Number of builders	Number of dwellings	Percent of total dwellings	Group average (dwellings per builder)
A. Those who build 20 or more dwellings in the whole period	122	5,350	23.0	43.85
B. Those who built 5 or more dwellings in some one year, but fewer than 20 in the whole period	279	2,498	11.0	8.95
C. Those who built 2–4 dwellings in some one year, but less than 20 in the whole period	1,949	7,542	32.7	3.87
D. Those who built no more than 1 dwelling in any year and fewer than 20 in the whole period	6,680	7,683	33.3	1.15
Total	9,030	23,073	100.0	—

SOURCE: Sam Bass Warner, Jr. *Streetcar Suburbs, p. 184.*

Table 7.2
Builders Classified by the Size of Their Operations Middleton, North
Reading, and Wilmington, 1960–69

Type of Builder	Number of builders	Number of dwellings	Percent of dwellings	Dwellings per builder
MIDDLETON				
A. 20 units +	1	34	12.8	34.0
B. 5+ in year	4	39	14.7	9.75
C. 2–4 in year	5	22	8.3	4.4
D. 1 per year	114	116	43.8	1.0
Public Housing	1	54	21.4	
TOTAL	125	265	100.0	
NORTH READING				
A. 20 units +	5	411	54.4	82.2
B. 5+ in year	11	124	16.5	11.3
C. 2–4 in year	13	65	8.6	5.0
D. 1 per year	68	72	9.6	1.0
Apartments	1	82	10.9	—
TOTAL	98	754	100.0	
WILMINGTON				
A. 20 units +	5	590	55.8	118.0
B. 5+ in year	21	245	23.2	11.7
C. 2–4 in year	28	101	9.6	3.6
D. 1 per year	107	122	12.4	1.1
TOTAL	161	1,058	100.0	—

SOURCE: Paul David Brophy, Property Taxation Effects on Suburban Development. Thesis for Bachelor of Science, MIT 1970.
Data from Building Permits.

Middleton, only a small percentage of dwellings were built by developers of this scale. However, as Brophy points out, the town of Middleton had a uniquely high effective tax rate for suburban towns in the Boston area.[4])

However, even today many suburban developers, even those producing twenty to a couple of hundred units in one town, qualify as relatively small businesses, not large enough to exert much monopoly control over the process of development at the metropolitan or even the town level. Only one developer in Brophy's sample was large enough to be a producer of several hundred homes. Thus to some extent Warner's conclusion may still hold: construction of small homes is not a monopolized activity in the Boston area.

But the building of homes is not the only phase of the building of sub-urbs. Providing transport access and utilities, and subdividing the farms and woods for small-scale builders to purchase, are also part of the sub-urbanization process. It is here that government policies, and the social conflicts that shape them, both have their main effects. And *it is at this stage that large-scale developers—the subdividers of land rather than the actual builders of dwellings—have had an important influence* on the form of the suburbs, as well as garnering a large portion of the profits generated.

Three of the most successful developers in the history of Boston were: Harrison Gray Otis in the 1790s and early 1800s; Henry Whitney and the West End Street Railway Co. in the 1880s and 1890s; and Cabot, Cabot and Forbes (CCF) in the 1950s and 1960s. All of these developers had a considerable impact on the shape of the metropolitan area: Otis through the development of Beacon Hill and several waterfront and bridge sites, Whitney through the development of Beacon Street as a locus of luxury apartments and homes in Brookline, and CCF through the build-ing of peripheral industrial parks that earned returns far above those of the typical homeowners discussed in part I.

We discuss these three cases in detail for two reasons. First, consid-eration of these developers qualifies the simple account of suburban growth, which made that process appear simply a natural evolution. Sec-ond, it gives some perspective on the low returns earned by the home-owners.

A. Harrison Gray Otis and Walking City Expansion[5]

The expansion of Boston in the early years of the republic was largely a process of development of land within walking distance of the port. Hills were leveled, bridges built, and marshes filled to make more land usable for residence and business. One of the leading shapers of this ex-pansion, both as politician and investor, was Harrison Gray Otis. Otis is best known as the developer of Beacon Hill for luxury housing, but he was also active in the development of other areas of the walking city.

Otis was a member of an upper-class Boston family: grandson of a noted lawyer, Colonel James Otis, nephew of the patriot leader James Otis Jr., and the son of a merchant who had received contracts for clothing the

Continental Army in 1777. Although Samuel A. Otis's business fell into bankruptcy after the war ended, both father and son were taken care of by their fellow members of the elite. Samuel A. Otis was named Secretary of the United States Senate, an uncle was appointed Collector of the Port of Falmouth, and young Harry was taken without charge as a pupil in the law offices of John Lowell, "out of friendship for the Otis family." In 1786, Lowell turned over to Harry his practice in the lower courts. Otis was even subsequently elected to the state legislature.[6]

In the early 1790s, Harrison Gray Otis began to expand his own capital through marriage to Sally Foster, the daughter of a leading merchant, and through a series of lawsuits by which he recovered debts owed his maternal grandfather, Harrison Gray, a Tory who had returned to England. In 1796, Otis served as United States District Attorney for Massachusetts, and became director of the Boston Branch of the United States Bank. Later that year, he was elected to the U.S. House of Representatives. In 1801, Otis returned to Boston, and thereafter played a major role in the city's development, as well as in Federalist Party politics.[7]

Samuel Eliot Morison has written of Otis:

> A long head for business he evidently had, since mainly by wise investments in real estate his estate grew from nothing at all in 1786 to a considerable fortune in 1810. There were few forms of local enterprise with which he was not connected.[8]

Business acumen, however, was always supplemented by political contacts. Otis was not only involved in investing in new real estate developments; he was simultaneously working in many political organizations and institutions to assure policies helpful to his economic interests.

One example of this occurred in 1793. Andrew Craigie, who had sold some western lands, bought up 300 acres at Lechmere Point, across the Charles River from Boston, and organized a company to build a bridge. Otis, as a state legislator, offered to use eminent domain on a piece of land needed by Craigie for a road to Cambridge. The legislature balked, but Otis meanwhile was able to purchase 39 of the 60 shares in Craigie's company.[9]

Otis's role in the development of Beacon Hill is a better known story. In 1795, Otis formed a syndicate, the Mount Vernon Proprietors, with

Jonathan Mason, another Federalist political leader, and several other stockholders. In 1798, the Mount Vernon Proprietors purchased from John Copley 18½ acres on Beacon Hill for $18,500. Interestingly, Otis had been chosen the previous year as a member of the committee to procure a site for a new State House in Boston. Perhaps not by coincidence, the land that was purchased for the State House was next to the land Otis and his partners had purchased. The Mount Vernon Proprietors then developed the Copley site as housing for Boston's elite, making a substantial profit.[10]

The development of Beacon Hill was perhaps an obvious decision. In the 1790s, the older sections of Boston were becoming overcrowded, and had been plagued by a series of fires. There was an evident desire by members of the merchant class to build new homes, outside of the developed area but still near enough to walk. The high ground that included Beacon Hill fit the need, and could be bought cheaply. Apart from these considerations, the choice of a site for the statehouse may have been influenced by the availability of a tract of land next to the common owned by the estate of John Hancock. Nonetheless, Otis's role in the case attracted considerable criticism. Copley's land had been sold not by the artist himself, but by his agent and son-in-law, Gardiner Greene. Greene was later a partner with Otis in other real estate ventures. Copley, who was in England at the time, disavowed the sale, and a series of lawsuits followed. Otis kept the land, although some payments were made to a man to whom Copley claimed he had sold it, and to the heirs of a claimant whose deed supposedly antedated Copley's. The incident led to a longstanding feud between Copley and the Boston establishment. (Less was said at the time about another aspect of the Hancock site: the Hancock estate owed money to the estate of Otis's Tory grandfather, Harrison Gray.) In 1795, when Hancock's widow remarried, Otis and an uncle recovered about a thousand pounds on this debt.[11]

The Copley purchase was quickly followed by purchases of adjoining lands on the hill owned by James Allen, the heir of Enoch Brown and Zachariah Phillips. This gave the proprietors title to most of the Trimountain region, with its undeveloped pasture lands, multiple peaks, and rich potential.[12]

The development of Mount Vernon, the westernmost hill of the region, was, wrote Chamberlain, "the most important real estate development enterprise until then ever undertaken in Boston. . . . On the commanding heights of Mt. Vernon, overlooking the Common on one hand, and the broad expanse of the Charles River on the other, there was ample room for the development of a court end of high distinction."[13] Walter M. Whitehill substantiates the importance of the Copley purchase: "This venture . . . was the largest land transaction ever to have been undertaken in Boston at that time, for it involved a sudden change in the character of an entire region."[14]

Other stages of Beacon Hill development also involved politics of a less covert sort. The building of Charles Street, along Beacon Hill on the side away from the Common and State Capitol, involved use of dirt taken from the leveling of part of Beacon Hill, to fill a marsh. Although it was a private venture, it received city approval because the area involved included a red light district the city wanted cleared. Later Boston's second mayor would personally lead a raid on vice in the area, opening the bulk of the Hill for respectable development by the owners. After Charles Street was built, the city appointed a commission to investigate filling the nearby Mill Pond, which had been dammed some 160 years and had become a sanitation problem. Otis, Charles Bulfinch, and Uriah Cotting formed a corporation to fill the pond using more of the earth that Otis wanted removed from Beacon Hill, in return for title to seven-eighths of the new land. The city got the rest.[15]

Another example of Otis's influence was the development of the Dorchester Neck area, across an inlet to the south of Boston. With land growing scarce in the city, the Selectmen of Boston, a group with strong commercial interests, presented a plan to develop the Neck. On May 22, 1801, a committee of six was appointed by the town meeting to serve with the selectmen, to "lease and manage said lands in such a manner as shall appear to them for the interest of the town." With the matter out of the hands of the town meeting as a whole, the field was free for political maneuvering.

Between 1800 and 1803, Otis had his associates also purchase several parcels of land on the Neck. On March 6, 1804, a state act annexing Dorchester Neck to Boston was signed. The state also chartered a company to build a toll bridge to south Boston, as the Neck was renamed. Otis and three associates were named as proprietors for the South Bridge, which they built the next year.[16]

Otis was also a partner in the Proprietors of India Wharf, a project for which his political connections may also have proven crucial. The wharf development was begun in the midst of an economic upswing in Boston just after 1800. In 1807 all 32 stores were sold off, with the proprietors sharing $206,000 in proceeds.[17] Otis was involved in 36 sales transactions involving 51 parcels of land in the South Wharf area. In 1807 he made $285,600.00 or more on land sales.[18] The bulk of these sales transactions occurred just before the Jefferson Embargo of December 22, 1807 drastically intefered with Boston's commerce. It is unlikely that Otis influenced the timing of the embargo, but his political connections undoubtedly gave him unusually good information that it was a possibility. Thus, one may conclude, with Morris:

> It is difficult to regard the dates of the sale of the wharf and the beginning of the embargo as a coincidence. Aside from being investors in the development of the wharf, Harrison Gray Otis and James Lloyd (one of his partners) maintained direct political connections to national politics. Otis and Lloyd having been elected to positions in government . . . it is logical that the Proprietors of India Wharf timed their transactions to events occurring at the national level.[19]

These and Otis's other ventures exerted considerable influence on the specific shape of city development both during and after Otis's period of activity. The success of Beacon Hill as an upper-class area of mansions directed future upper-income development into the wedge to the west of the city, in which it has tended to persist since. The redevelopment of the waterfront, by Otis's Broad Street Association and by the Proprietors of India Wharf, increased the separation of residences from commerce in the older city.

The development of East Cambridge and South Boston proved less successful, although Otis did make some profits there. Commercial owners in the south cove area prevented Otis from building the South Boston Bridge in his preferred location, and the area became one of commerce and wharves, warehouses, and working-class housing. A similar fate eventually befell the Craigie lands in East Cambridge. But both of these partial failures increased the availability of space to Boston investors and their workers, and set patterns for land use north and south of the city. It appears, therefore, that Warner's weave of small patterns was, to a large extent, woven on Otis's loom!

Otis's investments had a coherence which suggests that his connec-

tions gave him an accurate long-run view of Boston's development possibilities. "The key," writes Morris, "seems to lie in Otis's belief that the
insularity of Boston was for all practices past: every investment he made
involved the waters in and around Boston and developments concerning
them."[20] Having this view, Otis would frequently buy lands near potential bridge sites, and hold them until bridges were later developed. Once
development of Beacon Hill was begun, Otis and his associates continued to buy land there for long-term appreciation.

Otis's overall financial position also was an advantage. Following the
embargo of 1807, Otis was still able to speculate in land. During this
time of crisis, many people found it difficult just to maintain economic
position. Many bankruptcies occurred and many fortunes were lost.
Harrison Gray Otis not only maintained his position, but was also able
to exploit the losses of others and continue to speculate in land investments without the benefit of inflow revenue throughout the period.

Otis's personal gains from these investments were considerable. Morison refers to his considerable fortune. Kirker and Kirker refer to him as
the most successful man in Bulfinch's town. In 1837, Otis estimated the
value of his property at $533,000, of which about $400,000 was invested
in real estate, and the rest in cotton mills. In 1846, a pamphlet on "the
first men of Boston" estimated Otis's wealth at $800,000, making him
the thirteenth richest man in Boston.[21]

Jane Goldstein Morris has analyzed Otis's real estate transactions, and
estimated the appreciation of the land he owned and developed.[22] Her
study involved all pre-1823 transactions listed in the Suffolk County registry of deeds in which Otis was a principal. The analysis suggests the
overall magnitude of Otis's land value investments in the city of Boston,
as well as their location, timing, and success (see table 7.3).

Morris's estimates are only approximations. First, the analysis covers
transactions undertaken by Otis both alone and with partners. Morris's
data reveal that in about 79 percent of his buying transactions, Otis was
purchasing by himself. However, in *major* periods of development, this
was often not the case. In the period of the Copley purchase (1795–96),
his "alone" percentage dropped to 71.4 percent. In the 1802–3 wharf
development period, his "alone" percentage dropped to 58.6, perhaps
indicating his desire to share development costs. Second, the data also
exclude cost of land improvements, which were high in the case of Beacon Hill, and ignore any possible interest cost to Otis of borrowing money.

Table 7.3
Harrison Gray Otis and Partners: Purchases and Sales in Dollars

Year	Total Purchases (−)	Total Sales (+)	Annual Total	Cumulative Total
1785	inc. data	0	inc. −	− inc.
1786	0	0	0	− inc.
1787	855.00	0	− 855.00	− 855.00
1788	0	1,500.00	+ 1,500.00	+ 645.00
1789	0	0	0	+ 645.00
1790	1,800.00	1,620.00	− 180.00	+ 465.00
1791	2,070.00	0	− 2,070.00	− 1,605.00
1792	1,822.50	0	− 1,822.50	− 3,427.50
1793	9,432.00	0	− 9,432.00	− 12,859.50
1794	9,382.50	10,395.00	+ 1,012.50	− 11,847.00
1795	15,310.50	6,050.00	− 9,260.50	− 21,107.50
1796	51,980.00	27,700.00	− 24,280.00	− 45,387.50
1797	56,810.00	6,852.50	− 49,957.50	− 95,345.00
1798	6,726.00	22,781.66	+ 16,055.66	− 79,289.34
1799	4,560.00	15,814.00	+ 11,254.00	− 68,035.34
1800	1,475.00	5,605.00 +	+ 4,130.00	− 63,905.34
1801	4,502.72	23,471.00	+ 18,968.28	− 44,937.06
1802	105,340.00	53,541.00 +	− 51,799.00	− 96,736.06
1803	18,602.00	12,576.00	− 6,026.00	− 102,762.06
1804	2,246.00	80,806.00	+ 78,560.00	− 24,202.06
1805	37,983.16	128.449.60	+ 90,466.44	+ 66,264.38
1806	28,640.97	25,687.50	− 2,953.47	+ 63,310.91
1807	26,835.00	285,600.00 +	+ 258,765.00	+ 322,075.91
1808	37,374.50	3,000.00 +	− 34,374.50	+ 287,701.41
1809	22,816.90	25,505.00	+ 2,688.10	+ 290.389.51
1810	43,939.20	1,500.00 +	− 42,439.20	+ 247,950.31
1811	6,505.00	18,700.00	+ 12,195.00	+ 260,145.31
1812	6.00	10.00 +	+ 4.00	+ 260,149.31
1813	0	340.00 +	+ 340.00	+ 260,489.31
1814	0	5,500.00	+ 5,500.00	+ 265,989.31
1815	2,705.00	9,630.00	+ 6,925.00	+ 272,914.31
1816	0	29,000.00	+ 29,000.00	+ 301,914.31
1817	19,805.00	3,340.80	− 16,464.20	+ 285,450.11
1818	0	5,425.00	+ 5,425.00	+ 290,875.11
1819	10,500.00	7,000.00 +	− 3,500.00	+ 287,375.11
1820	1.00	8,019.00	+ 8,018.00	+ 295,393.11
1821	938.00	+	+ inc. +	+ 294,455.11
1822	0	5,024.00	+ 5,024.00	+ 299,479.11
1823	12,236.25	23,872.31 +	+ 11,636.06	+ 311,115.17

SOURCE: Jane Goldstein Morris, *Harrison Gray Otis and the Development of Boston Real Estate.*

The table shows an excess of $311,115 of sales over purchases of $543,199, a gain of just under 60 percent.

B. Henry M. Whitney and Brookline's Development[23]

In 1887, Henry M. Whitney, a steamship operator, banker, and real estate developer, formed a syndicate out of his small West End Street Railway Company, and bought up large amounts of stock in five other horsecar lines. The system Whitney put together was sizable and reflects how important the horsecar had become to the urban environment. In 1889, the year before the electric streetcars were to begin operating in Boston on a regular basis, the West End Street Railway operated 253 miles of track, had 1,841 cars and 7,728 horses, carried 104 million riders over 16.5 million car miles. If the system operated its lines on the average of eighteen hours a day, seven days a week, these figures imply that there was a streetcar about every six minutes on every line, and that every Bostonian including babes in arms took slightly over two round trips every week.[24]

The traction industry which Whitney inherited was not entirely sound. Horse-drawn street railways had begun in the 1850s and "a wave of entrepreneurial enthusiasm"[25] over the subsequent twenty years produced an industry characterized by cutthroat competition and overexpansion. By 1873, the streetcar lines had extended the limits of urban Boston 2½ miles from City Hall. The chaos had been reduced somewhat by some consolidation of companies, but even then the streets of downtown Boston were too narrow to accommodate all the streetcar traffic still passing over them. Moreover, because the downtown routes were more profitable to operate than suburban lines, there was a constant fight to control the downtown tracks.

Over the next 14 years, expanding streetcar service extended the limits of the city to about four miles from City Hall. There were only four major companies operating lines in Boston by the time Whitney entered the field. Street congestion downtown had grown intolerable, and Whitney's 1887 petition to the legislature for consolidation of all Boston lines into one company was based on his perception of consolidation as the only reasonable solution to this "blockade problem." Although the Metropolitan, the biggest line in Boston, opposed Whitney's move, "the ad-

Two developers of Beacon Street. Housing on Harrison Gray Otis' Beacon Hill and in Henry Whitney's Brookline still preserve genteel amenity.

Photo by Elliott Sclar.

Housing along Beacon Street on Beacon Hill, 1984.

Photo by Elliott Sclar.

Housing along Beacon Street in Brookline near Cleveland Circle, 1984.

vantage of the new line to the public [and to the legislature] was evident and irresistible,[26] and Whitney persuaded the legislature to allow the creation of a traction monopoly.

Whitney did not rely solely on his access to the public and political ears to promote his consolidation scheme, however. In 1887, the Metropolitan and the Cambridge Railway Companies began to arrange a consolidation of their own. The West End management became alarmed, and within a few weeks had bought a controlling interest in the stock of all the old Boston companies except the Lynn and Boston. Whitney then offered to combine all the companies into one by an exchange of stock in the old companies for stock in the West End. He managed to convince the stockholders that both the "blockages" and the financial problems of the lines would be solved by eliminating unprofitable competition.[27]

Before the merger, the capital of the West End Co. had been a relatively small $80,000. After consolidation, the company's capital included $6 million in preferred stock, $1.5 million in common stock, and $1.5 million in outstanding bonds, in addition to all the rolling stock. Once it had a virtual monopoly on street railway transportation in the city, the company grew rapidly.[28]

Consolidation did increase the rate of improvement in street railway transportation for a time. Service became more rational, and street blockades downtown became less serious. Whitney converted the system to electric power, with the first electric service starting on the Beacon Street line in 1889. Electric streetcars, or trolleys, were faster and more comfortable than horse cars, and electrification extended the range of convenient service to six miles from City Hall.[29]

The street railroads, however, soon ran into financial trouble. One side effect of the merger had been that the newly formed company contained all the stock of the former companies, much of which was "watered." Financial trickery accompanied the growth of the horsecar companies. The paper value of the company which emerged bore little resemblance to the productive value of the company's physical assets. By World War I, the company was bankrupt.[30]

Many observers have suggested that Whitney and other developers expanded the transit system in an uneconomical manner. For example, Warner has written:

Whitney continued two historic policies of street railway management. First, he was more interested in increasing the total number of fares on his system than in watching the relationship of distance, cost, and fare per ride. He, like his fellow streetcar managers the state over, was so convinced that the key to profit lay in the endless expansion of the numbers of passengers that, with little regard to costs, he constantly expanded the service area of the West End. . . .

Second, Whitney, like all horsecar managers before him, was an ardent believer in the five-cent fare. Thus expansion of service took place without additional charge to the commuter. As crosstown lines were built, free transfer points were added, so that the nickle fare was almost a universal in 1900.[31]

This criticism raises an interesting question. Why should Whitney, who demonstrated such business acumen in other areas, act irrationally in the area of the street railway? The answer is that he was a far sharper operator than a mere look at his behavior in street railway management would suggest. If that behavior is put in the context of his overall activities, which Warner himself points out included real estate development, then his behavior becomes economically rational. Whitney apparently saw the electric streetcar as a means of developing outlying real estate. If the motive was real estate development, then the idea of keeping fares down and extending lines as far as possible was quite rational.

In the summer of 1886, Whitney told a small group of fellow Cohasset summer residents about his plans for the development of Beacon Street, then a popular country drive in Brookline. Whitney had begun buying parcels of land along Beacon Street as early as 1868, but his major purchases were made in 1886. He had bought about 4 million square feet of land in Brookline and Brighton by November of that year. That fall, Whitney and a few associates formed the West End Land Company as a real estate development syndicate, and title to 3,828,804.8 square feet of the land Whitney had bought was transferred to the West End Land Company. The company made two other purchases after 1886, adding another million square feet of land to its holdings and completing its total real estate acquisitions by 1895.

Also during the fall of 1886, Whitney and a slightly larger group of capitalists, including some of the same men who were involved in the Land Company, were granted a legislative charter to form the original

West End Railway Company for the purpose of providing streetcar service to Brookline. In August 1886, 100 Brookline citizens had petitioned the Town Selectmen to take over control of Beacon Street from the state, changing it from a "country way" to a "townway." The street then would be laid out by the town as a tree-lined, 200-foot wide boulevard with a central strip for the West End Company's streetcar tracks.[32]

There was some opposition to this plan from the Metropolitan Railroad, which in 1884 had had its petition to build a streetcar line from Brookline to Boston denied by the legislature. Apparently, Whitney had enough political clout to overcome this opposition, for the Town Meeting gave almost unanimous approval to the scheme, and by early 1887, the legislature also had approved it. The inducements Whitney offered were considerable. He gave 630,000 square feet of his own land to the town, about half the total land required for the widening. Whitney also individually pledged $100,000 to help finance the project, which ultimately cost the town about $465,000 to complete. Thus, by investing only about 12 percent of his total land holdings and by paying for part of the project, Whitney convinced the Town of Brookline to help create the conditions by which the value of his real estate would be greatly increased.[33]

Barbara Sproat and Robert Miller have examined Whitney's Brookline real estate career. Their work covers the 1868–1910 period, and covers all of the land along Beacon Street from the Boston city limits to Cleveland Circle, near Brookline's western boundary. Miller has analyzed tax assessment records for Whitney and the West End Railway Company prior to the electrification of the streetcars. His data show that land values were already appreciating during this period, when Whitney was buying up his land and developing the first section of Beacon Street (see table 7.4).[34]

Sproat analyzed data on Whitney's land dealings contained in the Norfolk County Registry of Deeds. Every piece of land bought or sold by Whitney before 1910 was labeled with location, land area, price, and transaction date(s).[35] Her findings show that Whitney followed a fairly clear development strategy in his Brookline real estate dealings. Although his purchases of land stretched the whole length of Beacon Street, from one town line to the other, his properties were far from equally distributed among the three sections of Beacon Street. Figure 7.1 shows all of Whitney's purchases, with each parcel delineated in its approxi-

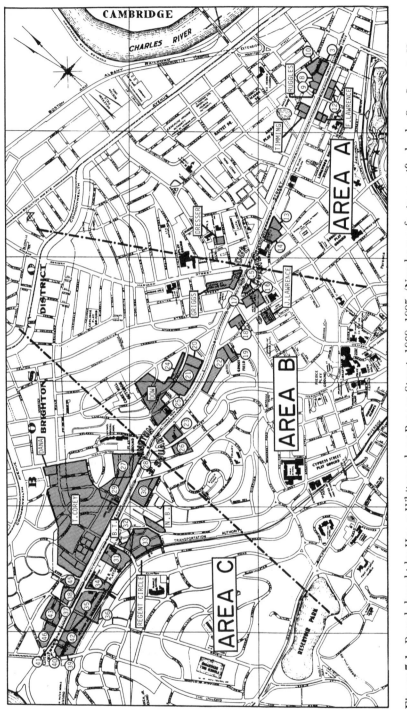

Figure 7.1. Parcels bought by Henry Whitney along Beacon Street, 1868–1895. (Numbers refer to specific deeds. See Sproat, Henry Whitney's Streetcar Suburb.)

Table 7.4
Assessments of Properties of West End Land Co. of
H.M. Whitney

Year	Properties	Sq. Feet	Land Assessment in $
1884	3	368	16.5
1885	3	368	17.5
1886	3	368	24.0
1887	28	2,487	761.5
1888	20	2,367	904.9

Brookline Assessment Records, tabulated by Robert Miller.

mate original form. The map also indicates the boundaries of the three areas of Beacon Street which Sproat defined for purposes of analysis: Area A at the eastern end of Beacon Street to Harvard Street, Area B between Harvard Street and Washington Street, and Area C from Washington Street west to Cleveland Circle (see table 7.5).

Some differences in Whitney's operation in the three areas are immediately obvious. The timing of his sales of land seemed to follow an east-to-west pattern. He would sell off large numbers of parcels in one general location all around the same time and then move on to sales in

Table 7.5
Amounts and Distribution of Land Acquired by Whitney in Brookline, 1868–1903

	Period of Purchase	Total Sq. Ft.	In Area A	In Area B	In Area C
West End Land Co.	by 1886 (Howe deed)	3,199,067.9	370,583.9	874,119.0	1,954,365.0
	1887–1895	1,021,899.6	—	—	1,021,899.6
Whitney alone	by 11/1886	284,237.0	40,036.0	105,876.0	138,325.0
	12/1886– 1903	516,668.5	59,652.1	368,524.0	88,492.4
	1898 (by fore closure)	191,672.0	—	—	191,672.0
TOTAL		5,213,545.0	470,272 *	1,348,519.0	3,394,754.0

*plus land Whitney inherited (square feet unknown)

another location. Farther out from town, where land was cheaper, new plots were purchased, and Whitney's total investments increased in scale.

The average price paid by Whitney for land he purchased in Brookline over the whole period was $0.36 per square foot; the total base value of his purchases (5,021,873 square feet) was $1,808,000, though his cash investment was considerably less, as many of his purchases were financed in part by mortgages. Correcting for two foreclosed mortgages, the total value of his investment in land in Brookline was $1,992,000.

Whitney sold most of his land for residential use. Two general patterns were discernible as well, one for land fronting on Beacon Street, and another for land along streets behind Beacon. Some of the land fronting directly on Beacon Street was sold in large parcels to other developers, although many smaller parcels on Beacon Street also were sold. Land which did not front on Beacon Street was more often sold in lots sized for individual houses; deeds for such land often carried restrictions which limited buildings to single-family houses, whereas apartment buildings were generally allowed on Beacon. Henry Whitney understood zoning: the restrictions he placed on the use of the land he sold almost always included a ban on public stables or any other business offensive to a neighborhood of dwelling houses, and they usually established a minimum value for any house to be built on the property.

One of the most frequent purchasers of large parcels from Whitney was Robert W. Lord of Boston. In several cases, Lord divided the property into two or three parcels, which he then sold to even smaller-scale developers, thus acting as a kind of intermediary in the development process. In addition, Lord was usually the "straw" through which land was transferred from the West End Land Company to Whitney individually. Although Robert Lord himself was not listed as an original stockholder in the West End Land Company, a George C. Lord was listed, and Robert Lord was clearly a close associate of Whitney.

Smaller individual house lots located back from Beacon Street usually were sold to individuals. Occasionally a purchaser would buy two or three of these small lots, but such purchases clearly represented small-scale housing investments rather than major development schemes. Whitney was a land speculator, not a housing developer. With only one major exception, he sold his property as vacant land and left the erection of buildings to his purchasers.

Whitney's enterprise illustrates that large-scale developers with access to certain key resources capture a large portion of the capital gains from rising real estate values. His access to the necessary resources was excellent. He obviously had good access to capital: the value of his total investment in Brookline land (exclusive of his other interests, which included Boston's entire trolley system) was about $2 million. Second, he gained and maintained control over the market by buying a large proportion of the available land in the area he was interested in, by engineering the widening of Beacon Street to benefit his plans, and by using his political influence to gain control of the street railway industry in Boston and Brookline. Finally, he had access to information about the market. His development strategy shows that he clearly understood that the real profits in real estate are to be made by buying land at the fringe of the urbanized area, providing transport to that land (or buying just before someone else provides that transport), and then selling out relatively quickly and capturing the initial steep rise in land values.[36]

Table 7.6 presents Sproat's estimates of Whitney's annual rate of return from the decades between 1880 and 1910. The table also shows the typical annual return enjoyed by individual homeowners on their investment in housing. Whitney's return on investment in Beacon Street land was consistently far higher than the normal return on homeownership in Brookline, which was in turn slightly higher than the average for the metropolitan area. Even the lowest average annual appreciation in the value of Whitney's land, 25.1 percent in the period 1900–1910, was almost four times greater than the average return for individual Brookline homeowners.

Table 7.6
Annual Rates of Return on Real Estate, 1880–1910 (in percent)

Period	Whitney			Individual Homeowners	
	Area A	Area B	Area C	Boston[a]	Brookline[b]
1880–89	29.7	—	—	3.4	—
1890–99	—	51.9	80.0	3.9	4.3
1900–1910	—	—	25.1	4.0	6.3

[a] City of Boston in 1880–89; Boston SMSA for other years. These rates of return are based on a sample of real estate transactions for random samples of Boston males drawn by Daniel Luria.

[b] Rates of return for Brookline are derived from a period-to-period index of house values, based on a sample of 32 Brookline houses between 1890 and 1970. See Lisa Dennen and Barbara Sproat, "Bedroom Community in Transition: Brookline, Massachusetts 1870–1970," Working Papers #19 in *Boston Studies in Urban Political Economy*.

Whitney did not, of course, put up the entire $2 million investment out of his own pocket; he borrowed a good deal of it. Thus a portion of his return went to paying off his own mortgages. We do not know, therefore, exactly what proportion of his return represented clear profit. We do know, however, that he used his land as collateral to raise additional capital, with which he could buy more land. Thus while part of his return went to pay interest, his rate of gain would probably be far higher than we have shown if his revenues after debt repayment were compared with his original equity alone.

C. Cabot, Cabot and Forbes and "Route 128"[37]

In 1945, the city of Boston had the reputation of being a "dead" city. No major building had gone up in nearly twenty years, and the Port of Boston was in decline. The traditional major industry of the region, textiles, had been in a state of serious decline for a decade and a half, and new industries weren't taking up the slack. There was no unused land in the core area of the metropolitan area for expanding industry, and the declining milltowns on the periphery were developing large pools of unemployed semi-skilled and skilled workers. It was against this grim background that enormous industrial development began to take place in the early 1950s.

This industrial development has been referred to as the rise of the "128 industries," although only some of the industries in Boston's suburbs really located there. Route 128 was built as a four-lane limited-access highway bypassing Boston and other business centers. Yet industrial development in nontraditional industries, such as electronics and aerospace, had begun to develop even beyond 128 well before the first four-lane version was completed. Individual plants had begun to move out from the core of the city, and new ones had come to Route 128 from out-of-state years before.[38]

Chapter 2 has shown how automobile suburbanization began in the 1920s, and how radial "parkways" were built in the 1930s. Within a month of V–J day in 1945, the Department of Public Works initiated an official study of road systems. The result, the Master Highway Plan, was released in 1948. Turning its back on any expansion of public transit, the Plan envisioned a series of three circumferential roads linked by radial connectors. First and most important was (and is) Route 128, a belt surrounding Boston at a distance of about 12 miles. This road was pushed so hard that its construction began a full year before the Master Plan was ever released. Second, the Plan called for a circumferential belt at a distance of 20 miles, Route 495. Finally, an inner belt, Route 295, was to be constructed to circle Boston's downtown at one to two miles distance. (Routes 128 and 495 were built. The inner belt, as will be seen in chapter 11, was unable to conquer a mighty, though short-lived, coalition of residents in the areas to be affected.[39]

The Master Plan is a good example of the use of public investment to support private investments. The Plan was metropolitan rather than urban: its concern was with access to Boston for suburbanites rather than with intracity access. The post-World War II technoboom had little use for Boston's urban blue-collar working class, and little more for its city patronage, white-collar labor force. The metropolitan capitalist class had been effectively barred from political power in Boston since 1910 by a parochial, Irish-based Democratic political machine. Suburbanization was for them a chance for a political end-run around the machine, their ticket for the reconquering of Boston. What is more, the new industries needed access to the growing, educated suburban population, and to the pliable, skilled labor of some of the outer ring industrial towns.[40]

In many respects, the development of Route 128 is the story of one firm, Cabot, Cabot and Forbes Company (CC & F), which began building industrial parks there in 1951. CC & F was originally a real estate management firm that managed trusts, estates, and properties of various members of the Boston "Brahmin" hierarchy of financiers, the Cabots, Forbes and their friends. In 1947 the only surviving member of the partnership was 73-year-old Murray Forbes. Forbes received a 26-year-old visitor in his office at 60 State Street, Gerald Blakely. Blakely explained that he thought a lot of money could be made in developing industrial parks, and asked for the use of the prestigious company name. Forbes put him on at $100 a week. He did not remain at that modest salary level for long.[41]

Blakely's development strategy was based on access to vacant land linked to Boston by the radial highways built in the 1930s and by the impending completion of Route 128. He expected a good market because of the presence in the area of MIT, electronics firms already established during the war, a pool of unemployed skilled workers, and military and aerospace money. He had made a study of where scientists wanted to live. The initial venture along Route 128 was a success because Forbes gave Blakely use of the CC & F name and access to venture capital. His development strategy met the approval of the banking and finance leaders in Boston who were looking for a way to revitalize the city and were willing to loan Blakely mortgage money. Tax laws favoring development investors sweetened the deal for them. Thus, an overall strategy that worked, based on access to capital and shrewd use of the opportunities afforded by tax laws to those with large amounts of capital, were crucial.

While Route 128 was in the planning stages, Gerald Blakely began his industrial development work. From 1947 to 1950, Cabot, Cabot & Forbes conducted an intensive educational campaign within the town of Needham to secure the zoning necessary for the creation of an industrial park. Initial land acquisition and development commenced in 1949. Rezoning occurred in 1953. By 1959, the New England Industrial Center (NEIC) included 38 firms employing more than 3,600 workers and was paying annual wages in excess of $12.2 million.[42]

Another early CC & F industrial development included the Waltham Industrial Center and the Waltham Research and Development Park, which face each other across Route 128. The former includes 175 acres, the latter 140. Taken together they constitute the largest CC & F development. Their development shows the use of political influence by a well-connected company. Waltham land was first acquired by CC & F in 1951. However, building was held up for some time because of delays in obtaining the required zoning from the city. Part of the difficulty resulted from the lack of an access road to Route 128. CC & F originally agreed to build at its own expense the necessary access road and interchange with Route 128. In 1956, however, Commissioner of Public Works John A. Volpe announced that CC & F would merely donate the land. The state would pay the construction cost of $305,000.

The land was acquired cheaply; much of it had been a pig farm and a portion of the remainder a swamp. The Cleveland-based Clevite firm had CC & F build a plant for them in the park. Clevite had conducted a national poll determining that scientists and engineers preferred work in the Boston and San Francisco areas. CC & F used this poll and Clevite's location choice in their marketing efforts. Another key advantage of the Waltham area was the highly skilled, precision work force left behind when the long established Waltham Watch Company moved out. Detailed electronics components assembly depends upon such a work force.

Another major attraction was the high unemployment in the old mill cities of Lowell and Lawrence, a short drive on good roads to the Northwest. Another factor that proved crucial in the Waltham case was the lay of the land. On one side of Route 128, the land was much lower adjacent to the highway and then rose to a knoll farther back. On the other side, the land rose steeply from the highway. CC & F capitalized on this and laid out the parks so that nearly every building could be seen from the highway. They carefully marketed the advertising value of this visibility to prospective tenants. In 1962, 40,000 travelers a day viewed the parks from 128. Highway access to the New England Region and Upstate New York was excellent, as was metropolitan area access. Airports were also nearby. Prospects for the park were so good that Boston Gas Company installed gas mains there at its own expense.[43]

CC & F also competed for shopping developments in Lexington and Wakefield, succeeding in the latter venture and being outdone by Filene Company in the former. Later developments were built in Woburn and Bedford.

By the mid-1960s, the industrial development boom on Route 128 had experienced a leveling-out period. CC & F switched its focus to some redevelopment in Cambridge, near MIT, and to new suburbs. Highway construction began in 1959 on a new Ring highway, Route 495, 88 miles in length, compared to 128's 65 miles. Route 495 was 90 percent paid for by the U.S. Government through its Highway Trust Fund for interstate roads. The total cost was $180 million. The new highway was completed in 1969. By March of 1971, 133 businesses had either located or were planning to locate in 22 communities along Route 495. During 1970, permits for construction of new industrial space were granted to 44 companies for expansion of their Route 128 facilities.[44]

The two major industrial developers on 495 were CC & F and State Properties, long the leading local developers of apartment complexes and suburban shopping centers. State Properties, with 1,000 acres of Westboro, where 495 crosses Route I-90 (the Massachusetts Turnpike), had the most advantageous location, since Route 90 goes straight into Boston. CC & F's major stake on 495 was its I-95 Industrial Center at 495, where the company owned 800 acres zoned as an industrial park at the intersection of the two highways joining Boston and Providence, on the main line of the Penn Central Railroad.

CC & F's location to the south of Boston was a disadvantage, since I-

95 goes north only as far as 128, 10 miles from the center of Boston. CC & F viewed this as a serious problem, since easy and speedy access to Boston is important to the distribution industry. Their efforts appeared headed for success during Volpe's governorship. CC & F, therefore, pressed for completion of I-95 south,[45] but their hopes were dashed on November 30, 1972, when Governor Francis Sargent decided against the construction of any more expressways in the core (see chapter 11). Like Harrison Gray Otis nearly two centuries earlier, CC & F ended up less successful in its ventures south of the city than it had to the west. But by then, CC & F was large enough to endure a project with only modest returns.

Since CC & F had not entered realty development as a publicly traded corporation limited by SEC regulations, full information on their returns is not available. But there are a number of estimates available of the scope of their gains. An economic impact study of Route 128, prepared at MIT, indicated that land for which CC & F paid $1,000–$1,500 per acre in 1951 was selling for $25,000 by the late fifties. The New England Industrial Center in Needham was assessed at $113,000 before its development, and at $6 million in 1957.[46] Another estimate, as of the late 1950s, was that the complex of industry, business, and homes that had been built along Route 128 was worth close to $500 million, and that CC & F held majority ownership of over $23 million in those assets, all on the base of $550,000 in 1950 investment capital.[47]

Christopher Rand estimated in 1963 that CC & F had built 75 percent of the plants along route 128. The next year, the Boston *Globe* reported the figure at 80 percent, including 13 of the 19 industrial parks. Blakely was believed to own 65 percent of the company.[48]

According to *Fortune* magazine, by the 1960s, Blakeley's personal wealth was in excess of $10 million. By the 1960s, CC & F was a mammoth enterprise, owning 21 subsidiaries and building industrial parks in Pennsylvania and California.[49] The 1971 prospectus for its first public subsidiary, CC & F Land Trust, listed properties having a gross appraised value of over $235 million. Blakely owned 56.8 percent of CC & F Land Trust and Paul Hellmuth—also a director of W.R. Grace and a trustee of the Boston Five Cent Savings Bank—held 26.2 percent.[50]

Information is available on specific industrial parks. In the case of the New England Industrial Center in Needham (Norfolk County), land for which CC & F paid $1,000–$1,500 per acre in 1951 was selling for $25,000 in 1959. CC & F itself made a profit of nearly 500 percent despite high land preparation costs. By 1967, per-acre prices were in the vicinity of $60,000.

Appreciation from 1967 to 1972 averaged 8 percent per year. *Fortune* has estimated that when all NEIC mortgages have been paid off, the partnership of Blakely-Linnell-Forbes will own properties valued at over $20 million.

Thomas Holzman has studied the land transactions in Waltham and other towns in Middlesex County which the firm and its legion of realty trusts made between 1950 and 1968.[52] Although it was impossible to estimate rental income, capital gains on land could be estimated using title deed records. Though these deeds did not give reliable price data on all transactions, a sample set of transactions was obtained for which the data give at least some estimate of transaction prices.

Return to investment can most quickly be realized through capital gains, and the purest, most reliable capital gains figures we have are on vacant land transactions. In addition, in transactions involving both land and buildings, we can estimate the value of the land part of the transaction by using the ratio of assessed value of the land to total assessed valuation as a proxy for the percentage of the transaction value involving the land. Using transactions involving land and buildings in this way allows a larger sample.

To begin to get an idea of CC & F's capital gains on suburban land, table 7.7 is suggestive. It shows the price paid and the price received

Table 7.7
Average prices of land purchased and sold by Cabot, Cabot and Forbes in Middlesex County, by town (1950–1971)

Town	Price paid for Land by CC & F	Price received for land by CC & F	Number of Observations	
			Price Paid	Price Rec'd
Cambridge	$0.02/ft.^{2}	$0.15/ft.^{2}	5	2
Waltham	0.08/ft.^{2}	0.50/ft.^{2}	11	19
Newton	0.01/ft.^{2}	1.00/ft.^{2}	2	1
Lexington	0.12/ft.^{2}	0.12/ft.^{2}	5	2
Burlington	0.10/ft.^{2}	0.33/ft.^{2}	1	2
Bedford	0.06/ft.^{2}	0.23/ft.^{2}	1	1
Woburn	0.18/ft.^{2}	—	2	—
Stoneham	—	0.80/ft.^{2}	—	1

SOURCE: Thomas Holzman, *Post-War Land Speculation in Middlesex County.*

Table 7.8
Average Capital Gain to Investment in Land by Cabot,
Cabot & Forbes

Town	Percent/Year	No. of Observations
Cambridge	10	2
Burlington	185	2
Lexington	100	1
		(composing about ½ of all owned land in the town)
Waltham	612	11

SOURCE: See Table 7.7.
[a]Confidence interval 55%–1169%. For other towns, data insufficient for confidence interval.

by CC & F for land.

Table 7.8 indicates the average return per year on investment in land. In each case, observations are used in which a price per square foot data are available for both transactions. Thus land purchased in Cambridge and Lexington but not resold later is excluded.

Table 7.8 makes clear the staggering capital gains CC & F was making along Route 128, particularly in Waltham.[53]

The relatively marked differences between tables 7.7 and 7.8 result mainly from adding the time element (how long the land is held) and by matching pairs of transactions to get prices on the same piece of land. The results in table 7.8 are explainable by the fact that the really expensive land in Technology Square and East Cambridge bought by CC & F was never sold, while the very cheap land acquired along Route 2 was. In Lexington, more than 50 percent of the total land acquired was sold in a single sale to Raytheon Corporation at a price of at least $0.12 per square foot, whereas ¾ of the land had been purchased by CC & F less than a year before at about $0.04 per square foot.

The pattern for Waltham shows purchases of enormous amounts of land at a low price, development of a minor part of the land and quick sale of much of the rest at a handsome profit. Lexington, the second largest development in Middlesex County, shows a somewhat similar pattern. Land was acquired cheaply in large amounts. Most of the land that was sold had been held less than a year. More land was purchased in 1960 and 1961 and developed, but almost none was sold.

In Cambridge, there are two patterns. The land on Route 2 was developed and sold much as land on Route 128 had been. Land in East Cambridge (as in Boston) was developed with high-rise buildings and not sold.[54]
Additional information on returns available in the core urbanized area is provided by the CC & F Land Trust prospectus of 1971, which discusses two CC & F urban developments: 28 State Street and Technology Square. For 28 State Street, completed in 1969, the original investment in the land was $1.5 million. The net cash flow in 1970 was about $0.6 million, a return on investment of 40 percent per year. The original investment for the land in Technology Square, Cambridge, amounted to about $1.7 million. Net cash flow was about $0.5 million in 1970, giving a rate of return of 30 percent.[55]
These returns may be understated, as it is likely that the depreciation deduction totally shelters net cash flow. Under the conservative assumptions of "straight-line declining" and 40-year useful life, the depreciation deduction would be $1.125 million annually, totally sheltering the net cash flow from taxes. In reality, the depreciation deduction was much larger, because CC & F probably uses a faster-than-linear depreciation and a shorter useful life.
Thus, urban and CBD developments can be quite lucrative, both in terms of providing direct income and indirectly by providing income through sheltering other income from taxes.
Even though these inner city returns are high, average return on investment in Waltham was considerably more than CC & F makes on investments in land and buildings in East Cambridge or the CBD. This raises the question of why CC & F invests in urban land and buildings, or in buildings on the periphery, when so much money can be made on land alone.
The answer is that investment in buildings on the periphery is part of the strategy of maximizing returns, by switching from the periphery to the CBD and back to the periphery. A good deal of money can be made quickly on the periphery as in Waltham. This income can be sheltered by depreciation and transferred to the CBD or East Cambridge, where it can be used to develop urban land. This developed urban land produces a steady, long-term stream of sizable rental income.
What is more, there is an aspect that involves political leverage. By putting up some buildings and getting large companies to occupy them (like Raytheon or New England Mutual Life), other firms are attracted

to the adjacent area: vacant land might not attract anyone. This in turn puts pressure on cities and towns to improve access, services, and zoning, thus raising the value of the land.

D. Builders of the Loom

Gerald Blakely and CC & F, like Whitney and the West End Street Railway, or Harrison Gray Otis and the Mount Vernon Proprietors, made exceptional profits from land development. Their analogues in other cities have also been studied. John Jacob Astor and Cornelius Vanderbilt in New York, Potter Palmer in Chicago, and Harrison Gray Otis (distant cousin of his Boston namesake) in Los Angeles are classic examples.[56] The Rockefeller interests in real estate in New York and elsewhere represent a similar expansion of wealth.[57] Other major developers in the Boston area could also be cited, from the Sumners of East Boston in the 1800s to the Rouses in downtown revitalization today.[58] Their returns might not equal those of Whitney or CC & F, but they exceed those available to the typical small businessman or homeowner.

Capturing the increased "rents" or land values generated by urban expansion is a classic case of individual reaping of "socially generated" wealth. Nineteenth-century reformers and political economists, from John Stuart Mill to Henry George, deplored these returns and sought to take them over for social uses, or to prevent the accumulation of permanent power by those who reap them.[59] A contemporary parallel is found in the work of Lester Thurow, who argues that the largest fortunes are the result of "lucky" capital asset inflation, rather than results of saving and investment at normal returns, and who therefore argues for inheritance taxes to reduce the size of the resulting fortunes.[60]

Certainly the generation of wealth inequalities is important. But it is only one effect of the activities of the large developers. They are also shapers of the pattern of urban growth. Through stimulation of or participation in transport investments, or the development of particular neighborhoods like Beacon Hill or the Route 128 suburbs, they shape the pattern of where metropolitan areas will expand. Through popularization of certain land-use styles—be they town houses, suburban tract homes, or industrial parks—they affect the demand and investment decisions of others. Their presence and power undercut the simple notion that suburbanization was just what "consumers" demanded.[61]

Nevertheless, even these developers operate within a larger milieu. Consumer demand is a partial limit to their power. Even Otis could not market the Dorchester Neck at a profit. So too is the power of government (even though at times developers may control government policy). Even CC & F could not get I-95 built south from downtown to Route 128. Finally, the developers—along with government and the market—are part of an overall economic system in which conflict between labor and capital may limit their ability to function or, conversely, give them new opportunities.

EIGHT

Fiscal Balkanization and
Suburban Devaluation

D EVELOPERS created many of Boston's suburbs. They opened
up new areas for business and for upper- or middle-class residents. They promoted a suburban way of life, through direct advertising
and through the creation of models for others to copy. They built part of
the transportation network that let people move out from the city. The
Charles River Bridge, the East Boston Ferry, the first suburban railroads, the trolley lines, the suburban electric network, and the suburban commercial malls and industrial parks were the work of private investment companies. These developers' profits were substantial. It is thus
tempting to see suburbanization as primarily their doing—and many
critical accounts of metropolitan expansion look to developer interest as
its cause.[1]

There are limits, however, to the degree to which suburbanization can
be credited to the Whitneys, the CC & Fs, and other major developers.
An orthodox economist would point out that a developer, no matter how
large, is ultimately only responding to consumers' demands: the consumer is ultimately the cause of suburbanization.[2] A Marxist economist,
while denying that consumers are sovereign over the economy, also sees
limits to the developers' power. The major decisions in the economy, in
the Marxist view, are made by a capitalist class, with interests in finance
and industry. This class needs to make and sell profitably a wide variety
of products, and to maintain labor discipline. This class may well desire
the building of suburbs, but if it finds suburbanization not to be in its
interest, developers will find themselves in conflict with even more
powerful members of their class. The power of developers to shape events

is thus circumscribed by broader needs of capitalists, and by the conflicts with labor to which capitalists also must respond.[3]

Recognition of the role of large developers does suggest that suburbanization was not *simply* the result of a completely free play of individual interests. The developers built some part, at least, of the loom on which weavers' small patterns were woven. We focus here on another set of builders of the loom—the various layers of government that oversee the Boston area. Like developers, these governments operate within an environment that limits their powers. Theories of voting behavior and public choice, operating on premises similar to those of market economics, suggest consumers' desires (reflected at the ballot box) place some limits on government.[4] Marxist analyses show that the needs of large investors are also a limiting factor. Yet governments do play a role in the suburbanization process. Viewed on a day-to-day basis, they are constantly creating the conditions within which people make their choices about moving to the suburbs, or staying where they are. Governments, like the big developers, are frequently the builders of the transportation systems and other public works that allow suburban development. They regulate most privately built works. Through the tax system and bank regulation, they greatly influence the private housing market. Taxes and public expenditures harm or benefit differentially those who live in different locations, and thus influence where people live. In some cases, these government actions may merely reinforce or reward decisions that would be taken anyway. In other cases, they shape the entire pattern of choices so as to produce outcomes that would not have emerged otherwise.

One way to appreciate the role of government in the suburbanization process is to look at the market forces which might tend to make people move to the suburbs, and then to consider ways in which the government affects those forces. This approach is partial: it leaves out the broader social conflicts and struggles that shape both the market and the government. (These will be dealt with in the next chapter.) Nonetheless, initial analysis of how government affects location incentives is a useful corrective to the view that suburbanization is exactly the pattern that everybody has individually selected through "free choice."

In chapter 1, we presented an analysis of a market model of suburbanization, with some indication of how government actions and financing accelerate a process of growth and devaluation which might occur to some extent even "on its own." Now, we attempt to quantify the role of government finance in the particular case of Boston's Balkanized metropolis. We also consider the history of how the region came to be so Balkanized, because that is an important historical specific, which, like the role of individual developers, has had an important effect in this particular metropolitan area.

A. The Balkanization of Boston

The most casual visitor to Boston will quickly notice its small size for a major city. Although Boston ranked eighth in population among the nation's metropolitan areas, as of 1978, it is 18th in area among central cities. As table 8.1 demonstrates, this disproportionality, though not unknown, is uncommon. Among the ten largest SMSAs, only Washington, D.C., and San Francisco have a similar disproportionate order of mag-

Table 8.1
The 10 Largest SMSAs Ranked by 1978 Metropolitan Population Size and Central City Size

Name of SMSA	SMSA Population Rank	Central City Size Rank by Population Rank	Land Area of Central City (sq. miles)
New York/ Northern N.J.	1	1	299.7
Los Angeles-Long Beach, Calif.	2	3	463.9
Chicago	3	2	222.8
Philadelphia/ Southern New Jersey	4	4	128.5
Detroit	5	6	138.0
San Francisco/ Oakland	6	16	45.4
Washington, D.C./ Maryland/Virginia	7	14	61.4
Boston	8[a]	*18*[a]	46.0
Dallas/Ft. Worth	9	7	498[b]
Houston	10	5	483.5

SOURCE: *Statistical Abstract of the United States:* 1980 (101st edition), U.S. Bureau of the Census, Washington, D.C., and *County and City Data Book*, 1977.
[a] Estimated by Interpolation.
[b] Dallas (270.4) and Ft. Worth (228.4) combined.

nitude ranking. In all three cases the cause is the same: a small-sized central city. The size of Washington, D.C., is set by the legislation which created the District from parts of Maryland and Virginia. To change its corporate limits would involve an act of Congress and the acquiescence of the two adjacent states. San Francisco's size is fixed in no small part by the extreme topography of mountain and water which characterize the peninsula upon which it sits and the bay area which surrounds it.

A part of the reason for Boston's small size is also topographical. As was discussed in chapter 2, Boston, like San Francisco, sits on a peninsula. But the waters that surround it do not have the width of San Francisco's bay. Some surrounding areas, across water and at the base of the peninsula, have been brought within city limits over the years. In the nineteenth century, attempts were made to annex surrounding areas. But this annexation movement soon waned. The reason is found in part in disputes over public finance and administration in the last half of the nineteenth century, but in part it goes back to the origins of European settlement in Massachusetts, and the institutions set up by the first Puritan colonists.

1. Origins of Subdivision

The initial settlement of the Massachusetts Bay Colony was a major experiment in theocratic democracy; for the pilgrim settlers, church and state were one. Central to the establishment of each town was the construction, use, and maintenance of a place of worship. The trip to the meeting-house was therefore an important part of the weekly social activities of the early residents.[5] As the population spread to remote reaches of the town, pressure began to build to duplicate vital public services, especially meeting houses, because of the significant travel needed to reach the center of town. Later, pressure for schools or roads became the issue which forced a subdivision; but in both cases it was a desire to pay for only those services used and to locate services near areas of population concentration which led to the many subdivisions which characterize contemporary metropolitan Boston.

The story of the early subdivisions has important similarities and differences to those which occur in the later nineteenth and earlier twentieth century during the first wave of suburbanization. The similarity is that subdivision came about essentially because of public finance and services disputes. The difference is that these early communities were far more integral as spatial units for living and working than would be the case during the era of suburbanization, when home and work became more separate.

The early history of Newton is illustrative of this process.[6] Newton was until well into the nineteenth century largely a farm community, with some industrial activity in the areas of its waterfalls where various mills could locate. Its early history could be described as a process of breaking large farm holdings into smaller ones. As the first settlers died, their holdings were divided among heirs.

Until it was established as a separate town in 1688, Newton was part of the town of Cambridge. It was then known as Cambridge Village. The first homesteader settled the area in 1639. By 1656 there were a sufficient number of inhabitants to avoid the long trek to Cambridge to attend worship services. Instead they met in the home of one of the more prosperous local residents. At that point they requested that the town of Cambridge remit their parish taxes so that they might build and maintain their own meeting house. The town refused and the General Court (the provincial legislature) sustained this refusal. The residents were not to be denied and in 1660 they built a new meeting house on land donated by one of their number. At that point the General Court allowed those living more than four miles from the Cambridge meeting house to be exempt from Cambridge church taxes. In 1664 eighty men and women then became the charter members of a new church in Cambridge Village.

Soon after the establishment of a separate parish, social isolation combined with geographic distance to create a desire for status as a separate town. A petition to that effect was brought before the General Court in 1672. The General Court deemed it advisable that Cambridge Village have three of its own selectmen and one constable but that it continue as part of the town of Cambridge. Another petition was brought to the court in 1678 and it too was turned down. Finally in 1688 the General Court became favorable to the petition for autonomy. On December 4, 1688, the town of New Cambridge was established. In 1691 the name of the town was formally changed to "Newtown" which soon became Newton.

At the same time that Boston was developing as a trading center, the

Table 8.2
Towns of Metropolitan Boston Established up to 1820

Year of Establishment as Town	Name	Year of Establishment as Town	Name
1630	Boston*	1713	Lexington
	Charlestown[a]*		Medway
	Dorchester[b]*		Weston
	Medford*	1719	Bellingham
	Roxbury[c]*	1724	Holliston
	Salem*		Walpole
	Watertown*	1725	Stoneham
1633	Scituate*	1726	Kingston
1635	Concord*		Stoughton
	Hingham*	1727	Hanover
	Weymouth*	1728	Middleton
1636	Cambridge*	1729	Bedford
	Dedham*	1730	Wilmington
1637	Duxbury*	1735	Acton
	Lynn*	1738	Waltham
1639	Sudbury*	1739	Chelsea
1640	Braintree	1752	Danvers
	Marshfield*	1754	Lincoln
1642	Woburn*	1765	Sharon
1643	Wenham	1770	Cohasset
1644	Hull*	1778	Foxborough
	Reading		Franklin
1645	Manchester	1780	Carlisle
1648	Topsfield		Wayland
1649	Malden*	1782	Lynnfield
	Marblehead	1783	Boxborough
1650	Medfield	1784	Dover
	Natick*	1792	Quincy
1662	Milton	1793	Hamilton
1668	Beverly		Randolph
1673	Wrentham	1797	Canton
1674	Sherborn*	1799	Burlington
1675	Framingham*	1807	Arlington
1688	Newton		Brighton[a]
1694	Boxford*	1812	Wakefield
1705	Brookline	1815	Saugus
1711	Needham	1820	Hanson
1712	Abington		
	Pembroke		

[a] Annexed to Boston in 1873.
[b] Annexed to Boston in 1869.
[c] Annexed to Boston in 1867.
*Town established as area of original settlement. Others were established through subdivision of previously established town.

surrounding region was also developing around agricultural and industrial bases. By 1700, the number of established towns had expanded from
28 to 35.[7] More significantly, as table 8.2 demonstrates, the manner of
establishment changed from that of the earlier period. All the new towns
resulted from the subdivision of previously existing towns. Previously,
most towns were established as areas of original settlement.

A perusal of table 8.2 indicates that this process of subdivision continued unabated until 1820. By that time, 72 of the 92 communities which
constitute the 1980 SMSA were established.

2. Nineteenth-Century Subdivision

After 1820 there was a 22-year hiatus until the next subdivision occurred, Somerville from Charlestown in 1842 (see table 8.3). By that time,
the insular independence of the towns had eroded under the impact of
industrialization, and a qualitatively new kind of subdivision had begun.
Although the basis for subdivision still remained disputes over services,
the era had changed from preindustrial to industrial and the later splits
are reflective of differences which have a social class and ethnic basis
rather than a purely locational one, as was the case in the earlier period.

Two different subdivisions help illustrate these new pressures. The cases
to be considered are Somerville, 1842, and Belmont, 1859.

By 1840, the town of Charlestown had essentially become two communities.[8] The area in the eastern section of town was a short ferry trip
across the harbor from the bustle and boom of growing Boston. The
coming of railroads, the growth of textile mills in the neighboring river
valleys, and a burgeoning workforce were creating lucrative economic
opportunities for those living in areas with good access to the scene of
all this activity. The eastern portion of the town was increasingly oriented toward the needs of the Boston economy. Its residents were most
concerned with spending their municipal revenues on those services and
capital improvements which would serve to enhance their economic position vis-à-vis Boston. The western portion of the town was still a locus
of agriculture and rural life.

The tensions between the two halves of the town had developed during the 1830s. There were two issues in particular which were the flash-
points for friction between the residents. One issue was the allocation of

Table 8.3
Towns of Metropolitan Boston
Established Between 1842 and 1897*

Year of Establishment	Name
1842	Somerville
1846	Ashland
	Revere
1849	Norwell
1850	Melrose
	Winchester
1851	West Roxbury[a]
1852	Swampscott
	Winthrop
1853	Nahant
	North Reading
1855	Peabody
1859	Belmont
1868	Hyde Park[b]
1870	Everett
	Norfolk
1872	Holbrook
	Norwood
1874	Rockland
1881	Wellesley
1885	Millis
1897	Westwood

*All towns in this period were established through
subdivision of previously established towns.
[a] Annexed to Boston in 1873.
[b] Annexed to Boston in 1911.

school expenditures between the two parts of town and the second was highway construction. The residents of the western portion of the town felt that the school expenditures on their portion of the town were inadequate both in terms of equity with the eastern part of town and the amount which they contributed to the local fisc. The merchants of the eastern part of town meanwhile wanted increased expenditures for the construction of roads and highways which would better serve their potential markets. These markets did not include the western part of town. In March 1842, after several attempts, the General Court finally granted the western residents their petition for separation as the town of Somerville.

In this case, the differences were those between rural, agricultural citizens and those who were now integrated into the urban, industrial economy. This is a different situation from the earlier subdivision between Newton and Cambridge in which all the residents were similarly situated socially but in which the geographic distances were the cause of tension in terms of services.

The town of Belmont could be described as a synthetic creation. At the time of its incorporation as a separate community in 1859, it was an area patched together from land in the towns of Cambridge, West Cambridge (later Arlington), and Watertown.[9] The basis for its incorporation appears to rest upon the desire of a group of affluent taxpayers and real estate speculators to create a residential enclave free from the costs of services for other classes of citizens. The area which became Belmont was sparsely inhabited (700 residents) when the Fitchburg railroad established station stops in the portion of West Cambridge which is now Belmont and at Waverly in the Watertown portion of the new community. The Fitchburg railroad ran from Fitchburg in the central part of the state through Waltham, Watertown, West Cambridge, and Cambridge, then over a bridge across the Charles River into the North End of Boston. As a result of the rail connection to Boston, the area became accessible to those groups who could afford the high cost of a daily commutation ticket. As was the case in Newton at this time, the Belmont area became home to a small group of wealthy families fleeing from the congestion, filth, and noise of the dense urban core. While the character of the area residents began to change, their total numbers did not increase rapidly. By 1853 there were 1,004 residents in the area. In 1854 the first petition for the separate incorporation of this area was brought before the General Court. This petition and similar ones were turned down until 1859, when it was finally accepted. A perusal of the recorded speeches pertaining to the issue makes clear that it was a group of wealthy residents and real estate developers who saw the potential for additional upper-class housing if the area could be set off as a separate tax and service jurisdiction.[10] It was the political influence which goes with wealth that eventually carried the day and led to subdivision.

At the time of petition, the area was immediately well off. It had a total of 3,648 acres, a population of 1,175, and a total valuation of more than $2 million. On a per capita basis that amounted to a valuation of $1,733 compared with $1,137 in West Cambridge, $756 in Watertown, and $695 in Waltham. Under the then-existing laws, state tax on domestic corporations was remitted back to the communities in which the stockholders resided in proportion to the amount of stock they held. For towns like Belmont that was a bonanza of additional revenue. In 1865 when the redistribution of this tax revenue amounted to $.91 per capita for the state as a whole, Belmont was receiving $3.04 per capita.[11] In addition, it must be remembered that poor relief was still a town responsibility. Consequently, communities like Belmont did not have to divert any of their wealth to this task, unlike the case in the industrial communities in which the new urban labor force was residing. As a result of such incorporations as Belmont, the rich were able to maximize their benefits and minimize their costs. The infrastructure built during this era created a town of services and charm sufficient to maintain its upper-class flavor through the era of trolley and automobile suburbanization.

The importance of the preceding two anecdotes lies not just in their typicality to other such subdivision stories, but also because of what they reveal about local governance in New England. In the rest of the nation, counties bear primary responsibility for local governance, with townships and unincorporated villages as refinements. In New England, the roles are reversed: counties provide refinements and towns bear primary responsibility. There is no provision for the unincorporated village. As a result, fiscal fights such as the ones described could only be resolved by the creation of more and more, smaller and smaller, antonomous units of government. While such a solution has much to recommend it as a contribution to participatory democracy and/or social class isolation, it is an inefficient way to organize urban services. It has the potential to lead to costly duplications of both physical infrastructure and service organizations. Such rising costs could have stopped the metropolitan urbanization of Boston dead in its tracks. If subdivision was the problem, then was annexation the solution?

3. The Annexation Era

Between 1868 and 1911, six towns were annexted to Boston, five of them in the short space of time between 1868 and 1873. The annexation movement was not unique to Boston. Other cities, particularly the older ports like Philadelphia and New York, experienced a similar rise and fall of annexation movements. But Boston's movement, and its collapse, were among the earliest major examples and to an extent pointed the way for other cities.

The annexation movement must be seen in the light of prior subdivisions. Massachusetts town subdivisions had roots in the desire of people to live close to those of a similar status. They also had a root in a desire of the more affluent to avoid supporting services for the less affluent when possible. Besides these class roots, there was also a racial one by the 1850s: the desire to avoid Irish immigrants as much as possible. This cut across class lines, and was present in poor and middle-class as well as upper-class native residents.

While subdivision provided a quick and simple answer to questions of exclusivity, it also avoided two more complex issues facing the region. The first was the need to build a range of public works and public agencies to permit metropolitan growth, so that all the economic benefits of urban growth could continue. The second was the political reality that if everyone withdrew from the city, the despised Irish would have dominance over the region's most precious economic and social resource: the city of Boston itself. The annexations of 1868–1873 represent an attempt to resolve these two impasses.

Consider first the impact of sheer numbers on the need for urban infrastructure. In 1820, the commonwealth's constitution was amended to permit towns to adopt a city form of government with an elected legislative council and an elected executive, the mayor. The impetus behind this amendment was the fact that direct democracy in the form of town meeting was falling apart under the weight of increasing numbers of people in several towns, the leading example being Boston itself.[12] Attempts to shore up town meeting governance by providing for elected selectmen to oversee municipal matters between town meetings were not working. But giving Boston a mayor, while it facilitated some public works like the clearance of the north slope of Beacon Hill, did not resolve all of the city's problems.

From Boston's establishment as a city until the middle of the 1840s, city governance could be characterized as more efficient administration for an overgrown town.[13] Beginning in the 1840s, there was a qualitative change in the numbers and kinds of services needed. This change was precipitated by the fact that as the living density of the area increased, it became increasingly difficult to meet the needs of more people merely by extending and expanding existing services. Rather a reorganization was needed which usually involved expending large sums for capital improvements. Such capital budgeting and long-range planning involved the development of whole new perspectives on provision of services and spatial relations. Hence it is in the 1840s that city government similar to the modern style begins to emerge. The first area of need in which this change becomes apparent is water supply.

The original relocation of the Boston settlement to the Shawmut Peninsula was based on a water supply problem. From that time (1630), until 1825, the question of water supply was a settled issue. The high water table, surrounding rivers, and low levels of industrial activity made the problem nonexistent. However, the rapid population growth of the early nineteenth century combined with the rising river pollution caused by industrialization in and around the city began to make water supply a problem. In 1825 the first of several reports calling for the systematic organization and delivery of water to the city began to circulate. After approximately twenty years of controversy and delay, a plan was agreed upon for piping water into the city from Long Pond (now Lake Cochituate) in Natick, twelve miles west of the city. Beginning in 1846, the cost of water was added to the list of municipal expenditures.[14]

The impact upon the finances of the city was both instantaneous and sizable. In 1845, total municipal expenditures were $974,102. In 1846 this jumped by 79 percent, to $1,742,947. Approximately 86 percent of the increase in expenditures could be attributed to infrastructure: the new water system, streets and sewers. Expenditures in any particular category of municipal activity will exhibit cyclical behavior because of the unevenness of capital expenditures; nonetheless, the city was now embarked on a series of expenditures which, whatever their cyclical behavior, had a very clear upward secular trend. In 1840, the city spent $6.78 per capita for all its activities. By 1865 that figure had jumped to $25.94 per capita, a 5.35 percent annual compounded growth rate.[15]

To some extent, the impressive growth in per capita spending is still an understatement. It must be remembered that population was also growing steadily. In the 25 years in question, it grew from 93,383 to 192,318, a compound growth rate of 2.95 percent per year. The absolute spending level rose 909%, or 9.69 percent per annum, compounded. Infrastructure spending—streets, sewers, bridges, water and lights—rose even more rapidly: by 11.92 percent per annum compounded. In 1840

236

Table 8.4
Infrastructure as a Proportion of
Total Municipal Expenditures:
Boston 1840–1865

Year	Proportion
1840	13.50%
1845	24.73
1850	42.67
1855	33.11
1860	40.73
1865	22.34

SOURCE: Derived from Charles P. Huse, *The
Financial History of Boston from May 1, 1822
to January 31, 1907.* (1916; rpt. New York: Russell & Russell, 1967.)

infrastructure expenditures were only 13.5 percent of the total budget.
In 1865 they were 22.34 percent but in the intervening years they had
been more than two-fifths of the budget, as is demonstrated in table 8.4.

As a way of easing into the revenue side of the ledger to complete this
brief excursion into Boston financial history, it is worth noting the fateful
decision made by the city at Mayor Josiah Quincy's prodding. The decision was to have the water system built and maintained by the city
rather than a private water company. A group of capitalists was ready to
undertake the venture. The difficulty would have been that private undertakings need to earn private profits. Public undertakings, on the other
hand, can yield more generalized benefits in a far different and usually
longer time frame. In the case of the water system, in only one year in
the 62-year period from 1846 to 1908 did revenues exceed expenditures.
It was unambiguously a subsidized service. A private company would have
had to charge at least enough to cover costs. Governments, by providing
subsidized water and other municipal services, contributed to the robustness of the regional economy.

That robustness, in turn, was repaid to the city in rising property values and hence tax base. The 9.69 percent annual rate of growth in total
spending, with all its contributions to the population's living standard,
was partially funded through the rise in property values. Between 1840
and 1865 the tax rate rose from $5.50 per $1,000 of property value to
$15.80 per $1,000; a rise of only 4.31 percent per annum. The gap between the rate of spending growth and tax rate growth was filled by a

Government support for development. Physical infrastructure was essential for suburbanization. The question of which local tax base should pay for this public investment led to controversy. Annexations, town subdivisions and the creation of metropolitan districts were all tried.

The Water Works at Chestnut Hill, ca. 1890. Originally built by the City of Boston and later incorporated in the Metropolitan Water District.

Early Urban Infrastructure, ca. 1890. Note the wood sidewalk and street utilities.

5.63 percent annual growth rate in total property valuation, much of it new property.

Boston's favored position in the search for water gave it an advantage over some of the smaller surrounding towns which could not afford equivalently expensive systems. For these towns, infrastructure require-ments suggested a need, literally, to tap into the urban center's infras-tructure. For a time in the mid-1800s, the way to do this seemed to be annexation to the city.

While its water system was making Boston an attraction for surround-ing towns, another factor was also becoming important. The city, and its budget, became the stakes in an emerging ethnic conflict (with class overtones) between the old "Yankee" elite of Massachusetts and new Irish immigrants.

At the time of Boston's establishment as a city, the number of Irish arriving at the port of Boston was notable but small. In 1821 there were 827 passengers arriving from Ireland. The 1820 population of the city was 43,298. The major influx of Irish did not begin until after 1840. Ta-ble 8.5 summarizes the Irish migrations to Boston for the 20-year period 1841–1861. As the table makes clear, the 10-year period from 1846 to 1856 was the time when the influx of Irish to Boston was at its peak. After that, it subsided greatly.[16]

This migration had a major impact upon all the cities and towns of the then-metropolitan area, as table 8.6 demonstrates. By 1865, approxi-

Table 8.5
Passengers Entering Boston by Sea 1841–1861

Year	Origin in Ireland	Total	Irish as Percentage of Total
1841	10,157	36,741	27.64%
1846	65,556	112,664	58.19
1851	63,831	117,505	54.32
1856	22,681	69,923	32.44
1861	6,973	42,721	16.32

SOURCE: Adapted from Handlin, *Boston's Immigrants* (Cambridge: Har-vard University Press, *rev. ed.* 1959) p. 242. The numbers in the table are not necessarily the number of actual immigrants, but the place or origin of arrivees at the port. Thus, for example, in 1841, of the total arrivees, 7,177 listed the United States as their place of origin. Nonetheless, the number does reflect the flow and ebb of Irish Immigration to the Boston region, if not the exact count.

Table 8.6
Population of Metropolitan Boston by Irish and Non-Irish Nativity for 1865

	Irish Nativity		U.S. Nativity			
Community	Number	% of Total	Number	% of Total	Total Population	Irish & U.S. as % of Total
Brighton	820	21.28%	2,840	73.69%	3,854	94.97%
Cambridge	5,588	19.19	21,063	72.35	29,112	91.54
Charlestown	4,443	16.83	20,423	77.36	26,399	94.19
Somerville	1,729	18.49	7,050	75.38	9,353	93.86
West Cambridge						
(Arlington)	551	19.98	2,039	73.93	2,758	93.91
Brookline	1,457	27.69	3,542	67.31	5,262	95.00
Dorchester	1,647	15.37	8,393	78.31	10,717	93.78
Roxbury	6,294	22.14	18,762	66.00	28,462	88.14
West Roxbury	1,426	20.63	5,029	72.76	6,912	93.39
Boston	46,225	24.04	126,432	65.74	192,318	89.78
Chelsea	1,655	11.49	11,551	80.20	14,403	91.69
North Chelsea						
(Revere)	101	11.77	720	83.92	858	95.69
Winthrop	129	13.74	465	73.46	633	87.20
TOTAL	72,065	21.77%	228,309	68.97%	331,005	90.74%

Adapted from Handlin, p. 246. (See Table 8.5).

mately one of every five area residents was of Irish birth. This Irish-born population was spread more or less proportionately among the area's cities and towns. The proportion of Irish nativity ranged from a low of about 11.5 percent in Chelsea to a high of almost 28 percent in Brookline. To some extent, these figures understate the degree of Irish influence in the area, because they do not separately count those people of American nativity but Irish parentage. The comparatively even spread of Irish among the municipalities of the region is reflective of the fact that low-wage factory and domestic work was far more widespread than it would be later, when cheap transit would make social separations along spatial lines even more distinct than the horsecars and railroad suburbanization ever could.

The impact of the Irish is even more powerful for another reason. As the last column of table 8.6 shows, the proportion of population of either U.S. or Irish nationality accounts for about 90 percent of the entire area population. The remaining 10 percent is spread over a wide range of nationalities. This meant that for the average non-Irish area resident, the terms "immigrant" and "Irish" were synonymous. Consequently, native mistrust of foreigners translated into mistrust of the Irish. Lastly, it is important to note the unique place of Boston in this. Approximately two-thirds of all the Irish-born population of the area resided in the city of Boston while only about half of the native-born population was similarly located. Thus for better or worse, Boston was viewed as the home of the Irish. This led Massachusetts leaders to fear that the city might fall into the hands of the new arrivals. To prevent this, annexation might be an option, if it could dilute the Irish percentage in a new, larger city.

These two factors of infrastructure development and ethnic composition came to the fore when it was proposed that Boston expand its territory by annexing surrounding cities and towns. Annexation was the complete opposite to the direction in which the area had been heading since its original settlement. Despite this break with tradition, the idea had much going for it. From the standpoint of the city fathers, it held the promise of allowing Boston to grow into a major city with ample land for industry, housing, and open space for parks. The process of building a new expansive city could also provide many interesting economic opportunities for enterprising city officials. To residents of the surrounding cities and towns, the chief advantage to be gained was the use of the growing Boston tax base to finance water, sewers, streets, lights, and schools for their communities.

The counterargument to this was voiced by groups in the several towns in question, which feared getting caught in the corruption and machinations of Boston politics; such politics were looking less and less desirable to middle-class New Englanders viewing it from the outside.

As with most such debates, there was a second agenda, less visible and less appealing to those of democratic values, but nonetheless real and most probably more important to the ultimate outcome. This hidden agenda involved the class and ethnic conflicts which swirled around the Irish residents of the city, who were increasingly becoming a force with which to reckon. The dilemma involving the Irish can be summarized as follows: If the city's boundaries were left alone, the Irish would soon become the dominant political group in the city. The central location of the city meant it was the locus of all the region's vital economic activities. The men who owned and controlled these valuable resources were not anxious to see even partial control over their property move into the hands of an Irish working-class political establishment. Annexation held out the promise that the city government might remain in native, middle-class hands, as the new electorate from the surrounding territories might be able to outvote the Irish wards of the central city. This second agenda became quite explicit on occasion, as the following quote from testimony by M. E. Ingalls before the General Court's committee on towns on April 18, 1870, illustrates:

> Again, Mr. Chairman, Boston cannot be commercially great unless she is numerically great, and has a healthy population, and sufficient room to expand and enlarge in. They tell us here that large cities become corrupt. What are the facts in this matter? Not that *large* cities breed corruption, but that *crowded* cities breed corruption . . . unless you give Boston room to expand and enlarge; unless you give her the opportunity to keep within her borders the bone and muscle which go to make up a good city government, she will not continue so. . . . What makes New York corrupt to-day? Is it because she has annexed territory? Is it because adjoining districts have been enclosed? No; it is because New York is an island, and there is no chance for annexation anywhere; and her bone and muscle her honest men go to Jersey and Brooklyn to live, and leave the City Government to be carried on by the crowds that dwell in the lower wards of the city. That is what makes New York corrupt today. It is not because she has got so much territory; it is because they have shut out the very men who make a good city government; and the policy of the gentlemen who appear here to oppose annexation is to make Boston in the future what New York is to-day. The only thing that can save her and make her in the future, as she has been in the past, an honest and virtuous city, is to enclose these surrounding towns, and keep within her borders the men who are the proper men to form a good and wise and honest government.[17]

In the year between 1868 and 1873, voters in the towns of Brighton, Charlestown, Dorchester, Roxbury, and West Roxbury were sufficiently convinced of the fiscal benefits of annexation to accept the plans developed in the state legislature. From that initial success, it would have appeared that a large regional city with its center on the Shawmut Peninsula was about to emerge. However, as quickly as the initial successes were achieved, the whole process came to a sudden and virtually complete halt when Brookline's voters declined the planned annexation of their town scheduled for 1873. That refusal, combined with the fiscal contractions precipitated by the national economic downtown of the 1870s, effectively ended the annexation movement. By the 1880s, the region's leaders began to turn to other devices to create regional infrastructure, and most of the potential candidate communities had begun developing their own capital-improvement projects. There was one final annexation—Hyde Park in 1911. Other than that, the annexation issue was a closed chapter.

To understand the social-class tensions which shaped the solutions of the 1880s and 1890s, it is worth perusing the transcript of A. D. Chandler, attorney for the anti-annexationists, when he testified before the legislature on the reasons for Brookline's refusal to be annexed. He first addressed himself to the question of political influence.

> It is claimed by annexationists, that because many Brookline
> men pay taxes in Boston they "should have a voice in the
> management of the city's affairs." Now I venture the asser-
> tion that the anti-annexationists pay far more taxes in Boston
> than the annexationists, and yet the anti-annexationists are
> quite content with the extent of their present influence in the
> management of Boston's affairs; and that influence is often
> powerful, though silent; quite as powerful as it would be if
> after annexation these tax payers attempted the farce of trying
> to outvote the 3,000 voters alone, now admitted by Bostoni-
> ans to be wrongfully on their registration lists.[18]

Chandler made quite clear what his views were on the electoral process in Boston. Of more interest is his ready assertion that the men of
Brookline were politically powerful in Boston without voting. If there
were any doubts that his clients were the region's movers and shakers,
this next quote lays such doubt to rest once and for all:

> Akin to this is the wearisome repetition of that erroneous and
> illogical assertion, that Brookline men make all their fortunes
> in Boston, or transact all their business there, and therefore
> ought to live in Boston. If the wealthy men of Brookline de-
> pended on Boston for their fortunes, or for their business,
> many of them might starve within a twelvemonth. Of all ar-
> guments advanced for annexation, no one is more readily an-
> swered than this. Take the case of a wholesale merchant. Be-
> fore leaving his home in Brookline he learns the state of the
> sugar market, for instance, from the morning paper and writes

or telegraphs at once to Cuba or elsewhere for the purchase of a cargo, which he afterwards sells in New York at great profit. How much of the money was made in the transaction out of Boston? Suppose the same person is in New York or Chicago on business, and the market reports justify his making a venture in indigo or wool; he telegraphs to India or Australia for the desired quantity and before the cargo is half way home, he has sold it at a profit in Liverpool. Every dollar of this was made in the Eastern Hemisphere, yet he is a Boston merchant living in Brookline, and for convenience puts his name down on the hotel register in New York or Chicago as from Boston. So with the manufacturers from Brookline, whose offices are in Boston, but whose factories are in Lowell, Lawrence, Lynn, Clinton, Taunton, Fall River, and elsewhere, and whose goods are sold in probably every State and Territory in the Union. Boston might be burnt up or sunk into the sea, and the manufacturers would go on as before, because their goods are made in other cities, and the market for them is the nation at large, Boston affording merely a convenient centre for counting and desk rooms. What might not be said of the wealth made out of land, railroads and mines in the West by Brookline men? But why pursue these illustrations. It is apparent that the great fortunes of the heavy tax payers of Brookline have been made largely outside of Boston, and not within it, otherwise Boston would not only be the Hub but the Whole of the Universe. The world at large, all parts of which have paid tribute to Boston merchants, would ridicule the monstrous conceit which attributed to Boston itself the fortunes its merchants have made.[19]

It is also worth noting who the specific clients were that Chandler represented. They were T. P. Chandler, Augustus Lowell, Ignatius Sargent, John L. Gardner, Amos A. Lawrence, Robert Amory, T. E. Francis, James S. Amory, John C. Abbott and Isaac Taylor—a blue-ribbon list of Boston area bluebloods.

On the annexation side of the debate in town was Henry A. Whitney, a leading Republican liberal of the era and the owner of the West End Street Railway. At the time of the debate, Whitney, as we have seen, was buying land on Beacon Street, Brookline's principal east–west artery. He was planning streetcar service down the length of Beacon Street and into the center of Boston.

Brookline's refusal to be annexed not only put the brakes on the entire annexation movement, but also lead to the recasting of the area's fiscal structure. The failure to annex this upper-class enclave indicated that "the proper men to form a good and wise and honest government" for Boston had no desire to take up the challenge. Rather they preferred to withdraw into their own community and underwrite its services. This gave them the best of two worlds: the benefits of living within three to four miles of downtown Boston without having any of the fiscal responsibilities for the social and economic costs of the area. However, as with most gains, there was cost. If the upper classes were not going to challenge the lower classes electorally for control of the city, then they would have to exercise more effectively that "powerful though silent" influence that Alfred Chandler alluded to in his brief against annexation.

This was done through the imposition of increasing state control over Boston's finances and municipal affairs during the 1890s and onward, and the development of regional agencies that would allow the taxation of Boston's economic base to expand regional infrastructure. However, before discussing these developments, let us first review the impact of the annexations which did occur upon Boston itself. From the standpoint of the annexed communities, the change led to a spurt in their population growth rates while that of the pre-annexation parts of the city slowed down. This can be seen in table 8.7. This growth was no doubt fostered by city spending for new services for these areas.

This can be seen in the jump in the cost of government. Before annexation, the per capita expenditure of the city had been $24.94 in 1865. By 1870, that had risen to $46.15. The national economic depression of the early 1870s had only a minimal effect on this growth in per capita spending. In 1875, spending per capita had only fallen slightly, to $42.92. In absolute terms, between 1865 and 1875, total city expenditures had

Table 8.7
Annual Population Growth Rates for Boston and the Annexed Communities 1855–1865 and 1865–1875 (in percent)

Decade	Boston	Roxbury	Dorchester	W. Roxbury	Brighton	Charlestown
1855–65	1.84	4.41	2.54	3.69	2.90	1.98
1865–75	1.54	5.90	3.95	5.48	4.87	2.40

SOURCE: Massachusetts censuses.

risen 142.24 percent, from $6,389,822 to $15,478,704. That translated into an annual growth rate of 9.25 percent for the decade. Despite this large increase in spending, the tax rate actually dropped about 15 percent over the decade from $15.80 per $1,000 assessed valuation, to $13.30. Once again, the offset was the increase in total valuation, which grew at 7.88 percent per year. Real estate valuations grew even faster, at an annual rate of 10.73 percent per annum. The growth of the city along with its tax base meant that Boston could deliver improved infrastructure and services to the newly annexed parts of the city.

While Boston was able to meet its commitments to its constituent communities, the collapse of the annexation movement effectively placed the large Boston tax base beyond the service of other parts of the region. Between 1865 and 1875, total property valuation in Boston rose from 37% of aggregate state valuation to 43 percent.[20] Furthermore, it must be remembered that large amounts of the commercial and industrial property in Boston were owned by businessmen who were increasingly making communities like Brookline, Belmont, and Newton their place of residence. These upper-class natives did not look with much favor upon the increasingly working-class and Irish composition of the city. All the elements were in place for some sort of change.

In 1875, the State Legislature, in a major break with approximately 250 years of home rule, imposed its first significant control on the ability of cities and towns to incur debt. The act placed limits on both short-term debt in anticipation of revenues and long-term debt. A ceiling of 3 percent of total valuation for total debt outstanding was imposed. Long-term debt could not extend beyond ten years with the exception of sewer construction, which was permitted twenty years for repayment. Debts for water supply and aid to railroads were exempt from any limitations at all. Sinking funds were made obligatory for the purpose of all debt retirement beyond temporary borrowings. This act and some minor ones passed later that year were held constitutional by the Massachusetts Supreme Court. This legislation thus established the principle that the state could regulate local finance.[21]

In 1885, the year in which the first Irish Catholic mayor assumed office in Boston, the debt limitation legislation was amended and Boston was singled out for special treatment. For all cities except Boston, the debt limit was lowered to 2½ percent of valuation; for Boston, the limit was set at 2 percent. The 1885 legislation also imposed municipal tax levy limits. The limits for the rest of the state was set at $12.00 per $1,000 of total valuation. For Boston, the limit was set at $9.00 per $1,000, 25 percent below the statewide limit.[22]

The debt and tax limitation laws had little more than symbolic value as the developing economy of the state required far more spending. The legislature found itself with a new occupation: granting special exemptions for one reason or another. They also continued to modify the terms of the legislation to make them more liberal. Furthermore, municipal accountants and clerks became quite adept at staying within the letter of the law if not always the spirit.

It is worth noting that in addition to the special debt and tax limitations that Boston was made subject to, it also lost the power to appoint its own police commissioner in 1885. The Boston police commissioner was appointed by the governor. The city did not regain this elementary power of home rule until 1968.

The arguments used to strip Boston of its fiscal and police autonomy were never explicitly put in anti-Irish terms, but the allusion to corruption and greedy individuals taking the place of public-spirited citizens in political life left little doubt about who the culprits were, ethnically speaking.

There is little doubt that Boston, as any large city, had its share of corruption, but the response to it seems out of proportion to the problem. A perusal of the expenditures and receipts of the city in comparison to the state of other cities similarly situated would not reveal any extraordinary problems to warrant the particular responses. Consider table 8.8. It compares the net (unfunded) debt as a proportion of total valuation for the years 1865, and 1871 through 1875, for Boston and the state as a whole. As the table reveals, Boston's debt proportion never exceeded the statewide average. Furthermore, it should be remembered that Boston's valuation was about two-fifths of the state total. Therefore, Boston must be viewed as the moderating influence in the state average. Yet it is these statewide ratios which are cited as evidence in the legislature's decision to impose debt limits with all their special impact on Boston.

The 1885 legislation, which was particularly hard on Boston, was instituted after a decade in which the city was especially prudent. The 1870s were years of national economic stagnation. Expenditure growth and debt growth were quite in line with the changes in the city's tax base. Table

Table 8.8
Ratio of Net Debt to Total Valuation for
Boston and Massachusetts

Year	State Ratio	City Ratio
1865	2.6%	2.6%
1871	2.6	2.4
1872	2.6	2.3
1873	3.0	2.4
1874	3.5	3.4
1875	3.8	3.4

SOURCES: (1) Royal S. Van de Woystyne, *State Control of Local Finance in Massachusetts* (Cambridge: Harvard University Press, 1934); (2) derived from data in appendix II of C. P. Huse, *The Financial History of Boston* (1916; rpt. New York: Russell and Russell, 1967).

8.9 summarizes the annual average growth rates for the key fiscal measures for the city in five-year intervals from 1850 to 1890. There is nothing in this table to arouse suspicion of irresponsibility out of the ordinary. It would be in the area of debt financing where one would expect to find evidence of serious pillage of the public treasury. Yet the only period of high debt growth was the period in which the city had high infrastructure costs for the annexed communities.

While limitations such as the 1875 and 1885 acts could satisfy punitive desires with respect to the perceived misbehavior of the upstart politicians who were coming into ascendency, they had little to do with the need to find mechanisms to make Boston part of a dynamic and growing

Table 8.9
Annual Growth Rates of Boston's Financial System 1850–1890

Period	Total Exped.	Total Valuation	Tax Rate	Net Fund Debt
1850–55	3.14%	6.09%	2.52%	0.75%
1855–60	5.09	2.73	3.85	4.26
1860–65	12.27	6.08	11.18	5.32
1865–70	14.36	9.45	−0.64	−0.58
1870–75	4.37	6.33	−2.18	23.49
1875–80	−3.44	−4.24	2.10	.47
1880–85	2.37	1.40	−3.38	−2.45
1885–90	3.97	3.70	0.77	4.78

SOURCE: Derived from Huse, see Table 8.8.

urban region even if the area was to be balkanized into several small cities and towns. In the 1890s, the problem would become central to the concerns of the area. This would be even more pressing because of the perfection of electric traction. Cheap, practical, and fast transit was available for the region to spread in the first wave of suburbanization. But annexation was not politically feasible.

The stalemate was resolved in the 1890s by the formation by the state of regional commissions. Water, sewer, and park commissions were formed. They were later merged into a metropolitan district commission, which today also runs some of the region's highways. A transit authority (now called the Massachusetts Bay Transit Authority) was created later as well. The impact of these authorities on suburban infrastructure was discussed in chapter 2. They did overcome some of the problems of balkanization, allowing taxes from different towns to be combined for public works. But they also created new splits in the metropolitan area, distinguishing high-contribution from low-contribution, or member from nonmember groups of towns.

Appendix E indicates that transportation financing for the MBTA and MDC taxes inner-ring towns more heavily than it does outer ring areas; outer ring commuters use the facilities more heavily than they contribute taxes. But this particular problem is part of a more general problem of tax and service inequality that balkanization brings about. This inequality, in turn, may bring about both a decline in property values (a devaluation of assets) in the disadvantaged communities, and an incentive to move to lower-tax (generally more suburban) towns.

B. Fiscal Consequences of Balkanization

In the public mind, a principal problem of Boston and its inner-ring communities is "high taxes." The real property tax has historically been the major source of local revenues in Massachusetts. In some of the communities of the metropolitan area, tax rates fell between 100 and 200 mills per dollar of assessed value (10–20 percent of value) until the recent state referendum to lower rates. Although assessment rates in the communities with highest taxes fell below market values, this still left tax rates at close to 10 percent of real values in some cases. In general, tax rates are higher in towns and cities with lower mean family incomes and in towns closer to the center of Boston.

Tax and expenditure differences between towns, and movement to evade taxes, are old stories in Massachusetts. Complaints have long been voiced that high taxes are causing an exodus of families (particularly the rich and the middle class), deterring investment and depressing property values. Less than twenty years after Independence, a merchant named Joseph Barrell had a house in South End of Boston but, "thinking himself unreasonably taxed by the town fathers bought another in Charlestown."[23] By 1889, migration from town to town to escape taxes was considered a major problem for the Commonwealth. Some towns had even been created by secession to be tax havens. As J. M. Benton Jr., complained:

> This system of town government, the most admirable system of local self-government for many purposes which ever existed, has, with the constantly increasing inequality of division of property, been constantly taken advantage of to enable wealth to avoid its fair share of the burdens of taxation. Wealthy men have either moved into existing towns and formed little communities of their own in one part of them, have induced the legislature to set them off into a new town, and have been assessed their property at less than its real value, and by massing large wealth in a small territory, have secured exceedingly low tax rates. This has induced other rich men to go into these towns, and the result has been a constantly decreasing tax rate in them with a consequent constantly increasing tax rate in others.[24]

A brief examination of tax inequality today and a century ago indicates some aspects of the problem, and the extent to which it has worsened. Table 8.10 compares the highest and lowest tax rates in each county of Massachusetts for 1873 and 1973. The table shows that the ratio between the highest and lowest rates in each county (except for Dukes) was greater in 1973 than in 1873, often by a considerable margin. These ratios, however, are for nominal tax rates on the assessed valuation of properties, and not on their true values, which often differ from assessments. Because assessment ratios differ among towns, differences in real tax among towns may not always follow the same pattern as differences among nominal tax rates.

Table 8.10
Tax Rate Inequality by Counties, 1873 and 1973

County and Year		High		Low		Ratio
BARNSTABLE	1873	Eastham	27.0	Mashpee	6.5	4.2:1
(real)	1973	Falmouth	42.4	Truro	14.6	2.9:1
(nom.)	1973	Falmouth	82.6	Barnstable	14.8	5.6:1
BERKSHIRE	1873	Florida	28.0	Dalton	8.1	3.5:1
(real)	1973	Florida	84.0	Tyring'm	17.0	4.9:1
(nom.)	1973	Richm'd	136.0	Tyring'm	17.0	8.0:1
BRISTOL	1873	New Bedford	16.2	Easton	10.0	1.6:1
(real)	1973	Fall River	86.0	Dartmouth	30.0	2.8:1
(nom.)	1973	Fairhaven	194.0	Dartmouth	30.0	6.5:1
DUKES	1873	Gay Head	30.0	Gosnold	8.6	3.5:1
(real)	1973	Gay Head	32.4	W. Tisbury	14.0	2.3:1
(nom.)	1973	Oak Bluff	85.0	Tisbury	25.0	3.4:1
ESSEX	1873	Rockport	21.0	Nahant	4.2	5.0:1
(real)	1973	Salem	69.9	Rockport	32.6	2.1:1
(nom.)	1973	Lynn	237.0	Rockport	37.0	6.4:1
FRANKLIN	1873	Monroe	32.0	Gill	12.0	2.7:1
(real)	1973	New Salem	72.2	Erving	27.0	2.7:1
(nom.)	1973	New Salem	164.0	Erving	27.0	6.1:1
HAMDEM	1873	Granville	21.5	Russell	10.0	2.1:1
(real)	1973	Springfield	73.8	Tolland	24.0	3.1:1
(nom.)	1973	Palmer	193.0	Southwick	34.0	5.7:1
HAMPSHIRE	1873	Pelham	34.0	Hatfield	9.0	3.8:1
(real)	1973	Williamsburg	62.0	Middlefield	31.0	2.0:1
(nom.)	1973	Huntington	186.0	Middlefield	32.0	5.8:1
MIDDLESEX	1873	Townsend	30.5	Stow	8.9	3.4:1
(real)	1973	Cambridge	94.0	Tewksbury	32.0	2.9:1
(nom.)	1973	Carlisle	224.0	Tewksbury	32.0	7.0:1
NORFOLK	1873	Medway, Foxboro	21.1	W. Roxbury	8.6	2.4:1
(real)	1973	Quincy	75.6	Dedham	36.5	2.1:1
(nom.)	1973	Plainville	170.0	Bellingham	39.0	4.4:1
PLYMOUTH	1873	Scituate	22.2	Kingston	5.5	4.0:1
(real)	1973	Brockton	95.0	Wareham	38.0	2.5:1
(nom.)	1973	Brockton	180.0	Wareham	38.0	4.7:1
SUFFOLK	1873	Chelsea	17.5	Winthrop	12.5	1.4:1
(real)	1973	Boston	163.3	Winthrop	55.6	2.9:1
(nom.)	1973	Boston	196.7	Winthrop	63.2	3.1:1
WORCESTER	1873	Clinton	23.5	Sutton	9.5	2.5:1
(real)	1973	Worcester	150.6	Douglas	30.0	5.0:1
(nom.)	1973	Oakham	314.0	Douglas	30.0	10.5:1
STATEWIDE	1873	Pelham	34.0	Nahant	4.2	8.1:1
(real)	1973	Boston	163.3	W. Tisbury	14.0	12.8:1
(nom.)	1973	Oakham	314.0	Barnstable	14.8	21.0:1

NOTE: 1873 figures cited by J. M. Benton, Jr., "Inequality of Tax Valuation in Massachusetts," Address delivered before the Beacon Society of Boston (Boston: Addison C. Gitchell, 1890). 1973 figures for nominal and real (corrected for valuation ratios) from Commonwealth of Massachusetts documents. All rates are in $/1000$ value.

Nantucket, which is a county with a single town, has been included with Dukes County.

Assessment ratios are not available for 1873, but contemporaries do not speak of these ratios as varying greatly at the time.[25] It may thus be more valid to compare the 1873 *nominal* figures with 1973 *real* tax rates. If this comparison is made, the ratio of inequality between highest and lowest town tax rates was greater in 1973 in seven counties out of the thirteen in table 8.10.

The increase in tax inequality was of particular concern both because of a sharp increase in average tax rates and because of a tendency for higher tax rates to be correlated with low incomes rather than with greater levels of service paid for by the taxes. The increasing burden of taxes overall is seen in the fact that the highest rates for 1873 were lower than the lowest nominal or real 1973 rates in eight of the thirteen counties considered, while the state average of 14.9 mills for 1873 is below all but one town's nomainl rate for 1973. In the 78 towns and cities of metropolitan Boston as defined in 1970, the mean nominal tax rate increased from 13.95 mills in 1870 to 75.14 in 1970. The real tax rate in 1970 (47.85 mills) was more than four times the real 1900 rate, the earliest such figure available.[26]

The correlations between tax rates and other town characteristics in the Boston area shown in table 8.11 illustrate the tendency for higher tax rates to fall on low-income communities rather than on those which tax themselves more heavily to provide better services. As the correlations show, tax rates have always been negatively correlated with teacher–student ratios (an indicator of service quality on which data are available for the entire century). The correlation is, to be sure, most highly negative in the early years of the twentieth century. However, as is discussed below, there is still considerable evidence that many taxes do not pay for wanted services. On the other hand, while higher taxes were positively associated with per capita personal property in 1870 (before suburbanization had advanced very far), the correlation was reversed by 1900. The correlation between family income and taxes apparently grew worse (more negative) over time, while the correlation between low taxes and a suburban location (distance from Boston) grew stronger.

These figures illustrate the problem of tax inequality and discrimination against low-income communities that arose in Massachusetts. But the effects of tax inequalities are not even fully captured in these simple comparisons of rates. Taxes may have effects on the distribution of population within the metropolitan area (either in terms of the pattern of

Table 8.11
Tax Rates in Metropolitan Boston, 1870–1970

	mean tax rate	std. dev.	correlations with:			
			per cap. personal property	mean[a] family income	tchr.- studn. ratio	miles from center
1870 (nominal)	13.95	3.62	+ .297	—	− .177	− .093
1900 (nominal)	15.47	3.59	− .629	− .187	− .500	− .240
1900 (effective)	11.02	3.24	− .595	− .217	− .533	− .368
1925 (nominal)	29.29	5.70	− .466	− .227	− .348	− .251
1925 (effective)	18.13	4.87	− .423	− .281	− .344	− .518
1950 (nominal)	44.38	8.45		− .215	− .207	− .220
1970 (nominal)	75.14	42.41	—	− .307	− .133	− .527
1970 (effective)	47.85	13.21	—	− .405	− .089	− .489

SOURCES: Nominal tax rates and 1970 effective tax rates from commonwealth of Massachusetts files, 1900 and 1925 effective rates calculated from our estimates of assessment ratios (see chapter 4 appendix). Personal property assessment and student teacher ratio from annual town reports. Mean family income and population from U.S. Censuses
[a] Before 1950, ratio of ratepayers to pollpayers used as proxy.

overall population densities or segregation between different income or occupational groups), on the pattern of land values in the region, or on the provision of public services such as education.

Differences in taxes do not, of course, always represent differences in the unattractiveness of different towns. Often, the higher taxes of one area go to pay for services the residents want to consume. Better snow removal and street conditions, and higher per capita police protection, are associated with higher income. This in turn suggests that the higher taxes to pay for these services are best seen as a voluntary user charge, adopted willingly by higher-income communities. Certainly, in the 1950s and early 1960s, many suburbs with high taxes for education were seen as attractive, because these taxes paid for schools that parents wanted their children to attend. During that period, school bonds, whose repayment was to be made out of taxes, were often voted for by a wide variety of communities. These considerations suggest that both taxes and expenditures must be considered, if the effect of public finance on the relative attractiveness of cities and suburbs is to be considered.

In economic theory, taxes and expenditures may affect the attractiveness of towns in two related ways. One is to affect the cost of living, or the direct attraction of living, in a town. If residence in an area means payment of higher taxes each year, some people may move away; if residence permits one to use particularly good schools or other attractive community facilities, then despite the tax costs involved, people may move in. But migration in and out of towns is not the only possible impact of public finance. Taxes and services may also affect property values. If taxes in an area are high, people may still be willing to move there *if* housing prices are marked down enough that the total of annual housing payments and taxes is not out of line with the cost of living in competing communities. Similarly, people may move to areas with poor public services if housing is cheap enough, and costly-enough housing may deter new entrants into areas with better services. In other words, prices of housing may absorb some or all of the impact of better or worse tax-service mixes; the process is known as *capitalization*.

Technically, since changes in taxes and services should affect what people are willing to pay to live in a town, it is *land* that one uses for one's house or apartment that bears the brunt of capitalization. Buying land, or renting space on land, is after all one's real ticket to enter a jurisdiction and use its services. It has long been known that a higher tax rate in an area will reduce the amount buyers will be willing to pay for land there, all other things being equal. With higher taxes, the amount a person or business is willing to pay annually to occupy land may not be affected, but since more of this payment is taken by the tax collector, less remains to pay off the purchase of the property. Thus taxes are said to be capitalized negatively into land values (nontax nuisances like air pollution may have a similar effect).

Since Massachusetts property taxes, like most others in the United States, are levied on buildings and other improvements as well as on the value of land itself, taxes may depress the market value of improvements as well. Since the building and maintenance of these improvements itself has a cost, taxes may also deter these expenditures. Other things being equal, a higher property tax will have the effect of reducing values of land, existing improvements, and those improvements that are still worth making; and in part it will reduce new investments, causing out-migration of capital and perhaps of residents. Much of the literature on local taxation has concerned the extent to which they deter investment.

Many people implicitly assume that taxes must have one or the other of these negative consequences. Recently, however, it has been shown that if taxes are used to pay for valued public services, a tax need not have a negative effect on values or investment. Wallace Oates showed, in a study of New Jersey communities, that educational expenditures added more to property values than the taxes that paid for them reduced those values.[27] In a subsequent paper, two of the authors of this book showed that under hypothetical conditions of competition between towns for residents (a market analogue originally set forth by Charles Tiebout), the value increases induced by desired services and the value reductions caused by taxes ought to balance each other *exactly*.[28] While the conditions for this to hold exactly are quite restricted, it is at least established that looking at taxes alone, without regard to how tax revenue is spent, is inappropriate. The question becomes one of which taxes are spent on desired services, which taxes are spent on items taxpayers do not value, and what services, if any, are not receiving as much revenue from taxes as consumers might desire. The entire tax service mix becomes a factor in the evolution of the property market. Thus even when an enactment like the recent Massachusetts Property Tax Limitation Initiative is in effect, unequal tax *bases* make "equal" tax rate the occasion for unequal provision of services.

To examine these factors, as they affected the land values discussed above in chapters 3 and 4, we here present a statistical analysis of some "causes" of those values. Regressions "explain" land values and median house values on the basis of tax rates, service mixes and a few housing characteristics. Tables 8.12 and 8.13 show some of the effects of taxes and expenditures to have been consistent throughout the twentieth century. Taxes consistently have a negative effect on property values, but the effect is strongest for 1930, the beginning of the Depression, and 1970, by which time the fiscal problem of towns had again apparently become serious. Of the expenditures whose effects offset taxes, *schooling* is the most consistently positive, though even its effects vary. Each dollar of school expenditures per pupil added $8 to house value in 1950, but less than half that amount in 1970. For 1940, the amount added to house value by school expenditures is not enough to offset the value loss from the taxes for schooling; for 1950 and 1960, periods of apparent shortages of schoolrooms and teachers, each tax dollar spent on schools clearly was more than repaid by the value of the schooling, as reflected, at least, by what parents were willing to pay for houses in districts with higher school expenditures. By 1970, however, with schools more prev-

Table 8.12
Marginal Contributions to Assessed Value ($1000/sq.mi)
(Beta coefficients from regression estimates)

	1900	1910	1930
Tax rate (mills)	−66	−75	−430††
School Expenditures ($/pupil)	+16.8	−27.7††	+5.4
Road Expenditure ($1000/sq.mi.)	+5	+226††	+74††
Welfare Expenditures ($/capita)	+259	+324††	+163††
General Govt. Expend. ($1000/cp)	+152	−34	−35
Police & Fire Exp. ($1000/capita)	n.a.	−173††	−58
Health & Sanitation Exp. (1000/cp)	n.a.	+8	+122
constant	6,956††	2,313††	11,512
distance (miles)	−1,465††	−727	−2,249††
distance^2	+90††	+48††	+139††
distance^3	−1.7††	−1.0††	−2.7††
density (population/sq.mi.)	+.296††	−.126†	−.164††
access to subcenter (d^{-2})	+548	+657†	+1,405†
zone effect (degrees from NS line)	−.54	−5.91†	+.14
R^2	.859	.941	.883

† = t greater than 1.60 but less than 2.00.
†† = t greater than 2.00.
n.a. = not available.

alent, the job market tightening, and taxes rising, it appears that school expenditures restored little more to house value than the taxes to pay for schools took away.

For other expenditures, effects are less uniformly positive. *Road maintenance* expenditures had a strongly positive effect on house values early in the century, but more recently, the effect has not been significantly different from zero. (It is not even positive for 1940 and 1950.) This confirms that much of the benefit from these expenditures goes to commuters driving through towns rather than to those paying for the maintanence. Some road expenditures, such as snow removal and filling of potholes on side streets, will benefit local residents; and it does vary among towns. But the cost of maintaining through routes may swamp these differences in the overall statistics. *Health and sanitation* expenditures had a positive effect for 1930 and 1940, but only a minimal influence on house values thereafter. Town differences in public health and garbage collection, that is to say, became small enough in the eyes of the consumer after World War II that they no longer influenced house prices, although towns continued to spend different amounts on these

Table 8.13
Marginal Contributions to House Value (Dollars)
(Data coefficients from regression analyses)

	1930	1940	1950	1960	1970
Tax Rate (mills)	−44	−24	−03	−09	−33
Education ($/pupil)	+12.3	+1.2	+8.0†	+5.8†	+3.8†
Health/Sanit. ($/capital)	+386†	+384††	+51	+52	+1
Highway Maint. (100$/sq.mile)	+3.3	−0.2	−2.4	+2.1·	+2.3
Police & Fire ($/capita)	−5.9	−28.5	+52.6	+56.9	+155.5††
Welfare ($/capita)	−271††	−72††	−22	−2	—ᵃ
General Gov. Exp. ($/capita)	−595††	−339††	−184†	−107	+78
Constant	6,250	6,016††	12,199††	27,571††	17,361†
Distance	+239	−41	−8	+737	+1,482
Distance²	−14.9	−6.1	−7.3	−81.7†	−85.5
Distance³	+.25	−.03	+.03	+2.29††	+1.30
Old Housing (prop over 30 yr)	−1,813	−73	−5,157††	−24,607††	−16,141††
New Housing (prop under 10 yr)	−5,808†	+11,015††	−2,110	−25,965††	−8,075
Homeownership	—ᵇ	−5.84	+.01	+8,468††	−22,309
R²	.593	.599	.281	.477	.36█

ᵃ Made a state function.
ᵇ Not available for all towns.
† t greater than 1.60.
†† t greater than 2.00.

services. On the other hand, *police and fire* expenditures, which are not reflected in higher house values before the same war, began to add to house value thereafter. Perhaps, up to 1940 these expenditures were viewed as necessary in large measure only in crowded or low-income areas, while in recent years, as more of the public became protection-conscious, people became willing to pay more to live in areas that appear better guarded.

Two additional expenditure categories considered in the tables are *welfare* and *general government expenditures*. The first had a negative effect on house values, if any, until it was taken over by the State in the 1960s. However, it is positively associated with assessed land values in the early part of the century. The paradoxical result, for 1930, that welfare had a positive effect according to table 8.12 and a negative effect according to table 8.13, is no doubt due to the concentration of welfare expenditures in areas of high population density, in which a low value of the individual house, even controlling for house age and distance to Boston, goes along with high land values. This relationship, rather than any real addition to land values through high demand to live in areas paying out more money in welfare, seems to account for the result observed. Nor did general expenditures—the costs of maintaining the basic bureaucracy of each city and town—have any significantly positive effect on house values; indeed, their effect was often significantly negative until the most recent census year. Not only do homebuyers consider their money spent on maintaining the "general government" a waste; they may even consider such expenditures to be actively harmful.

The analysis of tax and expenditure effects on house values shows that not all taxes are used for desired expenditures in such quantities that benefits and costs exactly balance. While educational expenditures—and, at times, some other expenses—return what taxes have taken away (and sometimes more) to real estate values, this is not true for all expenses. As a result, the prevalence of higher tax rates in central, more crowded, and less affluent parts of the metropolitan area, and the somewhat higher level of school expenditures in more affluent and suburban areas, can be seen to cause a reduction of property values in the less suburban areas, and possibly an increase or at least less of a decrease in the suburbs.

The magnitude of this redistribution cannot be read directly from tables 8.12 and 8.13. The coefficients there are marginal contributions to real estate values, which measure the effects of small changes in taxes or expenditures, all else being held constant. They do not necessarily measure whether the effect of a tax or expenditure change would be.so substantial that it moved a town outside of the present range of variation among towns. Nor do they take into account that changes in expenditure patterns might feed back onto the town characteristics that the statistical technique implicitly assumes constant. In other words, we cannot really tell from them what would happen if taxes and services did not exist, or even if they were equalized among towns at the current average levels for the whole metropolitan area. Nonetheless, the regressions allow a sort of "thought experiment" in which these alternatives are explored on the assumption that changes would affect values only in the limited ways measured by the regression coefficients. (Over the next few years, the impact of "Proposition 2½" tax limitation will allow observation of results of a somewhat related real-life experiment.)

One experiment involves comparison of the slopes of real estate value gradients as estimated by equations such as those of chapter 4, which leave tax and expenditure effects out as explanatory factors, with slopes of gradients estimated by equations (e.g., table 8.13) which consider them explicitly. By asking if value gradients for the latter equations, which control for tax effects, are steeper than those for the former equations, we can ask whether taxes and public expenditures are flattening the gradients in any census year. We can also see whether disparities increase or decrease over time. Figure 8.1 represents house value gradients for five census years, redrawn from figure 4.3, compared with gradients drawn using the slopes estimated controlling for tax and expenditure effects in table 8.13. The latter gradients, shown as broken lines, are drawn on the assumption that values remain constant three miles from the center of the metropolitan area. This is an arbitrary assumption: it simply involves setting values of the equalized fiscal variables such that gradients cross at this point. (Setting values of all taxes and expenditures equal to zero would yield gradients substantially below the actual gradients for 1960 and 1970, and substantially above the the actual for 1940, but it would

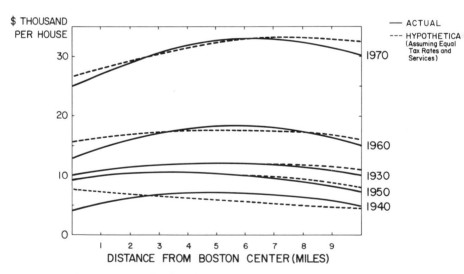

Figure 8.1   House Value Gradients Controlling for Fiscal Effects.

be premature to assume that the net effect of having governments in the area at all has become a net cost, since the assumed values of the fiscal variables are outside the range of the values used in the regression, and since *ceteris paribus* assumptions imply that all parameters would remain unchanged if government were abolished, which is absurd.) But the figure as drawn does allow consideration of relative fiscal effects at different distances from Boston Center.

What the figure suggests is that observed house values were most depressed by fiscal variables at the center of the metropolitan area in 1960 and 1970. Relative gains from the fiscal system were greatest (or losses least) at 3–8 miles from the center. This is consistent with a notion of fiscal transfer from the center of the area to at least some suburbs. For the previous three census years, differences were even smaller, and in 1940, the inner ring appears as a relative gainer in the comparison. Compared with effects of transport, fiscal disparities had a small effect on the slope of housing values up to 1950. But in 1960 and 1970, their effect was more noticeable.

The depression of house values in the higher-taxed core contributes to the process of neighborhood devaluation discussed in part I. But taxes may, under some circumstances, also contribute to the cycle by accelerating the pace of suburban migration. This is most likely if taxes are not fully capitalized into land value, a distinct possibility where property taxes cover improvements as well as site value. In Boston, tax rates prove, nonetheless, to have only a minor impact on total population migration, but they appear to have a more important effect on the relative migration of different classes within the population, and on occupational segregation.

Influences on population change in the Boston area are analyzed in table 8.14. The table gives regression estimates of several effects on population change per square mile over the intercensal decades from 1870 to 1970. Distance terms account, not surprisingly, for much of the observed variation, reflecting the general tendency for population to suburbanize. When distance is controlled for, population density also has a significant effect, with areas of denser population tending to attract more inhabitants before 1920, and to lose population thereafter. But the additional effects of taxes, once the terms for distance and original density are included, appear to be small. The initial tax rate during a decade does not have a significant effect on population change during any de-

Table 8.14
Determinants of Density Change, By Town, By Decade

date	const	DIS	DIS²	DIS³	DNSTY	TXRT	R²	ΔR From TXRT
1870–80	824 ††	−140 †	+7.31	−.1231	+231 ††	+2.19	.690	.002
1880–90	1647 ††	−236 ††	+10.69 †	−.1484	+.192 ††	−4.67	.775	.002
1890–00	2202 ††	−318 ††	+14.77 ††	−.2141	+.202 ††	−6.16	.813	.000
1900–10	2137 ††	−312 ††	+14.83 †	−.2309	+.047	+2.31	.545	.001
1910–20	1193	−140	+3.45	−.0051	+.119 ††	+6.61	.613	.000
1920–30	1349 †	+25	−12.80	+.3756	+.013	−0.55	.484	.001
1830–40	1032 ††	−38	−1.37	+.0641	−.066 ††	−7.88	.452	.018
1940–50	1508	−118	+2.97	−.0152	−.035 ††	−4.44	.249	.007
1950–60	−200	+319 ††	−25.68 ††	+.5304 ††	−.112 ††	+0.97	.744	.000
1960–70	650	+118 †	−11.14 ††	+.2465 ††	−.083 ††	−4.55	.543	.020

NOTE: Density is measured in population per square mile; Distance measured in miles; Tax Rate is measured in mills, using nominal rate on assessed valuation.
† = t between 1.60 and 2.00.
†† = t greater than 2.00.

Table 8.15
Effects on Changes in Composition of Resident Labor Force

group and date	CONST	ORIGINAL SHARE	HOUSE VALUE	TAX RATE	SCHOOL EXPEND.	R²
PROPRIETORS/PROFESSIONALS:						
1940–1950	.003	+.070	+.009	−.0006	−.0057	.466
1950–1960	.062	−.009	+.002	−.0002	+.0288 ††	.148
1960–1970	.046 †	+.011	+.001	−.0002	−.0012	.030
WHITE COLLAR WORKERS:						
1940–1950	.079	−.588 ††	+.003	+.0014 †	+.059 †	.592
1950–1960	.165 ††	−.310 ††	−.002	−.0001	−.011 ††	.413
1960–1970	.107 ††	−.099 †	−.001	+.0003 †	−.003	.125
BLUE COLLAR WORKERS:						
1940–1950	.111 ††	−.195 ††	−.013	+.0014 ††	−.038 †	.587
1950–1960	.068	−.269 ††	−.001	+.0011 ††	−.030 ††	.289
1960–1970	.015	−.126 ††	−.002	+.0002	−.005	.089

NOTE: The dependent variable was the change in proportion of the towns labor force in the type of job indicated, from U.S. censuses, subtracting original year decimal proportion from final year proportion. Original share proportion measured in same units. Thus, if the white-collar share in a town went from 30% to 35% over a decade, the value for original year variable is .300 and for the dependent variable is .050. House values (original year, from U.S. census) measured in $1000. Tax rates (nominal) from state reports, measured in $ per $1000 value. School expenditures from state reports, measured in $100 per pupil.
†t between 1.60 and 2.00.
††t greater than 2.00.

Table 8.16
Effects on Changes in Composition of Resident Labor Force, Controlling for
Density and Town Location

group and date	ORIGINAL SHARE AS RESIDUAL	regression coefficients for			
		HOUSE VALUE ($1000)	TAX RATE (mills)	SCHOOL EXPEND. ($100/p)	R^2
PROPRIETORS/PROFESSIONALS:					
1940–1950	−.026	+.0112 ††	+.0001	−.007	.634
1950–1960	−.059	+.0023	+.0002	+.023 ††	.462
1960–1970	−.030	+.0014	−.0002	−.003	.163
WHITE COLLAR WORKERS:					
1940–1950	−.668 ††	+.0018	+.0004	−.032	.787
1950–1960	−.347 ††	−.0012	+.0002	−.001	.468
1960–1970	−.259 ††	−.0008	+.0003	−.004	.242
BLUE COLLAR WORKERS:					
1940–1950	−.171 ††	−.0108 ††	+.0010	−.041 †	.630
1950–1960	−.218	+.0005	+.0005	−.016 †	.514
1960–1970	−.140 ††	−.0016	+.0002	−.003	.227

Variable definitions the same as for table 8.15 except that Distance, Distance^2 and Distance^3 (miles from Boston CBD), Density (persons per square mile) and Zonal Location (degrees off North-South line) are included as additional independent variables, and the original share variables used is a residual from regression of the share on the location variables and density.

cade before 1960; nor can it even be said the effect is always negative. The 1960s are the first decade in which tax rate differences can be shown to have affected gross population changes significantly. Even then, only two percentage points are added to the proportion of variance explained, and the marginal effect on population movements appears to have been small. A reduction of taxes of $10 per thousand dollars valuation would have attracted forty persons per square mile to a town.

Taxes do have a greater impact on the distribution of different population groups within the metropolitan area. Tables 8.15 and 8.16 analyze the effects of several factors, including taxes, on changes in the proportions of different towns' labor force engaged in occupations of different status. These changes are largely the result of movement of people between towns, but they also reflect, to some extent, the impact of individual career mobility by town residents, and intergenerational changes in status by nonmoving families. Explanatory equations are estimated for the past three intercensal decades for three status groups: blue-collar workers, white-collar workers, and proprietors-and-professionals. Marginal effects of taxes, housing values, and school expenditures are presented on two alternative assumptions. In table 8.15 the original share of each group in town populations is held constant in the equation for each decade; in table 8.16, density and town location are also held constant, so that more of the total variance between towns is explained.

The first table does indicate some difference between the reaction of different status groups to taxes. Higher tax rates do appear to increase the proportion of blue-collar workers in the population (and perhaps the white-collar proportion), while reducing the proportion of professionals and proprietors. The affluent or "upper middle class," that is to say, do seem to move to escape taxes. However, the effect is small. In the 1940s, the decade for which the highest marginal effect of taxes is indicated, a $10 difference in taxes would have increased the blue-collar and white collar percentages by only slightly more than one-tenth of a percentage point each. In the 1950s, it would have raised the blue-collar percentage similarly, but not the white-collar percentage. In the 1960s, the indicated effects are smaller, although this is the decade, as shown earlier, in which taxes began to have an effect on total population density. Table 8.16, in which density and location are controlled for, suggests the effects of taxes may have been even weaker than the previous table indicates. Attempts to measure the effects of tax rates on differential movement of population grouped by other criteria (income as reported by the census, or native vs. immigrant birth) revealed similar small effects for recent decades.

The direct effects of taxes as indicated here are, however, not their only effects. Two of the other factors analyzed in the tables—school expenditures and house values—may be affected by tax rates and, in turn, affect migration of different occupational groups among towns. A town with high taxes may be forced by fiscal pressures to skimp on educational expenditures. And high tax rates, particularly if they are not offset by school expenditures, will have a negative effect on house values. Low house values and low school expenditures will, in turn, add further to the share of blue-collar workers in the population, although the effects will be small, quantitatively. (In the 1940s, according to table 8.15, a house price differential of $10,000 and a per pupil school expenditure difference of $300 would each lead to an increase of only one-tenth of a percentage point in the blue-collar share of population.) Tax rate differentials thus seem to have major effects on the segregating of the Boston area population by occupational class.

C. Conclusions

Like the major developers who built the suburbs, governments have helped to build the framework within which individual decisions to move to suburbs have been made, and within which the suburbanization process has deteriorated the values of older, inner-city and inner-ring properties. While, to some extent, a movement to the suburbs might have occurred because of rising incomes and the simple aging of older buildings, these processes have been helped along considerably by the actions of state, local, and the federal governments.

We have considered only one aspect of the government's role: that of fiscal balkanization. There are other important aspects, too. The federal government's role in underwriting single-family housing, through tax deductions and support of the mortgage market, is often considerd a major factor in the growth of suburbs throughout the United States. In Massachusetts, the building and subsidizing of transport systems has greatly enhanced the individual benefits to those who moved to suburbs, and imposed costs on those who remained behind. (We consider this in Appendix E.) Urban renewal and the undermaintenance of public housing, in some cases, have exerted a direct push, expelling people from near the urban core. Differences in the tax–service mix between towns, while probably not as important as sometimes stated, have become a factor favoring the suburbs in recent years. As a result, it is hard to sustain the view that suburbanization was simply a mass movement that reflected what everybody wanted. If people did choose to move to suburbs, they made their choices in a situation in which incentives were slanted in favor of that move. Unless it can be shown that government policy itself was simply the sum of individual desires that everyone suburbanize, it is hard to credit the process to consumers' choice. And, as the next chapter will indicate, the origins and maintenance of government support for suburbanization were not just the result of a simple vote in favor of suburbs. They stemmed from a complex process of conflict and compromise among economic classes.

NINE

Origins of
the Suburban Compromise

WE have presented examples of ways in which land developers and/or governments have "pushed" at least some people into suburbanization. These examples cast doubt on the notion that suburbanization has been a simple sum of individual choices. But does this confirm the alternative theory, that suburban homeownership represented a manipulation of urban growth by capitalists, designed to ensnare a working class in a system of false mobility and real debts?

As chapter 6 argued, such a theory, while explaining some policies and some attempts to spread ideologies of property mobility, is too simplistic. A capitalist class may dominate the investments society makes, command the economy, and exercise considerable influence over the thoughts of others, but it does not do so in a vacuum. Workers, too, develop ideas and organizational power. There are two sides to a class conflict.

We argue here that the American capitalist class—as opposed to the real estate developers among their number—accepted suburbanization at least partly in response to workers' demands. Suburbanization, and spread of worker homeownership, was not the initial choice of the capitalists for housing their workers. Many of the specific policies that fostered suburbanization, in fact, were first proposed and fought for by labor radicals. Suburbanization, as it emerged, was a compromise solution between the demands of capital and of labor.

The suburban settlement pattern grew out of a struggle between capital and labor. The struggle ended in an arrangement or truce that gave some gains to labor (unevenly distributed among workers) and maintained capital's role as economic ruler. With some variations, this com-

A Natural Progression?

Boston Public Library, Print Dept.

Pedestrians, horses, trolleys and automobiles coexisted for a time on Boston's streets. These modes of transportation might at first seem to exemplify an inevitable march of technological progress. But the technologies themselves were products of political conflict. Cornhill at the corner of Washington Street, 1916.

promise has been in force in the United States for three-quarters of a century, although it may be breaking up now.

The origins of the compromise go back to the depression of the late nineteenth century, a period characterized by crowded immigrant quarters in cities, the eviction of farmers from a newly closed frontier, the concentration of industry into trusts, incipient labor unions, and infant radical political parties.[1] All these combined with generally weak markets to create an explosive economic and political situation. Immigrant politics in the cities took the form of socialist parties as well as of new machines in the major parties. Faced with political threats, American industrialists had to find a way to grant some concessions to labor that would not, at the same time, disrupt their own drive to greater power and growth.

This is a difficult task for any ruling class. But one felicitous way to do this is to reduce the cost of basic necessities of life for the workers. Living standards can then rise without the need for a wage increase. In the early nineteenth century the British ruling class countered the Chartist agitation with a drive to cheapen food by repeal of the Corn Law import duties.[2] In the America of the 1890s, a major strategy was to try to cheapen the cost of housing by developing trolley routes to open land around the towns. The more foresighted economic and political leaders backed this housing development by encouraging both state investigations of tenements and state "homestead commissions" to promote the suburban home ownership ideal. These "progressives" attacked streetcar owners and other monopolists who were hampering suburbanization for their own gain. But these capitalist reformers were not simply manipulating workers into a system designed for social control. They were responding to a situation in which alternatives—the tenement, the shanty, and the company town— had been ruled out by political opposition.

In some cases, the specifics of the reforms adopted were proposed by working-class movements. Even when this was not the case, reform became the best course because of disruptions and pressures from below. As implemented by the ruling American urban elites, suburbanization did lower housing costs and improve living standards. However, in doing so, it limited the push for further reform by breaking up the immigrant neighborhoods and company-towns-in-towns where agitation thrived. And the availability of public works jobs in construction helped cement the victory of the orthodox political parties over the socialist politics of the immigrant communities. Thus it was, for workers, only a partial victory.

A. Radical Urban Reform, 1884–1914

The origins of the suburban compromise lie in the two decades of intermittent depression, and/or urban and industrial conflict that followed the panic of 1873. In these years the industrial booms of the 1850s and the Civil War came to an end. Heavy industry continued to grow, intermittently, on the strength of mergers of smaller companies into large ones, but stable growth eluded the economy. Price relationships between city and country products within the United States fluctuated widely. The decline of small industrial firms and towns combined with both agricultural distress and immigration to drive large streams of population to the cities. New streams of immigration from Italy and Eastern Europe also swelled the metropolitan areas, where industrial employment was increasing, albeit sporadically. The combination of rapid urban growth with unstable employment and prices spawned conflict and—eventually—some degree of institutional reform.[3]

In 1877, the Baltimore and Ohio Railroad, caught in the depression, cut wages 10 percent. The strike that ensued spread quickly. Within days, strikers had stopped and seized the railroads, the nation's largest industry. Crowds of supporters won over first the police, then the state militias, and, in some cases, even federal troops sent to break the strike. In twelve major U.S. cities, general strikes broke out. In Boston, railroad workers struck for the first time.[4]

Although this "Great Upheaval" partially subsided, a second wave of militancy broke in the industrial depression of 1884. The movement for the eight-hour day, the peaking of membership of the Knights of Labor, and the founding of the American Federation of Labor followed in the next two years.[5] Specific labor distress and unrest triggered what, in our time, would be termed an "urban crisis." The fear of an urban uprising had been present in all capitalist countries, at least from the time of the Paris Commune. In the mid-eighties, it became more general in the United States. The increasing crowding of the cities and a perceived rise in crime and general unrest set the stage for this development. The entry of immigrant groups into politics achieved the election of the first Irish mayor of Boston, in 1884. A mild reformer, he was nonetheless perceived as a threat to the elite.[6] In 1886, the near-election of Henry George as Mayor of New York on an anti-monopoly labor platform, the election of a labor mayor in Milwaukee, and the May Day general strike by the Eight-Hour Movement convinced many that the crisis had indeed arrived. The eruption of violence at the Haymarket Rally in Chicago, although the apparent work of provocateurs and the police, added to this sense of impending disaster.[7]

The mood was not limited to those who saw the unrest as a threat to "civilization," or at least to their own interests. Frederick Engels proclaimed that

during these ten months a revolution has been accomplished in American society such as, in any other country, would have taken at least ten years. In February 1885, American public opinion was almost unanimous on this one point; that there was no working class, in the European sense of the word, in America; that consequently no class struggle between workmen and capitalists, such as wore European society to pieces, was possible in the American Republic; and that, therefore, Socialism was a thing of foreign importation which could never take root on American soil. . . . no one could then foresee that in such a short time the movement would burst out with such irresistable force, would spread with the rapidity of a prairie fire, would shake American society to its very foundations.[8]

Of course, American capitalism did survive the crisis of the 1880s. But it also changed in many ways, one of which involved a major extension of surburbs. In part, suburban flight by middle-class residents, and by some employers, was a direct response to the crisis in older cities. But suburbanization was also impelled by specific demands of working-class organizations which emerged from the crisis.

There were several such organizations. Engels, at the time, described three as competing for leadership: the Henry George Movement, the Knights of Labor, and the Socialist Labor Party ("of which only the latter," he commented, "has a platform in harmony with the modern European standpoint").[9] Further competitors for leadership, not mentioned by Engels, were the immigrant political leaders within the major parties, and the craft-union rivals of the Knights of Labor, who soon founded the AFL.

Only one of these movements, Henry George's "single tax" movement, placed urban reform, including suburbanization, at the center of its basic program. But all except the Knights of Labor, which disappeared soon after 1886, advocated programs which contributed to suburban growth.

1. The Henry George Movement

Henry George, a California-born printer, was the author of *Progress and Poverty*, a best-selling analysis of economic problems published in 1879.[10] George wrote from the viewpoint of a mixed group of workers

and small businessmen in frontier society, a group which saw no necessary conflict between labor and competitive capital, but which perceived
land speculators and monopolies as threats.

George described rent charged for land as parasitic, an unearned portion of the product of labor and capital. He saw this unearned rent increasing over time. Growing population and the progress of technology
would increase the demand for land and, in particular, widen the gap
between productivity at the frontier and in the most developed sections'
of the country. The growth of cities was particularly important in this:
closer cooperation in production there would make urban land particularly valuable, and rents would increase as a result. The landless would
be left worse off. Thus, George saw progress breeding poverty, widening the gap between rich and poor. What is more, increasing land prices
would also disrupt society by encouraging speculation. Movement to the
frontier would be artificially restricted by land monoplists seeking to hold
land back from the market to reap greater gains later.[11]

George's strategic proposal was that labor and competitive business
should unite around their common interest in preventing land monopoly.[12] Restricting that monopoly would not require confiscation of land,
or a socialist state, which George held would be extremely difficult to
achieve. To "make land common property," it was really only necessary
to tax away all of the rewards of land ownership.[13] A tax on land values
could, in George's view, remove the incentive to speculate and keep land
off the market, erase inequalities caused by property ownership, and make
unnecessary any tax on productive factors or products.

George's single tax views, propounded first in the late 1870s, were
picked up widely by the American labor movement during the 1880s.
Daniel DeLeon, the leader of the Socialist Labor Party, was a Single-
Taxer before becoming a Marxist.[14] According to Richard Ely, "tens of
thousands of industrial laborers had read *Progress and Poverty* who never
before looked between the covers of an economics book."[15] Although
George's original support within labor organizations came from men like
Terence Powderly, who were still concerned with the monopolization of
agricultural land and impediments to small property ownership, the base
of his support soon shifted to the cities. George himself had enough of a
following in New York City that the United Labor Party, in 1886, in-
vited him to be their mayoral candidate.

This party was organized by representatives of the Central Labor Union and the Knights of Labor in response to city repression of strikers and boycotters. It presented a platform of labor demands (eight-hour laws, abolition of child and convict labor, equal pay for equal work), working-class civil rights demands (abolition of property qualifications to vote, repeal of conspiracy laws), "free soil," and local and consumer issues (abolition of tenement house cigar-making, a ban on food speculation). When George became a candidate, plans for land nationalization and public ownership of transit were agreed to as a compromise between his land position and the socialists' desired confiscation of the means of production. George received 68,000 recorded votes, to 90,000 for Democrat Abraham Hewitt and 60,000 for Theodore Roosevelt, the Republican candidate. George's supporters believed that he would have won had the ballots been counted honestly.[16]

Although the extent of labor support within the George movement is a cloudy historical issue, it appears that he did have at least some wageworker support. Certainly, his campaign raised a number of urban reform issues to a prominent place among the demands of a variety of labor groups.[17] Even after the collapse of George's 1886 coalition, his followers became prominent advocates of cheap municipal transit and of active government intervention to restrict land monopoly and to promote public works.

All of these demands were part of the set of policies which would allow suburbanization to occur.

2. Municipal Socialism

During the 1890s, a number of socialist parties appeared in the industrial cities of the United States. In 1898, several of these merged to form the Social Democratic Party (SDP). In the party's first electoral contest, in 1900, a Harriman-Debs ticket drew 98,000 votes. Soon after, the SDP became the Socialist Party of America (SP). The SP counted among its members Americans from virtually every segment of the working class, including tens of thousands of trade unionists. The socialist press had a circulation in the millions, Socialists were elected to offices at every level but the presidency. Theodore Roosevelt called the growth of the SP "far more ominous than any populist movement in time past." The party grew rapidly until 1912, and then somewhat more slowly until World War I.[18]

Municipal Socialism, or "Sewer Socialism," was one of the early organizational themes of the new party. In towns and cities where there was a substantial trade union base of support, socialist parties had begun in the 1890s to run candidates for state or local office. Their program usually espoused municipal ownership. For example, Milwaukee's socialist platform of 1898 demanded municipally owned utilities, public works jobs for the unemployed, free medical services and textbooks, and the expansion of parks in place of slums. Since local government was generally funded by property taxes, municipal ownership frequently meant taxing property owners for the support of services. This program went beyond that of George, who did not advocate an expansion of government service; but the difference was not great. Although doctrinal and personal disagreements often prevented direct collaboration between single-tax and socialist parties, short-run cooperation was sometimes achieved. In 1901, some single-taxer groups were incorporated into the socialist party. The Texas and Oklahoma socialists, among the Party's strongest units, proposed full-rental-value taxes for uncultivated land as part of their program.[19]

Even in 1913, when Walter Lippman, then a member of the Socilist Party, criticized party leaders for not going beyond bourgeois reforms, he harked back to George's issues. Municipal reform, he held, was not anti-socialist, but neither was it necessarily anti-capitalist. The test he used, and on which he found the party wanting, was that it had in several cities refused to raise property tax rates to carry municipal programs further. The party's weakness, for him, was in not being Georgeite enough![20]

The SP did not unite the entire left. Daniel DeLeon's Socialist Labor Party (SLP) remained outside. DeLeon argued against alliances with other classes and against "ballot reforms" and other "sops and lures."[21] But his party was not opposed to supporting economic reforms: "The proletarian's chance to emerge from the bewildering woods of 'capitalist issues' is to keep his eyes riveted upon the economic interests of his own class— the public ownership of the land on which, and the tools with which, to work," he wrote.[22] And in 1893, the program that the SLP submitted to the AFL Convention had called for municipal ownership of streetcar, gas, and electric systems.[23]

Support for municipal programs was not unanimous within the new Socialist party either. The center–left, for example, argued against mu-

nicipal ownership on the grounds that it would mean low wages for utility workers. Although the party leadership insisted on retaining the right
to approve or disapprove local platforms and candidates, in practice few
candidacies were ever disapproved. The party achieved considerable
success in a number of large and industrial cities, including the election
of mayors in Schenectedy, Reading, Milwaukee, and Minneapolis.[24] Its
later decline, discussed below, came only after other parties had picked
up the municipal programs that had seemed too radical for business support when the George movement and the Socialists had first pushed them.

The Socialist Party, to be sure, did not build a strong base in all cities.
In Massachusetts, its main strength was in centers of the shoe industry,
where local capital was only slowly being displaced by national monopoly, and where a tradition of home ownership by artisan shoemakers was
still remembered. Socialists had elected mayors or state representatives
in Brockton and Haverhill in the 1890s. James Carey, a shoe-workers'
leader from Haverhill, received 34,000 votes for governor in 1902, while
other "third parties" on the left (populists and "nationalist" followers of
Edward Bellamy) had also elected mayors in Malden and Haverhill. In
the textile centers, where national corporations threatened factory clos-
ings, an electoral strategy was less popular than strike activity.[25]

In the municipal arena, the Socialist Party took on a variety of issues.
Limits on transit fares, regulation of public utility franchises, and public
control over utilities and transit lines, as well as direct municipal ownership, were frequent demands. Proposals for rent control and public or
cooperative housing did not become important in the Socialist program
until its declining period during and after World War I. But the program for utilities, as we shall show, would indirectly open new areas for
private housing. The party did not oppose individual homeownership for
workers.[26]

Friedberg has described the Socialist growth as "Marxism in America
finally allying with native radicalism and showing new strength."[27] Under American democratic socialism, "the proletariat could include the land-
owning farmer, professional man, or even small businessman."[28] The socialist position in America often resembled a kind of clean government,
left-populist reformism, linked to an anomalous program of factory organizing. But "sewer socialism," despite its inevitable drawbacks, was
not an unradical position. Friedberg writes that "the United States, like
England, was leaving competitive capitalism and entering an era of greater

social concern and progressive reform. The New Socialist movement, rather than stand aloof from and hostile to the reform sentiment sweeping the land, sought to lend Marxian structuring to prevalent moral concerns."[29]

Like the George Movement, municipal socialism was responding to needs expressed by working-class groups. Even DeLeon, who had stood against the watering-down of the Marxian program, agreed that a movement needed to advocate both "possibilist" and "impossibilist" positions.[30]

3. Political Machines

Even in its heyday, the Socialist Party did not attain a dominant hold on "working class politics," and thus much of the political advocacy of local working-class demands fell into the hands of local, often immigrant-based factions or "machines" within the bourgeois-dominated Democratic party. But even there, working-class and immigrant machine politics put forward some of the same issues pressed elsewhere by Georgeites and Socialists.

Boston presents one example of such a development. Unlike its shoe and textile producing satellites, Boston had no group of large manufacturing firms whose workers could become a focus for either Socialist or industrial union organizing. Even so, by 1929, 17 percent of the city's workers were unionized, as against an 11 percent national average. But the highly fragmented construction crafts were the main unions, and public employees were the other large group of workers who sought to unionize *en bloc*. Indeed, the most militant strike in the city between the 1880s and 1930s was conducted by the police in 1919. Separated from the Socialists' main industrial base, and dependent on city agencies, contracts, or franchises for jobs, most of Boston's workers stayed in the Democratic Party.[31]

Hugh O'Brien, the first Irish mayor of Boston, was elected in 1884 through an alliance between party leaders in the immigrant neighborhoods and the upper-class Mugwumps who had fled the Republican party. Over the next decade, the support of Patrick J. Maguire, the leading Irish political figure in the city, led to the election of several "genteel reformers" to the mayor's office and the state legislature. In return for that support, Mayor Nathan Matthews pushed a program of public works, proposed a municipally owned subway, and greatly increased municipal hiring as a relief measure during the 1894 depression. As a state legislator, Josiah Quincy IV put through bills for legal incorporation of trade unions and use of union labels, and bills on working conditions, child labor, and arbitration. Later, as mayor, Quincy increased municipal borrowing and expenditures, started a municipal printing plant headed by the president of the local printers' union, and extended public works using city laborers rather than hiring through contractors.

Quincy reached the limits of Brahmin collaboration with the rising Irish machine: he remained in the Democratic Party even after the Bryan nomination drove Matthews and most of the other Mugwumps back to Republicanism. He accepted the support of a new generation of Irish politicians who, unlike O'Brien and Maguire, were not also "respectable" businessmen. Steven E. Miller writes:

> A process of radicalization had converted him to a sort of municipal socialism which held that, while the principles of private enterprise were not to be violated, the state did not have to have to wait for private charity or business to deal with health, education, recreation, environmental and other social problems.[33]

But Quincy also was upper-class in his reform orientation. Many of his projects were directed at inner-city recreation. "It was almost a fetish with him that the poor should have as ample recreational facilities as the rich." He viewed recreation and cleanliness together as a program of moral uplift.[34] As he stated in dedicating one of the public baths he built, "If all bathed regularly . . . filthy tenement houses would disappear . . . crime and drunkenness would decrease."[35]

The machine politicians who succeeded Maguire, who died in 1896, were able to do without men like Quincy. After 1900, John J. Fitzgerald, James Michael Curley, and other mayors with strong Irish working-class followings improved city workers' salaries and working conditions, increased payrolls, and built more public works. Curley, in particular, frequently made use of assessment policy to raise real estate taxes on business, and raised the tax rate as high as the state would allow.[36] This was practical Georgeism without ideology. Business leaders may have escaped formal Socialist ideology in Boston (except perhaps when the police went on strike), but they were threatened by it *as a program*. They responded by continuing to disinvest in the city and by extending state control over local government

4. Labor Unions

Of the various working-class organizations, the trade unions, except through their Socialist political party affiliates, were the least directly concerned with municipal reform and housing issues. The AFL's decision to focus exclusively on wages and related workplace issues, and to eschew broader political alignment, meant housing and community issues would, at best, be secondary. True, the divorce was not complete. Several groups ocaasionally spoke on housing reform, and the AFL's 1893 convention endorsed municipal ownership of utilities as part of a compromise resolution which avoided broader socialist programs for general nationalization of industry.[37] In 1916, the AFL endorsed the new cooperative league in the U.S.A., but over the next decade very few unions attempted to develop cooperative housing.[38]

One union, the Amalgamated Clothing Workers, actually built major co-op housing developments in the late 1920s. But by then, to the extent that most unions had a position on housing, it was simply that a living wage should allow access to private homes at least for skilled workers.[39] By 1931, William Green, president of the AFL, had come to favor home ownership as desirable for workers:

> For working men and women particularly, a good home is all important. Because it can not be supplemented by clubs, travel, opportunities in independent living, the workman's home is definitely the center of family life, the formative influence on growing children.[40]

And home ownership had many advantages over renting. Green favored technological development to allow "mass production" of homes, and particularly cited the importance of financing arrangements.

Given depression conditions, Green stressed that "apartments and rented homes which will be equipped with modern comforts and appliances, and situated in suitable environments" were needed along with homes which can be purchased on easy terms. Even then, he stressed the importance of job security, calling for "steady work long enough to pay installments on a purchase if he wants to buy a home."

B. Conservative Urban Reform as a Response

Georgeites, machine politicians, and socialists all demanded better living conditions and an active municipal role in providing employment and public utilities. While they did not necessarily support individual home-ownership as the dominant form of new and better housing, nor the con-struction of the sort of public works that would extend the suburbs, nei-ther did they oppose them. Their active support was not necessary, for as it turned out, municipal reform itself led to a toppling of barriers to suburbanization. It might have done so even had capital been hostile to all its demands. But reforms, in practice, were so acceptable to business leaders that they compromised with, and later copied and shaped, work-ing-class programs. Urban reform became suburban growth.

The possibility of a compromise was not immediately apparent when the cities erupted in the mid-1880s. The immediate reaction of the mid-dle class was to wall itself off from urban unrest. David Gordon has shown that many factory owners responded by trying to remove *their* factories and *their* employees from the urban core.[42] Richard Sennett has sug-gested some middle-class Chicago neighborhoods responded by turning inward.[43] However, other families of the middle class fled to suburbs, following the wealthy and some middle-class members who had been moving out of the city long before the 1880s.[44] Nonetheless, this im-mediate panic might have subsided, or suburbanization might have been restricted to families of means, had labor pressure not led capitalists eventually to support a suburban housing option for at least a portion of the working class.

Before the 1880s, there was no major government or reform program for housing the working class. Workers rented quarters in older build-ings or in specially constructed private tenements, or they built their own shanties. Health and fire codes had just begun, and their scope was limited. To cope with urban agitation, government had sometimes tried to break up "unhealthy" concentrations of troublemarkers by repressing riots, campaigning against saloons, jailing leaders, tearing down neigh-borhoods, or encouraging the building of "model tenements" by "philanthrophic" corporations. These programs did not remove workers from the cities, although specific businesses frequently built company towns to keep their workers from being influenced by urban agitation.[45]

As members of the business elite slowly came to see the need for *some* housing program, they also began to consider what types of housing could be made available to workers. Since they were able to go into more detail than the labor radicals, their activity in large part shaped the suburbs.

Several specific options were open to the capitalists, apart from the *status quo* option of repressing dissent while doing nothing about urban conditions. "Tenement house reform," including the enactment of building codes was one; construction of company towns and other controlled workers' communities outside of the metropolitan centers, was another. All of these options were explored increasingly in the 1880s and 1890s, but all generated working-class opposition. Eventually, the response that emerged was the expansion and "democratization" of suburban home ownership.

We shall consider these options in turn. (A final possibility, involving public or cooperative housing, was not seriously pressed by working-class organizations at the time.)

1. Tenement Reform

Boston had undertaken a few programs even before the 1880s.[46] The 1868 Tenement House Act, for example, included fire and ventilation requirements, and cheap housing used by immigrant workers in Fort Hill had been demolished. But the housing shortage had frustrated attempts at code enforcement. A few local philanthropists had experimented with model tenement houses beginning in the 1870s. The Boston Cooperative Building Company, established in 1879, invested in 78 houses for 311 families; and there were a few others.[47]

The desire to tidy up the slums, as a minimal reform, incorporated a theory that social control over workers could be accomplished through a "sound" environment. The sanitary movement, having improved water supply as a defense against cholera, had turned its attention to the air. Parks ("the lungs of the city"), outings for poor children, and public baths, were touted as "social" as well as medical cures. The Boston YMCA's

"Country Week" claimed to provide its charges with "the moral stimulus which naturally comes to them through the influence of a more healthful environment and a contact with nature." Tenement-house reform was expected to eliminate immorality and rebellion.[48]

But the prime mover in several such projects, Robert T. Paine, eventually conceded they had "not succeeded in building houses at a lower cost." Paine concluded, in the end, that compared with private business speculators, the philanthrophic enterprises had an insignificant influence on the housing market.[49]

The unrest of the mid-1880s made the need for housing reform seem more urgent. In 1889, the Associated Charities of Boston commissioned a "sanitary inspection of certain tenement house districts of Boston." The report, by Dwight Porter, criticized overcrowding, the result of the "modern tendency towards a concentration of life at large centers." Porter claimed that for health reasons, density should not exceed 500 cubic feet of air space per occupant. "Existing overcrowding can be lessened only gradually," he noted, urging that the Board of Health be given broad discretionary powers, and a larger staff.[50] Also in 1889, Benjamin Flower founded *The Arena*, a nationally oriented but Boston-based liberal magazine "with special emphasis on the liberal or progressive ideals or the new and more conventional thought of the day." He conducted an extensive campaign against Boston's slums.[51]

In 1891, the legislature ordered the city's first "tenement house census" to be conducted by the Massachusetts Bureau of the Statistics of Labor and its chief, Horace G. Wadlin. The bureau's report found that the "Concentrated District" of slums consisted of the South Cove, Wards 11 and 19 of the South End, Ward 12 in South Boston, Ward 16, and the North End. Wadlin recommended that the Board of Health be strengthened by giving it power to demolish condemned buildings, greater discretion over sanitary facilities, and more building inspectors.[52] At least one of the Bureau's recommendations was acted upon. An act passed on April 1, 1897, broadened the Board of Health's control over unsanitary buildings from the power to issue vacating orders to the power to order their destruction.[53]

In 1893, the 20th Century Club was founded by Edwin D. Mead, with John Fiske, Edward E. Hale, and Robert Woods, to stimulate progressive housing reform in Boston. In 1898, the Club hired Harold K. Estabrook to do yet another survey of Boston's slums. The Estabrook report reviewed the activities of the Board of Health, lauding its increased power to vacate and demolish unfit buildings. It denounced the excessive profits of slum landlords, and appealed to the "public conscience" for action to stop them from exploiting the poor. One model tenement effort, the Boston Cooperative Building Company, was cited as an example of realistic alternatives to slum conditions, for providing improved housing at rents of $.72 to $1.05 per room per week.[54]

The reformers argued that better as well as cheaper housing was a realistic goal. However, the goal was not easily obtained. In 1899, Edwin Mead, chairman of the 20th Century Club, reviewed the progress made by the Board of Health in eliminating unsanitary tenements. Although 75 houses had been ordered vacated under the Act, far fewer had actually been destroyed.[55]

2. Model Company Towns

When model tenements, baths, and parks failed to sanitize the slums morally as well as physically, business leaders and other bourgeois reformers began to look to other environments to house their workers. Often they attempted to provide those environments themselves.

"Model dwellings" for workers—either cottages, row houses, or boarding houses—had been used in the United States since the beginnings of the textile industry. Lowell, Massachusetts, was designed by A. Lawrence Lowell and Kirk Boott to provide both inexpensive dwellings and a controllable "moral" environment for workers.[56] In the mid-nineteenth century, other New England mill towns had employed similar designs, with housing built and owned by employers. In some, as at the Amoskeag Manufacturing Company in New Hampshire, company loyalty was rewarded by low rents.[57] But the communities did not always ensure worker loyalty. In the face of rising militancy, companies often gave up on "buying cooperation" and turned from the attempt to provide model environments to the recruitment of whatever immigrant labor was least expensive.[58]

Between 1860 and 1884, according to Stuart D. Brandes, there was a "calm before the surge of modern welfare capitalism." In Massachusetts, the Waltham Watch Company and the Ludlow Manufacturing Company built major housing and community facilities in this period, but in general interest was low.[59]

More extended building began with George M. Pullman's new town outside Chicago, built in 1880. Copies followed over the next 14 years. Even in New York, company housing was built, by Steinway's piano works, among others. Even when company towns were not built, factories might still be relocated. Around the turn of the century, David M. Gordon writes, "New suburban manufacturing towns were being built in open space like movie sets." Gordon suggests the move was a response to urban labor unrest, and he considers it largely successful. He cites a 1915 study by Graham Taylor as showing that "decentralization served its purpose and the unions were much less successful than they had been in the central city districts."[60]

Yet control was not complete, and this was particularly apparent in the best-planned, most-supervised towns. In 1894, a major strike broke out at Pullman when the company cut wages but not rents. A nationwide strike followed when the American Railway Union refused to handle Pullman cars. After the U.S. Strike Commission, which investigated the incident, concluded that the company's paternalism bore much of the blame, the building of company towns subsided. Carnegie's Homestead Steel Works, which earlier had had a major strike, shifted emphasis from providing company housing to subsidizing individual home ownership for workers. This meant the suburban factory had to become part of a general process of suburbanization.[61] Although the company town survived at least until the 1930s for isolated rural industries, particularly in the South, it no longer was a leading contender as an urban housing alternative. Business interests came to support the single-family home or, as a temporary compromise, the three-decker. They advocated this interest by supporting expansion of utilities to suburbs, legislation against overcrowding, and propaganda for home ownership.

3. Homeownership and Suburbs

Like the idea of the company town, home ownership was not strictly a new proposal. Mayor Josiah Quincy III had proposed in 1871 that housing be provided in suburbs for at least some workers. In 1879, Edward E. Hale had proposed forming housing cooperatives to build new towns and relieve urban congestion. The Boston cooperative building society formed by Henry Bowditch in 1875 actually bought tracts of land and sold shares in the corporation; individuals capable of paying $3 per week could own their homes, plus some stock in the corporation, in six years. Cooperative banks such as the Pioneer Bank (1872) were also established to promote home ownership.[62]

After the mid-1880s, similar projects and proposals multiplied. Edward Atkinson, a businessman, economic writer, critic of Henry George, and an active Mugwump, popularized the goal of "each man his own landlord" as a cure for social unrest.[63] Developers of model housing projects for workers began to turn toward smaller buildings and suburban locations. The Workingmen's Building Association, founded in 1888, built single- and two-family houses in the outlying areas of the South End, Roxbury, and Dorchester.[64]

In 1893, ledaers of the Anti-Tenement House League—William D. Bliss, Robert T. Paine, and Arthur B. Ellis—founded the People's Building Association. Its purpose was to help poor laborers purchase homes in the suburbs at low weekly payments over a 15- to 21-year period. The depression of the 1890s, however, cut short the life of this organization.[65]

More than a decade later, the Economic Club of Boston condemned the city government's tolerance of gross inequities in Boston's distribution of population. Using data from the 1905 census, it found a density of 427 persons per acre in Wards 6 and 8, compared with 24 per acre citywide. In these crowded wards, 30,000 of the city's population lived in dwellings with less than 400 cubic feet of air space per person, "the lowest standard fixed as the minimum by any city in the United States or Europe which has undertaken to establish a minimum."[66] Unlike the earlier Mead and Estabrook reports, however, the Club did more than criticize the Board of Health for neglecting to enforce the housing code. It called for cooperative building associations to provide suburban residences for workers, improved suburban transit lines, and more rational control over the city's growth so immigrants could not congregate in unsafe numbers in the central city wards.

> The present haphazard system of intermingling dwellings, factories, stores, offices and other buildings in hopeless confusion must give way to a system of town planning on scientific lines. These include the defining of zones in which buildings of specified character and height can alone be erected.[67]

The report implied that both incentives to private developers and zoning for planning the city's growth were proper government spheres.[69]

The spirit of the Economic Club's report was embodied in Chapter 607 of the acts of 1911, the "Act to provide for establishing with the assistance of the Commonwealth homesteads for workingmen in the cities and towns." This act created the Homestead Commission, which was instructed to study and present to the legislature a plan by which mechanics, factory workers, and laborers could be assisted in purchasing small houses and plots of land in the suburbs.[69] In 1917, the Homestead Commission undertook the Lowell Homestead Project. This experiment, for which the legislature allocated $50,000, involved building and selling 50 homesteads at small down payments and monthly payments of $15. The legislature was reluctant to appropriate the funds requested by the Commission to carry on the project, however, and only 12 houses were actually completed. In 1919, the newly created Department of Public Welfare absorbed the Homestead Commission.[70]

More important than the Commission's housing development was its recommendation to establish city planning boards, which resulted in Boston's creation of such a board in 1914. In the 1920s, full-scale zoning ordinances began to enforce density limits. But density zoning could be used to keep lower-cost homes out of suburbs at least as easily as it could push population out of the city's inner core. The major thrust of suburbanization required actions that went beyond experiments with model dwellings, or incremental changes in health codes.

C. The Suburban Breakthrough

The development of working-class suburbanization required a response by investors, and by their allies in government, which is only explicable as a result of working-class pressure to do something about housing. Changes in transit technology, and major efforts to confront land and transit monopolies, were needed to impel the mass suburbanization of the 1890s and after. *Both* of these, we would argue, were responses to worker demands.

1. Transit Innovation

The development of the trolley car, and after it the electric subway and automobile, are usually thought to be pure technological advances

brought about by the accumulation of scientific knowledge. Undoubtedly, the trolley could not have been built without a series of earlier
inventions by people unconcerned with urban transit and, most likely,
these inventions would have been put together eventually into a working street vehicle, whatever the political climate. From mid-century, there
had been experiments with pneumatic, cable, and steam power for subways or street railways and a number of electrical systems had also been
tried. Nonetheless, as E. S. Mason says, "It is surprising, in view of the
fact that cars were run on rails by means of electrical motors as early as
1835, that the commercial use of the idea had to wait until the late
1880s."[71] It is surprising, that is, until one realizes that the "development" aspect of "research and development" requires capital investment; and not until the heightened urban tensions of the 1880s did businessmen begin to appreciate the possibilities of this investment.

   In May 1887, a group of New York capitalists gave Frank Julian Sprague
the contract that enabled him to develop the working prototype of the
trolley car. Their offer came after Sprague had searched five years for
backers. The contract was for building a line in Richmond, Virginia, but
the investors were certainly aware of the unrest in their own city, where
Henry George had been defeated only a few months before.[72] During
the two years from 1886 to 1888, others also attempted to develop electric railways, including Charles J. Van Depuele in Montgomery, Ala-
bama, Sidney H. Short in Denver, and the Thompson-Houston Electric
Company in Lynn, Massachusetts.[73]

   Sprague's model, powered by overhead wires, proved the most work-
able of several machines. It was soon adopted by Henry Whitney, who
had begun his investments in Brookline soon after O'Brien's election in
Boston. After the success of Whitney's lines, the trolley came into more
general use as a commuter vehicle.[74]

2. The Intervention of Government

   But development investment alone did not bring about massive suburban growth. Government action was needed both to control those monopolists who threatened to limit the use of the new technologies and to
use the power to tax real estate to provide basic infrastructure in the
suburbs. These actions went beyond what business had traditionally tol-

erated from government. But, after 1886, there was increasing pressure on business to allow new state activities. Radical municipal demands provoked a response. On the one hand, business was starting to recognize a common interest in preventing monopolies from cutting too deeply into other capitalist values. On the other hand, labor organization, and the threat of socialism, made some bread-and-butter concessions expedient for employers. Thus, the broad demands for municipal reform raised by the Single Tax, Socialist, and machine factions of the working class were, in a sanitized form, accepted by the capitalist class.

This acceptance developed only slowly and grudgingly among the capitalists, in response to workers' pressure. Their first reaction was both to try to crush all union activity and to limit the taxing power of local government. An "anti-double taxation" movement, for example, successfully removed financial assets from the property tax rolls.[75] Until the late nineteenth century, not only land and other real property were taxed, but also machinery and "intangibles" which included both financial assets and the value of an individual's trade. Taxing the building and machinery of a corporation in one town and shares in the corporation held in another town, critics asserted, amounted to levying two taxes on the same property, and was, therefore, inequitable. Removing financial assets from the tax base of cities and towns meant that, while land and building owners might still be vulnerable to fiscal pressure by working-class political movements, big capital was relatively immune from direct impact.

For those businessmen not particularly concerned with land investment, it was a small step from ending double taxation to advocating a Single Tax. A municipal property tax base allowed smaller tax-haven factory towns and affluent suburbs to escape city levies. Thus, the property tax itself was less a threat to business than a wealth tax that could be levied on all. And advocates of the Single Tax could also propose a more active role for city governments. In general, big business came to support city ownership, control over franchises, or direct subsidy to services, particularly after the strikes of 1894, the Bryan campaign of 1896, and the growth of Socialist programs in a number of cities.

In some places, business wholeheartedly accepted the Single Tax position. Tom Johnson, a street railway owner who said he had been converted to new views by reading *Progress and Poverty*, was elected Mayor of Cleveland in 1901. While some found it ironic that "he advocated the public ownership of street car systems before the same city councils from which he was soliciting franchises for himself," he nonetheless managed to introduce considerable regulation and tax reform in the city.[76] But even where explicit acceptance of Single Tax doctrine was absent, the major parties accepted a more active role for municipal government. By the outbreak of the First World War, a watered-down version of municipal socialism had been adopted by the so-called Progressives.[77]

The importance of an anti-monopoly program is seen clearly in the case of New York. At the time of the George campaign, the main commuter lines, the elevated railways, were controlled by Russell Sage and Jay Gould. Their company's refusal to experiment with electric vehicles, according to Frank Sprague's biographer, was due to Jay Gould's "prejudice against electric traction."[78] But that prejudice had its basis in a policy of maximizing profits by limiting service. Gould and Sage were later accused of preventing investors from bidding for franchise rights for a subway line when the city offered those rights in 1892. James Blaine Walker, the historian of the subways, notes that "Gould, of course, did not want a competitive transit line in the city and certainly was powerful enough, financially and politically, to interpose obstacles."[79]

Most of the street railway lines not controlled by Gould and Sage were run by another monopoly, the Metropolitan Traction Company controlled by William C. Whitney, Thomas Fortune Ryan, P. A. B. Widener, W. L. Elkins, and Thomas Dolan. These investors appear to have been more interested in mergers and stock watering than in developing new lines. They did not even install electric power as rapidly as Whitney's brother Henry had in the Boston area. The Metropolitan Traction Company did introduce transfers, and its competition held the elevateds down to a five-cent fare. But it joined the Gould interests in opposing city chartering or building of subways.[80]

A move against these monopolies began shortly after the 1886 election. The attack occurred on several fronts. The New York business community swung the vote in Congress for the Interstate Commerce Act. This support has been attributed to a desire to prevent price wars, but it was also to provide an entering wedge to attack Gould.[81] Meanwhile, the newly elected Democratic mayor, Abraham Hewitt, a respected iron manufacturer and leader of the Chamber of Commerce, proposed that the city finance an underground railway system which would then be leased by a private operator. After several years of opposition, the State

Legislature passed a watered-down bill in 1891, which called for the granting of a franchise to a private developer for a route laid out by a city board. In 1894, a new act allowed city financing of construction. The first line was finally built in 1904 by August Belmont's Interborough Rapid Transit Company, after the merger of New York with Brooklyn and three other suburban counties.[82]

The subways and the opening of new land to urban development in northern Manhattan, Brooklyn, the Bronx and Queens were, in many ways, the accomplishment of Hewitt, Belmont, William Steinway, and other leaders of the Chamber of Commerce. But they were motivated by the pressure of demands for housing, and the fear of radicalism in the congested inner city.

The response to labor demands also affected housing policy. The tenement house law governing New York's slums was also strengthened, requiring all bedrooms to have access to a window, after Henry George and Samuel Gompers joined with housing reformers for a large rally. A subsequent tenement house commission continued the movement toward building code reform.[83]

3. The Case of Massachusetts

A similar transition occured in Massachusetts in 1886. Opposition was the response to reform demands "from below." The state government, stepping in to protect the interests of the wealthy, took away Boston's control over its police force, placed limits on the city's debt and tax rates, ended "double taxation" of financial assets, and subjected city spending to the scrutiny of a finance commission. The timing of the police measure is most instructive: it occured immediately after the election of the first Irish mayor.[84]

Much of the rhetoric involved criticism of government spending and "waste." But the elite was *not* opposed to government spending for suburban expansion, and the suburban developers and politicians realized quickly the new demand for housing created by the urban turmoil of the mid-1880s. For example, William E. Russell, Mayor of Cambridge in 1884–1887, directed major new investments into street construction.[85] Even in Boston, the state was waiting to have general taxes used for development of the more suburban and underdeveloped southern wards.

Indeed, the legislature refused to let the city pay for street construction by assessments on adjacent properties, an alternative to general taxation that Mayor Matthews said was a routine practice in other cities.[86]

The introduction of public works was first justified in an extremely paternalistic manner, as in Mayor Quincy's advocacy of public baths. But when Representative Chase of Haverhill, a Socialist, defeated a combined Democratic and Republican "Citizens' ticket" on a platform stressing such improvements as grade crossings for railroads and new high schools, the conservative *Boston Traveller* wished he "were a Republican" so that it could support him.[87] Serious attention was being paid to the reforms proposed by workers.

Of course, support for suburban transport and improvements could take an anti-labor turn. Mayor Russell of Cambridge used the state National Guard against a strike of street railway workers in 1887.[88] Similarly, the establishment of "metropolitan" sewer, water, and park commissions allowed suburbs to develop infrastructure, while levying part of the cost on Boston.[89] By providing an alternative to annexation, which the suburbs rejected, the Metropolitan Commissions helped keep Boston, where working-class influence was strong, subservient. Nonetheless, the very development that the MDC fostered was itself providing some homes for workers.

Taxation and improvements were important, but the main battle came over the control and financing of street railroads. While private, horse-drawn railroads had become widespread before 1886, a new surge of development followed that year. An 1886 act authorized cable-drawn transit, an option that in practice never was introduced in Boston. In 1887, Henry Whitney's West End Street Railway was chartered by the state, with permission to use cable or electric traction. The company was, from the start, committed to expansion, both in terms of land development (in Brookline), and through acquisition of other lines.[90]

The charter of the street railway at first was presented simply as a traditional franchise to a private business using city streets. But from the start, Whitney and his propagandists claimed that the trolley cars he was building would suburbanize the poor and "provide a safety valve for the social pressures of the congested city," without the need for regulation or public expense.[91] But this invocation of public benefit quickly came to be held up as a criterion for street railway policy.

In 1890, Whitney received a franchise from the state for a downtown elevated line to link his into feeder routes. A legislator's complaint (based, it is alleged, on the line's threat to amenities around Boston Common) led to an investigation of the franchise's approval. Whitney's company, it turned out, had spent large sums lobbying and bribing legislators. Although Whitney was cleared of having acted illegally, the state was led to pass a law against future lobbying.[92] Further, the hearings led to an open discussion of various complaints against Whitney's operation of the rail system, free transfers between all of his merged lines, and his opposition to town taxation of his lines (which he claimed were merely part of the public street). At one hearing, the Mayor of Malden challenged Whitney's opposition to paying local taxes. Whitney claimed that his lines to Malden did not pay their way. A revocation of his franchise there would be welcome, he said. [93] Although the issue of town taxes was left unresolved, the legislature did act to protect cheap fares and free transfers.[94]

Despite Whitney's claim that regulation would discourage capital investment in new lines, some direct regulation of transit was undertaken. In 1894, the state enacted a statute forbidding a corporation to "withdraw or discontinue use of free transfers" without approval. The Boston Transit Commission was created, and the Public Utility Commission received new regulatory powers.[95] When neither Whitney nor any other developer would build an underground alternative to the unpopular elevateds near the Common, the city government built the tunnel itself, in 1896, leasing tracks to the private trolley lines. By 1898, the move toward public involvement was strong enough that a state commission openly debated public ownership either of the entire streetcar system, or at least of all of the tracks.[96] A study of municipal streetcars in Glasgow was undertaken. Although public ownership did not occur until the lines faced bankruptcy some years later, the entire progression suggests an incremental adoption of a Socialist—or at least a Georgeite—plank by the elite, under the continuing pressure of the working class for cheap fares.

Throughout the 1890s, at least, the projected drop in investment never occurred, and though profit rates fell, a major wave of construction and expansion followed. And after the 1907 business crisis, when many of the newer lines were in financial trouble, even so redoubtable a conservative as Henry Cabot Lodge saw danger in letting the New Haven railroad buy them all. He wrote that it would not be good "for New En-

gland, for Massachusetts, and—above all—for the city of Boston to have
the entire railroad system put under the control of a Connecticut corporation which is owned in New York."[97]

The battle for cheap transit was only part of the political struggle for
working-class suburbanization. Another aspect involved sturggles over
what residents and what forms of housing might be permitted in different suburbs. Joel Schwartz has described a "struggle for the corridors"
in which a number of different means were employed to limit the entry
of immigrant or working-class families. The prohibition of liquor sales,
which not-so-subtly masked an anti-Irish position, was an early attempt
to maintain "respectability."[98]

Informal covenants, Henry Whitney's restrictions on building on the
lands he sold in Brookline, and the later adoption of zoning laws were
urged for a similar end. Similar battles exist today, frequently centering
on "environmental" restrictions on housing size and open space.

Nonetheless, despite opposition, working-class residence was extended into more and more suburbs. By 1910, Winthrop, a peninsula to
the east of Boston, had been developed largely in tripledeckers. Several
towns toward the north, and the outlying wards of Boston itself, contained similar neighborhoods.[99] In a manuscript compiled between 1905
and 1914, the housing reformers Robert A. Woods and Albert J. Kennedy celebrated these "zones of emergence." They argued that the passage of property in these zones into the hands of immigrants was worthwhile:

> The lust for land and building institutes a stage through which
> all newcomers go. A house is large enough to signalize
> achievement in the most forceful way. it has a quality that
> bolsters a man with his neighbors as no other small owner-
> ship does. It furnishes an extremely valuable training in ac-
> quisition, and has great utility as automatically interesting the
> owner in government, neighborhood, and the general com-
> munity situation as nothing else does. Indeed analysis would
> show that this custom of buying a house constitutes one of
> the great educational forces in American life.[100]

Woods's espousal of working-class suburbanization—in opposition to
those who saw only deterioration—parallels his argument on unioniza-

tion. As S. B. Warner writes, "At a time when labor unions were widely thought to be instruments of revolution, settlement workers told the middle-class that economic unions like the American Federation of Labor were necessary devices in the protection of the worker and for the preservation of capitalism."[101] In both cases, upper-class reformers were accepting and modifying "solutions" developed "from below," rather than imposing them outright.

TEN

The Compromise Evaluated

ONCE business progressives accepted an idea of municipal reform which stressed individual ownership of housing, barriers to new construction were dismantled. The movement of transit, utilities, and housing beyond older built-up areas is well known, although often it is attributed simply to the invention of the trolley car. Sam Bass Warner Jr., who discusses suburbanization in Boston as a continuous process from the beginnings of the horse-drawn street railways, nonetheless documents a surge in building permits in three "streetcar suburbs" in the 1880s, and a level of construction in the 1880s that far surpasses the previous two decades.[1] Similar increases characterize other indicators of suburban investment for the Boston area, including street railway trackage and savings banks in suburbs (see table 10.1).

As we have shown, the Boston metropolitan area expanded greatly between 1890 and the end of 1920s. Most new housing built at the time was in the suburbs around Boston. While much of the new housing built was for homeowners, even much of the homeowner stock included rental units. Two- and particularly three-family structures were common.

Average rates of homeownership did not, in fact, rise for Massachusetts in the period between the turn of the century and 1920. (The rate was 34.9 percent in 1900, 34.8 percent in 1920.)[2] However, this stability was maintained despite an increase in the urban percentage of population, and despite the fact that at the turn of the century the rate at which rural residents owned homes was double that for non-farm residents.

For the United States, the overall homeownership rate increased from 45.1 percent in 1900 to 46.8 percent in 1930; the non-farm homeownership rate increased from 34.9 percent to 45.2 percent. By 1975, the

Fruits of the Suburban Compromise. For many workers, the development of suburbs allowed a move from the dirt, density, and dreariness of the older inner city, to somewhat more spacious quarters. But small house lots, commuting burdens, and isolation reduced the gains to partial ones. (See also page 294.)

Cleaning the Boston Slums, 1909.

Spring Street in the Old West End, 1907.

Boston Public Library, Print Dept.

Old West End, 1910.

A view of early suburbs.

Boston Elevated Railroad, courtesy of the
Bay State Society of Model Railroad Engineers.

More view of Early Suburbs

Table 10.1
Two Indices of Suburban Investment Activity in Metropolitan Boston
1880 to 1926

	Activity			
	Number of New Savings Banks[a]		Additional Miles of Street Railway Trackage[b]	
Time Period	Total	Boston	Total	Electric
1880–1884	7	2	—	—
1890–1889	38	5	—	—
1890–1894	16	3	4,035	2,452
1895–1899	5	3	7,161	7,038
1900–1904	—	—	11,934	11,934
1905–1909	—	—	13,654	13,654
1918–1926	—	—	12,550	12,550

[a] Peter Lemos with Daniel Luria, "Working Class Savings as Ruling Class Investment: The Rise of Massachusetts Banking" Working Paper #25 in *Boston: Studies in Urban Political Economy* (1974). Not available, 1900–1926.
[b] Edward Mason, *The Street Railway in Massachusetts*, (Cambridge, Harvard University Press, 1932).

metropolitan rate had increased to 61.2 percent, while the overall rate in 1977 was 64.8 percent.[3]

Average home ownership rates, even those limited to urban residents, understate the chances of home ownership for individuals. As Boston residents became homeowners, often moving to the suburbs, immigrants or younger Bostonians replaced them as tenants. But taking the sample of people who lived in Boston in 1880 used in chapter 5, we find that the percent owning homes rose from 6.7 percent in 1880 to 14.4 percent in 1890, 24.5 percent in 1900, and 34.5 percent in 1910. (Of those few traced beyond World War I, the majority became homeowners.)[4] This rise is paralleled by suburbanization. Average distance lived from Boston City Hall rose from 0.85 miles in 1880 to 1.29 miles in 1890, 2.46 miles in 1900, and 3.4 miles in 1910, while the population density of the ward or town of residence fell by one-quarter in thirty years, with most of the reduction coming in the 1900–1910 decade. For those remaining in Boston or in its older suburban districts or suburban towns, home ownership percentages rose only slowly.[5]

The late-century construction boom did not occur in Boston alone. David Harvey's estimates of investment in the "built environment" in

the United States show a greater percengage of national product devoted to building transport lines, housing, and other structures between
1890 and 1910 than at other times in American history.[6] Britain, which
also had access to the streetcar, had a much smaller construction boom,
and that about a decade later than in the United States. Clearly, a whole
complex of economic and political factors—trans-Atlantic cycles of investment and migration, working-class pressure on cities, and so on—
may have contributed to the differences; construction peaked at different times in different American cities as well[7] (see figure 10.1).

After business and government leaders had accepted a suburban version of labor's municipal demands, it is clear that, except during periods
of national depression, major housing investment was made. But, did
workers benefit economically from the variant of working-class reform
that centered on suburbanization and owner-occupancy?

Housing and urban land policies are not the only reforms which have
emerged as a response to incipient rebellion. Education, welfare, social
security, economic regulation, and union recognition have all been used
to placate or co-opt the demands of farmers or of employed or unem-

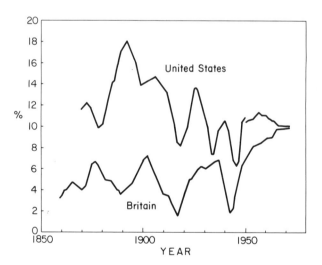

Figure 10.1 Different Rhythms of Investment: Britain and the United States:
Percent of GNP (U.S.A.) and GDP (Britain). Five-Year Moving Averages.
(*Source:* Adapted from David Harvey, "The Urban Process Under Capitalism: A
Framework for Analysis," in Michael Dear and Allen J. Scott, eds., *Urbaniza-
tion and Urban Planning in Capitalist Society* (London: Methuen, 1981).)

ployed workers. Often seen simply as either "progress for all" or as pure mechanisms for "regulating the poor," these programs are really uneasy compromises. They are outcomes of struggles, in which those in power are forced to yield some measure of economic benefit, in return for the maintenance of their political control. The important question is of course what are the long-term consequences of the change?

Every reform struggle contains a tension between immediate and long-term interests. Whether or not a reform will economically benefit the working class, or at least some employed or unemployed workers, has been addressed over and over again, in a number of contexts. What a reform will do to the *organization* of the working class is, however, a little-explored field. Theoretically this question has been discussed by Gramsci in the development of his concept of a "war of position" between classes, and in Gorz's distinction between "reformist" (or self-limiting) reforms, and "non-reformist reforms," which pave the way for greater working-class unity and organization as well as paying off in some economic terms.[8]

The expansion of suburbanization and homeownership in the United States is an example of a reform that was debated in the working class movement when it was proposed and whose eventual consequences may be evaluated in the light of history.

A. Economic Benefits to the Working Class

The demands that labor made in the 1880s—better and cheaper housing and generally improved urban conditions—were debated in terms of rival theories about the place of "rent" in the economy. These theories debated whether the price paid for land or its use (or for other resources) eventually fell upon wages, profits, or both, and whether a reduction of rents would increase or merely redistribute the total incomes or values produced by society.

1. The Rent Theory Debate

The orthodox tradition in economics has always held that monopoly could *in theory* pose a barrier to investment, raising prices and reducing production. But orthodox theorists have generally held these effects to be small. David Ricardo, the main developer of the theory of rent, argued that landlords were passive recipients of rents, *not* active agents interfering with the economy (except perhaps when they united to impose tariffs on Britain's grain imports). Land was expensive, he held, because food prices were high, not the reverse.[9] The same argument has generally applied to urban land—it is seen as costly because it is naturally scarce, and housing is costly to build, not the reverse. The moral, implicitly, is that land redistribution will not do much for the economy; while rent controls, zoning, and other limits to owners' rights will, if they have any effect, make everyone worse off.[10]

But economics also has a radical tradition, within which the power of landowners has sometimes been seen as important. In the United States, one version of this tradition was exemplified in the writings of Henry George, whose role in the working-class movement we have already described. George, as indicated above, saw land ownership and monopoly as posing a major barrier to investment, and as impoverishing both workers and small businessmen.[11]

The Marxist variant of the radical economic tradition has never placed as much of an emphasis on the landlord. According to Marx, the principal class conflict for workers in a capitalist era was not against landlords. Concern over either the price of products produced on the land or over access to land ownership was subordinated to direct conflict with capital over wages and hours (in the short run) and control of society (in the long run).

Friedrich Engels argued such a position against land reformers like Henry George. But he went further, to argue that a spread of ownership, at least in the housing sector, would not merely be secondary, it would be economically useless and politically harmful. Considering a proposal that workers should own their own homes, Engels states:

> Let us assume that in a given industrial area it has become the rule that each worker owns his own little house. In this case, *the working class of that area lives rent free;* expenses for rent no longer enter into the value of its labor power. Every reduction in the cost of production of labor power, that is to say, every permanent price reduction in the workers' necessities of life is equivalent "on the basis of the iron laws of political economy" to a reduction in the value of labor power

and will therefore finally result in a corresponding fall of wages. Wages would fall on an average corresponding to the average sum saved on rent, that is, the worker would pay rent for his own house, but not, as formerly, in money to the house owners, but in unpaid labor to the factory owner for whom he works.[12]

Engels generalized the point to argue that any saving by consumers will be to capitalist advantage. The worker with a small garden plot who produced some food could be paid below the cost of subsistence. The effect of cheating by shopkeepers, if generalized, would be reflected in average wage rates; thus the introduction of consumer cooperatives would benefit employers. Indeed, Engels presented as applicable in all capitalist situations the argument that reforms affecting the cost of living cannot help the working class. "Either they become general and then they are followed by a corresponding reduction of wages, or they remain quite isolated experiments, and then their very existence as isolated exceptions proves that their realization on a general scale is incompatible with the existing capitalist mode of production."[13]

Engels's specific defense of this view was based on his analysis of German and English conditions, and a denial that capitalists could provide owner-occupied housing for workers within a diversified urban labor market. He did not envision that an attack on land monopolists, combined with rapid development of urban transit systems, could allow wide production of cheap suburban housing.

Such a conclusion is, however, not foreordained by Marxist theory. Marx suggested labor might benefit from access to land or to cheaper commodities in certain cases. While seeking these goals might be a distraction from the main business of confronting capital, Marx was able to recognize the advantages to labor of pursuing some of these goals in a particular situation. It was futile to warn labor away from them as a point of principle.

One example was frontier settlement. Marx indicated that areas of new "colonization" did not provide good ground for the capitalist exploitation of labor, because workers could utilize the new land for survival. Capitalists could respond by preventing access to land, or restricting laborers' freedom to leave their employers. This struggle over land tenure or freedom of labor might occur.[14] This argument suggests that in a frontier society such as the United States, access by workers to land ownership might lead to higher wages for those workers remaining in industrial employ. But it does not deny that in the German situation, analyzed by Engels, giving workers land might in fact depress wages by entrapping them as peasants who could not earn a full living from their farms. One could not, that is to say, decide whether land ownership could favor workers without analyzing the specifics of a case.

The same was true on the issue of food prices. Marx's theory of rent distinguished between two major types of rent. The first, "differential rent," merely gave the landowner the right to receive the *excess* value produced on land which was more fertile, better located, or better suited for investment. Changing or restricting ownership or its rights could not affect this rent, within a capitalist system. Nor did differential rent actively affect prices or investment possibilities. However, another type of rent existed. "Absolute rent" was exacted by a landholding class and could raise the price of basic foods and restrict investment in their production.[15] By an extension of this argument, Marxist economics has identified a series of "absolute" and "monopoly" rents which can affect the values or costs of production, including workers' necessities of life.[16]

Which type of rent is involved in a particular situation, and whether rent or price reductions can benefit the working class is therefore a matter for specific analysis.

In Volume II of *Capital*, Marx suggested a case in which reduced prices for consumption goods had benefited the working class. The entry of cheap grain from the frontier regions had allowed increased consumption levels in England, he stated, "It is not true that consumption of necessities does not increase as they become cheaper. The abolition of the Corn Laws in England proved the reverse to be the case."[17]

This was a reversal of an earlier opinion that free trade could not benefit workers, and that cheaper food imports would only lead to lower wages.[18] (This earlier argument may have been the basis of Engels's position on housing.)

Other passages in *Capital* make it clear that Marx did not think improved living standards *automatically* followed free trade or the abolition of monopolies, nor did he propose that labor ally with capitalists to seek these gains. In Volume I, he analyzed the political alliances that had pressed reforms in England. He suggested there that the ability of labor to ally with landlords against capital enabled some gains to be won.[19] In other words, his analysis amounted to a view that labor had been able to win something from the abolition of tariffs only because it had *not* subordinated itself to capital in seeking to implement the reform.

Nor did Marx think that gains in the standard of living would be permanent. Eventually, a falling rate of accumulation and the replenishment of the pool of the unemployed would force capitalists to counterattack, and give them a means to force wages down. This would even occur in the "favored" United States once the frontier was closed. As new possibilities for technical advance and accumulation within capitalism declined—as the system came up against its own limits—economistic struggles would no longer yield labor economic gains within the system. For the long run, revolutionary demands alone could save the working class from eventual misery.

In the short run, however, Marx did not think that gains from trade union activities were impossible, much less undesirable. This is clear from his criticism elaborated in *Wages, Price and Profit* of the "iron law of wages" which was purported to make union demands for higher pay meaningless.[20]

If this was true about trade union struggles over wages, Marx's arguments on the frontier and on free trade must imply that, in certain circumstances, struggle over rents and tariffs also could yield short-term gains. A labor position in favor of abolishing barriers to production of basic necessities—for the abolition of absolute rent—was admissible as long as one recognized that winning them would require a simultaneous struggle against capitalists.[21]

The possibility raised by Marx that an anti-monopoly or consumer strategy might sometimes be appropriate for labor is not, in itself, proof that an urban reform program was a good one for labor in the late nineteenth century. The conditions under which such a strategy makes sense must be examined closely. If there is no absolute rent raising the price of housing to the working class, or no barrier to capital investment restricting production of this necessary consumer good, then there is no gain to be won through an anti-monopoly strategy. If (as Engels assumed) there is no technology that can build a sufficiently increased supply of cheap urban housing, there is no way to win anything by demanding its availability. If, on the other hand, that technology is *inevitably* going to be applied, as has often been said about traction and automotive commuting technologies, there is also no need for wasting political energies demanding them. Only if a barrier to existing or potential systems of construction exists, and if that barrier can be removed politically, is a consumer struggle economically justifiable. Even then, it may be undesirable if it is incompatible with concurrent struggles against employers to secure for workers at least a portion of the gains from the removal of monopoly barriers or absolute rent.

2. Economic Gains in Boston's Suburbanization

Both Marx's theory of rent and George's theory of speculation allow the possibility that the working class can benefit from the removal of barriers to land use. If one of the necessities of life can be produced more cheaply, or better, on the newly opened land, and if (in Marx's theory) capitalists can be prevented from taking all the gains, the workers' standard of living may rise. The "opening" of suburbs may have been, historically, such a case. The removal of barriers to use of suburban land, and to the use of new transit systems that could make it accessible, created a condition in which working-class housing could be produced more cheaply. The benefits of this saving may in part have gone to workers' employers, because an increase in wages that would have been required by rising rents was staved off. But wages remained high enough that at least some of the benefit could go to workers in the form of more spacious housing.

The expansion of a metropolitan area generally involves at least some increase in land values. As population, employment, or housing standards increase, new space is required to accommodate the new demand. If no new land can be added to the city, the price of existing urban space will be bid up, often precipitously.[22] If land can be converted from agricultural to urban uses, its value is often increased, although if enough land is available for conversion, land sellers competition keep price increases to a minimum.

Frequently, a large jump in land values occurs at the point of subdivision, when utilities are connected up to a new area of a city. This sudden increase would not occur if a gradual expansion of the supply of urban land were keeping pace exactly with demand. Its existence suggests that something is holding investment back. Developers are holding back on their projects until enough pent-up demand exists to allow unusually high returns, or speculators are holding undeveloped land, awaiting some presumed future jump in values. At other times, developers and land speculators or assemblers themselves may be held back, by an inability to assemble the proper-sized parcels or to receive the permission of cities to install utilities or to build. In these cases, the reduced supply of developed housing that results may increase rents both to owners of the existing stock of dwellings and, particularly, to those few who are able to control new construction and capitalize the future higher rents.[23]

If any of these barriers exists, and is inflating the price of working-class housing, then municipal control over suburbanization—advocated by "Sewer Socialists"—or taxation to reduce the gains to speculators—advocated by the Single Taxers—might restrict such monopoly control and thus reduce the real housing costs.

Monopoly control was reduced in Boston. To demonstrate this, one need only compare the sorts of returns that transit and land development brought in Henry Whitney's early development of Beacon Street as a unique luxury project with the returns to development in the 1890s from towns like Somerville in which the tripledecker predominated. In Brookline, as shown in chapter 7, assessed land value doubled from 1885 to 1890. Some of Whitney's own land tripled in value. In two areas of Brookline, annual rates of land appreciation were calculated at or above 25 percent in the 1880s and 1900s, and at 51.9 percent and 80 percent annual rates during the 1890s. While these figures do not adjust for the costs of trolley lines themselves, the lines built on Beacon Street and two cross streets cannot have represented an investment of more than half a million dollars (or a 25 percent mark-up on land cost, at most), which was recouped on fares and on the later sale of the line.[24]

Later lines, however, do not seem to have yielded equivalent profit. Mason, in his study, indicates an eventual economic failure of the street railways, preceded by a slow fall of dividends between 1890 and 1910.[25] This evidence, however, is not particularly relevant, since the returns at issue include not only those of the lines, but also those of real estate developers besides Whitney who were involved in real estate. Warner, for example, mentions that real estate developers in southern Boston held directorships in transit companies.[26] More to the point is the difference in the pace of land value development once broader-scale investment began to take place, particularly in the late 1890s.

While Brookline land values doubled in five years, values in the ring affected by street railway electrification (3–7 miles out, particularly) grew

only by about 25 percent in the 1890s (see chapter 4). We can use Somerville, which included in its western wards a large area opened to
commuter settlement by trolley lines in the 1890s, to represent this ring.
According to the price index in chapter 3, values in Somerville rose 46
percent between 1890–1894 and 1900–1904. Since land values per square
mile in Somerville were about $6 million ($26 million for the entire town
of 4.2 square miles) in 1900, estimates of 25 percent or 46 percent for
value increases during the 1890s would imply a value increase per square
mile of $1.3 to $2 million.

This clearly exceeds the cost of the rail systems. There were 32 miles
of track in Somerville, or 7.6 miles per square mile of land area. Using
Mason's capitalization estimate for street railways of $39,000 per square
mile, this would indicate an investment of less than $400,000 per square
mile of the city.[27] Even if transit developers owned all the land served
by their lines (which they did not), their rate of gain would have been
less than Whitney's. Assuming the 46 percent value increase for land,
an investment of $4.3 million in land and $0.4 million in railway development would yield $1.6 million in profit. This is a very attractive re-
turn, but it is considerably less than the rate of appreciation Whitney
enjoyed from his Beacon Street investments.

It is not hard to see that Whitney, like Gould and Sage in New York,
had an incentive to limit development so as not to spoil his market. It
was only after the loosening of Whitney's monopoly that development of
rail lines in the new suburban areas reached its maximum pace.

The partial breaking up of the transit monopoly is a case where political action led to lower returns for a particular set of investors, and thus
released a supply of land for housing. The case is one in which an attack
on a land monopoly bore some fruit.

The question of who ultimately pays or benefits still arises. Engels implied that a reduction in housing costs would benefit capital by allowing
wage reductions. George, while expecting labor and competitive business both to benefit, acknowledged that the benefits might all go to
monopolies. In other words, reduced costs of living would not *necessarily* help labor. However, the four decades of municipal growth that began in 1890 lead one to conclude that, at least for some workers, the
extension of services meant a long-term increase in consumption standards. Residential crowding did decrease, public health facilities did improve, commuter transport at least temporarily did become less burden-
some for many workers.

To what extent this improvement was available to at least some workers at the turn of the century, and to what extent it had to await the
suburban booms that followed World War I and World War II, is a matter of interpretation. The average population density in the center of the
metropolitan area did not begin to decline until the 1930s, although in
certain wards of Boston, like the West End, a decline began in 1900.[28]
On the other hand, with total population in the metropolitan area growing rapidly, a better index may be whether population density at the center
is growing more rapidly than the area's total population.

Table 10.2 shows that estimated central density grew more than twice
as rapidly as total population in the 1880s. In the 1890s, despite an increased growth rate of total population, central density grew no more
rapidly than in the previous decade, and in the 1900–1910 decade it grew
less rapidly than total population—a relationship reversed only in the
construction-slump decade, 1910–1920. Certainly, from the turn of the
century, a growing percentage of the population lived at lower densities
than during the 1890s.[29]

Contemporary reports, such as Woods's and Kennedy's accounts of the
zone of emergence, suggest some housing improvement at the time, for
the middle stratum of the working class. Woods's other studies of the
inner city make it clear that, for many workers, intense crowding and
slum life still prevailed and were growing worse.[30]

Table 10.2
Regression Estimates of Population Density Gradient

Year	A	b_1	b_2	b_3	R^2	gA	gF
1870	5952	−1048	+61	−1.13	.454	—	—
1880	8176	−1432	+83	−1.53	.499	37%	52%
1890	11326	−1949	+110	−1.99	.574	39%	18%
1900	15737	−2666	+147	−2.61	.641	39%	30%
1910	18643	−3102	+169	−2.97	.689	18%	20%
1920	22188	−3612	+193	−3.31	.709	19%	15%
1930	23964	−3629	+182	−2.96	.738	7%	18%
1940	23139	−3417	+168	−2.69	.753	−3%	2%
1950	23639	−3407	+164	−2.60	.774	2%	9%
1960	20853	−2709	+120	−1.78	.776	−12%	8%
1970	19399	−2350	+98	−1.37	.781	−7%	6%

NOTE: Population per square mile estimated using regression form DENSITY $= A + b_1$ DIST $+ b_2$
DIST$^2 + b_3$ DIST$^3 + e$ where DIST is straight line mileage from Boston center.
  The figure gA is the percentage change in A over previous decades, while gF is the percentage change
in total population of the area.
  All t and F statistics significant at .01 level.

Table 10.3
Housing Prices, Rents and Incomes

Year (or Mid-Year) of Period	Average Family Income	Average Value of New Houses	Year's Income Needed for Purchase	Rent as % of Income
1880	950	1,760	1.85	17%
1890	901	2,464	2.73	19%
1910	1,248	3,464	2.78	21%
1925	2,122	5,774	2.72	22%
1935	1,700	5,145	3.03	20%
1980	19,800	70,000	3.50	—

SOURCES: Lloyd Rodwin, *Housing and Economic Progress*, pp. 17.32. Updated from H.U.D. estimates.

The relationship of housing prices and rents to incomes, presented by Rodwin, also gives a mixed picture of progress (see Table 10.3). The ratio of new housing prices to family incomes, which had increased by approximately 50 percent between 1800 and 1890 in his estimates, remains constant thereafter through the 1920s. There is a small increase in the 1930s, because of falling incomes, but the pre-depression ratio appears to have been reestablished, or possibly even reduced, after the war.

Progress was apparently limited, however, for those who could not partake of the new opportunities for suburbanization or home ownership. Rodwin estimates apartments' rent–income ratios to have increased from 17 percent in 1880 to 19 percent in 1890. They continued to increase through the mid-1920s and declined only slightly into the 1930s. Since population densities at the center of the metropolitan area did not decline until the Depression, it appears that benefits in terms of rents *or* housing densities did not "trickle down" to the inner-city renters until after World War II. Even then, benefits did not reach all workers.[31]

B. Political Costs to Labor

The economic gains that accrued to part of the working class suggest that labor's support of municipal reform had some reason on its side. The simple view that suburbanization was either unreasonable individual striving or that it was simply a manipulation by the capitalist elite is untenable. From a viewpoint of labor strategy, however, the value of the working-class attack on rent must also be measured against its contribution to labor unity and to a class-conscious political movement. By this criterion, turn of the century suburbanization is less praiseworthy. The pattern of suburban home ownership that was set up had unequal effects on different strata of workers. It entrapped its beneficiaries in a mesh of depreciating investments, giving them individual stakes in differential and competing properties. But even these economic divisions—like those inherent in labor union demands—could have been excused, from the viewpoint of radical theory, if the struggle to attain the demands had helped create a class-based political movement. Unfortunately for working-class development, this did not happen. "Sewer socialism" did not built a lasting socialist party; the growth of suburbs, indeed, undercut socialism's political base.

Several theories have attempted to explain why the Socialist Party, which had grown so rapidly in the first decade of the century, declined thereafter. One is that the party turned to the right in 1912, and came to be a nonmilitant, petit bourgeois party which lost its appeal to workers. This line of argument is inaccurate. The party was still gaining in membership and electoral strength between 1912 and 1917. It opposed the World War. It made many post-1912 efforts to attract black Americans, and did much of the work that resulted in women's suffrage. Explicitly anti-imperialist, it remained a radical political party until its death in 1924.

Another, and more interesting, argument, is that the fall of the Socialist Party was largely due to repression by the State. This is no doubt partly correct. Harrassment of party members, impoundment of Socialist newspapers by the U.S. Post Office, and campaign sabotage took a heavy toll on the party. But what is more important is that such open repression failed. The fate of the party was not decided until Progressive Era reform cut much of the ground out from under moderate socialists. Some even suggest that a principal goal of the Progressive movement was to smash the S.P.

A third explanation points to the increasingly "un-American" character of the party. According to this view, an immigrant-dominated socialist party fell easy prey to the more "European" appeal of the Communist organizations from 1918 onward. This position confuses outcome and process. The success of CP raids on the S.P.'s foreign language federations is not evidence that the S.P. was in trouble, but only that its urban immigrant base was not its strongest point.[32]

A different reason seems just as likely to us. The peculiar history of American political parties has seriously blocked third parties for over a century. With both capitalist parties formed in times of comparative labor weakness, and with the success of "bread-and-butter" trade unionism in a generally dynamic economy, there has been little room at the federal level for electoral alternatives. This situation has created a well-nigh inexorable force driving the American left to a local electoral strategy. The Socialist Party tried municipal socialism because that was where it could build a base at the turn of the century.

Municipal reform, however, led to an exodus from the cities. We hypothesize that the decline of the S.P. can, to some important extent, be explained by the migration of its early constituency to the suburbs, where the party was not established and where the class mix ruled out local socialist political organization on any significant scale. We test this hypothesis formally in appendix F.

Comparing Socialist voting strength in a sample of 145 U.S. cities from 1900 to 1916, we find that the more the suburbanization, the weaker the Socialist electoral strength in local elections. On the other hand, suburbanization did not reduce votes for the party's presidential candidate, Eugene V. Debs. Comparing the period of party decline, 1916 to 1922, with the pre-1916 era, the decline in local vote still correlates with suburbanization. Taking the local vote as reflecting upon the party organization, it appears that suburbanization had a destructive effect. Changes in the vote for Debs between 1912 and 1920 do not, however, correlate with suburbanization, suggesting continuing *ideological* support for socialism. Thus organizational weakening antedates any possible ideological conservatizing attributed to suburban life. Indeed, the data suggest that psychological conservatism resulted from the lack of an organized movement, rather than from the economic gains of suburbia.

The organizational decline of the Socialist Party is, however, a very important effect of suburbanization. And this suggests that, strategically, the party erred to the extent that it allowed its demands for municipal reform, better housing, and cheaper utilities to be diverted into programs simply for suburbanization. It is on this ground, rather than that of its reformism *per se*, that it can be criticized.

Certainly, from a viewpoint of working-class organization, a pattern of expansion through municipal housing developments built on the urban fringe might have been more conducive to holding a Socialist Party together. This, at least, has been the experience of the British Labour Party and some of the other Social Democrat movements of Western Europe.[33] But such a housing pattern was not considered very seriously by the Socialist leadership before World War I. Right after the War, rent control campaigns and public housing demands had a brief vogue, and Milwaukee's city government built a few houses. In the 1920s, when public housing was being built throughout Europe, there were few demands for it from the surviving fragments of American socialism. The Amalgamated Clothing Workers, in New York, built the first significant cooperative project in 1927.[34]

Before World War I, indeed, the issue of the form of housing was raised in the S.P. by only one significant group: socialist feminists considering collective alternatives to housework. Ending the isolation of the housewife, they reasoned, would help organizing. Charlotte Perkins Gilman called for the building of apartment communities with centralized professional cooking, laundry and child-care facilities. Meta Stein Lilienthal described plans for communal cooking, while K. W. Baker argued for "futurist" communal child-rearing. And a group in Greenwich Village actually drew up plans for a cooperatively run apartment house.[35] But these proposals did not receive much of a hearing. John Spargo, for example, while advocating that some household chores be performed by outside agencies, opposed communal living. "A glorified Waldorf-Astoria is inferior to a simple cottage with an old-fashioned garden," he wrote.[36] And even among women, others, like Caroline Hunt, "believed in the family home with a roof of its own and a plot of its own" so firmly that she considered its importance beyond argument.[37]

Even with home ownership as the norm, different financial and taxpaying arrangements might have made housing more clearly a consumer good and less a financial asset subject to speculative investment, hopes of capital gain, and frequent disillusionment through asset depreciation. And a more active awareness of a need to build organizations among working-class homeowners might have helped preserve a socialist party. Victor Berger's more conservative branch of the party in Milwaukee was able to do that at least for a while.[38] A more ideological labor union movement, less divided by craft union and ethnic distinctions, might have held a movement together despite the original spread to the suburbs.

By the time of the suburban boom after World War II it was too late to think of alternative forms of suburban housing for the United States. The Socialist Party had fallen apart; the Communist Party never came to play a major role in urban or suburban politics as it has in some Western European cities (most successfully in Bologna, Italy). Public housing was discredited by being built as a last resort, rather than as a model for private developers. Labor unions that still sought to keep their members housed together did so through cooperative high-rise projects, and these were a success only in New York. When labor demanded more jobs, in the Depression and after World War II, they were accommodated by more suburbanization helped by cheap credit and government highway construction. Until the early 1960s, the suburban compromise worked smoothly. Labor or radical movements did not have to think of a housing or suburban strategy at all.

It was only when the suburban compromise began to fall apart in the 1960s that strategic discussion of rent and land value issues returned to the agenda of American radicalism. The confusions that resulted—and the real conflicts that underlay them—will be analyzed in the next, and final, chapter.

ELEVEN

Compromise Lost

THE suburban compromise remained a dominant factor in American economic and political life from the turn of the century through the 1960s. Today, however, it has lost its power to compel the allegiance of many groups in American society. Discontent by the participant groups and general economic conditions have undermined its effectiveness. Whether it can be reconstructed in anything like its historic form is highly doubtful.

In this final chapter, we chronicle the continuing decline of the compromise, which began in the 1960s. We first describe the contradictions that emerged within the suburbanization process during that decade. These included technical limits to the continued extension of suburbs, around at least the older central cities, which became apparent and led to an intensification of conflict over urban lands. They also included social limits to suburbanization, and to the ability of suburbanization and devaluation to ensure social stability. These social limits stemmed from dissatisfactions felt both by suburban residents themelves and by those left behind or trapped by metropolitan growth. These contradictions created severe problems for further suburbanization, but did not completely end it.

We next describe the further problems for suburbanization and devaluation that emerged with the general economic crisis of the 1970s. These problems included both the limitations to new suburban construction caused by economic austerity, and the inflation of housing values in a general inflationary period, which temporarily disrupted the use of asset devaluation as an orderly process to ensure class stability. We show that the apparent recovery of housing values does not, however, mean a permanent end to the mechanisms that have in the past been expressed as asset devaluation. Rather we show that the general economic crisis intensifies, even as it masks, the contradictions that emerged in the earlier decade.

Finally we discuss the role of working class demands and pressures (or at least of demands put forward tentatively in the name of the working class) in the urban spatial politics of the past two decades. We discuss the strengths and limits of antimonopoly and community defense demands that made up the staple activities of "left" activism in this period. We conclude with a discussion of possible directions for urban evolution and for left- and working-class activity under possible projections of either continued economic austerity or recovery over the next decade or two. We suggest that suburbanization—and housing policy generally—is unlikely to play the same central role it did in the past two cycles of economic expansion, but that community and housing policy must at least be taken into account in any emerging strategy.

A. Contradictions of the Consensus

The suburban compromise was the dominant social arrangement in American cities when the 1960s began. Federal policy had lost any potential for constructing moderate-income housing which could keep better-paid workers within central cities. The Highway Trust Fund, established in 1956, allowed urban areas to expand their commuter radius using federal money. The end of the deep 1956–58 recession, and the post-Sputnik expansion of educational opportunities, created apparent economic opportunities to match the housing opportunities afforded by the suburbs. Little visible unrest or conflict marred the mood of the country: critics of the society in general and of suburbia in particular complained only of apathy and anxiety rather than misery and the nonfulfillment of basic expectations.[1]

The few complaints that emerged from the suburbs were easy to dismiss, as in Raymond Vernon's 1961 claim that supposed urban problems were really myths.[2] Vernon did not expect that the middle class could be aroused to crisis policies for the cities or to tax revolt, and even suggested that serious trouble was unlikely in the ghetto. "The trend," he wrote, "is not clearly retrogressive. . . . There is no clear evidence of the taut stretching of a rubber band close to its breaking point."[3]

It was not long, however, before the band did snap. Uprisings swept Watts, Hough, Detroit, and other ghettos. They were followed by a wave of protests against urban renewal, property taxes, and other policies in the surrounding moderate-income white areas. But Vernon's view was not his alone. Even so sympathetic a depiction of the older neighborhoods as Herbert Gans's *The Urban Villagers* showed a community unable to rouse itself to active protest when threatened with demolition. Although Gans did suggest that forcing city residents to join the suburban migration would harm them, his evidence suggests few manifestations of opposition as of the late 1950s.[4] If urban renewal forced unwilling participants into the suburbanization process, it seemed at worst to be compelling a small minority to go along with a trend that the majority wanted.

Even the principal problem cited by Vernon, the weakness of the old functions of the central business district, seemed to be near solution by the early 1960s. Although the older downtown shopping centers and manufacturing districts continued to decline, new business and institutional activities arose to take their place. Office towers, hospital and university complexes, and civic centers, as well as highways, were new competitors for central city land. Their construction offered some hope of coherence to a new spread city or megalopolis; their taking of land simply pushed the last few laggards onto the suburban escalator.[5]

When, in due course, the ghettos did erupt, suburbanization was still seen as the answer. Through 1963, urban unrest was scattered and unfocused, and could be dismissed as the result of gangs or of individual deviants. To the extent that social workers or social scientists saw the causes of such "deviance" as social, the slum environment itself could be blamed. If the problem was one of slums, then suburban dispersal seemed at least as likely a cure as the building of more public housing within the city. Overcoming barriers to housing integration, through rational argumentation—as in the claim that Blacks did *not* lower property values— or through legal action, was seen as a long-run solution. Even advocates of a community development approach saw its benefit as making young people fit to "graduate" from the slums.[6]

After the riots began, the chorus of experts favoring a suburban solution to the ghetto problem swelled still more. A typical example was Edward S. Mason's comment at an international conference that "the only practical solution is to lift the ghettoites out of the ghetto and rehouse them at the periphery where the jobs are and where there is access to them."[7]

There was, to be sure, some criticism of these policies. Some argued that politically they amounted to an attempt to disperse centers of opposition to those in power, and that they would defuse pressures for greater change by draining leaders from the black communities of the city. From a radical viewpoint, a strategy of community economic development for the ghetto was sometimes counterposed as more conducive to holding together and strengthening pressures for change. But there were economic difficulties with the "development" strategy. And radicals also came to recognize this strategy was imperfect because leaders could be drawn into "black capitalist" activities or machine politics and become a conservative local elite. Eventually, talk of community-development alternatives became less common.[8]

Herbert Gans's endorsement of suburbanization as the nearest thing to a solution is representative of the acceptance even by a supporter of the inner-city community of the view that a repetition of the old compromise was the best that could be hoped for.[9]

There was, however, a problem in this view: *the possibilities for further suburbanization were reaching their limits.* These limits were both technical and social. From a *technical* viewpoint, the space that could be used for new housing developments within an acceptable commuting range of the central city was limited. Even before fuel prices began to rise in the 1970s, the ecological limits of increased automobile use were growing problematic. Moreover, attempts to extend these limits were encountering difficulty. True, radial highways could be widened, allowing higher commuting speeds and extending the radius available for suburbs. But this drew protests from communities that were demolished, disrupted, or polluted by the new highways. Alternatively, the move to the suburbs could be extended by locating factories and other sources of employment in hitherto residential districts. But this too drew an angry response from existing suburban communities threatened by new developments or by increased housing densities.

These technical limits were not necessarily unsolvable. Had residents both of inner-city communities and of older suburbs remained willing to sell their properties and move to ever newer suburban areas, the technical limits would have been extendable. But the rising cost of new suburbs, which required this relocation, revealed social contradictions implicit in the suburban compromise even in its periods of greatest success.[10]

As we have indicated in the previous chapters, suburbanization had given many working-class and "lower-middle-class" Americans a chance to acquire more and better housing. It had also meant access, at least for some, to local amenities—better schools, parks, and more valued neighborhoods themselves. But the process had also meant isolation from a community in which work and residence were located together, in which one's co-workers and neighbors were the same group, and in which stable class ties might develop. For a long time the living standard thus acquired was valued. But over time, at least some residents came to believe that suburban mobility would deliver, at best, only part of what it had promised. For some residents of the upper-middle-class or more affluent suburbs, the result would be an angry rejection of suburban lifestyle entirely, a rejection which has been well debated in the literature.[11] For residents of the less affluent suburbs—the newer tract communities and the aging suburbs of the inner ring—another rejection occurred. People did not reject their own communities, or renounce the goals of housing quality and amenity through homeownership. Rather, they ceased to believe that they could achieve these goals in full by moving ever farther into the suburbs. Knowing full well the limits to housing quality and to local amenity in the areas in which they lived, they came to feel that this would be the best they could achieve. In their own neighborhoods, they had at least some communal ties. They had at least some amenities, compared to the lowest income inner-city areas. Rather than trading up—a tactic which they were beginning to learn might be made illusory by neighborhood devaluation—they sought to hold on to what they already had. The disillusionment which for the more affluent became community rejection became for the less affluent the basis of community defense.

The defense generally took the form of struggles against different levels of government, although at time other targets (landlords or private land developers) also were attacked. The expressed aim was usually the conservation of a perceived *status quo* under attack, but the anger that fed the defense usually also found expression in a statement that the immediate issue was part of a larger history of "having been pushed around

Boston Public Library, Print Dept.

Traffic jam at Boylston and Tremont Street in 1921.

Boston Public Library, Print Dept.

Traffic Jam at the Sumner Tunnel in 1948.

The slow breakdown of urban transportation, under the pressure of the automobile. By 1963, traffic problems became so severe that Boston actually suffered from a 12 hour traffic jam!

Boston Public Library, Print Dept.

Traffic Jam at Haymarket Square in 1961.

too much," of being the victimized "little man." This reflected a real
yearning for a more egalitarian society, in the sense of wanting more respect and a leveling of power and wealth—even as it involved a desire
to protect privilege from the parallel egalitarian yearnings of those below
them.[12]

Since land use and housing expenses frequently were issues in these
disputes, suburbanization itself became an issue. Here, too, the demands were often confused. On the one hand, demands amounted to
calls for continuing and perfecting the trend toward more homeownership and better suburban conditions—i.e., people sought to preserve or
extend those aspects of their communities which involved suburban
amenities or the dream of mobility through housing and education. On
the other hand, the weaknesses of suburbanization were openly attacked, and certain investments necessary for its continuation—such as
highway construction—were actually stopped.

In this solution, working-class communities came into conflict with each
other, as well as with the upper classes. Local elites were able to ma-
neuver, to grant concessions here and there while minimizing the need
for major compromises, and to provoke intercommunal disputes, thus
buying time. What they were *unable* to do was to *impose* a policy that
would ensure both continued accumulation and create enough visible
benefit to reestablish the legitimacy of the suburban pattern. Thus, continuing waves of community struggle, of demands for more and better
housing and for improved neighborhood conditions exposed more and
more the contradictions of the suburban compromise.

B. Boston Aroused

The urban crisis of the 1960s affected many American cities, even some
whose major growth had come in the era of automobile suburbanization.
But the contradictions behind that crisis were particularly strong in Boston. There, the pace of suburban transformation and downtown renewal
in the late 1950s and in the 1960s marked more of a change from previous decades than for most other cities.

What is more, Boston's economic structure, involving more professional institutions and small-shop manufacturing occupations and fewer
large and concentrated industries than many other cities, tended to fo-

cus discontent at the community level. Industrial unionism had not generated cross-neighborhood working-class organizations to create a coun-
terpoint to parochial struggles over turf. Student and professional
radicalism, unusually strong in the area in the 1960s, was also a fractioning force. "New Left" groups either operated as a separate "youth" or
"anti-war" constituency, or took part in local struggles with an ideological commitment to the local community as the unit of organization. Thus,
Boston was, to some extent, unique—but it was unique in ways which
made it a harbinger of conflicts that were soon to arise elsewhere.

Because many of Boston's community issues have been reported at
length elsewhere, we shall discuss them only schematically. Neighborhood discontent in Boston, as elsewhere, emerged first in the form of
separate struggles in black and white communities, although the separation was, until the 1970s, not as clear as in some other cities. Early
black discontent was not focused into one major uprising: the city suffered two rounds of riots, but the disturbances were smaller than those
in other major cities. The smaller size of the minority community in Boston
than in Detroit, New York, and other northern centers made its struggles appear merely as one among a number of interethnic neighborhood
battles.

The local organization of the black community in Boston focused on
two issues: education and housing location. In common with blacks in
much of the country, Boston's minority leadership through the 1950s had
focused primarily on the issues of school integration and open housing.
Both were seen as matters of *exclusion* from the suburbanization process. Since exclusion was the central diagnosis, approaches such as support for fair housing laws and for integrated quality education in those
towns such as Cambridge, to which some blacks could move from the
ghetto, seemed appropriate as tactics. In Massachusetts, they had some
success. The Taubers' census tract analyses showed Cambridge as one of
the least segregated cities in the United States in 1960.[13] Massachusetts
has one of the strongest laws in the nation against housing discrimination, and by the late 1960s it would add a law allowing the state to void
local "snob-zoning" ordinances. Some suburban communities were willing, when pressed, to admit a small number of inner-city black children
as part of a private, voluntary busing program called "Operation Exodus."[14] However, when the state passed its strong school integration and
busing law in 1965, it carefully excluded intermunicipal (metropolitan)

busing, in effect exempting the white suburbs.[15] And despite all laws, the overwhelming majority of blacks (as well as Hispanic families who moved into Boston in large numbers in the late 1960s) remained in the inner-city neighborhoods of the South End, Roxbury, and Dorchester.

New demands thus arose, reflecting disillusionment with the integration strategy. In 1962, a campaign for improved schools in Roxbury was begun, culminating in a major school boycott by blacks and Hispanics the following year. The initial effect of that boycott was to increase, for about the next five years, the proportion of total school system resources directed to schools in black neighborhoods, *rather than* any effective integration.[16] Similarly, a controversy over the form of urban renewal in the Washington Park section of Roxbury allowed some black leaders to push successfully for the construction there of new housing for higher-income black families.[17] Upgrading of housing and education was thus, at least for a time, presented as a successful alternative to integration.

These initial campaigns were followed by campaigns for community-controlled housing in the South End, for tenant control in the Columbia Point housing project, and for access to the land cleared under Boston's highway plan in the "southwest corridor" for community-run housing or businesses. A new generation of political leaders articulated a more general version of the demand for community control, and it became the centerpiece of the program of minority groups in Boston in the late 1960s.[18]

Meanwhile, organization over neighborhood issues began to spread in the white communities of the inner ring. The rapid growth of new technological industries, hospitals, universities, and financial institutions in the metropolitan area was requiring new land for institutional expansion. It also was creating new demands for housing from groups never firmly committed to suburban residence: single individuals, childless couples, and young, small families, all of whom sought out inner-city neighborhoods where high-quality housing could be found or built. The city interpreted their new wants as a demand for urban renewal. A massive highway system was planned and begun, to knit the area together. All of these new demands led to massive demolition programs by the administrations of Governor John Volpe, Mayor John Collins of Boston, and their counterparts in some suburban towns. Much of the demolition was concentrated in low-income white ethnic communities surrounding downtown Boston and Cambridge.

Two generations of political movement.

Boston Public Library, Print Dept.

The inauguration of James Michael Curley as Governor in 1935 symbolized the coming to full power of the Massachusetts Irish.

Boston Public Library, Print Dept.

Martin Luther King's march through Boston in April 1965 marked the awakening of the Black community, which is only now beginning to achieve a measure of similar power. The scene is Columbus Avenue.

The extreme visibility of the destruction of the West End in 1959 may have made the dangers most apparent. The threatened communities began to organize a resistance.

In 1963, a small neighborhood located behind Harvard University's stadium and business school hung out a large sign proclaiming "TO HELL WITH URBAN RENEWAL" in response to threatened demolition. Their ten-year struggle to avoid eviction, although eventually unsuccessful, served notice that groups could fight the bulldozers. The idea spread rapidly. In Cambridge, a community coalition formed to oppose the construction of the "Inner Belt" highway, which would have cut through several working-class neighborhoods as well as some areas of student residence. Jamaica Plain, Somerville, and other communities threatened by the other links in the highway plan also began protests. Charlestown, a predominantly Irish neighborhood, voted down an urban renewal program even after being told that it would involve mostly rehabilitation loans to residents. East Boston's predominantly Italian community organized against expansion of Logan Airport runways and against the building of new ground transportation links that would have also brought more traffic to the airport area. Lynn, an industrial city in the northern part of the metropolitan area, was the scene of still more protests against urban renewal and highway building. Numerous neighborhoods fought expansion of specific universities and other institutions.[19]

Nor did the protests focus only on demolition, though that was their main target. Some neighborhoods were threatened by an influx of students and professionals into the rental housing market; this, combined with demolitions, drove up rents, and so demands for rent control began to be heard. Similarly, with taxes on housing driven up by rising government costs, the beginnings of tax revolt made themselves felt. Even the demand for direct community ownership of local resources was occasionally voiced, as when East Boston residents organized a community development corporation, one of the few white groups designated for federal aid under the Office of Economic Opportunity's Special Impact Program.

The demands made by different communities were generally spontaneous and specific. They were for the defense of homes and occasionally for the provision of specific public facilities seen as necessary for *local* wellbeing. The organizations that pushed for them were populist coalitions in the sense that working-class residents were often allied with shopkeepers, students, professionals, and others. Leadership was often, though not always, exercised by middle-class residents. Student radical organizers and "advocate planners" sometimes helped to articulate goals, but despite the claims of right-wing politicians and business spokesmen, the protests were not simply the work of a few well-off troublemakers and outside agitators. When there were leaders, local support was very broad; in all cases, the issues were locally generated.

Some of the community demands were successful in the late 1960s and early 1970s. This was particularly true when different communities began to band together. In the fall of 1971, delegations from several Boston-area communities marched on the state house demanding an end to all highway construction within the Boston metropolitan area. Represented were inner-city areas, working-class towns of the old streetcar ring, and a few affluent suburbs and inner-ring university enclaves. Black and white communities were there; city officials and student radicals were, for once, allied. It was a heady experience for all concerned. And it won the immediate demand for a ban on new construction. Governor Francis Sargent, turning against his predecessor (who had just become U.S. Secretary of Transportation) imposed a highway moratorium; the committee that he then appointed went on to cancel most of the planned highways within the Route 128 radius, and to scale down the few that remained.[20]

The success of the highway moratorium campaign suggested that unity among the different communities of the Boston area was possible, that a movement linking black and white working-class areas and even some sympathizers from outside could indeed be organized.

A few other successes in intercommunity organizing could be cited as well. Harvard students fighting the University administration had made common cause with community groups resisting the University's expansion. The latter had brought their demands to the campus in demonstrations at graduation exercises. Some of the white students had joined with black residents in blocking evictions. And in Italo-American East Boston, protests against airport expansion had drawn support from an unexpected ally:

> On three separate occasions that spring and summer, East Boston citizens—those already activists and others new at the game—slowed traffic to a crawl both at the airport and on the MPA's Mystic River Bridge nearby. The last demonstration

. . . included student sympathizers . . . and representatives from the South End, Roxbury and Jamaica Plain. One East Bostonian pulled out of the demonstration shouting, "This is a disgrace. We don't need outside agitators to participate." Standing quietly nearby were three or four blacks, including Chuck Turner in his dashiki, not an everyday sight for the sons and grandchildren of Naples, Abruzzi, Calabria, and Palermo. "We should be thankful they're here," one woman yelled, and no others pulled out of the line.[21]

Community coalitions had also forced the state legislature to pass an enabling act for local-option rent control, and set up a "master tax plan commission" to propose alternatives to the property tax.[22]

But hopes for a new populist coalition were quickly shattered. By the fall of 1974, black and white communities within the city of Boston were battling over school integration. Outer-ring suburbs were busily investigating whether environmental protection laws would enable them to zone out *lower income* developments. The new rent control laws were being watered down; Lynn's law was actually repealed. Voters turned down the tax commission's proposal for a graduated income tax designed to replace or reduce local property levies over the next year. As soaring gasoline prices brought home the message that suburban commuting options were dwindling and as rising unemployment ended the "miracle" of downtown job development, thoughts of a united community defense movement gave way to a struggle of neighborhood against neighborhood, each fighting only for its own preservation.

C. Boston Divided

The conservative turn taken by Boston's community movements is shown most clearly in two movements: opposition to high school busing, and the so-called "tax revolt."

The dispute over school busing drew national attention when it escalated into violence by the mid-1970s. Several Boston white communities, which resisted court-ordered school integration, argued that it would transfer benefits away from them and to black neighborhoods. The Massachusetts Racial Balance Act had defined the issue as busing between communities within the city—excluding the suburbs. By the early 1970s,

gaps in the allocation of resources to city schools were no longer narrow-
ing, and battles over allocation of pupils replaced battles over funds.
The parameters of conflict were fairly well-known to the public; resources were limited. The suburban schools and tax bases were off limits
to reform efforts in the city of Boston. Lower income white communities
saw their few resources, including their local schools, devaluing. As one
radical organizer commented, the force behind anti-black positions came
at least partly from desperation.[23] The school superintendent of Boston ·
called the issue "a class problem."

> We have a suburban ring around the city that likes to think
> of itself as liberal, and dissociates itself from the problems of
> the working class. They like to shift the problems of integra-
> tion onto the city. So the people in the city felt everything is
> against them. They feel if they could just raise an extra $5,000
> to cross the river and move, it would solve all their prob-
> lems. So they flee. But those who are left are stuck with all
> the problems—they feel trapped.[24]

But knowledge that class was involved did not prevent intercommunity
battles within the city from reaching a high level of explicitly racial violence.[25]

A similar turn was taken in tax reform. In the early 1970s the State
Legislature's Master Tax Plan Commission proposed revisions in Massachusetts taxes. Several radical and liberal groups responded with calls
for a more progressive tax alternative, involving a graduated income tax,
higher taxes on business, and a large reduction in property taxes, which
were (as indicated in chapter 8) regressively distributed among towns.
Two of the authors of this book were involved in one reform group, the
Ad Hoc Committee for Fair Taxation, which sought to build on the community activities of the anti-highway fight and other local issues to form
a coalition against regressive taxes.

The attempt failed. By far the principal reason for failure was the great
gap between the way we argued the issue, and the way the issue was
perceived by people.

> This experience can perhaps be seen most vividly in the in-
> cident encountered by Ted Behr during one of his public
> speaking engagements. We received a call from a civic asso-
> ciation in Dorchester, a working-class neighborhood of Bos-

ton, whose members were very upset about their tax situation and wanted to discuss the possibilities of a tax strike. Ted went to their meeting with a set of charts which showed how the people of the city of Boston were being milked by the tax system in Massachusetts, and how unfair the property tax was. He found out that the people were not so angry about their tax burden (though this was part of it), as they were about the lack of services that they were supposedly paying for. If they got the services, they were willing to pay the taxes. Ted's rap about how unfair the tax system was just did not go over. They just wanted to find out if they could refuse to pay their property taxes to the city of Boston until they got the level of services that they felt they should have.[26]

A subsequent attempt to carry a tax-reform initiative, to replace the flat rate income tax by a graduated tax, was defeated in a referendum in 1972 by a 2-to-1 majority. The League of Women Voters, which was the main supporter of the referendum campaign, argued that a graduated income tax was fairer than the existing state income tax and that it would save the middle and lower income family some money. The slogan was, "Let's Stop Paying the Fat Cat's Share."

The corporate opposition countered with a massive media campaign based on two points: (1) the graduated tax would mean higher taxes and (2) government spending was getting out of hand and a vote against the graduated tax would tell the governor and the legislature that people wanted spending kept in check. One subway advertisement featured the heading, "DON'T BE FOOLED—The Graduated Income Tax is just another tax increase." Below it said, "It means more for them, and less for you . . . Again!" These appeals were much less abstract and spoke directly to the frustrations, anger, and distrust of politicians that was felt by the general public.[27]

A state-wide telephone poll four months before the referendum found that 90 percent of the people felt that the graduated tax was fairer than the flat-rate income tax. At the same time, two-thirds of the people preferred a cut in government spending to the graduated tax. These were not contradictory responses; simply, the electorate understood how taxes work theoretically, but they also knew that liberal tax reforms did not necessarily mean tax relief for them given the way that state government operates.[28]

In 1978, another tax reform group, Fair Share, secured passage of a classification referendum, which allowed local governments to tax commercial property at higher rates than residential property. But proposals for partial income tax relief for low-income groups and for higher business taxes were defeated.

Two years later, the conservatives took their version of tax reform directly to the public. A ceiling on state and local spending had been proposed in 1972 by the First National Bank of Boston, a central institution of the Massachusetts financial elite.[29] Now, following California's passage of "Proposition 13," an initiative referendum to roll back local property taxes directly, dubbed "Proposition 2½" (for the proposed maximum tax rate of 2.5% of full market value) was proposed. In 1980, it was passed by a 3–2 margin, touching off a massive round of local-government spending cutbacks. The inner-ring vote was split on the referendum. Some of the more organized community groups kept their voters opposed to the changes, because of the cuts involved. But other voters seem to have felt that they were not receiving much in government services anyway. In Somerville, Proposition 2½ received a 1,000-vote plurality. According to one account, the proposition's sponsors, called The Citizens for Limited Taxation, were "able to rely on inflation, escalating tax bills, and anger at public officials to do its organizing."[30]

Proposition 2½ cuts hit all groups at least to some extent, but they were most devastating for the inner-city poor. Thus, like the school reform movement, tax reform had, by the end, been turned into a movement which set the lower income communities (at least in part) in opposition to the poor.

But there were other examples as well of reforms which ended up turning community against community. One battle concerned tax assessments in the city of Boston. It was revealed that property tax assessments were lower for one, two, and three family homes than for other properties. Because fewer blacks than whites are homeowners, black neighborhoods tended to have higher assessment ratios than white. As a result, the NAACP sued, demanding that full-value assessment be implemented uniformly. Opposition emerged, not so much because taxation on a "highest and best use" basis would have driven large numbers of residents out of some ethnic neighborhoods near the very center of the city, but because ethnic politics were involved. The city assessor, an Italian-American resident of one such neighborhood, was attacked for supposed "Mafia" ties during a mayoral campaign. Thus, a simple issue of tax allocation was politicized by charges of anti-black and anti-Italian discrimination.[31]

Even the highway controversy, which drew inner-city and inner-ring communities into a strong coalition pushing for a moratorium on construction, involved aspects of intercommunity contradiction. The battle emerged in the mid-1960s only after some sections of the planned highway network had been completed. The middle-belt circumferential (Route 128) and some radial routes were already in place or nearly so. The outer belt, also under construction, was not an issue. But several other radial routes, as well as the inner belt, were not yet under construction. The priorities in building, up to that time, had followed the traditional Boston land-use pattern of strengthening the traditional thrust of higher-income suburbs out to the west. Thus the prime residential suburbs and the leading Route 128 industrial park sites, all to the west of Boston, were already well connected to downtown Boston and to Cambridge, through the Massachusetts Turnpike extension and the rebuilding of Routes 2 and 9, before the moratorium was achieved. These roads not only had had strong suburban and business lobbies favoring them, they also had required displacement of fewer homes than would the highways built through working-class areas to the north and south of the downtown. These latter roads had both less of a lobby for them and were delayed by detailed battles over their locations. The delay gave the threatened communities time to organize total resistance to them, and to stop the construction of several links completely.

This solution removed an immediate threat to several communities; but it also created problems for the newer, but still relatively high-density, working-class suburbs to the north and southwest of Boston. These areas had been built up, around a core of earlier working-class factory centers and streetcar suburbs, on land served by some of the highways built by the Metropolitan District Commission in the 1930s. These highways, and other routes to the center such as the newer Southeast Expressway and several local streets, were already overcrowded commuter arteries by the mid-1960s. Their crowding probably accounted for the relative slump in values noted to the north and south of Boston in our statistical analysis (in chapter 4). It certainly imposed real costs on the workers who lived there. Even in the inner-ring communities saved from demolition, the solution involved continued presence of large numbers of commuters' cars on local streets. Thus, for the inner ring, cohesion was achieved *at the expense* of a more congested, less suburban street environment. Hence, the inner ring and the suburbs to the north and south were left in direct conflict.

These divisions and conflicts, whether open or merely latent (as in the case of highways), suggest that there were real limitations to the possibilities of intercommunity coalitions. The opposition of neighborhoods to their own devaluation, and a willingness to fight rather than emigrate to further suburban frontiers, took a progressive form in the 1960s, faced with attacks from urban renewal, and in a situation in which government funds to expand services were potentially available to the organized. The *same resistence* to devaluation, and to community destruction, set group against group, neighborhood against neighborhood, in the subsequent decade. If a compromise based on voluntary suburban migration was waning, its replacement was not, at least in the short term, to be a working-class or intercommunal movement united to demand more in the way of housing and services, much less a revival of a neighborhood-based municipal socialism.

D. Real Estate Boom and Economic Crisis

The fight against neighborhood devaluation dominated the urban scene in the late 1970s. It helped illuminate the way in which the market had frustrated mobility. But just as these struggles were coming to a head, the real estate market took a new turn: a boom in property values built upon accelerating general inflation. Stagnant or declining house values gave way to rapid increases in values. Home owners saw the market value of their equities soar, while other families began to fear they could not afford homes. By the end of the 1970s it appeared that the pattern of house values described in this book might be a matter of history, with little current relevance.

1. From Devaluation to Boom?

A closer examination of the real estate boom, however, suggests that *devaluation* of middle class assets is still a basic pattern in American society. While real estate values in some areas were soaring, other areas were being abandoned. And assets other than housing were declining in real value. The returns to education, job skills and experience were eroding under the impact of economic decline. Pension fund assets were falling behind inflation's impact. Rising unemployment, and the overall effects of price inflation were taking their toll. Indeed, whole areas of the country appeared to be devaluing, as industry contacted or moved out. While the Midwest, particularly the automobile production areas around Detroit, was the hardest hit by this devaluation, the Northeast also suffered. Thus the Boston real estate market showed, in the 1970s, a mixed picture of gains and declines in real value. More important, the continuing weakness of the economy suggested that those real value increases that had occurred in the 1970s might be transitory: falling real incomes could eventually lead to a collapse of the market, a repetition of the boom and bust pattern that had characterized real estate during the 1920s and 1930s.

In this situation, we suggest, real estate price movements are less important than they were previously as a regulator of society. But they do play a role in keeping the working class divided and in transfering assets from the working class to other segments of society. The role of housing prices must be considered in any discussion of social arrangements which may emerge, whether these involve new compromises, repression, or fundamental shifts in class power.

We may begin by reviewing briefly what occurred during the late 1960s and 1970s in the values of urban land. Starting in the mid to late 1960s, apartment rents and then housing values began to increase rapidly in certain areas, under the impact of demand from a population which was expanding in the age brackets at which households form. The first of the "baby boom generation," born in the late 1940s and 1950s, reached college age in the 1960s. The expansion of education within that generation, in addition to their general numbers, greatly expanded university enrollments. Thus the first major increases in housing demand were in college towns. Rising rents led to tenant movements in such college towns as Ann Arbor and Madison. Within the Boston area, new housing demand from students, and from graduates employed in research institutions, was focused primarily on the areas around Harvard, MIT, and Boston University. Rents in Cambridge, Somerville, Brookline, and the Back Bay section of Boston rose rapidly.[32]

The pressure of student demand for housing became one of the threats to local neighborhoods—particularly to renter neighborhoods—against which communities rallied in the late 1960s. Rising rents, rehabilitation, and renewal displaced many previous tenants. The interest of both student tenants and long-term resident tenants in staving off increases led to apparent student-community unity in some rent-control campaigns, and control or regulation statutes were enacted in several Boston-area cities early in the 1970s.

Students and local residents also cooperated in some campaigns against urban renewal, but this unity did not cure the basic contradiction between student and working-class demands for the same living space. The fractioning of the rent-control coalition later in the 1970s became part of the general fragmenting of community-defense movements.

If the interest of working-class tenants was complicated (because of the need to ally with students who were their competitors to get any rent control), the situation of homeowners and small landlords in the area was also complicated. While real estate values did rise rapidly, suggesting that landowners could reap large benefits, such benefits did not always accrue to long-term resident owners. The new renters frequently needed small housing units (except where they would accept sharing of space in nonfamily "households") but the previous tenants had been large families who had wanted large apartments. To the extent that younger professionals emerged as a force in the rental market, they desired rehabilitated apartments. But rehabilitation and interior redesign of large apartments into groups of small apartments requires capital. This the previous owners of buildings frequently did not have. A new group of redeveloper–rehabilitators emerged, which was able to reap much of the profit from housing conversion, while the previous owners who sold reaped more modest gains. In the South End, a wave of title transfers preceded the wave of value increases that followed the building of the Prudential Center and the beginning of gentrification of the area.[33] Real estate capital gains for Cambridge, analyzed in chapter 3, show that rising values did not necessarily mean high capital gains for long-term owners.

Consider tables 11.1 and 11.2. They contain data on the decade-long change in equalized assessed valuations and median house values for the cities and towns of metropolitan Boston.[34] Both the house value data drawn from the census survey of self-reported house values and the state estimates of actual land and building valuations have an almost equal order

332

Table 11.1
Mean Changes in Per Square Mile Equalized Valuations for Metropolitan
Boston, 1970–1980

Distance from Center (in Miles)	0 to 5	6 to 10	11 to 15	16 to 20	Beyond 20
Absolute Increase	$73,835.10	$41,971.80	$26,390.79	$17,594.71	$10,869.30
Proportionate Increase	131.3%	145.8%	192.6%	208.4%	245.2%
No. of Communities	10	15	19	24	10

SOURCE: Massachusetts Department of Corporations and Taxation Data.

of magnitude of real-estate appreciation for areas within 10 miles of downtown Boston. Beyond that point the series diverge with rates of equalized valuation displaying a more rapid increase than rates of house value appreciation. The divergence in those areas beyond 10 miles of the center is understandable if we remember that the base of total real estate valuation there was far lower at the beginning of the decade. As a result the increases in all types of building activity at the periphery had the effect of pushing up equalized valuations at a far greater rate in the outer suburbs than in the more centralized areas. This is demonstrated by the fact that even though equalized valuations grew over 245 percent in the most distant suburbs and only 131 percent at the center, the absolute increment to center equalized valuations was seven times as large as its far suburban counterpart.

In terms of the house value data, the absolute increments grow as we move from the center toward the periphery, peaking in the area 16 to 20 miles from downtown Boston. Thus in both absolute and relative terms house values performed better the farther one went from the center. This performance is reflective of two facts. First, on average the suburbs historically contained more of the newer housing stock. Second, through-

Table 11.2
Mean Changes in Median House Values for Metropolitan Boston, 1970–1980

Distance from Center (in Miles)	0 to 5	6 to 10	11 to 15	16 to 20	Beyond 20
Absolute Increase	$29,030	$34,620	$37,494	$41,867	$37,705
Proportionate Increase	129.0%	136.1%	143.6%	152.6%	155.9%
No. of Communities	10	15	16	24	10

SOURCE: U.S. Census of Housing 1970–1980.

out the 1970s the periphery had most of the population growth and hence most of the new residential construction. The consequence of this uneven construction means that, although the gains in value everywhere are faster than the rate of inflation as measured by the Consumer Price Index (CPI), the observed increases should not be interpreted as simply appreciation of existing assets. Rather they must be interpreted as a combination of increased appreciation and new construction. To the extent that generalization is possible, a larger proportion of the increase. closer to the center represents measured appreciation on existing stock and more of the increase in peripheral areas represents the effect of new building. If we consider the magnitude of inflation over the decade, the meaning of the impressive increases is greatly lessened. The increase in prices between 1970 and 1980 was 112 percent. Therefore the rate of *real* increase in property values measured by either index in the core communities was less than 2 percent per year. In the communities 6 to 10 miles from the periphery, the growth of real estate values is just about appropriate to what economists have called the "real rate of interest" (inflation plus approximately 3 percent). It is only in the areas of the newer suburbs with the newer construction that we observe rates of increase in excess of such low-risk alternatives as savings accounts.

The data contained in tables 11.3 and 11.4 are growth-rate increases for each of our value indices (equalized valuations and median house values). They are derived from regression estimates which used distance north–south and east–west of the center as independent variables. The technique for creating these variables was described in chapter 4. These

Table 11.3
Percentage Change in Regression Estimates of Equalized Valuations Among North-South and East-West Locations for Metropolitan Boston, 1970–1980†

Distances North/South	Distances East/West					
	0	5	10	15	20	25
0	111.84%	134.77%	157.69%	180.62%	203.55%	226.47%
5	131.57%	154.50	177.42	200.35	223.28	246.20
10	151.30	174.22	197.15	220.08	243.01	265.93
15	171.03	193.96	216.88	239.81	262.73	285.66
20	190.76	213.69	236.61	259.54	282.46	305.39
25	210.49	233.41	256.34	279.27	302.19	325.12

†% Δ EQ VAL. = 111.84 + 3.9 N/S + 4.6 E/W R^2 = .34

334

Table 11.4
Percentage Change in Regression Estimates of Median House Values Among
North-South and East-West Locations for Metropolitan Boston, 1970–1980†

Distances North/South	Distances East/West					
	0	5	10	15	20	25
0	122.83%	128.09%	133.34%	138.60%	143.85%	149.11%
5	128.62%	133.88	139.13	144.39	149.64	154.90
10	134.41	139.67	144.92	150.18	155.43	160.69
15	140.20	145.46	150.71	155.97	161.22	166.48
20	145.92	151.25	156.50	161.76	167.01	172.27
25	151.78	157.04	162.29	167.55	172.80	178.06

†% Δ MED. HSE VALUE = 122.83 + 1.16 N/S + 1.05 E/W R^2 = .18

two tables present a more ambiguous picture of the impact of direction on value appreciation than had been the case in chapter 4. In that chapter values along the east–west plane always exceeded those with a north–south orientation. Let us consider each in turn.

As in earlier decades, equalized valuations (table 11.3) grew more rapidly along the east–west plane than did valuations along a north–south plane. However, a similar equation for the median house value appreciation leads to an almost opposite conclusion (table 11.4). In that case, the north–south plane slightly exceeds the east–west plane.

To understand the implications of these data, consider table 11.5. That table is based upon the data in the previous tables. It converts appreciation estimates obtained from the regression into annualized compounded rates of growth for the decade 1970–1980. For purposes of comparison, the consumer price indices for the nation as a whole and metropolitan Boston are presented as well as the index of homeownership costs. The homeownership index excludes costs of home purchase and is consequently a gauge of operating costs. The comparison is quite revealing. For the region as a whole, each location listed had a rate of growth that exceeded both the national and regional CPI. In comparison to early decades, this is a better performance, though the center locations did not exceed inflation by very much. In fact, when we look at specific locations rather than the regression estimates we find that there were places in which equalized valuations did not even keep up with inflation. For example, the City of Chelsea, which experienced much abandonment and arson, had a growth rate of only 6.11 percent. Chelsea

Table 11.5
Annual Compounded Growth Rates for Various Price Indices and Indices of Equalized
Property Valuations and Median House Values at Selected Boston Area Locations,
1970–1980

Price Index	Growth Rate
National Consumer Price Index	7.81%
Boston Consumer Price Index	7.48
Index of Homeownership Costs	9.34

Location	Eq. Prop. Valuation Growth Rate	Median House Value Growth Rate	Location	Eq. Prop. Value	Median House Value
Center	7.80%	8.34%	—	—	—
Miles N/S	8.76	8.62	5 miles E/W	8.91%	8.60%
Miles N/S	9.65	8.89	10 miles E/W	9.93	8.84
Miles N/S	10.48	9.15	15 miles E/W	10.87	9.09
Miles N/S	11.26	9.42	20 miles E/W	11.74	9.32
Miles N/S	12.00	9.67	25 miles E/W	12.56	9.56

is located three miles north of Boston. The Town of Milton, eight miles south of Boston, had a rate of growth of equalized valuations of 5.95 percent. Milton, unlike Chelsea, is a stable middle-class community which lost little population and had little housing construction. It was established as a streetcar community in the first wave of suburbanization. Its relatively slow growth must be attributed to the fact that values were appreciating more slowly on average than is usually thought.

Even the high-income town of Brookline, with its stock of fine housing located on well-designed streets located as a literal enclave embedded in the City of Boston, exhibited a growth rate scarcely better than the inflation rate: 7.96 percent. The rate for Boston itself was somewhat higher: 10.11 percent. However, it must be remembered that this was the decade in which Boston added much new office and hotel space to its core. Consequently its superior performance as measured by equalized valuations is more reflective of this new downtown construction than significant appreciation of house values in its neighborhoods.

It is in the suburbs in which the performance is on average superior to that of the rate of inflation. However, if we consider that a home is not an asset which is maintained in a costless manner and compare appreciation to the cost of asset maintenance, the relative increase in value does not begin to exceed costs until we move out from the center to suburbs at some distance from the center. Once again it is worth bearing in mind that these estimates are based upon averages with wide variance in the underlying data set.

The overall conclusion to be drawn from these data are that the decade was indeed one in which property values did rise both absolutely and more important, relatively, to the rate of inflation. However, the growth rates in decade-long perspective arc not as great as one would assume from just a reading of the experience in the period between 1976 and 1981, when values took a quick speculative leap. Rather the entire decade as well as the present looks much more like the long-term trend in property values which we have found in this study.[35]

2. Devaluation and the Limits of the Boom

Even the "winners" in the inflation game, those whose homes' value went up at a pace exceeding the general increase in costs of living, were not freed from continuing worry about the devaluation of their properties. No one knew for how long the inflation would continue. If uncertainty led some people to rush to buy houses for fear of increases later, it left others unable to sell and move to new locations, even in the face of possible job opportunities or reductions in commuting cost, because of the burden of new mortgage debt that a move would require. For those who did buy, higher ratios of initial mortgage payments to monthly income involved a gamble that inflation, and in particular their own wage increases, would continue until the ratio was brought down over time.

Rising property values were also seen as bearing a risk of higher property taxes. The fear that the higher nominal values would lead to greater real demands on current income fed the tax revolt, which culminated, in Massachusetts, in the passage of Proposition 2½. On the other hand, austerity in public services brought about by general economic recession and intensified by the tax revolt brought about a fear that neighborhood deterioration might threaten housing investments. Thus the pattern of entrapment in a neighborhood, and fear of property devaluation, that had characterized the suburban compromise, was continued into the period of real estate inflation.

What is more, there were reasons to expect that the property boom could not continue as it had in the 1970s. The relationship of the housing market to other sources of income, particularly wages, suggests incomes are a limit to housing prices. Factors affecting housing supply similarly suggest limits.

Housing (even homeownership) is for most workers paid for out of current income. Except where a home is owned clear of mortgage obligations, monthly payments must be made by a homeowner as well as by a renter. If incomes are interrupted, payments will not be made and mortgages will be foreclosed, as occurred widely in the 1930s. Owners and tenants alike are subject to eviction if long-term unemployment outruns the availability of social insurance and savings. True, a homeowner may be able to stave off problems by selling a house voluntarily, to cash in his equity in the home. Or he may adjust his own housing standard downward by taking in lodgers, borders, or tenants to earn some extra income. But if unemployment is widespread enough, and particularly if some homes are already being foreclosed, sale prices realized may drop rapidly. In the present situation, where consumer debt is high, and where people have been buying homes and assuming high mortgage obligations on the assumption of rising future incomes, even a freeze in cash wage levels or a reduction in hours worked might start a series of mortgage defaults. The vulnerability of the housing boom to the economic cycle is readily apparent.[36]

Even if there is not major downturn, other considerations suggest that housing prices are not likely to continue rising faster than other prices. In a capitalist system, housing is a commodity produced for profit. If housing prices rise, eventually this will affect the profitability of supplying more houses, and increasing new supplies will drive price increases back toward the general inflation level. Apart from its land value component, price is, in some sense, regulated by the real labor cost of new housing constructions. House values in this sense may have risen relative to values of other commodities, because of organizational and technical factors in the different industrial sectors. But whatever permanent shift in the value of housing has occurred relative to other goods has probably already been capitalized into prices of existing houses. A continuing situation in which housing prices rise faster than other prices is thus improbable.

To be sure, either monopolies in financial (mortgage) markets or in the construction industry may impede the process of profit equalization and price stabilization. Shortages of appropriate land, or its monopolization, may do the same. We argue above they did so in the 1880s. Some such barriers in the land market and the construction industry may exist now, but it is doubtful they are great enough to lead to continually rising relative construction costs. Capital is mobile, and if appropriate land is scarce or monopolized around Northern cities, capital will move elsewhere (e.g., to the sunbelt) in search of lower costs. The resulting regional recession would lower land costs in the north. At present, only a truly national monopoly could raise housing costs generally.[37]

Mortgage costs may, to be sure, continue to induce shortages. But if the shortages increase housing's scarcity, and thus its price, interest costs will themselves cut into realizable sale prices for buildings, and generally high interest rates will induce recessions that in turn cut demand for homes. Thus it is unlikely that even continuing problems in the financing of homes can be the source of continuing housing value increase.

There is only one situation in which it is likely that housing prices can continue to rise. That is a situation in which there is a general deterioration of worker living standards, to the extent that housing that now can be afforded by one family must accommodate a larger number of individuals. Such a condition of crowding marked the inner cities at the time of the urban crisis of the 1880s. If a similar level of housing crowding reemerges, the pooled rents of a larger number of individuals might allow continuing increase of the real value of housing. Thus, a full consideration of prospects for house values requires that we examine possible outcomes of general class struggle over the next decade.

E. Housing and Working-Class Strategy

1. The Crisis of the 1980s in Historical Perspective

As the nation approaches the centenary of the first urban crisis, it is apparent that working- and "middle-"class living standards, and the prospects for accumulation by capitalist institutions, are in severe difficulty. In this emerging general crisis, sections of both the working class, and of the capitalist class, are struggling to preserve their shares of an apparently stagnant shrinking pie. In this "zero sum" society, home ownership, suburban location, or other factors of housing access may play a role in the degree to which workers can defend their positions, individually or as a united class.[38] But housing conditions may also have some relevance to whether the conditions can be re-created for general economic advancement—a new wave of accumulation—within some variant of the present economic system.[39]

The present majority strategy of the capitalist class seems to be an attempt to restore profitability and growth primarily through reduction in working-class living standards. The Reagan administration's attacks on organized labor, the toleration of high unemployment rates, and the reduction of social services and social insurance in federal and stage budgets are all interpretable as such a strategy.[40]

These programs are presented, at least at times, as a necessary temporary sacrifice, which ought to be accepted by labor, as it will lead to eventual recovery and accelerated economic progress. Within such an austerity program, stringency in housing construction, initiated in Lyndon Johnson's "credit crunch" and largely in effect since then, might be seen as a reasonable aspect of general sacrifice for a common good.

Unfortunately, there is, as this is written, little evidence that falling living standards alone can create the conditions for recovery. A partial "recovery" is underway, but it appears to be a short-cycle readjustment aided by the Keynesian effects of an anti-Keynesian's military deficit, rather than a vigorous boom led by investment as would be expected in a long-cycle upturn. Corporate behavior suggests that increasing earnings are being used for financial manipulation or exported, rather than being invested in modernization of national industry. Even accelerated foreign investment is accompanied by so high a military expense that it is doubtful the nation can earn back enough to guarantee even a favored stratum among workers a good living as international rentiers. There is no guarantee that reduction of U.S. living standards, whether to British, Italian, or even Third World levels, will necessarily increase competitiveness to the point of generating a strong investment boom.

The experience of the long turn-of-century and midcentury investment booms suggest that an interconnected set of innovations, which allow rising standards of living to coexist with improved profitability, gives the best chance of capitalist prosperity. But no such set of innovations has yet emerged to allow investors confidence in the outlines of an "end of century" boom. Despite evident advances in automatic control and data processing, the shape of a new industrial order which can generate abundance has not emerged. Severe doubts exist as to what sources of energy should be utilized to power any new plant, and what the cost of that energy might be. The form of cities remains in doubt: continued suburban spread, downtown revival, and a replacement of cities by small towns as a center for residence and production all have their proponents. Even the size and composition of households in the future remains a source of great uncertainty and controversy. Regional patterns of growth are similarly a source of uncertainty, as sunbelt growth responds to short-term wage differences or temporary abundance of oil, rather than to any long-term vision of where resources can most efficiently be utilized. Nor has there been any serious attempt—even comparable to some of the "New Deal" committees of the 1930s—to plan for a national investment strategy, be it "public" or "private" in its direction.[41]

The present situation of short-term struggle and austerity, combined with long-term uncertainty, suggests that a study of housing and suburbanization should conclude by examining whether patterns of house building, housing ownership, or housing location can play a role either in affecting the balance of class power, or in creating the conditions for compromise around a new investment strategy. We have argued they did so in the previous two booms. Can they do so this time?

2. Housing, Rent and Investment Possibilities

We first may consider whether anything in the housing sector can play the kind of role in the creation of a new boom that streetcar suburbanization and the attack on land and transit monopoly played in the turn-of-century boom, or that federally assisted automobile suburbanization played after World War II. Such a consideration requires that two questions be answered. One is whether monopolies exist that are keeping costs high, so that an attack on their rents could remove barriers to investment and allow both profits and living standards to rise. The second is whether possibilities exist for reductions in the real cost (or, in Marxian terms, the value) of housing, which could also allow profits to be made while reducing the cost of living, and serve to generate jobs and investments.

Over the past decade or more, there has been no lack of effort by radical scholars to identify monopoly barriers in the housing and home finance markets. The fractioning of neighborhood organizations, and their confrontations over turf and external resources, has given organizers a stake in finding external enemies deserving of a unified attack. This has been particularly true when changing credit conditions have led either to apparently speculative neighborhood renewal and "gentrification," or to deterioration of redlined areas. Community activism, as David Harvey has commented, has been "interest-rate sensitive." Harvey describes an example from Baltimore where community groups came to realize that financial institutions, by denying conventional mortgage funds while financing speculator-landlords, were the controlling influence in the situation. "The community group began to unravel these through a process of political exploration. And at the end of the road, the community came face to face with what appears to be the dominant power of finance capital."[42]

Attacks on "redlining" have the advantage of laying the blame for bad housing on a highly visible elite, and the attack can often unify rather than divide diverse local constituencies. In addition, the recent rise of redlining practices links the housing struggle with other struggles over service cutbacks associated with the scarcities of the growing fiscal crisis of the cities.

If financial monopolies are making working-class housing scarce, as Michael Stone and Emily Achtenberg have argued,[43] then an anti-monopoly strategy, involving state housing, banks, anti-redlining laws, and mortgage-payment moratoria, makes good sense.

Such monopoly barriers *have* in the past been an important source of absolute rent and hence a meaningful target for working-class struggles, especially in the 1880s and 1890s. However, in our view, recent changes in the financial situation itself have made financial barriers to housing appear more important than they in fact are.

Throughout the long postwar wave of growth running through the early 1960s, cheap mortgages for suburban housing were widely available; financial barriers affected only minorities. Nor did the onset of a more stagnant economy in the mid- to late-1960s change this very much, as declining industrial investment opportunities led banks to seek mortgage borrowers. But the funds available were no longer able to support low- to moderate-income housing, because real *incomes* were beginning to stagnate. Indeed, the very availability of funding *reduced* low-income housing supply by allowing urban renewal, which often involved the demolition of low-income areas. Suburbanization had led to a relative decline in land value in the inner city, and banks realized that this was the time to build there; any hesitation would cost money. It was this conjunction of events which began to convince many observers that the banks were out to destroy urban housing.

The conviction grew into an unquestioned credo as stagnation continued. Growing debt drove up interest rates. As debts produced insolvencies, banks became the arbiters of who was and who was not to be bailed out, of which activities would be able to expand and which would not. Banks, it seemed, were taking over—and housing, especially in working-class areas, was apparently on their hit list.

In our view, however, these apparent financial barriers merely reflected the higher costs and obstacles to economic growth created by the economic crisis itself. The culprit is not monopoly by a specific financial fraction of capital, but the inherent limits of capitalist growth.[44]

The question, then, is whether struggles in the housing area can restore capitalist growth. We believe that they cannot, because: (1) transport scale economies have given way to fiscal-crisis–ridden diseconomies; (2) the suburban frontier has been replaced by metropolitan land saturation; and (3) reduced living costs as a result of new housing have become *increased* living costs, as new housing merely replaces livable older housing, thereby *raising* overall shelter costs. In a word, the 1980s are a far cry from the 1880s. What was once productive investment for new accumulation has become an investment drain.

If long-run cost considerations, rather than specific financial barriers or other sources of monopoly rents are, as we believe, the primary cause of high housing costs, it follows that strategies designed simply to reduce these rents cannot reduce housing costs. It then follows that, to the extent that reductions in the cost of basic necessities are necessary for reestablishment of profitable accumulation, an anti-monopoly housing strategy—even if it were successful—would not be sufficient to restore growth.[45]

3. Housing and Class Unity

If the housing sector and local services cannot generate conditions for a new boom, housing problems and local fiscal crises will persist unless a new boom generated elsewhere can allow resources to be diverted into these sectors. In the meantime, it is likely that housing struggles will continue, as different groups seek to better or defend their housing standards, to seek profit opportunities, or to stave off devaluation of housing equities. Such struggles are, in a sense, secondary to more global conflict between capital and labor over living standards, working conditions, and the control and use of economic surplus. But being secondary, they are not necessarily unimportant.

If the economy remains stagnant, working-class unity and combativeness are important to maintaining any decent living standards. If a new boom is to be generated in other sectors of the economy, working-class unity may affect the directions of that boom. And if a new boom continually fails to materialize, working-class strength and consciousness would be a necessary condition for any attempt at noncapitalist solutions. As we have seen in our history of the suburban compromise, housing-related struggles were important in developing a working-class movement at the turn of the century. Suburbanization, in turn, weakened the working-class socialist base, even as it achieved many of the economic goals of that movement. And the mobility-devaluation mechanism of suburbanization helped control and divide labor in the later phases of the two booms. But these events occurred in a situation in which housing was more central to accumulation than it may be in the present crisis and any possible recovery. What role may housing play in the present situation?

A number of writers on the left have argued in recent years that homeowner–renter differences, and struggles between neighborhoods that have received differential benefits from the suburbanization process, can be a serious impediment to working-class unity. In the face of major attacks on working-class power and living standards, such divisions are of serious concern. Unity among neighborhoods in the face of a reactionary onslaught may be both more necessary and more difficult than populist coalitions among neighborhoods would be to an attack on monopolies.

Unity may be threatened if different groups in the working class have different real interests in preservation of portions of the status quo. According to some analysts, important differences involve housing and neighborhood services. Thus, Elliott Currie, Robert Dunn, and David Fogarty have argued that there has been a "curiously fragmented and often seemingly irrational political response to the erosion of material well-being" because "stagflation has struck very unevenly at different groups

within the working class."[46] Housing is one area where these divisions
may occur:

> The crisis in housing starkly exhibits the new divisions that
> stagflation has produced among working people. Inflation has
> not proven such an unmixed blessing for people who already
> own their homes as some writers have argued; for other costs
> have risen dramatically in the past decade as well. Mainte-
> nance and repair costs rose 118% between 1970–1975 alone,
> and property taxes rose 105% in the same years. For people
> with limited or fixed incomes, these costs can tip the balance
> between being able to keep a home or being forced back into
> the rental market. But it remains true that those who already
> have a strong foothold in the housing market have seen their
> homes appreciate wildly in value and their relative mortgage
> costs decline, often dramatically. And this has created one of
> the keepest divisions between winners and losers in the stag-
> flation era.[47]

A more formal argument to the same effect is made by Peter Saunders, who argues that property ownership by a worker may be a "a crucial source of revenue" obtained "outside the work situation," and thus
affect class standing.[48] Saunders sees this as particularly important if
housing prices rise faster than the general rate of inflation. In this situation, homeownership becomes a form of "accumulation potential" which
can give the worker with housing equities interests distinct from those
without such equities.[49] There may be a material basis to a class schism
between homeowning and renter factions of the working class.

Even before the acceleration of inflation, differential access to housing
was sometimes presented as the basis of divisions among workers. Rex
and Moore analyzed what they called "housing classes" in England.[50] In
the United States, David Harvey argued that different working-class
groups might suffer differentially from monopoly rents. Harvey maintained that racial minorities, immigrants, and other subgroups might face
so limited a choice of residences that they were forced to pay rent that
drives their living standard below the level that underlies the normal
value of labor power.[51]

In other neighborhoods, housing costs might be lowered because of
monopoly of the land by the users, who manage to keep out other groups
that could bid up the price. Local financial institutions might also be part

of the monopoly, restricting credit to ensure purchasers are acceptable. The lower financing costs involved in keeping property in use among members of a cohesive community may allow real income gains (in the form of housing, rather than cash) to be achieved by community members. Harvey suggests this for Baltimore, where

> The white ethnic areas are dominated by homeownership which is financed mainly by small community-based savings and loan associations which operate without a strong profit orientation and which really do offer a community service. As a consequence little class monopoly rent is realized in this submarket and reasonably good housing is obtained at fairly low purchase price, considering the fairly low incomes of the residents.[52]

The existence of local privileges of this sort might be a material basis for the tenacity with which some neighborhoods keep out minority buyers, and to make intercommunity alliances impossible.

A similar analysis has been raised over the most troublesome of Boston's intercommunity conflicts, the school bussing issue. Alan Hunter and James Green have argued

> There is a material basis to white working class racism in Boston and elsewhere. . . . White working-class people oppose integrated education as a way of defending their material advantage over Blacks. Most white working-class people are against busing white children to Black schools because in a racist society Black schools are poorer schools.[53]

In this view, the availability of better schools in some (white) communities is equivalent to possession of a monopoly rent, achieved by excluding others; and benefited communities will defend their monopoly position.

If these conflicts split the working class during the period of community populism of the late 1960s, and if inflation divided the working class between homeowners and renters, as well as along other new lines of stratification, it would appear that the prospect for unity might be a strategy to forcibly share the misery within the working class. Hunter and Green argued the need for a direct onslaught on privilege within the working class, although this onslaught appeared to the white working-class communities to mean a reduction in their own standards of ed-

The material basis of disunity. Working class housing of about the same era, and about the same distance from downtown Boston shows the diverse effects of a century of political division. Aluminum-sided tripledeckers in Brookline preserve their value, reflecting that community's advantageous tax base, trans-

Photo by Elliott Sclar.

Left: Tripledecker in Brookline, 1984.

portation access, and political cohesion. Three-story brick apartment buildings about 1 mile away in Boston are abandoned despite good transit access to downtown; reflecting the undesirability of high taxes, poor services and public schools torn by racial strife.

Photo by Elliott Sclar.

Abandoned Building on Chilcott Place off Washington Street, Boston, 1984.

ucation with no resulting gains in overall opportunities.[54] Such an argument could easily become, as Marya Levinson argued about the Hunter and Green argument, "condescending" to workers and apt to "polarize them to the right."[55]

Fortunately for working-class prospects, however, we do not see divisions in the working class as deepening, at least around housing issues, over the course of the economic slump. The reason is found precisely in our analysis of the devaluation process, which we have analyzed in this book. To the extent that the process divides workers during prosperity, we have argued, it is because the process is one of creation, as well as devaluation, of equities. Mobility occurs, at least for some workers. It is this mobility which makes them at least partially contented. Devaluation, if it sometimes leads workers to feel competitive with those below them, is primarily a process which keeps mobility from leading to any real alteration of class structures. The onset of economic crisis increases devaluation, and thus for a time makes conflict among working-class groups more intense, as each seeks to hold on to the gains it has made during the previous prosperity. But if prosperity is not quickly restored, further mobility is not possible. As devaluation continues, that process itself (rather than campaigns by the poor) erodes the bases of privilege within the working class. In the case of housing, homeownership values will be threatened by more general economic collapse, and homeowners' equities and living standards will be imperiled by reductions in labor earnings. In the case of local government services, the spread of general austerity will mean that the service advantages of some communities over others will diminish. Already, the suburbs are coming to suffer from "urban" fiscal problems.

A major depression in a capitalist economy is always a time of danger, as well as of immediate suffering. Middle-class support for Nazi and other fascist movements in Europe in the 1930s shows how the division and resentments of groups outside the capitalist ruling class can be mobilized for repressive ends. Certainly the way in which mobility and devaluation of assets have both created and threatened a "middle-class" segment in American society can create such a threat here. But the longer recovery is delayed, the weaker the bases of privileges to defend will be, and the greater the chance that the different working- and middle-class segments can come to understand the source of their difficulties lies not in whatever gains other such segments have made or preserved, but in the working of the overall system. It is to such an understanding that, we hope, our analysis of the mobility–devaluation cycle and the historical development of the suburban compromise can contribute.

It is not our place here to predict whether working-class unity and pressure can force capitalism to find a compromise solution, involving the development of new technologies and social institutions, as an alternative to greater austerity in the resolution of its crisis. We do not know if a new "trolley" and some analogue to the suburban solution is in the cards. Nor do we know whether, if this compromise is not achieved, the resulting confrontation will end in working-class victory or defeat. But we believe that the history we have examined suggests that working-class unity, pressure, and strategy are active elements in the determination of change. The extent to which an American working-class movement is to operate effectively can only be enhanced by an understanding of its past record of strategies, and of gains, losses and compromises.

APPENDIX A

A Principal Components Analysis
of Suburbanization

In chapter 2, we traced the general contours of urban development in Boston. Different parts of the metropolitan area, we have shown, were built up at different times, as the region's economic base and its possibilities for transporting people evolved. The growth of new neighborhoods meant the old ones were faced with competition. Part of the basis of decline of some of the older neighborhoods can be grasped from this simple account. The decline of the South End, faced with the competition of the Back Bay, and the later filtering down of the inner ring of old streetcar suburbs, are incidents in this historical process. Specific causes, such as the roles of land developers, of government policy, and of political struggles, detailed in part II, are also part of the pattern.

Sorting out the different strands is not always easy. Sometimes, two communities that seem to be similar in location, will evolve in different ways.

The suburbs of Boston present the same smorgasbord as those around Philadelphia, Los Angeles, and other major cities. Just outside Route 128 and next to each other are the towns of Bedford and Lincoln. Both towns cover about 14 square miles in area. Both were originally farm towns with populations between 1,000 and 1,500. Both have direct rail access to Boston, and both towns attracted a few hardy commuters in the interwar years who wanted to live in the country. By 1940, Bedford had a population of 3,800; Lincoln was half the size. The willingness to be part of the metropolitan scene has always exemplified Bedford, while Lincoln steadily opted for the solitude of the rural atmosphere. Thus, even though

Lincoln has the better road access to Boston and Cambridge and the more frequent rail service, Bedford has consistently outscored Lincoln in population and industrial growth. By 1965, Bedford had a population of over 10,000 and a higher employment-to-population ratio than even the City of Boston. Meanwhile, Lincoln had a population of just 4,400, and one of the lowest employment-to-population ratios in the metropolitan area, a ratio about one-tenth that of Bedford. Few can afford the luxury of Lincoln's rural solitude; thus, the town's population has higher family incomes, lower fertility rates, and more years of schooling than the residents of neighboring Bedford.

While the differences between other adjacent metropolitan towns may be less extreme, they do exist everywhere. In the automobile age it is particularly clear these differences are not just a function of transportation access. Since there are paved roads everywhere, the development of automobile-based suburbs does not follow any particular highway or other road net patterns. The fact that one suburb grows faster than its neighbor is not just a matter of location, but rather one of local policy. A community can effectively control its growth through zoning ordinances and building permits. Yet even these policies may be the result of prior population characteristics or developers' preferences. Even before the automobile and the introduction of formal zoning, political and business concerns differentiated the Back Bay from the South End, or the western streetcar suburbs from those to the north.

To demonstrate and help explain the rise and decline of different towns in the actual complexity of metropolitan Boston, we attempt here to rank them by their degree of "suburbanization" and "affluence." For this we use principal component analysis. This statistical technique takes data on a variety of characteristics of a sample (towns in this case). It simplifies the data into the best separate index scores. That is, the first, second (and possibly higher number) principal components are indices that do not correlate with each other, but correlate as closely as possible with the raw data.

We constructed principal components indices for the 78 towns and cities of the 1970 Boston SMSA, using data from several census years. The characteristics used in the index were:

1) Median House Value (or, before 1930, per capita personal property assessments).
2) Distance from Boston.

3) Zone Score (representing the location of town in relation to the socially more prestigious East–West axis through Boston).
4) Population density (and, for 1940, manufacturing density).
5) Per pupil educational expenditures of the public schools.
6) Road expenditures per unit area.
7) Effective tax rate.
8) Median family income (or, per capita welfare expenditures).
9) Percent of pupils in Catholic schools.
10) Percent of housing units under ten years old.

We then used a principal component analysis to determine the linear combination of these variables which best explained the underlying relationship between them. (For example, in 1970, the first principal component explained 43 percent of the pooled variance, and yielded the weights given in column 1 of table A.1. The second principal component was found which explained an additional 21 percent of the remaining variance, and yielded the weights of column 2.)

The importance of variables like density and distance as well as fiscal variables and housing age in the first component suggests it measures something akin to the "suburbanness" of towns, while the second principal component's weights suggest it is a measure of how wealthy a com-

Table A.1
Factor Loadings (Weights) for 1970

Variable	Factor 1 (suburbanization) Weight	Factor 2 (wealth)
Median House Value	.26535	.87974
Distance from center	.83386	−.31074
Zone (angle from NS)	.11754	.66772
Population Density	−.90523	.14688
Educ. Exp/Pupil	.42478	.33115
Road Exp/Sq. Mi.	−.72058	.40984
Effective Prop. Tax Rt.	−.70622	−.02319
Median Family Income	.56040	.70311
Pct. Catholic Schools	−.77425	.04146
Pct. Housing New	.79349	−.18084
Cumulative fraction of variance explained	.434	.648 (adds 21%)

NOTE: A third factor, interpretable as representing "tax haven" town policies, raised cumulative variance explained to .737. Adding to more factors, not as easily interpretable, raised cumulative variance explained to .8762.

munity is, measured in such a way that suburbanness is not counted as part of richness. (The 1970 first principal component is the measure of suburbanization used in chapter 5 to measure the suburban mobility of Somerville residents.)

Suburbanization and affluence emerge from the data also as identifiable principal components for the earlier census years studied. The weights for 1890 and 1940 are shown in table A.2.

In all cases, the first principal component, which explains more than 30 percent of the variance, is readily interpretable as ranking down on an axis of suburbanness–urbanness. (In the case of 1890, it actually seems to measure rurality–urbanness.) The second factor has something to do with affluence in all cases.

The principal component index weights can be applied to specific communities to give their score and ranking on both the "suburbanization" and "wealth" components for the different years.

The rankings for the towns and cities of metropolitan Boston (as defined in 1970) for the two components are given for 1890, 1940, and 1970

Table A.2
Factor Loadings (Weights) for 1890 and 1940

	Weights for 1890		Weights for 1940	
Variable	Factor 1 (suburban)	Factor 2 (affluent)	Factor 1 (suburban)	Factor 2 (affluent)
Median House Value	—	—	.04435	.78980
Distance from Center	.84241	.16785	.71414	−.43542
Zone (angle from NS)	−.08098	.43947	.13129	.60449
Road Exp/Sq. Mi.	−.77721	.04580	−.83425	.35832
Pct. Housing New	−.65585	−.36216	.76577	.30202
Personal Property Assessment/Cap.	−.27334	.82371	—	—
Welfare Exp/Capita	—	—	−.38032	−.52266
Educ. Exp/Pupil	−.43332	.67138	.18934	.30788
Pct. Catholic Sch.	−.42295	−.16581	−.77418	.06232
Prop. Tax Rate	−.04818	−.74933	−.59140	−.39766
Population Density	−.75038	−.22350	−.86994	.25224
Manufact. Density	—	—	−.54502	−.07273
Cum. Fraction of Variance Expl.	.306	.535 (adds .229)	.363	.545 (adds .182)

NOTE: For 1890, a third factor, with high weights for Catholic schools and EW location, raised cumulative variance explained to .642. For 1940, three additional factors raise cumulative variance explained to .816.

in Tables A.3 and A.4. The dates allow comparisons of the towns before the first wave of massive suburbanization, between the two waves, and after the second wave. Not surprisingly, there is some degree of stability in the ranking for suburbanness, because geographical location factors have considerable weight in the index. In the case of the affluence index, location (in North–South or East–West direction) is also something of a factor. In addition, it is not unexpected that certain towns maintained high or low status over time. Nonetheless, there are also a large number of dramatic changes in ranking over time, which suggest the patterns of rising and falling "value" (here considered in a very broad sociogeographical sense of relative rankings) we have hypothesized.

Consider first the suburbanness factor. There are some towns which, beginning as the most rural, remain highly suburban up to 1970. Duxbury and Westwood are never out of the top dozen. Similarly, and unsurprisingly, only two of the most urban twelve in 1890 end up outside the most urban twelve in 1970. But there are also dramatic changes. Considering only cases where towns change by fifteen or more in the rankings between 1890 and 1940, or between 1940 and 1970, we find that a group of towns rise sharply over time. Bedford, Dover, Concord, and Weston have gone from middle ranks to being among the most suburban. Manchester and Canton rise from lower ranks to well into the more suburban half. There are several dramatic rises in the first wave of suburbanization which are at least partially reversed in the second wave. Cohasset, Needham, Belmont, Milton, Nahant, Wellesley and Arlington all follow this pattern. These are, in many cases, towns in which large estates were broken up, initiating a period as suburbs with favored amenities, and then a later period of increased building, and decline of amenities. In some cases, like Wellesley, even some decline leaves them at a quite high suburbanness ranking, but in other cases, like Nahant, the final rank is not very suburban at all. Devaluation of a similar, very suburban, status is found in some towns in the first suburban wave as well, although some of the towns then regain their earlier suburban status in 1970. Beverly (which includes the estate enclave of Pride's Crossing) falls from 21 to 62 on the 1940 list, and then recovers only to 49th place. But Pembroke, Hanover, Sherborn, Danvers, Framingham, Peabody, Norwood, and, to a partial extent, Natick, show a stronger recovery on the list. In the 1940–1970 round, Scituate, Ashland, Hingham, and Millis also become more urban.

The affluence factor shows even more instability. Several communities

Table A.3
Rank Ordering of Towns on "Suburbanness" Factor

Town	1890	1940	1970	Town	1890	1940	1970
Duxbury	1	4	8	Burlington	41	36	19
Marshfield	2	7	15	Weymouth	42	56	52
Pembroke	3	20	7	Needham	43	19	37
Westwood	4	2	11	Peabody	44	61	38
Scituate	5	12	27	Weston	45	14	4
Norfolk	6	8	13	Saugus	46	44	45
Hanover	7	31	12	Norwood	47	63	46
Ashland	8	6	23	Hull	48	51	65
Hingham	9	10	40	Dedham	49	50	47
Sudbury	10	16	2	Wakefield	50	49	54
Sherborn	11	34	3	Swampscott	51	53	58
Hamilton	12	17	18	Stoneham	52	55	50
Topsfield	13	25	5	Wellesley	53	1	25
Wenham	14	11	24	Melrose	54	57	62
Medfield	15	18	9	Winchester	55	39	48
Middleton	16	33	29	Woburn	56	60	60
Norwell	17	26	17	Belmont	57	38	53
Millis	18	15	34	Manchester	58	23	22
N. Reading	19	37	33	Salem	59	73	67
Wilmington	20	32	28	Medford	60	65	71
Beverly	21	62	49	Quincy	61	69	63
Sharon	22	21	20	Milton	62	27	55
Wayland	23	22	10	Nahant	63	46	59
Lynnfield	24	24	36	Arlington	64	59	66
Randolph	25	40	43	Canton	65	58	30
Danvers	26	45	31	Newton	66	54	61
Bedford	27	9	4	Revere	67	67	64
Rockland	28	48	56	Waltham	68	68	57
Natick	29	47	41	Winthrop	69	66	72
Holbrook	30	42	51	Watertown	70	70	70
Framingham	31	52	21	Lynn	71	71	69
Marblehead	32	35	39	Everett	72	72	74
Cohasset	33	13	32	Malden	73	74	73
Dover	34	5	1	Cambridge	74	77	75
Concord	35	28	6	Chelsea	75	78	78
Lexington	36	30	35	Somerville	76	75	76
Braintree	37	41	42	Brookline	77	64	68
Walpole	38	29	26	Boston	78	76	77
Lincoln	39	3	16				
Reading	40	43	44				

Rank Order Correlations: 1890–1940 = .768
1940–1970 = .837
1890–1970 = .799

Table A.4
Rank Ordering of Towns on "Affluence" Factor

Town	1890	1940	1970	Town	1890	1940	1970
Manchester	1	46	63	Ashland	41	29	36
Nahant	2	28	41	Norfolk	42	39	58
Weston	3	17	1	Arlington	43	14	16
Milton	4	12	20	Waltham	44	22	22
Lincoln	5	10	25	Peabody	45	72	66
Brookline	6	1	2	Natick	46	41	27
Cohasset	7	21	34	Marshfield	47	64	69
Dover	8	9	13	Salem	48	60	55
Wellesley	9	2	3	Hingham	49	20	29
Westwood	10	13	19	Winthrop	50	6	10
Swampscott	11	7	17	Weymouth	51	63	64
Belmont	12	4	5	Medford	52	25	31
Wayland	13	33	6	Somerville	53	15	44
Hamilton	14	53	67	Marblehead	54	27	14
Newton	15	3	4	Norwood	55	44	43
Sudbury	16	34	9	Pembroke	56	75	75
Medfield	17	32	42	Cambridge	57	18	18
Concord	18	23	8	Middleton	58	67	72
Burlington	19	54	54	Canton	59	57	48
Lexington	20	16	7	Beverly	60	69	56
Sherborn	21	66	21	Quincy	61	47	53
Wenham	22	43	74	Danvers	62	70	61
Dedham	23	37	30	N. Reading	63	74	70
Topsfield	24	61	35	Woburn	64	62	51
Norwell	25	65	62	Melrose	65	26	37
Scituate	26	49	52	Reading	66	50	47
Hull	27	30	33	Lynn	67	51	60
Millis	28	36	68	Braintree	68	56	40
Needham	29	8	12	Wakefield	69	45	50
Bedford	30	24	23	Revere	70	58	46
Duxbury	31	71	73	Randolph	71	77	78
Sharon	32	48	38	Stoneham	72	35	49
Watertown	33	11	11	Chelsea	73	31	39
Hanover	34	76	59	Saugus	74	52	65
Boston	35	19	28	Holbrook	75	73	77
Framington	36	38	26	Malden	76	55	57
Winchester	37	5	10	Rockland	77	78	76
Lynnfield	38	40	24	Everett	78	59	32
Walpole	39	42	45				
Wilmington	40	68	71				

Rank Order Correlations: 1890–1940 = .513
1940–1970 = .833
1890–1970 = .482

become decidedly less affluent over time. In Middleton and Nahant, a very sharp devaluation in the first wave is followed by continuing decline in the second. Noticeable drops are found also for Cohasset, Burlington, Norfolk, Norwell, Peabody, and Pembroke. (Lincoln drops also, but still remains in the most affluent third of the list.) A decline in affluence followed by recovery is noted for Weston, Wayland, Sudbury, Topsfield, and (most dramatically) Sherborn. A decline and partial recovery occur for Sharon and Hanover.

On the other hand, a number of communities which are not initially among the more affluent rise sharply in status. These include Winchester, Arlington, Waltham, Hingham, Medford, Marblehead, Cambridge, Braintree, Malden, Reading, Everett, and Winthrop. In addition, Boston, Chelsea, Stoneham, and Wakefield rise in the first period, and show a moderate weakening in the second. Framingham, Lynnfield, and Natick show an increase in affluence only in the second period.

An increase in affluence in the first wave of suburbanization, followed by a sharper decline in the second, is shown for Revere, Lynn, Saugus, Melrose, and most dramatically for Somerville, which rises in affluence from 53 to 15 and then slips back to 44. This is the clearest case of a mobility and devaluation cycle. In chapters 3 and 5 we take Somerville's decline as an example for further study. The factor analysis suggests it may be extreme in some respects, but certainly declines in status occur in other places as well.

Use of the principal component analysis, and the rank ordering of scores, cannot be taken as a definitive study of change in the Boston area. All of the problems a factor analysis has for establishing overall rankings have been made abundantly clear by the controversy over IQ. Our aim is certainly not to create a suburbanness quotient or an amenity quotient for use in public policy. But our results are suggestive of the fact that communities in Boston have been and are at high risk of devaluation of their degree of affluence or of suburban amenity, whether they be older estate enclaves like Nahant or Milton, or middle-rank towns like Somerville or Beverly.

APPENDIX B

Measuring Value and Change
in Twice Sold Properties

This appendix describes how resold house indices for Brookline, Somerville, and Cambridge—as well as the subdivision and rehab indices for Cambridge—were formed.[1] Following Bailey, et al. and Engle, the problem of controlling for the many diverse characteristics of houses is eliminated by comparing prices of the same house in different periods.[2] Each pair of prices on each house is used to construct a price relative, the more recent observed price divided by the previous price. These relatives are then combined, via regression, into an index.

In Engle's version of the model,[3]

(1a) $P_{it} = P_{io}B_tV_{it}$
where P_{it} is the price of the ith house in period t
P_{io} is the price of the ith house in period 0, the base period.
B_t (to be estimated) is the value of the price index in period t ($B_o = 1$)
V_{it} is the error of the observed price in period t (it has an expected value of unity)

Engle assumed that the property in his sample received normal maintenance and underwent no basic changes during the time his index covers.

For the first price on house i in period t:

(1) $P_{it} = P_{io} B_t V_{it}$
and for the second price on the same house i in a later period t:
(2) $P_{it'} = P_{io} B_{t'} V_{it'}$

Form a price relative by dividing equation (2) by equation (1):

$$\frac{P_{it'}}{P_{it}} = \frac{B_{t'}}{B_t} \frac{V_{it'}}{V_{it}}$$

Take the logarithm of both sides:

$$(3) \quad ln \ \frac{P_{it'}}{P_{it}} = ln \ B_{t'} - ln \ B_t + ln\frac{V_{it'}}{V_{it}}$$

For convenience rename

$ln \ \dfrac{P_{it'}}{P_{it}}$ by $r_{itt'}$

$ln \ B_{t'}$ by $b_{t'}$

$ln \ B_t$ by b_t

$ln \ \dfrac{V_{it'}}{V_{it}}$ by $e_{itt'}$,

so equation (3) becomes

$$(4) \quad r_{itt'} = b_{t'} - b_t + e_{itt'}$$

Now, construct a vector χ_i for the ith house:

$$\chi_i = (\chi_{i1}, \ \chi_{i2}, \dots, \ \chi_{it}, \dots, \ \chi_{it'}, \dots, \ \chi_{ik}),$$

which will serve as a "dummy" vector for the time periods 1, 2, ..., t, ..., t', ..., k. Giving the χ_i's the value of -1 for period t, $+1$ for period t', and 0 for all other periods, equation (4) in vector notation becomes:

$$(5) \quad r_{itt'} = \chi_i \ b + e_{itt'},$$

where χ_i is a row vector and b is a column vector:

$$b = (b_1, \ b_2, \dots, b_t, \ 111, \ b_{t'}, \dots, \ b_k)$$

Expand, or "stack" (5) to include observations on n houses, and you get, in matrix notation:

$$(6) \quad r = \chi b + e \text{ where } r \text{ is an } n \times 1 \text{ matrix}$$
$$\chi \text{ is an } n \times \ k \text{ matrix}$$
$$b \text{ is a } k \times 1 \text{ matrix}$$
$$e \text{ is a } n \times 1 \text{ matrix}$$

Note that the base period $t_i = 0$, does not appear in the χ and b matrices, since B_0 is set equal to unity and $b_0 = ln \ B_0 = ln \ l = 0$.

By making the usual assumptions, equation (6) fits the model for ordinary least squares regression.

The logarithms of the estimated price index are given by $\hat{b} = (\chi'X)^{-1}\chi'r$, so that $\hat{B} = $ antilog $(\hat{b})$.

Engle was able to use the model $(1a)$ because he assumed that the properties in his sample underwent no basic changes. Equation (1a) shows that only time (embodied in the index value) affects price.

But *for the properties which were subdivided or rehabbed,* equation (1a) is not correct, because any physical alteration of the property should change its price.

For these indices, we used the model

$$(1b) \quad P_{it} = \left(1 + \frac{C}{VT}\right)^{\lambda} P_{io} \, B_t \, V_{it}$$

where C is the estimated cost of construction (it is estimated by the owner and appears on the building permit).

T is the period in which the property is subdivided.

V_T is the estimated value of the property in period T, the value the property has before subdivision. It is obtained by applying the Engel index to a prior price:

If $T > t$, the term: $\left(1 + \frac{C}{V_T}\right)$ is set equal to unity.

The model can be estimated by using the same procedure as in the Engle model. The additional estimated parameter, $\lambda = \dfrac{d(P_{it})}{P_{it}} \Big/ \dfrac{dc}{V+C}$ can be thought of as an investment elasticity of price. If subdivision is a profitable venture, λ should be greater than unity.

The assumption that the error terms are independent of one another is valid when a single pair of price observations is used for each house, as is used in the Engle index. In constructing the rehabilitation and subdivision indices for Cambridge, however, there were often many price observations for each house, and all possible price relatives were constructed. In this case, the errors are not independent of one another. For example, suppose the first observed price on a house is low. Then *all* the price relatives which are formed by dividing successive prices by the first price are likely to be larger than the average, or "true" price relative.

This problem can be ameliorated by employing a slightly different regression model, general least squares. For our indices, a packaged computer program called the Cochrane-Orcutt iterative technique was used.[4] The Cochrane-Orcutt method does not provide the perfect solution to the error problem, however. This regression model assumes a constant correlation between an error and the preceeding error. Clearly, this is not the case in the above index model. For instance, there is no theoretical correlation between the error of the first price-relation observation of one house and the preceeding error of the last observation of another house. Similarly, there will be no correlation between errors of price relatives of the same house which do not include a common time period.[5]

The problem of correlated errors in this model is a theoretically difficult one and impossible to solve without making some questionable assumptions. Ordinary least squares estimates, at least, are not biased, and although they underestimate the variance of the regression coefficients, they may still be the most practicable.

Tables B.1–B.6 present the data and indices for Somerville and Brookline which underline the analysis in figure 3.3.

Table B.1
Return on Housing Investment, Somerville (sample)

House No.	Date of Resale	Years Since Previous Sale	Resale Price	Previous Price	Average Annual Rate of Increase
01	1939	19	3,000	2,000	.026
	1956	17	11,000	3,000	.157
	1970	14	22,500	11,000	.075
02	Insufficient data				
03	1892	22	725	450	.028
	1914	22	300	725	−.027
	1923	9	400	300	.037
	1927	4	1,600	400	.750
04	1919	24	4,500	1,000	.146
	1929	10	10,000	4,500	.122
	1943	14	8,800	10,000	−.009
07	1906	30	8,000	14,000	−.014
	1915	9	3,000	8,000	−.069
	1925	10	2,500	3,000	−.017
08	1934	9	8,000	15,500	−.054
	1936	2	8,500	8,000	.031
	1950	14	142	8,500	−.070
	1951	1	142	142	.000
	1956	5	12,000	142	16.701
09	1965	1	17,500	20,000	−.125
10	1884	12	4,200	5,000	−.013
	1901	5	7,000	4,200	.133
	1923	22	12,000	7,000	.032
	1924	1	10,500	12,000	−.125
	1949	25	5,650	10,500	−.018
11	1953	74	6,500	2,800	.018
13	1946	25	6,600	2,500	.066
14	1884	6	1,700	2,150	−.035
	1934	50	2,400	1,700	.008
	1934	1	2,500	2,400	.042
15	1951	45	12,000	2,500	.084
	1956	5	19,000	12,000	.117
18	1912	24	1,000	432	.057
19	1940	36	7,500	7,500	.000
	1954	14	20,900	7,500	.128
	1958	4	16,950	20,900	−.047

House No.	Date of Resale	Years Since Previous Sale	Resale Price	Previous Price	Average Annual Rate of Increase
20	1905	25	41	422	−.036
	1920	15	1,000	41	1.559
	1922	2	1,500	1,000	.500
	1941	19	2,000	1,500	.018
	1961	20	4,500	2,000	.063
21	1920	11	5,000	3,855	.027
	1925	5	9,000	5,000	.160
	1925	1	10,000	9,000	.111
23	1938	18	3,000	1,000	.111
	1941	3	4,400	3,000	.156
	1945	4	2,750	4,400	−.094
	1945	1	5,500	2,750	1.000
	1946	1	9,350	5,500	.700
	1950	4	1,500	9,350	−.210
	1952	2	3,500	1,500	.667
	1961	9	17,000	3,500	.429
25	1887	3	7,000	3,000	.444
	1930	43	4,000	7,000	−.010
26	1933	7	55,000	26,000	.159
	1941	8	44,000	55,000	−.025
	1960	19	82,500	44,000	.046
	1969	9	134,000	82,500	.069
	1973	4	116,280	134,000	−.033
27	1901	9	1,200	831	.049
	1918	17	103	1,200	−.054
	1920	2	600	103	2.413
	1920	1	99	600	−.835
	1922	2	500	99	2.025
	1932	10	1,000	500	.100
	1932	1	3,500	1,000	2.500
	1936	4	7,000	3,500	.250
	1942	6	7,700	7,000	.017
	1942	1	99	7,700	−.987
	1943	1	3,300	99	32.333
	1950	7	6,600	3,300	.143
	1953	3	8,450	6,600	.093
	1961	8	5,691	8,450	−.041
	1963	2	5,750	5,691	.005
28	1962	16	3,850	4,400	−.008
29	1963	43	36,500	21,000	.017
	1965	2	37,500	36,500	.014
	1967	2	39,200	37,500	.023
30	1958	15	8,800	6,000	.031

House No.	Date of Resale	Years Since Previous Sale	Resale Price	Previous Price	Average Annual Rate of Increase
31	1923	1	3,000	4,900	−.388
	1926	3	3,000	3,000	.000
32	1943	26	7,250	9,500	−.009
	1950	7	11,000	7,250	.074
33	1927	2	8,000	7,000	.071
	1946	19	11,000	8,000	.020
	1955	9	15,500	11,000	.045
	1966	11	22,000	15,500	.038
	1969	3	21,000	22,000	−.015
36	1885	2	4,550	4,600	−.005
	1942	57	3,500	4,550	−.004
	1968	26	5,500	3,500	.022
37	1931	1	12,500	12,500	.000
	1947	16	11,500	12,500	−.005
38	1954	10	9,500	5,000	.090
	1956	2	11,000	9,500	.079
39	1955	20	12,000	3,000	.150
41	1922	21	13,000	12,500	.002
	1934	14	8,000	13,000	−.027
	1942	8	4,115	8,000	−.061
	1962	20	11,000	4,115	.084
	1967	5	14,000	11,000	.055
42	1918	42	3,000	3,050	−.000
	1945	27	6,600	3,000	.044
43	1920	1	2,000	2,000	.000
44	1918	9	3,000	3,500	−.016
	1919	1	5,000	3,000	.667
	1956	37	17,600	5,000	.068
	1968	12	30,000	17,600	.059
45	1907	3	11,300	7,550	.166
	1937	30	50,000	11,300	.114
	1944	7	37,400	50,000	−.036
	1945	1	10,450	37,400	−.721
	1972	27	51,000	10,450	.144

SOURCE: Charles Levenstein, "House Prices in an Inner-Ring Suburb: An Index for Somerville, Mass., 1870–1970." *Boston: Studies in Urban Political Economy* (1972).

Table B.2
Return on Housing Investment, Brookline Sample

House No.	Date of Resale	Years Since Previous Sale	Resale Price	Previous Price	Average Annual Rate of Increase
1	1920	4	16,000	11,950	8.47%
	1952	32	11,200	16,000	-0.94
	1968	16	45,000	11,200	18.86
2	1961	45	45,000	20,145	2.74
3	1945	52	5,500	6,625	-0.33
	1953	8	22,000	5,500	37.50
	1955	2	23,000	22,000	2.27
	1964	9	22,500	23,000	-0.24
4	1956	7	48,000	28,000	10.20
	1970	14	115,000	48,000	9.97
5	1960	6	27,925	23,000	3.57
6	1920	10	21,500	20,500	0.49
	1925	5	20,000	21,500	-1.40
	1930	5	11,800	20,000	-8.20
	1966	36	96,000	11,800	19.82
7	1916	25	7,325	6,800	0.29
	1922	6	10,000	7,325	6.09
	1970	48	30,000	10,000	4.17
8	1927	11	15,000	14,00	0.97
9	1955	8	20,000	11,000	10.23
10	1912	11	6,000	5,000	1.82
	1969	57	24,000	6,000	5.26
11	1942	13	11,500	23,000	-3.85
	1968	26	48,000	11,500	12.21
12	1936	7	11,000	10,000	1.43
	1949	13	19,250	11,000	5.77
13	1920	19	8,000	8,826	-0.49
	1927	7	8,700	8,000	1.25
	1934	7	7,956	8,700	-1.22
	1944	10	7,000	7,956	-1.20
	1970	26	31,000	7,000	13.19
14	1962	5	234,000	176,500	6.52
15	1925	2	18,000	8,000	6.25
	1953	28	11,500	18,000	-1.29
	1961	8	16,000	11,500	4.89

House No.	Date of Resale	Years Since Previous Sale	Resale Price	Previous Price	Average Annual Rate of Increase
16	1922	21	37,000	25,000	2.29
	1937	15	37,500	37,000	0.09
	1963	26	43,000	37,500	0.56
	1967	4	107,496	43,000	37.50
	1972	5	140,000	107,496	6.05
17	1948	6	9,000	4,000	20.83
	1951	3	13,000	9,000	14.81
	1962	11	18,000	13,000	3.50
18	1899	7	8,200	7,000	2.45
	1921	22	8,000	8,200	−0.11
	1937	16	6,500	8,000	−1.17
	1944	7	5,500	6,500	−2.20
	1948	4	11,500	5,500	27.27
	1958	10	12,409	11,500	0.79
19	1943	39	16,000	29,000	−2.08
20	1941	15	7,300	5,800	1.72
	1951	10	12,000	7,300	6.44
21	1921	27	9,400	8,500	0.39
	1941	20	10,000	9,400	0.32
	1962	21	20,000	10,000	4.76
22	1955	26	22,000	13,000	2.66
23	1955	27	15,500	6,000	5.86
24	1969	42	47,500	29,000	1.52
25	1964	35	55,000	20,000	5.00
	1967	3	65,000	55,000	6.06
26	1951	4	30,000	17,409	18.08
27	1922	3	28,500	13,865	35.18
28	1950	25	18,500	15,000	0.93
	1970	20	53,000	18,500	9.32
29	1955	20	25,500	9,000	9.17
	1971	16	44,000	25,500	4.53
30	1913	4	4,000	4,000	0.0
	1920	7	4,000	4,000	0.0
	1928	8	6,000	4,000	6.25
	1944	16	6,500	6,000	0.52
	1966	22	55,000	6,500	33.92
31	1934	5	5,000	10,000	−10.00
	1943	9	8,500	5,000	7.78
32	1929	5	170,000	64,000	33.13
	1958	29	180,000	170,000	0.20
	1963	5	180,000	180,000	0.0

SOURCE: Lisa Dennen and Barbara Sproat, "Bedroom Community in Transition: Brookline, Massachusetts, 1870–1970." *Boston Studies in Urban Political Economy.*

Table B.3
Changes in House Values Index for Somerville
1870 to 1973

Period	Index	Changes in Index	% Change in Index	% Change Per Year
1870–74	1.00	—	—	—
1875–79	0.54	− 0.46	− 46%	− 9.2%
1880–84	1.15	+ 0.61	+ 113	+ 22.6
1885–89	1.28	+ 0.13	+ 11	+ 2.3
1890–94	0.97	− 0.31	− 24	− 4.8
1895–99	0.14	− 0.83	− 86	− 17.2
1900–04	1.43	+ 1.29	+ 921	+ 184.3
1905–09	0.46	− 0.93	− 65	− 13.0
1910–14	0.83	+ 0.37	+ 80	+ 16.0
1915–19	0.52	− 0.31	− 37	− 7.4
1920–24	1.49	+ 0.98	+ 188	+ 37.7
1925–29	1.61	+ 0.12	+ 8	+ 1.6
1930–34	1.59	− 0.02	− 12	− 0.2
1935–39	3.75	+ 2.16	+ 136	+ 27.0
1940–44	1.73	− 2.02	− 53	− 10.8
1945–49	2.03	+ 0.30	+ 17	+ 3.4
1950–54	1.34	− 0.69	− 34	− 6.8
1955–59	4.74	+ 3.40	+ 254	+ 50.8
1960–64	4.19	− 0.55	− 12	− 2.4
1965–69	4.91	+ 0.72	+ 17	+ 3.4
1970–73	6.21	+ 1.30	+ 26	+ 6.5

Table B.4
Changes in Somerville House Values from Initial Period to 1965–69

Period	Index	No. Years	Change in Index to 1965–69	% Change in Index	% Change Per Year in Index
1870–74	1.00	95	3.91	391%	4.12%
1875–79	0.54	90	4.37	809	8.99
1880–84	1.15	85	3.76	327	3.85
1885–89	1.28	80	3.63	284	3.54
1890–94	0.97	75	3.94	406	5.42
1895–99	0.14	70	4.77	3407	48.67
1900–04	1.43	65	3.48	243	3.74
1905–09	0.46	60	4.45	967	16.12
1910–14	0.83	55	4.08	492	8.94
1915–19	0.52	50	4.39	844	16.88
1920–24	1.49	45	3.42	230	5.10
1925–29	1.61	40	3.30	205	5.12
1930–34	1.59	35	3.32	209	5.97
1935–39	3.75	30	1.16	31	1.03
1940–44	1.73	25	3.18	184	7.35
1945–49	2.03	20	2.88	142	7.09
1950–54	1.34	15	3.57	266	17.76
1955–59	4.74	10	0.17	4	.36
1960–64	4.19	5	0.72	17	3.44
1965–69	4.91	0	—	—	—

Table B.5
Changes in House Values Index for Brookline
1890–1972

Period	Index	Change in Index	% Change in Index	% Change Per Year Index
1890–94	1.00	—	—	—
1895–99	1.31	+0.31	+31.0%	+6.2%
1900–04	1.15	−0.16	−12.2	−2.4
1905–09	0.78	−0.37	−32.2	−6.4
1910–14	1.02	+0.24	+30.8	+6.2
1915–19	1.11	+0.09	+8.8	+1.8
1920–24	1.20	+0.09	+8.1	+1.6
1925–29	1.43	+0.23	+19.2	+3.8
1930–34	0.87	−0.56	−39.2	−7.8
1935–39	1.19	+0.32	+36.8	+7.4
1940–44	1.00	−0.19	−16.0	−3.2
1945–49	1.37	+0.37	+37.0	+7.4
1950–54	1.93	+0.56	+40.9	+8.2
1955–59	2.44	+0.51	+26.4	+5.3
1960–64	2.47	+0.03	+1.2	+0.2
1965–69	5.44	+2.97	+120.2	+24.0
1970–72	4.97	−0.47	−8.6	−1.7

Table B.6
Changes in Brookline House Values from Initial Period to 1970–1972

Period	Index	No. Years	Change in Index	% Change in Index	% Change Per Year in Index
1890–94	1.00	80	+3.97	+397.00%	+4.96%
1895–99	1.31	75	+3.66	+279.39	+3.73
1900–04	1.15	70	+3.82	+332.17	+4.75
1905–09	0.78	65	+4.19	+537.18	+8.26
1910–14	1.02	60	+3.95	+387.25	+6.45
1915–19	1.11	55	+3.86	+347.75	+6.32
1920–24	1.20	50	+3.77	+314.17	+6.28
1925–29	1.43	45	+3.54	+247.55	+5.50
1930–34	0.87	40	+4.10	+471.26	+11.78
1935–39	1.19	35	+3.78	+317.65	+9.08
1940–44	1.00	30	+3.97	+397.00	+13.23
1945–49	1.37	25	+3.60	+262.77	+10.51
1950–54	1.93	20	+3.04	+157.51	+7.88
1955–59	2.44	15	+2.53	⏐103.69	+6.91
1960–64	2.47	10	+2.50	+101.21	+10.12
1965–69	5.44	5	−0.47	−8.64	−1.73
1970–72	4.97	—	—	—	—

APPENDIX C

Assessment-to-Sales Ratios, 1900 and 1925[1]

The assessed valuation assigned by a town's assessors to a piece of property rarely reflects the full market value of that property. To analyze the relative land values of the cities and towns in the metropolitan area, it became important to develop a series of land value estimates for the communities at several points in time. The series had to be able to reflect market value and intrametropolitan relative values more accurately than did assessed valuations. It is well known that assessed value tends to be lower than market values, but it it impossible to know the exact relationship between the two.

The only real source of market values is selling prices. At various times and in several ways, these prices are recorded on deeds at the time individual pieces of property change hands. Our technique for measuring the average divergence between assessed values and market values was to sample the prices recorded on deeds on property sold in each town in specified years and to compare the assessed value to the sale value of each parcel of land in the sample.

The necessary data were found in the Registry of Deeds in each of the five counties in the Boston SMSA. There, using deeds books from 1900 and 1925, we drew samples of 50 property transactions in each year for each of the 78 cities and towns in the SMSA.[2] For each observation, as much of the following data as was available was recorded: the town in which the property was located; the street and/or lot numbers of the property being sold; the full names of the buyer and seller; the size of the lot and the presence and type of buildings, if any; the value of any tax stamps affixed to the deed; the cash consideration recorded, if any; any prior mortgages being taken over by the buyer; and the total sale value of that property, which was the total of cash transaction plus mortgages. Appended mortgages on the property were also noted (represented by separate documents, usually closely following the original deed, in which the buyer "sells" his new property to a bank or to another party for part of the total sale value recorded in the original deed). If an appended mortgage was found, it often helped in determining whether the original deed represented a "straight" sale—if the appended mortgage was for $5,000, for example, and the sale itself had been only $1,000, it was assumed that the sale was an arrangement, for example between relatives, for which the price recorded on the deed did not represent the true market value of the property. Tax stamps were an important tool in estimating the sale price of the property, for the cash consideration listed on the deed was rarely meaningful—it was most often listed as "$1.00 and other considerations." In each property transaction, however, $.50 worth of tax had to be paid on each $500 of cash transaction, and stamps representing the total amount of tax paid had to be affixed to the deed. Thus for every $.50 worth of tax stamps on a deed, we could assume that $500 had been paid. If a cash consideration was also listed and it seemed to correspond to the amount represented by the tax stamps, the actual cash consideration listed was used in computing the ratio for that observation; but for the most part, tax stamps were relied upon to indicate the cash value of the transaction.

After a sample of 50 transactions was drawn for a town, that sample was taken to the Assessors Office in the town, where the assessed valuation on each property was looked up for the year in which it was sold (or one year earlier or later if the assessment could not be found in the same year the property changed hands). Locating each piece of property at the assessor's office was often difficult, because of several factors, but a goal was set of at least thirty completed observations out of an original sample of fifty. The assessed value of the land, of the buildings, if any, and the total assessed value of the property were listed for each property which was found in the assessment records.

When a sample was completed for a town, the ratio of assessed value to sale value was calculated for each transaction. The mean of the ratios was then calculated, as well as the median, the standard deviation from the mean, and the 95 percent confidence interval. This mean ratio was then used to adjust all the assessed valuations of the town in question to an estimate of market value.

The sampling method used involved drawing the first fifty deeds recorded in 1900 and 1925 for each town in the SMSA. In the case of some of the smaller, outlying towns, fewer than fifty property transactions sometimes took place in a town, particularly in 1900. In these cases, the data collectors simply took as many transactions as they could find on record, but this situation did contribute to the wide variation in sample size with which we ended up. Another problem encountered in working in the Registry of Deeds involved the existence of "funny deals"—for example, cases in which a person sold his property to someone in the same family for a price usually far below full market value. Even if such a "funny deal" did not involve people with the same name, it was often possible to identify the problem if the assessed value of the property was much greater than the sale value, in which case the transaction was discarded from the sample. Another variation on this problem was the case of a land owner dividing a large parcel of land into small, equal-sized lots and selling them all at approximately the same time for the same price. If a large number of these transactions was included in a town's sample, they would throw off the balance of the sample. Because the process of identifying these cases often did not take place until after the assessed values had been collected and the data were being analyzed, the sample size suffered if it included a large number of such deals.

A final problem encountered in collecting data from the Registry of Deeds was that tax stamps were evidently not uniformly used throughout the SMSA, or in all years. In particular, in Essex County, the collectors finally had to include deeds without tax stamps because they were finding so few deeds with them. As it turned out, Essex County also seemed to record the actual cash consideration paid more frequently than other counties, so it was still possible to obtain large enough samples from those towns. In some cases, however, the irregular use of tax stamps became more of a problem. For example, assessment records for 1900 were unavailable in Millis; 1905 was the earliest year in which they were available. When we attempted to draw a 1905 deeds sample for Millis, however, we discovered that tax stamps had been out of use after 1904 for a number of years, at least in Norfolk County, and there was thus no way we could obtain a sample for Millis any time near 1900.

By far the biggest hindrances to our efforts to complete our samples were problems encountered in using assessment records. There were a number of problems in finding and identifying the correct property in the assessors' records in each town, and in general, it seemed that the more steps involved in locating the piece of property in the assessment records, the more observations dropped out of the sample.

One problem was that each town's assessment records were different. There seemed to be three main kinds of valuation records, each of which had to be used differently: one lists town residents and their holdings alphabetically, with a section toward the end of the book for nonresidents; one lists town residents and their holdings by ward and precinct according to the location of the property, but alphabetically within wards and precincts; and one lists properties according to their location on the streets and lists the streets alphabetically by ward and precinct. In order to use the latter two types of records, it was necessary to obtain a street list which indicated which wards and precincts contain which streets, since the deeds did not list the properties by ward or precinct. Such street lists were not always available for the years in question, in which case lists from other years had to be used.

In addition to the problem of the organization of each town's assessment records, there were other problems involved in actually identifying the property in question. For example, the land areas indicated on the deed and in the assessment books often were only rough estimates and did not always match up with each other; in addition, the measurements often were given in different units, which necessitated converting rods to square rods to acres to square feet, etc. Another obstacle was that the land sold might represent only part of all the land owned by the buyer or seller, and the individual pieces of property owned by each person were not always itemized in a town's valuation books. It was frequently necessary to look in the years preceding and following the date of sale to try to determine what part of the seller's property seemed to have disappeared from his assessment and appeared on the buyer's assessment. Another identification problem involved the names of the buyers and sellers: if only the last names had been recorded at the deeds office and there were a number of people with that last name in the town, it was that much harder to identify the correct property. Even if the full name had been recorded from the deed, the assessment was frequently listed in the name of another family member.

A common finding was that when a parcel of land was sold in 1900 or

1925, it had no buildings on it, but by the time it was assessed for that year a building had been partially or completely erected on the site. It became important to watch for these cases, in order to compare the assessed value of the *land* alone with the sale value; and even then, the value of the land alone might have increased simply by virtue of the addition of a building. In addition, either the deeds or the data collectors often did not specify whether there were buildings on the property being transacted, and even if they did specify "buildings," the assessment record might mention a house, a barn, and outbuildings, for instance, and it was impossible to know whether all of those buildings existed at the time of the sale.

Probably the most difficult problem overall encountered at the assessors' offices involved some assessors. We encountered different types of negative responses in larger cities and in small towns. In the cities, the assessors often claimed that they were too busy to take people down to the vault to find records but that they could not allow the data collectors in the vaults alone. In small towns, the assessors often work only part-time, which made it harder to arrange times to use the records, and which often meant that assessment recorded tended to be more disorganized. Persistence became the golden virtue of data collectors; we usually found that if we called back enough times and emphasized our needs, our knowledge of how to use the records so as to inconvenience the assessor as little as possible, and our right to inspect their records, we won. Given the constraints of time and money, however, we occasionally chose to give up, and concentrate on what seemed to be the more important towns. This decision accounts for missing data in four towns.

The other major cause of missing ratios was assessment records which were missing altogether. In a number of cases, there had been fires which destroyed the town's records; in other cases, the disappearance of records was unexplained. This problem was most common in 1900, although 1925 records were missing in three towns. In 1900, we failed to find assessment data in eight towns, and in one other town, the very few deeds which could be found for those towns were not located in the assessment books.

Finally, after the raw data had been collected and were ready to be analyzed, there were some other problems. One is the tremendous variation in final sample size for different towns. It was particularly difficult to find fifty transactions in small towns, as mentioned above, and even harder to locate the assessed values of all the properties in each town. As a result, our sample sizes vary from three observations in Bedford in 1900, to 56 in Beverly in 1925 (aside from Boston, whose sample was purposely larger). In addition, the various problems in collecting accurate data caused the reliability of the results to vary (the size of the standard deviation), and even large sample sizes did not always produce smaller standard deviations.

Another problem we found after the data had been collected was that a large number of transactions, particularly in 1900 and in smaller towns, showed tax stamp values of $500 (one $.50 tax stamp on the deed). Since $.50 was the smallest denomination of tax stamp available, a $.50 tax stamp represented a cash transaction of any amount up to $500. Thus a piece of property could appear to have been sold for $500 but have an assessed value of $30. If there was a large number of these cases in a town's sample, the mean ratio was likely to appear lower than it might have been in reality.

Tables C.1–C.4 show, respectively, the mean ratio of assessed to market value in each town for 1900 and 1925, as well as the standard deviation from that mean in each sample, and the number of observations from which the mean was calculated; a list of the towns for which data are missing, with an explanation of the situation for each town; and the published aggregate assessed land valuation, real estate valuation, and total property valuation for each town in 1900 and 1925, and the corrected value for each of these figures. These corrected valuations represent our approximation of market value of all the land, real estate, and total property in each town in each year, as derived by applying the assessment-to-sales ratio to the town's published assessed valuations.

Table C.1
Assessment Sales Ratios for Boston Area
Cities and Towns, 1900 & 1925

Cities & Towns	County	1900 Mean Ratio	1900 Stan. Dev.	1900 N	1925 Mean Ratio	1925 Stan. Dev.	1925 N
Arlington	M	.60	.28	27	.68	.25	31
Ashland	M	—	—	—	—	—	—
Bedford	M	.67	.21	3	.64	.22	15
Belmont	M	.65	.24	31	.65	.21	32
Beverly	E	.61	.29	43	.63	.16	56
Boston	S	.80	.25	117	.70	.18	210
Braintree	N	.73	.29	21	.60	.23	33
Brookline	N	.82	.18	31	.88	.18	42
Burlington	M	—	—	—	.66	.24	27
Cambridge	M	.83	.25	21	.60	.23	32
Canton	N	.69	.20	19	.56	.23	34
Chelsea	S	—	—	—	.91	.13	20
Cohasset	N	—	—	—	.69	.19	29
Concord	M	.74	.27	21	.53	.19	21
Danvers	E	.75	.29	37	.65	.19	48
Dedham	N	.69	.29	36	.67	.25	32
Dover	N	.52	.26	10	.62	.24	9
Duxbury	P	.68	.31	24	.54	.26	.38
Everett	M	.84	.20	38	.74	.18	37
Framingham	M	.68	.32	21	.57	.15	27
Hamilton	E	.60	.31	27	.57	.29	39
Hanover	P	—	—	—	—	—	—
Hingham	P	.63	.30	24	.72	.22	39
Holbrook	N	—	—	—	.56	.21	41
Hull	P	.61	.21	27	.66	.21	17
Lexington	M	.77	.28	25	.58	.21	29
Lincoln	M	.51	.38	5	.51	.20	11
Lynn	E	.87	.24	31	.56	.17	47
Medfield	E	.55	.28	20	.46	.16	32
Malden	M	.79	.24	29	.61	.24	35
Manchester	E	.46	.24	46	.51	.24	42
Marblehead	E	.60	.27	33	.59	.20	49
Marshfield	P	.80	.17	24	.58	.21	32
Medfield	N	—	—	—	.61	.23	17
Medford	M	.84	.24	17	.71	.18	23
Melrose	M	.84	.26	37	.73	.24	25
Middleton	E	.81	.35	7	.52	.26	37
Millis	N	—	—	—	.45	.23	9
Milton	N	.65	.24	35	.58	.15	31
Nahant	E	.74	.27	26	.55	.27	42
Natick	M	.65	.25	31	.49	.22	24
Needham	N	.62	.32	39	.59	.26	39

Cities & Towns	County	1900			1925		
		Mean Ratio	Stan. Dev.	N	Mean Ratio	Stan. Dev.	N
Newton	M	.68	.29	25	.61	.13	32
Norfolk	N	.65	.35	8	.38	.22	6
North Reading	M	.82	.32	12	.58	.31	27
Norwell	P	.59	.33	18	.58	.27	19
Norwood	N	.68	.29	33	.61	.28	37
Peabody	E	.68	.31	38	.57	.17	51
Pembroke	P	.75	.33	25	—	—	—
Quincy	N	.68	.22	40	.87	.22	29
Randolph	N	.73	.23	27	.66	.31	39
Reading	M	.77	.24	25	.70	.27	29
Revere	S	.82	.24	33	.75	.29	36
Rockland	P	.64	.31	28	.61	.19	36
Salem	E	.81	.24	36	.66	.14	49
Saugus	E	.65	.33	35	.63	.22	47
Scituate	P	.71	.28	21	.67	.22	38
Sharon	N	.65	.28	40	.75	.24	39
Sherborn	M	.59	.38	8	.57	.18	8
Somerville	M	.76	.23	23	.64	.18	30
Stoneham	M	.87	.20	29	.62	.27	31
Sudbury	M	—	—	—	.46	.24	15
Swampscott	E	.78	.28	33	.61	.18	49
Topsfield	E	.55	.27	9	.47	.20	15
Wakefield	M	.71	.28	30	.65	.28	33
Walpole	N	.69	.31	13	.50	.20	35
Waltham	M	.80	.21	30	.71	.24	34
Watertown	M	.67	.29	32	.59	.19	34
Wayland	M	.76	.27	9	.55	.24	31
Wellesley	N	.54	.23	42	.62	.26	41
Wenham	E	.49	.28	26	.53	.31	17
Weston	M	.78	.26	18	.59	.20	17
Westwood	N	—	—	—	.58	.27	14
Weymouth	N	—	—	—	—	—	—
Wilmington	M	—	—	—	—	—	—
Winchester	M	.57	.25	24	.80	.20	33
Winthrop	S	.80	.24	18	.74	.24	26
Woburn	M	—	—	—	.49	.20	38
Bost. Proper		.82	.23	28	.81	.16	63
Allston		.63	.36	10	.69	.20	12
Charlestown		.94	.14	5	—	—	—
E. Boston		.84	.22	11	.63	.13	19
Dorchester		.80	.24	29	.64	.17	46
Roxbury		.84	.24	10	.68	.19	23
W. Roxbury		—	—	—	.67	.17	33
S. Boston		.78	.26	24	.67	.20	14

Table C.2
Holes in the Assessment Data

Ashland: 1900 and 1925—the assessor was uncooperative.

Burlington: 1900—only two deeds found at Registry; neither property could be found in assessment books.

Canton: 1900 and 1925—could not contact assesor.

Charlestown: 1925—only two usable deeds, neither of which could be located in assessment records.

Chelsea: 1900—assessment records missing; probably lost in a fire.

Cohasset: 1900—assessment records missing.

Hanover: 1900 and 1925—the assessor was uncooperative.

Medfield: 1900—assessment records lost in a fire.

Millis: 1900—earliest assessment records available were for 1905.

Pembroke: 1925—records (assessments) missing (total of about 30 years' worth of valuations missing).

Randolph: 1925—could not contact assessor.

Sudbury: 1900—assessment records lost in a fire.

West Roxbury: 1900—no usable deeds in original sample.

Westwood: 1900—assessment records missing.

Weymouth: 1900 and 1925—closest available records were 1903 and 1929.

Wilmington: 1900 and 1925—deeds are in Lowell Registry, not Cambridge. did not pursue.

Woburn: 1900—earliest assessments were 1906.

Table C.3
Metropolitan Boston Published and Effective Total Valuations, 1900 and 1925

Cities & Towns	1900		1925	
	Pub. Total Val.	Eff. Total Val.	Pub. Total Val.	Eff. Total Val.
Arlington	$ 8,748,206	14,580,343	42,287,387	62,187,333
Ashland	1,039,354	—	2,281,210	—
Bedford	1,104,477	1,648,473	2,568,533	4,013,333
Belmont	5,211,725	8,018,038	26,079,175	40,121,807
Beverly	16,135,475	26,451,598	45,686,725	72,518,611
Boston	1,129,175,832	1,411,469,790	1,862,799,900	2,661,142,715
Braintree	4,638,650	6,354,315	16,674,250	27,790,416
Brookline	77,952,900	95,064,512	136,797,100	155,451,250
Burlington	574,932	—	2,065,085	3,128,917
Cambridge	94,465,930	113,814,373	166,483,200	277,472,000
Canton	3,957,630	5,735,696	8,191,990	14,628,553
Chelsea	23,711,750	—	52,701,950	57,914,230
Cohasset	5,550,262	—	9,363,410	13,570,159
Concord	4,684,363	6,330,220	8,217,039	15,503,847
Danvers	5,227,990	6,970,653	11,177,425	17,196,038
Dedham	8,807,220	12,764,086	19,729,100	29,446,417
Dover	860,300	1,654,423	3,353,289	5,408,531
Duxbury	1,652,851	2,430,663	5,219,980	9,666,630
Everett	18,705,100	22,276,976	55,627,150	75,171,824
Framingham	8,809,900	12,955,735	28,003,359	49,128,700
Hamilton	2,299,870	3,833,117	5,166,848	9,064,646
Hanover	1,231,009	—	2,533,410	—
Hingham	4,152,059	6,590,570	13,435,260	18,660,083
Holbrook	1,217,680	1,581,403	2,881,154	5,144,918
Hull	4,118,111	6,751,002	16,972,715	27,716,234
Lexington	5,182,060	6,729,948	14,648,461	25,255,967
Lincoln	2,237,295	4,386,853	2,348,836	4,605,561
Lynn	51,593,386	59,302,742	119,821,665	213,967,258
Lynnfield	672,245	1,222,264	2,700,197	5,869,993
Malden	27,287,540	34,541,189	59,323,350	97,251,393
Manchester	8,723,604	18,964,356	12,126,280	23,777,019
Marblehead	6,515,279	10,858,798	16,927,010	28,689,847
Marshfield	1,329,245	1,661,556	5,155,975	8,889,612
Medfield	1,452,656	—	2,391,112	3,919,856
Medford	19,776,400	23,543,333	59,441,500	83,720,422
Melrose	12,778,365	15,212,339	28,757,700	39,394,109
Middleton	569,923	703,608	1,505,638	2,895,458
Millis	698,375	—	2,701,154	6,002,564
Milton	20,848,999	32,075,383	27,636,615	47,649,336
Nahant	5,374,540	7,262,892	4,695,412	8,537,113
Natick	5,989,075	9,213,962	10,694,025	21,824,540
Needham	3,406,360	5,494,129	15,691,843	26,596,344
Newton	57,634,720	84,756,941	117,850,800	193,198,032

Cities & Towns	1900		1925	
	Pub. Total Val.	Eff. Total Val.	Pub. Total Val.	Eff. Total Val.
Norfolk	598,715	921,100	1,509,015	3,971,092
North Reading	555,429	677,352	2,010,070	3,465,638
Norwell	850,074	1,440,803	1,724,790	2,973,776
Norwood	4,476,809	6,583,543	24,089,870	39,491,590
Peabody	8,143,520	11,975,764	22,159,840	38,876,912
Pembroke	623,410	831,213	2,519,555	—
Quincy	20,291,376	29,840,258	109,053,625	125,348,994
Randolph	1,904,450	2,608,836	4,482,950	6,792,348
Reading	4,412,574	5,730,616	13,283,985	18,977,121
Revere	10,217,460	12,460,317	38,021,400	50,695,200
Rockland	3,176,644	4,963,506	7,839,110	12,851,000
Salem	27,876,291	34,415,174	52,401,290	79,395,893
Saugus	3,676,839	5,656,675	11,893,902	18,879,209
Scituate	2,642,700	3,722,113	11,083,375	16,542,350
Sharon	1,840,700	2,831,846	5,286,000	7,048,000
Sherborn	836,170	1,417,237	1,659,467	2,911,346
Somerville	52,513,400	69,096,578	104,769,800	163,702,812
Stoneham	5,143,300	5,911,839	10,603,375	17,102,217
Sudbury	1,176,572	—	1,857,540	4,038,130
Swampscott	5,585,175	7,160,480	19,513,791	31,989,821
Topsfield	859,435	1,562,609	2,797,743	5,952,645
Wakefield	7,765,215	10,936,922	19,985,335	30,743,592
Walpole	2,665,680	3,863,304	10,943,549	21,897,098
Waltham	20,049,939	25,062,423	48,843,350	68,793,450
Watertown	10,743,242	16,034,689	38,695,847	65,586,181
Wayland	1,649,275	2,170,099	4,648,114	8,451,116
Wellesley	8,936,675	16,549,398	27,705,925	44,686,975
Wenham	1,032,000	2,106,122	2,905,687	5,652,240
Weston	4,435,527	5,686,573	7,377,347	12,503,977
Westwood	1,314,895	—	3,808,374	6,566,162
Weymouth	6,694,088	—	30,759,443	—
Wilmington	1,095,877	—	3,311,771	—
Winchester	8,483,680	14,883,649	26,249,300	32,811,625
Winthrop	6,998,225	8,747,781	22,659,000	30,620,270
Woburn	10,555,975	—	18,713,731	38,191,287
Boston Proper	744,888,600	908,400,731	810,035,700	1,000,044,000
Allston-Bri.	31,045,400	49,278,413	64,314,400	93,209,275
Charlestown	36,437,100	38,762,872	33,737,900	48,197,000†
E. Boston	26,015,000	30,970,238	20,902,500	33,178,571
Dorchester	65,872,900	82,341,125	119,523,000	186,754,680
Roxbury	94,790,100	112,845,357	347,215,300	510,610,730
W. Roxbury	56,742,900	70,928,625†	56,761,100	84,718,059
S. Boston	36,647,700	46,984,231	172,096,600	256,860,590
Jamaica Plain	24,795,000	30,993,750†	13,412,900	20,019,253
Hyde Park	10,554,250	—	21,126,600	31,532,238

†No 1900 sample for W. Roxbury/Jamaica Plain; ratio is total Boston ratio, 1900. No 1925 sample for Charlestown; ratio used is total Boston ratio, 1925.

Table C.4 (continued)
Metropolitan Boston Published and Effective Land and Total Valuations, 1925

Cities & Towns	1925			
	Pub. Land Vals.	Eff. Land Vals.	Pub. R.E. Vals.	Eff. R.E. Vals.
Arlington	$ 8,046,837	11,833,584	38,115,587	56,052,334
Ashland	481,255	—	1,869,025	—
Bedford	774,253	1,209,770	2,258,193	3,528,427
Belmont	5,926,379	9,117,506	23,933,690	36,821,062
Beverly	14,565,100	23,119,206	38,854,050	61,673,095
Boston	884,606,300	1,263,723,200	1,685,597,700	2,407,996,700
Braintree	4,293,275	7,155,458	14,971,675	24,952,791
Brookline	41,042,100	46,638,750	118,880,800	135,091,810
Burlington	866,361	1,312,668	1,777,818	2,693,664
Cambridge	58,063,300	96,772,166	146,132,200	243,553,667
Canton	1,955,070	3,491,196	6,209,220	11,087,892
Chelsea	10,185,800	11,193,186	44,852,050	49,287,967
Cohasset	3,515,238	5,094,548	8,530,263	12,362,700
Concord	2,104,082	3,969,966	6,856,454	12,936,705
Denvers	2,427,875	3,735,192	9,718,475	14,951,500
Dedham	5,442,025	8,122,425	16,319,675	24,357,723
Dover	764,200	1,232,581	2,765,725	4,460,847
Duxbury	1,431,864	2,651,600	4,821,157	8,928,069
Everett	10,752,600	14,530,540	46,237,150	62,482,635
Framingham	5,828,060	10,224,666	22,571,090	39,598,403
Hamilton	1,487,720	2,610,035	4,475,395	7,851,570
Hanover	471,330	—	1,991,290	—
Higham	3,697,450	5,135,347	11,831,200	16,432,222
Holbrook	516,560	922,428	2,401,160	4,287,786
Hull	5,314,460	8,052,212	15,563,705	23,581,371
Lexington	3,694,549	6,369,912	12,871,090	22,191,534
Lincoln	712,765	1,397,578	2,019,475	3,959,755
Lynn	35,786,685	63,904,794	102,056,235	182,243,260
Lynnfield	786,965	1,710,793	2,398,990	5,215,196
Malden	13,945,050	22,860,737	50,705,750	83,124,180
Manchester	5,040,960	9,884,235	10,385,475	20,363,676
Marblehead	7,281,700	12,341,864	15,476,700	26,231,694
Marshfield	1,326,000	2,286,207	4,836,650	8,339,052
Medfield	514,657	843,700	1,957,173	3,208,480
Medford	13,926,750	19,615,140	53,851,850	75,847,676
Melrose	6,875,500	9,418,493	25,574,500	35,033,561
Middleton	316,330	608,326	1,356,030	2,607,750
Millis	386,985	859,967	2,152,535	4,783,411
Milton	7,850,325	13,535,043	24,388,275	42,048,750
Nahant	1,785,046	3,245,538	4,304,451	7,826,275
Natick	2,224,075	4,538,929	8,914,850	18,193,571
Needham	4,133,850	7,006,525	13,814,450	23,414,322
Newton	30,848.750	50,571,721	101,498,800	166,391,470
Norfolk	316,115	831,881	1,091,810	2,873,184
North Reading	584,645	1,008,009	1,812,030	3,124,190

Table C.4 (continued)
Metropolitan Boston Published and Effective Land and Total Valuations, 1925

Cities & Towns	Pub. Land Vals.	Eff. Land Vals.	Pub. R.E. Vals.	Eff. R.E. Vals.
		1925		
Norwell	381,940	658,517	1,471,775	2,537,543
Norwood	5,427,690	8,897,852	19,612,360	32,151,409
Peabody	4,246,650	7,450,263	17,236,050	30,238,684
Pembroke	724,360	—	2,100,520	—
Quincy	35,565,650	40,891,551	95,937,700	110,273,210
Randolph	1,088,050	1,648,561	3,673,180	6,565,370
Reading	3,600,655	5,143,793	11,749,305	16,784,721
Revere	11,906,150	15,074,866	34,548,650	46,064,866
Rockland	1,710,784	2,804,564	6,367,355	10,438,286
Salem	13,098,375	19,846,022	41,556,270	62,933,742
Saugus	3,468,519	5,505,586	10,739,570	17,046,936
Scituate	3,161,600	4,718,806	9,693,195	14,467,455
Sharon	1,152,053	1,536,077	4,420,923	5,894,564
Sherborn	506,575	888,728	1,395,550	2,448,353
Somerville	26,624,850	41,601,328	95,027,000	148,479,680
Stoneham	2,872,500	4,633,065	9,308,875	15,014,314
Sudbury	530,190	1,152,587	1,586,905	3,449,793
Swampscott	6,706,391	10,904,083	17,870,147	29,295,322
Topsfield	1,033,350	2,198,617	2,444,658	5,201,400
Wakefield	3,855,365	5,931,331	16,944,075	26,067,807
Walpole	1,448,479	2,896,958	7,373,858	14,747,716
Waltham	10,331,550	14,551,478	38,100,300	53,662,394
Watertown	8,235,870	13,959,101	33,894,030	57,447,508
Wayland	1,585,777	2,883,231	4,060,165	7,563,036
Wellesley	7,542,600	12,168,483	24,664,575	39,781,372
Wenham	634,245	1,196,689	2,541,745	4,795,745
Weston	2,477,000	4,198,305	6,296,200	10,671,525
Westwood	1,063,755	1,834,060	3,100,995	5,346,543
Weymouth	4,513,335	—	22,226,236	—
Wilmington	725,464	—	2,924,544	—
Winchester	6,299,775	7,874,719	22,999,650	28,749,562
Winthrop	5,711,550	7,718,311	21,124,200	28,546,216
Woburn	3,974,640	8,111,510	15,102,430	30,821,285
Boston Proper	493,463,400	609,214,070	703,419,400	868,419,019
Allston–Bri.	17,392,200	25,206,086	59,605,000	86,384,057
Charlestown *	14,386,700	20,552,428	31,356,800	44,795,428
E. Boston	7,804,200	12,387,619	19,309,900	30,650,634
Dorchester	36,902,500	57,660,156	113,384,000	117,162,500
Roxbury	158,712,400	233,400,580	317,764,000	467,300,000
W. Roxbury	15,306,600	22,845,671	53,184,700	79,380,149
S. Boston	86,010,500	128,373,880	165,639,600	247,223,280
Jamaica Plain	3,922,300	5,854,179	12,572,100	18,764,328
Hyde Park	4,389,400	6,551,343	20,288,800	30,281,791

*No 1925 sample for Charlestown; ratio used is total Boston ratio, 1925.

APPENDIX D

Measures of Social Class

The analysis of mobility, 1880–1920, in chapter 5 employed a constructed variable for class position. Four issues are raised by the use of these variables and by the way they have been labeled.

The first issue is the quantifiability of social class. In theory, social class is certainly quantifiable, inasmuch as it is an amalgam of objective descriptions of people in a particular historical context. Unfortunately, though, most of what is interesting about class is not objective: relationship to capitalist private property, role in the social institutions of an epoch, attitudinal identifications.

Second, defining an index poses technical as well as methodological difficulties. Even if many of the elements which go to make up an individual's relative position in society can be ascertained and then quantified, it is by no means obvious how these elements should be combined in the construction of an overall measure.

Third, if an index of social position is to be used in studies which cover a span of years, there is always the danger that it may be distorted by index number problems if the relative contributions of the elements of the index change over time.

A fourth issue concerns grouping. If the measurement technique results in a ranking of individuals along a continuum, then for the theory to be useful some means must be found to group these ranks, as there must exist fewer class or strata than individuals.

Five indices were devised, one for each decennial year from 1880 to 1920. While these indices must inevitably fail to grasp subjective aspects of class and class structure, they have a number of advantages over alternative measures in their completeness of data inclusion.

384

APPENDIXES

The technique employed is called factor analysis, or principal component analysis.[1] Factor analysis begins where most analysis-of-variance techniques end—with the correlation matrix, the table of simple correlations between the original variables. Analyzing the correlation matrix, factor analysis constructs the first principal component, the linear combination of the variables which accounts for the maximum of what the original variables have in common.[2] The first principal component, then, is the single best summary of the common variance of those variables.

Since the variables for which data were gathered were selected as being among the criteria of social position, the first principal component ought to represent a summary measure of how much each variable contributes

Table D.1
Components of the Social Class Measure, 1880–1920

Variable	First Principal Component in t =				
	1880	1890	1900	1910	1920
Born in U.S.?	.701	.755††	.592†††	.508††	.380†††
Born in Mass.?	.500	.581†††	.420†††	.427	.341††
Wife or mother born in U.S.?	.789	.809	.786	.701†††	.650
Wife or mother born in Mass.?	.654	.638	.597	.512††	.458
Father born in U.S.?	.813	.824	.806	.712†††	.688
Father born in Mass.?	.586	.620	.583	.562	.557
Protestant?	.651	.667	.600††	.537†	.540
Occupation$_t$	.494	.377†††	.425†	.511††	.551
Father's occupation	.445	.399†	.547†††	.654†††	.716†
Non-home wealth	.555	.252†††	.379†††	.588†††	.661††
Father's property	.414	.309†††	.485†††	.588†††	.661††
Lots owned$_t$	.523	.191†††	.284†††	.531†††	.647†††
Homeowner$_t$?	.379	.027†††	.096††	.185†††	.360†††
Number in sample:	358	241	226	191	151
Proportion of relationship between the variables explained by first principal component (%)	28.1	25.8	24.3	26.9	30.1

†Change from preceding decade significant at 10%.
††Change from preceding decade significant at 5%.
†††Change from preceding decade significant at 1%.
SOURCE: Daniel Luria, *Suburbanization, Homeownership and Working-Class Consciousness* Ph.D. Dissertation Univ. of Mass. Anherst, 1976.

to the underlying communality of all the variables, i.e., how much each "weighs" in explaining the "pooled variance" in the data as a whole.[3] Table D.1 presents the first principal component for each of the five decennial years. The 1880 weights suggest the importance of national origin and religion in determining sample members' relative positions. They accord with the fact that the area elite in 1880 was homogeneously Protestant and native-born. Occupational and property variables have somewhat smaller weights. The relative contribution to social position of the various components shifts between 1880 and 1890. Nativity and religion remain important with upward occupational mobility slowing and being reflected in a smaller weight. The pattern of returns to land and home ownership also produced some leveling in the wealth distribution. After 1890, the weights on nativity variables and religion decline, while those on measures of economic attainment rise. With increasing residential dispersion and falling rates of European immigration, the reduced importance of personal background makes good sense. The growth of suburbs and service industry produced a boom period from 1897 to 1908; wage disparities increased, and hence the weights on occupation and wealth.

These considerations suggest that the weights captured many important contours of the changing Boston social structure. Scores for each sample member in each of the five years were generated as follows:

$$\text{SCORE} \frac{\text{person } j}{\text{year } i} = \text{Weight}_{\text{variable } 1} \frac{\text{variable } 1^j - \overline{\text{variable } 1}}{\text{std.dev.}_{\text{variable } 1}}$$

$$+ \ldots + \text{weight}_{\text{variable } 13}$$

$$\frac{\text{variable } 13^j - \overline{\text{variable } 13}}{\text{std.dev.}_{\text{variable } 13}}$$

$$\div \text{pooled variance of 1st principal component}$$

NB: this procedure results in a series mean of zero and standard deviation of one.

Given-year weights were used in constructing each index. To make sure there was no problem with this procedure, 1880 weights were applied to 1920 data. The resulting ranking of sample members were compared with the ranking produced by 1930 weights applied to 1920 data. The Spearman's R of 0.977 was significant at 1 percent: there was no index number problem.

Finally, a means was needed for grouping the scores in a theoretically meaningful way. Remarkably, the frequency distribution of each index exhibited three natural breaks, the first slightly below the mean, the second a little more than one standard deviation above the mean, and a third break just over two standard deviations above the average. This provided four categories; each was coded at the value of its internal median, and then scaled. Exact groupings of variables CLASS80 to CLASS20 into CLG80 to CLG20 are shown in table D.2 below.

Finally, it seemed desirable to generate series for class score for the fathers of sample members, so as to make possible intergenerational comparisons (table D.3). This was accomplished as follows. First, an average was taken on the weights on father's property in the five principal

Table D.2
Class Score Groupings

CLASS80		CLG80
lowest to -0.215	=	-0.90
-0.214 thru 1.25	=	0.54
1.26 thru 2.3	=	1.45
2.36 thru 3.6	=	2.50
CLASS90		CLG90
lowest to -0.005	=	-0.90
-0.044 thru 1.26	=	0.54
1.265 thru 1.73	=	1.45
1.78 thru 2.5	=	2.5
CLASS00		CLG00
lowest to $-.005$	=	-0.90
$-.004$ thru 1.254	=	0.54
1.255 thru 1.96	=	1.45
1.97 thru 2.5	=	2.5
CLASS10		CLG10
lowest to -0.06	=	-0.90
$-.055$ thru 1.05	=	0.54
1.1 thru 2.5	=	1.45
2.51 thru 2.8	=	2.5
CLASS20		CLG20
lowest to $-.061$	=	-0.90
$-.06$ thru 1.0	=	0.54
1.05 thru 1.8	=	1.45
1.9 thru 3.2	=	2.5

SOURCE: See Table D.1.

Table D.3
Distributions of the Class Measure

A. 1880

Category	Median	n	%	Code
1	1.101	95	50.0%	2
2	2.507	74	39.0	5
3	3.682	17	8.9	7
4	5.006	4	2.1	10

B. 1890

Category	Median	n	%	Code
1	0.878	93	49.7%	2
2	2.303	73	39.0	5
3	3.615	16	8.6	7
4	4.984	5	2.7	10

C. 1900

Category	Median	n	%	Code
1	0.936	92	50.0%	2
2	2.400	71	38.6	5
3	3.468	18	9.8	7
4	4.610	3	1.6	10

D. 1910

Category	Median	n	%	Code
1	0.942	96	50.5%	2
2	2.390	72	37.9	5
3	3.505	17	9.0	7
4	4.699	5	2.6	10

E. 1920

Category	Median	n	%	Code
1	0.950	93	52.0%	2
2	2.365	69	38.5	5
3	3.454	13	7.3	7
4	4.733	4	2.2	10

SOURCE: See Table D.1.

components. The same was done to the weights on father's occupation. Father's raw class score *(FCL)* was computed as

$$FCL^k = 0.49 \; \frac{FPROP^k - \overline{FPROP}}{\sigma FPROP} + 0.55 \; \frac{FOCC^k - FOCC}{\sigma FOCC}.$$

While this measure was less rigorously devised than the series for sample members' own scores, its distribution also exhibited three natural breaks; the four categories were coded with the same values as the *CLG* groupings.

APPENDIX E

Government and Transportation

In chapter 2, we showed how transport investments opened up new areas to residence over the past two centuries. Some of these were private investments, encouraged by the liberal provision of government charters. Charters for new bridges in competition with old ones were upheld by the U.S. Supreme Court in the landmark Charles River Bridge case.[1] Street railway franchises were handed out liberally. Today, commuter airlines are encouraged by charters for new routes and by "deregulation."

Government has also played a more direct role. Landfill and the laying out of avenues in the Back Bay and the Boston "Neck" were partially financed by government from the start. The first subway tunnel was built by the city after private investors could not be found. Where private investment created the initial routes, government showed itself ready to take over operation or to subsidize operations when services could no longer be maintained profitably. Thus the bridges over the Charles, the ferries to East Boston, the street railways, and many bus lines have come under government operation, while subsidies are paid to the remaining private commuter railroads. More recently, the suburban highway network has been built with state and federal funds. And throughout, government has built and maintained most local streets.

Where government subsidy has been involved, it has often meant the subsidization of the suburban commuter by taxes levied on the inner city. As early as the 1890s, Mayor Nathan Matthews Jr. of Boston complained that the city was obligated to build streets in newly annexed areas which were being developed for the first time. Unlike other cities, Boston did not have the power to levy assessments on the properties in the benefited area to cover those costs, and the state legislature would not alter the city's charter to permit such assessments to be made until after much of the street network was already built.[2] More recently, the system of metropolitan regional commissions—the Metropolitan District Commission, which controls regional highways, parks and water supply, and the Massachusetts Bay Transportation Authority, which runs subways, buses and subsidizes commuter rail—have placed much of the cost of running metropolitan-wide systems on the inner cities of the area.[3,4]

A. Government Transport Outlays

The financing of the transportation system is worth particular attention as an example of how financing is directed to favor suburbs over more central cities and towns in the Boston area.[4] As of the late 1960s, this financing came to more than $188 million annually for the 79 towns included in the MBTA district.

Transportation financing here refers to those systems through which the public aspects of transportation are financed. Thus the costs of gasoline or of transit fares are excluded from the figure, as privately paid transportation costs. The specific figures of table E.1 also exclude public costs embedded in nontransportation budgets, such as traffic police and court costs, and the portion of planning and administrative costs for transportation which communities generally absorb as part of general government costs. But the major costs included—for highway construction, road maintenance by the Metropolitan District Commission and by the towns—and the subsidies given to the Massachusetts Bay Transport Authority, are substantial enough to indicate that a large amount of public money is involved in turn, indicating the importance of their distri-

Table E.1
Estimates of Boston Area Transportation Costs for 1967

Portion of State Highway Fund expended in BMA	$ 91,497,244.94
MDC Highway Maintenance Costs	15,490,819.02
Total MBTA Net Cost of Service	25,429,087.17
Cost to Communities for Highway Maintenance	56,120,007.00
TOTAL COST	$188,537,158.13

SOURCE: Elliott Sclar "The Public Financing of Transportation in the Greater Boston Area" Unpublished Ph.D. Dissertation, Tufts University, 1971.

bution among the different towns of the region. Our conclusion is that the costs of the transportation system are skewed so that more urban, and generally lower income, towns within the metropolitan area pick up most of the cost. Since much of the transport is for commuters from the outer ring of towns, and since the dominant mode of transport, the automobile, is used to more than an average degree by suburban residents, it is doubtful that this distribution of costs is matched by a concentration of the benefits in those same locations.

Indeed, as shown in chapter 4, the pattern of highway building has enhanced most the value of land in the suburbs, particular those to the west, where upper income groups live and in which the principal financial interests have invested (along Route 128). The impact of highways on land values to the north and south has been at least partially nullified by subsequent congestion, just as earlier impacts on land values by privately built trolley lines were removed when those lines were allowed to close, or partially removed if lines were left to be subsidized from the local tax base. Not only has the transport system bestowed the greatest gains on the well off; the process of financing has also left a greater burden on the working-class homeowners of the inner ring and the north and south suburbs.

1. State Highway Construction Outlays.

The $91.5 million listed in Table E.1 as state spending on highways in the Boston metropolitan area is basically a cost of construction of new highways, or the reconstruction of older highways. More than 95 percent of the money in the fund came directly from gasoline taxes paid by automobile users, making it appear that no significant subsidies are involved. However, in 1967, Massachusetts was to some extent subsidizing the Federal Highway Fund, rather than receiving a net subsidy: federal gas tax collections in the state were $90.5 million, $21.8 million more than the state received from the fund, and Massachusetts automobile users also paid an estimated $18.2 million in products taxes on tires, tubes, tread rubber, parts and accessories, trucks, buses, and trailers. Second, the Boston metropolitan area was subsidizing the rest of the state to the tune of $20.1 million by paying in a larger share of the tax than it received from the state.[5]

Subsidization of some towns by others also occurred to some extent *within* the metropolitan area, because per capita auto registrations are slightly higher in the outer-ring, more affluent suburbs than in inner-city or inner-ring area. True, some of the 1960s highway construction was occurring in the inner ring—particularly in the rebuilding of some of the radial highways (and in the abortive land clearance effort for others that never were built)—so that some of the inner-ring towns undoubtedly got more money from the highway fund than their residents contributed. However, as shown in table E.2, annual per capita state highway aid and per capita new highway outlays were negatively correlated with the density of communities, and positively correlated with median income: the richer, more suburban communities got more per person.[6]

Table E.2
Correlation of Traffic-Related Magnitudes with Density, Commuter Flow and Income (1960–1963)

Correlation of/with	Density in Population/Sq. Mi.	Flow of Commuters/Sq. Mi.	Median Income
per square mile:			
Highway Maintenance Expenditure	.871	.598	−.303
Police Expenditures	.940	.762	−.407
Traffic Tickets Issued	.607	.564	−.239
New Highway Outlays	.733	.459	−.199
Accidents	.954	.843	−.429
Area in Streets	.856	.613	−.237
State Highway Aid	.989	.751	−.377
MBTA Assessment	.878	.828	−.383
MDC Assessment	.945	.688	−.324
per capita			
(per vehicle) insurance rate	.812	.704	−.503
Highway Maintenance Expend.	.376	.240	−.098
Police Expenditures	.107	.112	−.115
Traffic Tickets Issued	−.155	−.056	−.042
New Highway Outlays	−.126	−.159	.290
Accidents	−.249	.007	−.080
State Highway Aid	−.463	−.305	.214
MBTA Assessment	.812	.712	−.312
MDC Assessment	.516	.310	.070

SOURCES: Boston Redevelopment Administration, *Transportation Facts for the Boston Area* (Boston: BRA, 1963) John Gardiner, *Traffic and the Police* (Cambridge: Harvard University Press, 1969); and Commonwealth of Massachusetts, statistical files. Number of observations = 64.

2. Metropolitan District Commission Highway Maintenance.

The Metropolitan District Commission (MDC) maintains approximately 184 miles of roadway within the Boston area. These roads constitute a vital element in the region's transportation network. In 1967, the cost of maintaining this system was $15.5 million. The state paid $9.5 million from the Highway Fund, while the other $6 million was assessed against the 37 cities and towns which were members of the MDC Parks District because of a state law that requires the state to pay 61 percent of the cost (60% from Highway Fund sources and 1% from General Fund sources) and the 37 communities pay $6 million of the cost for a road network which clearly benefits the entire region.

The 39 percent paid by the 37 communities is assessed one-third in proportion to their populations, and the remaining two-thirds in proportion to their property valuation. The range of variation is explainable by differences in per capita property valuations among the communities in question. Because such valuations tend to be higher in higher-income and more suburban communities, the MDC assessments are somewhat progressive on a per capita basis, though when the 37 communities are divided along urban–suburban lines, the differences are virtually nonexistent.

But these per capita differences are of little importance in terms of who actually pays the assessment, because the assessment is not raised on a per capita basis but rather through the general tax on property, which is the main source of revenue for local communities. Even though higher income communities within the district pay slightly more per capita, they pay less *per dollar of average assessed valuation*, and thus in tax rate terms the lower income communities pay more than an equal rate.

Of course, since more than half of the metropolitan area communities pay nothing into the MDC funds, if contributions for the entire metropolitan area are compared, as in table E.2, the MDC assessment per capita (or per per square mile of town area) proves to be higher in towns with higher population density and higher commuter flowthrough.

3. Net Cost of MBTA Service.

The Massachusetts Bay Transportation Authority is the political subdivision of the Commonwealth responsible for the provision of public transportation service in the Boston Metropolitan area. If its operating income is inadequate to cover the expenses entailed in the provision of transportation, it is permitted to assess its member communities for the difference, called the "net cost of service." The net cost of service is the most important public expenditure for the provision of mass transit made in the region. Thus we need only analyze the burden of this cost in order to learn who is actually paying for public transportation.

There are five distinct components to the total net cost of service (see table E.3). Each has its own assessment formula. Generally speaking, the formulas attempt to distribute the assessment burden so that it approximates the direct benefits of the system: each municipality is assessed in accordance with measures based upon number of commuters or ridership, so that its assessment will bear a close resemblance to the activity which the municipality generates for the MBTA.

The two largest items (local service—14 cities and towns, and service on the MTA debt) account for 84.7 percent of the total. These two items also are paid for by only the 14 of the 79 MBTA communities which were part of a preceding transit district, the MTA. This in itself indicates that the net cost of service burden is highly skewed; but these 14 communities also pay a portion of the express service cost and the commuter rail subsidy. Thus, in 1967, the 14 MTA communities actually paid 90.6 percent of the total MBTA net cost of service. Considering that these 14 communities comprise only 50.33 percent of the district's population, it becomes clear that, unlike the MDC assessments, these are not even close to being equalized on a per capita basis.

Table E.3
MBTA Costs, 1967

		Percent
Express Service	$ 1,985,753.68	7.02
The Service on the MTA Debt	2,472,650.27	8.74
Commuter Paid Subsidy	418,725.27	1.48
Local Service (14 cities and towns)	21,493,104.30	75.96
Local Service (65 cities and towns)	1,924,508.32	6.80
Total	$28,294,741.84	100.00

SOURCE: See table E.1.

Of the 14 communities in the old MTA, the seven low-income ones containing 36.58 percent of the MBTA district's population paid 78.07 percent of its net cost of service. Boston, with 23.57 percent of the district's population, paid 57.25 percent; while the other six low-income communities (Cambridge, Chelsea, Everett, Malden, Revere, and Somerville), with only 13.31 percent of the population, paid 20.83 percent. Compare these figures with the remaining seven communities (Arlington, Belmont, Brookline, Medford, Milton, Newton and Watertown) which, with 13.75 percent of the population, paid 12.53 percent of the net cost of service. Finally, the remaining 65 cities and towns paid only 9.4 percent of the net cost of service, while they contained 49.77 percent of the district's population. Thus, in addition to the skewed shape of the distribution, it is also highly regressive in a fiscal sense. What is more, just as with the MDC assessments, the MBTA assessments are not only regressive between communities, but within communities because they are paid from the property tax.[7]

4. Local Highway and Police Costs.

One of the largest items of cost for towns is the maintenance of their streets and highways. Even though the state pays for the construction of many major arteries through the State Highway Fund, towns are responsible for much of the routine maintenance of all but MDC highways. They must also maintain the local streets that they themselves build, even though these may bear some of the load of commuter flowthrough. And again, except for the MDC highways, they must police the traffic on the roads. In 1967, town highway upkeep expenditures in the metropolitan area totaled $56.1 million, most of which had to be raised from local sources—principally the property tax. Similarly, police expenditures, which were incurred because of highway usage, were locally supported, except to the extent to which traffic fines contributed to costs.

Highway and police expenditures, as is shown in Table E.2, are both considerably higher (in per square mile terms) in towns with higher population densities, or with more commuters flowing through them, and lower in higher income towns. In per capita terms, the same relations hold, even though police and highway expenditures go for many functions (like rapid snow removal) which rise with income. What little state highway aid there is, furthermore, appears to be greatest in per capita terms in the low-density, low-flowthrough, and higher income communities.

5. Other Expenditures.

Other categories of public financing, smaller in scope, also work against the inner-core communities. For example, the traffic court system is financed by county taxes. In at least two of the counties, Suffolk and Essex, older cities (Boston and Lynn, respectively) pay disproportionate shares of the cost.

In addition to these public-sector costs, some private-sector or non-market costs must be borne by the less suburban portions of the metropolitan area. Automobile accidents and insurance rates (which until recently were in part based on local accident rates) tended to bear heaviest on the inner core. So does air pollution, which is in part the result of automobile usage.

B. Regression Analysis of Expenses

Regression analysis can be used to further examine the relationship between local expenditures and towns' positions in the Boston commuting system. Data are from the sources cited in table E.2.

Highway and police expenditures per square mile are closely related to high population density and vehicle flowthrough. But the two factors are themselves collinear. The relation can be expressed in either of two least-squares regressions:

$FLOW = -.933 + .0012\ DENSITY\ (R^2 = .608)$
$DENSITY = 2567 + 4.00\ FLOW\ (R^2 = .631)$

In explaining highway and police expenditures (in dollars per square mile), multicollinearity prevented independent use of these two variables. Density alone explained much of the variance in both:

$HIGHWAY\ EXPENSE = 9345.57 + 9.15\ DENSITY\ (R^2 = .759)$
$POLICE\ EXPENSE = -2415 + 15.55\ DENSITY\ (R^2 = .883)$

Adding flowthrough as a separate variable did not increase explanatory power significantly, and *FLOW* alone explained slightly less than *DENSITY* alone. However, if *FLOW* is assumed to have the greatest possible effect independent of density, by using *FLOW* and the residual from regressing *DENSITY* on *FLOW* as independent variables, it appears that *FLOW* of commuters may have a significant effect in the observed pattern.

$$HIGHWAY\ EXP = 34857 + 31.62\ FLOW + 11.27\ RESIDUAL\ DENSITY$$
$$R^2 = .784$$
$$POLICE\ EXP = -36975 + 63.57\ FLOW + 14.98\ RESIDUAL\ DENSITY$$
$$R^2 = .884$$

Addition of a term for median per-family income had no significant effect.

Police expenditures, of course, include many nontraffic activities. To get some idea of the traffic-related element alone, the number of traffic tickets in a year, compiled by Gardiner, was used in a separate regression:

$$TICKETS = 13.47 + .126\ DENSITY + .036\ FLOW + .002\ INCOME$$
$$(R^2 = .387)$$

Incidentally, estimation of possible effects of police expenditures on traffic ticketing, and of police expenditures or traffic tickets on accidents showed no significant effects, whether the variables were used directly as explanatory variables, or replaced by their residuals when regressed on *DENSITY, FLOW,* and *INCOME.*

Thus, although the separate effects of *FLOW* and *DENSITY* cannot really be separated, their joint effect on local costs is significant. The location of commerce and industry combined with the residential patterns of the region are such that the traffic generated by the region's economy passes through the older, densely populated industrial towns and "streetcar suburbs" and additional street and highway maintenance, police, and snow removal expenditures for them. These inner-core communities must bear the additional costs associated with the larger quantity of traffic as well as the heavier vehicle weights which an economic center of necessity generates. In addition, there is the land lost to tax base in these inner-core communities for roads and parking. The net effect of these additional expenditures is to place additional pressure upon this inner-core tax base.

In the outer suburbs, even when they have commerce and industry, the additional costs generated are not comparable. The industry which located along Route 128 is close by the road and as a consequence the traffic generated by these businesses only minimally uses the municipal streets and roads. Whereas, in the inner core, the location of business is such that the workforce and truck traffic must flow through the center of these communities.

As a result of the additional flowthrough which the high-density communities must bear, it is not surprising that they also have the highest accident rates per square mile in the region.

$ACC = 2.67 + .021\ DENSITY\ (R^2 = .911)$
$ACC = 33.58 + .021\quad DENSITY - .004\quad INCOME + .026\quad (RESIDUAL\ FLOW)$
$(R^2 = .932)$

One effect of the higher accident rates was (until a recent reform) to raise insurance rates in those communities with the highest densities significantly above that in the rest of the region. The rates were set not on the basis of where the accident occurred but rather on the basis of the residence of the party at fault. However, given that greater number of motorists drive through the high-density areas, in addition to those generated by the high-density population alone, the probability of a resident of the high density region being in an accident and at fault is that much enhanced.

Statistically, the insurance rate was explained about as well by density, flowthrough, and income as it was by the accident rate. When the effect of driving safety alone is added, by use of the residual from regressing *ACC* (accidents per square mile) on *DENSITY*, *FLOW*, and *INCOME*, the separate effect of this residual is significantly positive, and R^2 is raised slightly.

$INS = 37.43 + .117\ ACC\ (R^2 = .699)$
$INS = 59.68 + .002\ DENSITY + .002\ FLOW - .003\ INCOME\ R^2 = .703$
$INS = 59.67 + .002\ DENSITY + .002\ FLOW - .002\ INCOME + .083\ (RESIDUAL\ ACC)\ (R^2 = .727)$

As a consequence, the insurance rates set upon this experience and upon this basis led to a further subsidy from the inner-core resident to the suburban resident. Automobile insurance represents a very significant portion of the yearly expense of operating a car. As a result of this process, the suburbanite was encouraged to drive and the inner-core resident discouraged.

State finance and metropolitan subsidy arrangements do not improve the financial condition of the low-income, high-density communities and their residents. State highway aid to towns is distributed under antiquated formulae which favor the outer suburbs, and is small in any event.

The maintenance cost for the MDC road system, an integral part of the region's entire commuter network is partly financed by a special assessment upon the 36 cities and towns in the MDC's Parks District. Not only does this mean that the burden is regressive among the communities of the SMSA, given the income characteristics of these communities, but it is also regressive within the district. The lowest income communities must bear higher effective tax rates for this particular expenditure than is the case for the higher income communities.

In a similar manner, the cost of the public transit deficit is borne by all the cities and towns of the SMSA through an assessment paid from the local property tax levy. Here, too, the assessment procedure is such that the largest portion of the burden falls upon the lowest income communities of the region. Even the primary highway system itself, which is not financed from property taxes, also involves a subsidy to the suburbanites from the inner-core residents. As Meyer, Kain, and Wohl have demonstrated, it is the peak-hour highway user who is being subsidized not only by the off-peak user but by the non-highway-driving motorist as well.[8] Since the peak-hour user is most likely to be an outer-ring suburbanite, this, too, represents an additional subsidy to the suburban resident.

The insurance subsidy and highway subsidy, as well as the property tax differentials caused by highway costs, involve a burdening of the higher density, inner-core, and poorer communities, and a benefit to the more suburban areas.

It is thus clear that the transportation system, which opened opportunities for suburbanization, has also (through its financing and external effects) increased the cost of living in inner-core areas, adding to the incentive to move to suburbs and further devaluing property in the inner ring.

APPENDIX F

Suburbanization and
the Socialist Party Base

This appendix presents a test of the hypothesis, suggested in chapter 10, that suburbanization weakened the socialist party base. This hypothesis is of some importance in considering political strategy, as well as in evaluating suburbanization itself.

Consider what it would mean if suburbanization were found to be a significant part of the explanation of the decline of the Socialist Party as an American radical mass party. The party's inability to build a mass base in the major urban centers of the U.S., instead of being symptomatic of a rejection of the notion that socialism must be based on the urban proletariat, could be understood as a result of the spatial instability of the native-born urban working class itself. Finally, the success of Communist Party raiding on the S.P.'s foreign language federations after the 1917 revolution in Russia could be seen, not as the result of the ideological cogency or organizational form of the CP, but as the result of the residential segregation of the recent immigrants in the nation's urban centers.

The hypothesis has a number of distinct if interrelated pieces. First, was Socialist Party local organization based more on native- or on foreign-born workers? Second, were slow rates of native-born suburbanization associated with party strength and tenure? Did suburbanization itself reduce socialist consciousness? If not, why didn't suburbanizers build suburban party organizations? Third, did nonpartisan city reforms hurt the S.P.? If so, did they do so through usurpation of socialist programs or by diminishing class consciousness?

These and other aspects of the hypothesis are tested in the following sections. Tables at the end give sources and notes on the statistical data used in the least squares regressions. All regressions are based on data covering 145 U.S. cities from 1900 to 1922.[1]

Following Bogue and Schnore, we can measure rates of suburbanization indirectly by looking at the position of cities in their metropolitan areas.[2] A city whose population constitutes the major part of its SMAS is one which has not undergone massive suburbanization. A city which dominates its SMSA *over time* is one which is not being suburbanized. In explaining pre-1916 local socialist voting strength, regression analysis yielded the following result. Numbers in parenthesis are *t*-statistics.

(1) $VLOCB = 4.44 + 2.45U12 - 0.65PRESSB +$
    (3.10) (3.00)   (−0.80)
    $0.015FORBOR10 - 1.18RELPOPOO +$
    (0.79)   (−0.63)
    $14.80DRELPOP01$
    (2.39)

$$R^2 = 0.102$$

Local electoral strength is positively predicted by union support and low rates of suburbanization. The SP vote was low in cities on the east coast, where suburbanization already had proceeded far by 1900. The city's population relative to that of its SMSA, and its "Americanness," had little to do with local party performance between 1911 and 1916.

But how did slower-than-average suburbanization help the party? Was it by holding urban party organization together, or did suburbanization imply a loss of socialist consciousness by those who suburbanized? Regression analysis of Debs's 1912 presidential vote shows that suburbanization hurt party organization, but that the radicalism of suburbanizers did not decline.

(2) $VDEBS12 = 9.03 + 2.45PRESSB + 8.89U12 -$
    (2.33) (1.78)   (2.95)
    $0.14 FORBOR10 - 2.40 RELPOPOO +$
    −1.38)   (−1.19)
    $5.97 DRELPOP01 - 8.31 NP12$
    (0.65)   (−1.69)

$$R^2 = 0.15$$

Debs ran best in rural cities with relatively few foreign-born voters. A strong left press and union support helped his vote significantly.

Suburbanization had little effect on Debs's vote; nonpartisan city elections hurt him by weakening the party's local organization.

Kipnis, Friedberg, and others aver that the S.P. never recovered after World War I. Viewing, as they do, the S.P.'s anti-war position as a pandering to recent European immigrants rather than as principled socialist opposition to imperialist war, they depict the Party after 1917 as increasingly conservative and petit bourgeois in both membership and appeal.[3] But, as the equation below must be taken to suggest, local socialist support after the War relied increasingly on labor endorsement.

(3) $VLOCA = 6.15 + 8.15\ U20 - 0.64\ PRESSB + 1.94\ DPRESS$
    (1.82) (3.62)   (−0.26)   (0.60)
    $-0.19\ FORBOR20 + 2.20\ RELPOP10 + 36.07\ DRELPOP12$
    (−0.46)   (0.43)   (1.97)

$$R^2 = 0.11$$

Despite its anti-war stand, the local S.P. vote between 1917 and 1921 had nothing to do with the proportion of foreign-born in the electorate. Again, only union support and the existence of a stable native-born base were significant predictors of local party success. Of some interest is that the sign on $RELPOP10$, the measure of the city's 1910 position in its SMSA, has changed: support for socialists was becoming a more urban— and hence a more east-coast—phenomenon.

(4) $VDEBS20 = 6.60 + 6.91\ U20 + 0.85\ PRESSB + 3.59\ DPRESS$
    (1.88) (2.20)   (0.39)   (1.63)
    $-0.25\ FORBOR20 + 4.89\ RELPOP10 + 16.40\ DRELPOP12$
    (−0.42)   (1.86)   (1.50)
    $-11.06\ NP20$
    (2.03)

$$R^2 = 0.16$$

Though damaged by the effect of nonpartisan city administration, Debs ran well in 1920 in urban areas, especially those in which suburbanization was proceeding relatively slowly and better still if both unions and the left press lent him their support.

Suburbanization, then, hurt local S.P. organization, but did not imply in itself a decline in the radical consciousness of the suburbanizing native-born working class. Though the S.P. came, after 1917, to be increasingly immigrant-dominated, it did no better in cities counting a high proportion of recent arrivals. That is, immigrant domination of party

Table F.1
List of Variables Used

Variable Description	Name Used
City population 1900	$CITYPOP00$
1910	10
1920	20
Change in city pop., 1900–1910	$DCITPOP01 = CITYPOP10 - CITYPOP00$
1910–1920	12 20 10
Metropolitan area population 1900	$METPOP00$
1910	10
1920	20
Change in met. area pop., 1900–1910	$DMETPOP01 = METPOP10 - METPOP00$
1910–1920	12 20 10
City pop. as percent of met. area pop., 1900	$RELPOP00 = CITYPOP00/METPOP00$
1910	10 10 10
1920	20 20 20
Change in city as % of met. area, 1900–10	$DRELPOP01 = RELPOP10 - RELPOP00$
1910–20	12 20 10
Percent foreign-born in city, 1900	$FORBOR00$
1910	10
1920	20
Change in percent foreign-born, 1900–1910	$DFORBOR01 = FORBOR10 - FORBOR00$
1910–1920	12 20 10
Union support dummy variable, 1911–1915	$U12$
1917–1922	$U20$
Maximum Pre-war local S.P. vote (1911–1916)	$VLOCB$
Maximum Postwar local S.P. vote (1918–1922)	$VLOCA$
Change in local S.P. vote, 1911–1922	$DVLOC = VLOCA - VLOCB$
Nonpartisan election dummy variable, 1912	$NP12$
1920	$NP20$
Change, 1912–20	DNP
Debs vote for President 1912	$VDEBS12$
1920	$VDEBS20$
Change in Deb's vote, 1912–1920	$DVDEBS = VDEBS20 - VDEBS12$
dummy variable for socialist newspaper/periodical; pre-1916	$PRESSB$
Postwar (1917–22)	$PRESSA$
Change in socialist press status	$DPRESS = PRESSA - PRESSB$

SOURCES: Demographic data from U.S. Censuses, 1900, 1910, 1920 and D. J. Bogue, *Population Growth in Standard Metropolitan Areas* (Washington: GPO, 1953). Data on union activity and voting are described at length in Daniel Luria, "Suburbanization, Homeownership and Working Class Consciousness" (PhD. diss. University of Massachusetts, 1966).

membership obscures the fact of immigrant nondominance in the parliamentary base. Finally the requirement of trade union support for the party contradicts the stereotype of the petit bourgeois party.

It remains to see whether the process of suburbanization *over time* was associated with the decline of the Socialist Party of America. In the case of the local S.P. vote, we can see that this indeed was the case.

(5) $DVLOC = 0.40 + 0.15\ VLOCB + 5.29\ U20 + 0.41\ PRESSB$
$\quad\quad\quad (0.13)\ (0.72)\quad\quad\quad (2.53)\quad\quad (0.18)$
$\quad\quad + 2.51\ DPRESS - 0.13\ DRORBOR12 + 1.76\ RELPOP10$
$\quad\quad\ \ (0.87)\quad\quad\quad (-0.45)\quad\quad\quad\quad\quad (0.37)$
$\quad\quad + 28.54\ DRELPOP12$
$\quad\quad\ \ (.21)$

$$R^2 = 0.10$$

Not only are low rates or suburbanization associated with relative *SP* gains, but the power of this spatial force is underlined by the poor performance of the pre-war vote as a predictor. Changes in population distribution outweigh in importance the tradition of previous performance in explaining the progress of the party.

In the case of Debs's gain from 1912 to 1920, we see again the importance of tradition and of labor support. Most of the damage done by nonpartisan election reforms had been wrought by 1912; spatial changes wrought their effect on local organiztion rather than on socialist identification itself.

(6) $DVDEBS = 1.62 + 0.58\ VDEBS12 + 11.06\ U20 + 1.11\ PRESSB$
$\quad\quad\quad\quad (0.73)\ (1.71)\quad\quad\quad (3.89)\quad\quad (0.62)$
$\quad\quad + 2.98\ DPRESS - 0.15\ DFORBOR12 + 4.23\ RELPOP10$
$\quad\quad\ \ (0.98)\quad\quad\quad (-0.43)\quad\quad\quad\quad\quad (1.50)$
$\quad\quad + 9.37\ DRELPOP12 - 8.66\ NP12 - 6.45\ DNP$
$\quad\quad\ \ (0.82)\quad\quad\quad\quad (-1.89)\quad (-0.99)$

$$R^2 \quad = 0.139$$
$$F(9,67) = 2.96$$

Consider the six equations and the conclusions which emerge therefrom. We see from equation (1) that low rates or suburbanization aided union-backed local socialist candidates. Far from implying that suburbanization was a conservatizing influence on native-born workers, equation (2) shows that Debs ran better in 1912 in cities where the local party organization was strong, regardless of whether suburbanization was fast or slow. After the War, the S.P.'s appeal did not move to the right but, as equation (3) shows, continued to rely heavily on labor support. Equation (4) suggests that the party became increasingly urban, but that this owed more to the birth of an urban American proletariat than to the concentration of immigrants in the center cities. Taken together, equations (5) and (6) make clear the effect of Progressive-era electoral reform, as well as the contra-organizational impact of a party bsae in the process of dispersing. Local S.P. organization flourished most where unions remained progressive and the base remained urban. Debs's strength in city-dominated SMSA's, whether or not they had a high proportion of recent immigrants, suggests that the party did not collapse because of defections to the CP or to anywhere else.

There are, then, good grounds for accepting the hypothesis that the decline of American socialism owed much to the process by which the party's base became geographically diffuse.

NOTES

INTRODUCTION

1. Time Magazine, *"Housing:* It's Outasight," Sept. 12, 1977, p. 50.
2. 61.2% of metropolitan households and 72.1% of nonmetropolitan households owned homes in 1975 according to U.S. Department of Housing and Urban Development, *1975 Annual Housing Survey.*
3. *Ibid.* 85% of all two-person households headed by a 45–64 year old owned homes.
4. James Follain, Jane Katz and Raymond D. Struyk, "Programmatic Options to Encourage Homeownership," *H.U.D. Occasional Papers in Housing and Community Affairs* (1978), vol. 2.
5. U.S. Internal Revenue Service *Statistics of Income 1967: Individual Income Tax Returns* (Washington: G.P.O., 1969).
6. Peter Marcuse, "Home Ownership for Low Income Families," *Land Economics* (May 1962); John P. Shelton, "The Cost of Renting vs. Owning Home," *Land Economics* (Feb. 1968).
7. For example, "Our House," as recorded by Crosby, Stills, Nash and Young.
8. Subway advertising poster, Kent Cigarettes, early 1970s.
9. Charles Abrams, *Home Ownership for the Poor* (New York: Praeger, 1970), p. 197.
10. Daniel J. de Benedictus, *The Complete Real Estate Advisor* (New York: Pocket Books, 1970), p. 171.
11. *Ibid.,* p. 169.
12. *Boston Globe,* December 16, 1972, p. 24.
13. John McClaughry et al., *Expanded Ownership* (Fond du Lac, Wisc.: the Sabre Foundation, 1972).
14. *Time,* "Housing," p. 57.
15. Constance Perin, *Everything in its Place* (Princeton, N.J.: Princeton University Press, 1978), p. 32.
16. Erma Bombeck, *The Grass is Always Greener Over the Septic Tank* (New York: McGraw-Hill, 1976); Howard, Jarvis, cited in "Fury Over Taxes," *Time* magazine, June 19, 1978, pp. 12–16, 21.
17. Ann R. Markusen, "City Spatial Structure, Women's Household Work and National 'Urban Policy'" and Susan Saegert, "Masculine Cities and Feminine

Suburbs," in Catherine R. Stimpson, et al., eds., *Women and the American City* (Chicago: University of Chicago Press, 1980), pp. 20–41, 93–108.

18. Raymond Vernon, *The Myth and Reality of our Urban Problems* (Cambridge: Harvard University Press, 1964).

19. *Ibid.*

20. Christopher Jencks, "Why Worry About Inflation," in *Working Papers for a New Society* (Sept.–Oct. 1978) 6(5):9.

21. Leo F. Schnore and Peter R. Knights, "Residence and Social Structure: Boston in the Ante-Bellum Period," in S. Thernstrom and R. Sennett, *Nineteenth Century Cities* (New Haven: Yale University Press, 1971), pp. 247–57.

22. See, e.g., Lloyd Rodwin, *Housing and Economic Progress* (Cambridge: Harvard University Press, 1961); Stephan Thernstrom, *The Other Bostonians* (Cambridge: Harvard University Press, 1973); Sam Bass Warner, Jr., *Streetcar Suburbs* (Cambridge: Harvard University Press, 1960); Walter Muir Whitehill, *Boston: A Topographical History* (Cambridge: Harvard University Press, 1981); Walter Firey, *Land Use in Central Boston* (Cambridge: Harvard University Press, 1947).

23. The small township, rather than the county, is the basic exhaustive unit of administration and geographic division in New England.

24. Warner, *Streetcar Suburbs.*

25. Thernstrom, *Other Bostonians.*

26. The "Down Escalator" motif has been applied to the U.S. class structure recently by Paul Blumberg, *Inequality in an Age of Decline* (New York: Oxford University Press, 1980). Blumberg applies the notion to the system in a period of decline while we see it as working within the normal operation of American capitalism, even in the growth phase of long swings.

1. MOBILITY AND ENTRAPMENT

1. Richard Sennett and Jonathan Cobb, *The Hidden Injuries of Class* (New York: Knopf, 1972).

2. *Ibid.*

3. Arthur Miller, *Death of a Salesman* (New York: Viking Press, 1949); and Philip Hayes Dean, *Freeman* (presented at the American Place Theater, New York, 1973).

4. Lilian E. Rubin, *Worlds of Pain* (New York: Basic Books, 1976).

5. David M. Gordon, *Theories of Poverty and Underemployment* (Lexington Mass.: D. C. Heath, 1972); Frances Fox Piven and Richard A. Cloward, *Regulating the Poor* (New York: Random House, 1971)

6. Gordon, *Theories of Poverty,* p. 72.

7. Piven and Cloward, *Regulating the Poor,* p. 22.

8. *Ibid.,* p. 33.

9. Some other studies in this vein include, on education, Samuel Bowles and Herbert Gintis, *Schooling in Capitalist America* (New York: Basic Books, 1976); and on conspicuous consumption, Stuart Ewen, *Captains of Consciousness* (New York: McGraw Hill, 1976).

10. Gordon, *Theories of Poverty*, p. 79; Sennett and Cobb, *Hidden Injuries*, p. 153; Bennett Berger, *Working Class Suburbs* (Berkeley: University of California Press, 1960).

11. Jonathan Cobb, "Afterword," in Sennett and Cobb, *Hidden Injuries*.

12. Berger, *Working Class Suburbs*, and Eli Chinoy, *Automobile Workers and the American Dream* (Boston: Beacon Press, 1955).

13. Ivar Berg, *Education and Jobs: The Great Training Robbery* (New York: Praeger, 1972); Bowles and Gintis, *Schooling*.

14. Sennett and Cobb, *Hidden Injuries*.

15. Gary Becker, *Human Capital* (New York: Columbia University Press, 1964) is the principal reference.

16. Edward F. Dennison, *Accounting for United States Economic Growth, 1929–1969* (Washington: Brookings Institution, 1974).

17. Richard B. Freeman, *The Overeducated American* (New York: Academic Press, 1976).

18. Christopher Jencks et al., *Inequality* (New York: Basic Books, 1974).

19. Ivar Berg, *Education and Jobs*, pp. 47, 59.

20. Paul H. Douglas, *Real Wages in the United States* (Boston: Houghton Mifflin, 1930), pp. 395–98.

21. Albert Szymanski, "Trends in the American Working Class," *Socialist Revolution* (July–August 1972) 10:116.

22. Sennett and Cobb, *Hidden Injuries*.

23. Stanley Lebergott, *Manpower in Economic Growth* (New York: McGraw-Hill, 1964).

24. Dale Hiestand, *Economic Growth and Opportunities for Minorities* (New York: Columbia University Press, 1964).

25. Lloyd Fallers, "A Note on the Trickle Effect," in Perry Bliss, ed., *Marketing and the Behavioral Sciences* (Boston: Allyn and Bacon, 1963), pp. 208–216.

26. Benjamin Franklin, *Autobiography*, cited in John W. Gardner, *Self-Renewal: The Individual and the Innovative Society* (New York: Harper and Row, 1964), p. 106.

27. *Ibid.*

28. Gardner, *Ibid.*

29. Franklin paid £ 70 down, and had paid off a mortgage for the rest of the price by his death in 1744.

30. Nathaniel B. Shurtleff, *Topographical and Historical Description of Boston* (Boston: Rockwell and Churchill, 1891), pp. 630–33.

31. Friedrich Engels, *The Housing Question* (New York: International Publishers, n.d.).

32. David Harvey, *Social Justice and the City* (Baltimore: Johns Hopkins U. Press, 1973), ch. 4.

33. The following sections present a market model of metropolitan growth as developed in the urban economics literature, including, among others, Wilbur Thompson, *A Preface to Urban Economics* (Baltimore: Johns Hopkins University Press, 1965); Richard F. Muth, *Urban Economics* (New York: Harper and Row,

1975); Werner Z. Hirsch, *Urban Economics Analysis* (New York: McGraw Hill, 1973); Matthew Edel and Jerome Rothenberg, eds., *Readings in Urban Economics* (New York: Macmillan, 1972).

34. The role of cities as regional headquarters is developed in Roderick D. McKenzie, *The Metropolitan Community* (New York: McGraw Hill, 1933) and Stephen Hymer, "The Multinational Corporation and the Law of Uneven Development," in Jagdish Bhagwati, ed., *Economics and World Order* (New York: The Free Press, 1972), pp. 113–140.

35. Andre Gorz, *Strategy for Labor* (Boston: Beacon Press, 1964).

36. Margery Davies, "Women's Place is at the Typewriter: the Feminization of the Clerical Labor Force," *Radical America* (July–Aug. 1974) 7:1–28.

37. Ivar Berg, *Education and Jobs.*

38. T. Caplow, "Urban Structure in France," *America Sociological Review* (October, 1952) 17:544–50; T. Caplow, "The Social Ecology of Guatamala City," *Social Forces* (December 1949), vol. 28.

39. William Alonso, *Location and Land Use* (Cambridge: Harvard University Press, 1964).

40. For a sampling of the literature, see Charles M. Haar, ed., *An End to Innocence: A Suburban Anthology* (Glenview, Ill.: Scott Foresman, 1972).

41. Richard Muth, *Cities and Housing* (Chicago: University of Chicago Press, 1969).

42. Robert Lampman, *The Share of Top Wealth Holders in National Wealth 1922–1957.* (Princeton, N.J.: Princeton University Press, 1962).

43. Wallace F. Smith, *Filtering and Neighborhood Change* (Berkeley: University of California Center for Real Estate and Urban Economics, 1964); Ira S. Lowry, "Filtering and Housing Standards: A Conceptual Analysis," *Land Economics* (Nov. 1960) 36:362–70.

44. Matthew Edel, "Filtering in a Private Housing Market," in M. Edel and J. Rothenberg, *Readings in Urban Economics* (New York: Macmillan, 1972), pp. 204–14.

45. Jerome Rothenberg, "Urban Renewal Porgrams," in Robert Dorfman, ed., *Measuring Benefits of Government Programs* (Washington: Brookings Institution, 1965).

46. Lowry, "Filtering."

47. K. H. Schaeffer and E. D. Sclar, *Access for All*, rev. ed. (New York: Columbia University Press, 1980).

48. Henry Aaron, *Shelter and Subsidies* (Washington: Brookings Institution, 1972).

49. On urban renewal in Boston, see particularly the film by R. Boardman, *Mission Hill and the Miracle of Boston.* See also Chester Hartman, "The Housing of Relocated Families," in *Journal of the American Institute of Planners* (Nov. 1964) 30(4):266–86; Marc Fried, "Grieving for a Lost Home," in L. J. Duhl, *The Urban Condition* (New York: Basic Books, 1963), ch. 12.

50. On "redlining" see National Commission on Neighborhoods, *People Building Neighborhoods: Final Report to the President and Congress* (Washington: GPO, 1979).

51. Alonso, *Location and Land Use;* Lowdon Wingo, *Transportation and Urban Land* (Baltimore: Johns Hopkins University Press, for Resources for the Future, 1961).

2. UNEVEN DEVELOPMENT OF METROPOLITAN BOSTON

1. Commonwealth of Massachusetts, *Historical Data Relating to Counties, Cities and Towns in Massachusetts* (Boston: Secretary of the Commonwealth, 1975).

2. Walter Muir Whitehill, *Boston: A Topographical History*, 2d ed. (Cambridge: Harvard University Press, 1968), ch. 1.

3. Provincial Census, cited in *Boston Year Book 1923–1924* (Boston: City of Boston Printing Dept., 1924).

4. All census figures from here on refer to the U.S. Decennial Federal Census.

5. Whitehill, *Boston*, pp. 60–63.

6. Oscar Handlin, *Boston's Immigrants: A Study in Acculturation*, rev. ed. (Cambridge: Harvard University Press, 1959), p. 82.

7. Jerry Greer, "East Boston: A Study in Development," unpublished term paper, MIT, 1971.

8. Whitehill, *Boston*.

9. Henry K. Rowe, *Tercentary History of Newton 1630–1930* (City of Newton, 1930), p. 94.

10. The case of Belmont will be discussed in chapter 8.

11. A Visit to Old Sturbridge Village in Sturbridge, Massachusetts. should illustrate this independence most vividly through its historical re-creation of village life in the 1840s.

12. Walter Firey, *Land Use in Central Boston* (Cambridge: Harvard University Press, 1968).

13. Albert B. Wolfe, *The Lodging House Problem in Boston* (Cambridge: Harvard University Press, 1906), pp. 36–37.

14. Stephan Thernstrom, *The Other Bostonians: Poverty and Progress in the American Metropolis, 1880–1970* (Cambridge: Harvard University Press, 1973).

15. Daniel Luria, "Stuck Inside Boston with the Mobile Blues Again," in *Boston: Studies in Urban Political Economy*, Working Paper #11.

16. Sam Bass Warner, Jr. *Streetcar Suburbs: The Process of Growth in Boston, 1870–1900* (Cambridge: Harvard University Press, 1960; rpt, New York: Atheneum, 1968).

17. K. H. Schaeffer and Elliott Sclar, *Access for All: Transportation and Urban Growth* (New York: Columbia University Press, 1980).

18. Frederick A. Bushee, *Ethnic Factors in the Population of Boston* (1903; rpt. New York: Arno Press, 1970), ch. 5.

19. Robert K. Lamb, "The Entrepreneur and the Community," in William Miller, ed., *Men in Business* (Cambridge: Harvard University Press, 1952); R. K. Lamb, "Remarks for the Nieman Fellows," (unpublished ms, 1948).

20. Geoffrey Blodgett, *The Gentle Reformers: Massachusetts Democrats in the Cleveland Era* (Cambridge: Harvard University Press, 1960), p. 115.

21. *Ibid.*, p. 74.

22. Steven Miller, "The Boston Irish Political Machines, 1870–1973," *Boston: Studies in Urban Political Economy,* Working Paper #15.

23. Schaefer and Sclar, *Access for All,* ch. 6.

24. Edward S. Mason, *The Street Railway in Massachusetts: The Rise and Decline of an Industry* (Cambridge: Harvard University Press, 1932), p. 13.

25. Schaefer and Sclar, *Access for All,* ch. 8.

26. Marc D. Draisen, "Regionalism versus Localism in Metropolitan Agencies: The Metropolitan District Commission as a Case Study," unpublished senior honors thesis, Brandeis University, Waltham, Mass., 1978.

27. Peter Skerry, "The Political Economy of the Metropolitan District Commission," report of the Massachusetts Public Finance Project, Lynn, Massachusetts, 1974.

28. Commonwealth of Massachusetts, Mass Transportation Commission, "The Boston Regional Survey," (Boston: April 1973), pp. 90–92.

29. Miller, "Boston Political Machines," p. 129.

3. REAL ESTATE VALUES

1. On early development of South End, see Fred E. Hays, "Historical Chapter II," in Robert A. Woods, ed., *The City Wilderness: A Settlement Study* (Boston: Houghton Mifflin, 1898); Walter Muir Whitehill, *Boston, A Topographical History* (Cambridge: Harvard University Press, 1968), chs. 4, 5, 6; Nathaniel B. Shurtleff, *Topographical and Historical Description of Boston* (Boston: Rockwell and Churchill, 1891). On the turn-of-the-century period, see A. B. Wolfe, *The Lodging House Problem in Boston* (Cambridge: Harvard University Press, 1906).

2. Hays, *ibid.*, says of Harrison Avenue in the South End (1804) that "the agreement of the owners to build no structure less than ten feet from the street was probably the first instance in Boston of a restriction upon real estate that had in view the symmetry and general appearance of a street lined with buildings."

3. Shurtleff, *Topographical and Historical Description,* pp. 430–450.

4. Wolfe, *Lodging House Problem,* p. 37.

5. Urban Field Service and Urban Planning Aid, *Report on South End Urban Renewal Plan,* prepared for Boston City Council Hearing, March 25, 1968.

6. Alexander S. Porter, "Changes of Values in Real Estate in Boston," *Collections of the Bostonian Society* (1888) 1(3):57–70.

7. John C. Kiley, "Changes in Realty Values in the Nineteenth and Twentieth Centuries," *Bulletin of the Business Historical Society,* June 1941.

8. *Ibid.*, p. 9.

9. Henry Whitmore, "Real Estate Values in Boston," with comments by James R. Carey and Dudley P. Bailey, *American Statistical Association* New Series (March 1896) 37:1–17.

10. Robert F. Engle and John Avault, *Residential Property Market Values in Boston* (Boston: Boston Redevelopment Authority Research Department, 1973);

Robert F. Engle, "De Facto Discrimination in Residential Assessments," *National Tax Journal* (December 1975) 27(4):445–51.

11. Mason Gaffney, "Adequacy of Land as a Tax Base," in Daniel Holland, ed., *The Assessment of Land Value* (Madison: University of Wisconsin Press, 1970), pp. 157–212.

12. Porter, "Changes of Values"; Whitmore, "Real Estate Values."

13. This section is based on Lisa Dennen and Barbara Sproat, "Bedroom Community in Transition: Brookline Massachusetts 1879–1970," in *Boston: Studies in Urban Political Economy* #19, and Charles Levenstein, "House Prices in an Inner-Ring Suburb: An Index for Somerville, Mass., 1879–1970," in *ibid.* # 16.

14. This section is based on Alan Mathews, *A Study of Rehabilitated Homes in Cambridge.* Unpublished BA thesis, MIT, 1973.

15. U.S. Census, 1950, 1960, 1970.

16. Gregory Palm, et al, *A Study of Rents in the Boston Metropolitan Areas,* unpublished seminar report, MIT, 1969.

17. Mathews, *Study of Rehabilitated Homes.*

18. Mathews, *ibid.* Analysis of Cambridge city building permits.

19. Construction of the index is described in Appendix B.

20. A value-laden term, "speculation" has many meanings. If the meaning implies "gambling" that uncertain price changes will occur, not all subdividers are truly "speculators": some would have subdivided had they expected overall prices *not* to rise, because there was a gap in values between subdivided and unsubdivided homes. Such developers are perhaps better thought of as "arbitragers," moving a good *between* two markets. For a discussion of the issue in another redevelopment market in the same period, see Sharon Zukin *Loft Living in New York City* (Baltimore: Johns Hopkins University Press, 1982).

21. For calculations, see Mathews, *Study of Rehabilitated Homes.*

4. REAL ESTATE VALUE CHANGES

1. Jere Chapman, Elliott Sclar, and Raymond Torto, *The Rich Get Richer and the Rest Pay Taxes: A Massachusetts Tax Primer* (Lynn: Massachusetts Public Finance Project, 1974).

2. L. Kish and J. Lansing, "Response Errors in Estimating the Value of Homes," *Journal of the American Statistical Association* (1954) 49: 520–38.

3. See, e.g., Richard Muth, *Cities and Housing* (Chicago: University of Chicago Press, 1969).

4. Robert Engle and Robert Richter, Unpublished town estimates of housing price change (MIT Dept. of Economics, 1971). The method used in these analyses is similar to that discussed in appendix B.

5. George Sternlieb, *The Tenement Landlord* (New Brunswick, N.J.: Rutgers University Press, 1966).

6. R. J. Lampman, *The Share of Top Wealth-Holders in National Wealth, 1922–1956* (Princeton: Princeton University Press, 1962).

5. THE REALITY OF SUBURBAN ENTRAPMENT

1. Horacio Caminos, John F. C. Turner, and John A. Steffian, *Urban Dwelling Environments* (Cambridge: MIT Press, 1969), pp. vi, ix.

2. *Ibid.*, pp. vii, ix.

3. These figures are taken as representative of the 1950–1970 period, based on "Where to Live?" *Business Week*, December 1, 1976. A similar exercise undertaken around 1980 would show similar results, with prices doubled or tripled.

4. U.S. Bureau of Labor Statistics, *Rent or Buy?*, Bulletin 1823 (Washington: G.P.O., 1974).

5. See Stephen A. Marglin, "What Do Bosses Do?—Part II," *Review of Radical Political Economics* (1975) 7(1):22–23.

6. For further discussion of the assumptions, see Daniel Luria, "Suburbanization, Homeownership, and Working Class Consciousness," Ph.D. diss., University of Massachusetts, Amherst, 1976, pp. 15–17.

7. Matthew Edel and Elliott Sclar, "The Distribution of Real Estate Value Changes: Metropolitan Boston, 1870–1970," *Boston: Studies in Urban Political Economy*, Working Paper #4, p. 2.

8. Caminos, et al. Urban Dwelling Environments, p. ix.

9. Stephan Thernstrom, *Poverty and Progress* (New York: Atheneum, 1969), p. 1955.

10. Thernstrom, *The Other Bostonians* (Cambridge: Harvard University Press, 1973), pp. 101–3.

11. Full methodology is described in Luria, "Suburbanization."

12. Table 5.2 does not, of course, report on the true spatial distribution of the population, based as it is on a male-only 1880 sample. But it does follow the same people through space and time, hence capturing the movement to the suburbs, which characterized the period. In fact, it does conform closely by 1910 with census data, summarized in Thernstrom's *The Other Bostonians*, p. 11, which reports Boston's population as a percent of its SMSA as 44, 43, 42 in 1890, 1900, and 1910, respectively.

13. Marglin, "What Do Bosses Do"; Daniel D. Luria, "Wealth, Capital and Power: The Social Meaning of Homeownership," *Journal of Interdisciplinary History* (Autumn 1976) 7(2):261–82.

14. Compiling a series for owner's equity—and hence for "non-home wealth,"—was no easy task. A fifty-year trace of each sample unit through county Grantee indexes and deed books allowed identification of real estate owners and purchase price. Following Warner, *Streetcar Suburbs*, p. 200, it was assumed that owner's equity was 52% of the most recent assessor's valuation. Finally, city directories provided street addresses which allowed identification of which real estate purchases were purchases of owner's home.

15. The estimations also make possible an analysis of the various direct and indirect effects of paternal homeownership on son's class group. Combining equations (2), (3), and (4), we get son's 1910 class group $= 1.390 + 0.239\text{FOCC}$

$+ 0.065OCC10$ (FPROP, FOCC, FHOME) $+ 0.0099PROP10$ (FPROP, FUS, FHOME, OCC10) $- 0.003FHOME$

Where
CLG10 = son's 1910 class group
FHOME = father's homeownership
OCCID = son's 1910 occupation
PROP10 = son's 1910 wealth
    and
FOCC   = father's occupation
differentiating totally, we get:

$$\frac{dCLG10}{dFHOME} = \frac{\delta CLG10}{\delta FHOME} + \frac{\delta CLG10}{\delta OCC10}\frac{dOCC10}{dFHOME} + \frac{\delta CLGL0}{\delta PROP10}\frac{dPROP10}{dFHOME}$$
$$+ \frac{\delta CLG10}{\delta PROP10}\left[\frac{PROP10}{OCC10}\frac{dOCC10}{dFHOME}\right] + \frac{CLG10}{FOCC}\frac{dFOCC}{dFHOME} + \frac{CLG10}{OCC10}$$
$$\left[\frac{\delta OCC10}{\delta FOCC}\frac{dFOCC}{dFHOME}\right] + \frac{\delta CLG10}{\delta PROP10}\frac{\delta PROP10}{\delta OCC10}\left[\frac{\delta OCC10}{\delta FOCC}\frac{dFOCC}{dFHOME}\right]$$
$$= -0.1334$$

From the above, it can be seen that the total effect of FHOME on CLG10 is composed of the direct association plus six indirect effects which can be measured using information gleaned from table 5.11. Partitioning the correlation between father's homeownership and Son's 1910 Class Group, we get:

Effect	Percent Explained
Direct	1.08%
Via father's job	54.49
Via son's 1919 job	7.19
Via son's 1919 wealth	28.27
Via son's wealth via son's job	2.71
Via son's wealth via son's job via father's job	1.69
Via son's job via father's job	4.58

Father's job and son's property together explain nearly 83% of the correlation between father's homeownership and son's class. Of the 13% of son's class explained by father's homeownership, nearly five-sixths is explained by the adverse effects of paternal homeowning on the father's job and on the son's wealth.

16. Equation (4) also was estimated without FHOME as a predictor, as the inclusion of insigifnicant predictors often biases the estimates of the other coefficients. Its omission, however, produced virtually no change, either in the other coefficients or in the overall performance of the equation.

17. Charles Levenstein, "Class, Assimilation, and Suburbanization," in *Boston: Studies in Urban Political Economy"* Working Paper #20; Charles Leven-

stein, *Class, Suburbanization and Ethnic Homogenization: Towards a Theory of Social/Spatial Stratification*, Ph.D. diss., MIT, 1975.

18. Charles Levenstein, "Occupation, Homeownership and Residential Persistence in a Working Class Suburb," *Boston: Studies in Urban Political Economy* Working Paper #22.

19. Charles Levenstein, "Assimilation, Homogenization, and Intermarriage," *Boston: Studies in Urban Political Economy* Working Paper #21. See also, Charles Levenstein, "The Political Economy of Suburbanization" (Summer 1981) 13:2.

20. This section is based on Sandy Altman, Steven Karp, Thomas Holzman and Minna Strumpf, *Brookline, Somerville and Lexington: A Study in Comparative Suburbanization 1880–1970*, unpublished paper, Boston Suburbanization Project, 1972, and Michael J. Haran, *Entrapment and the Somerville Schools*, unpublished thesis, Cambridge-Goddard School, 1973.

21. Altman, et al., *Brookline, Somerville and Lexington*, p. 6; J. G. Curtis, *History of the Town of Brookline Mass.* (Boston: Houghton Mifflin Co., 1933), p. 79; Amalie Hofer, *Brookline Schools*, 1896.

22. City Report, Somerville, Mass., 1890, p. 134; Harran, *Entrapment*.

23. Harran, *Ibid*.

24. Educational Survey of the Public Schools of Brookline, Mass., 1917.

25. Somerville Annual Town Report, 1920; Altman, et al., *Brookline, Somerville and Lexington*.

26. Altman, et al., *ibid.*; Harran, *Entrapment*.

27. Altamn, et al., *ibid.*, p. 11.

28. *Ibid;*

29. *Ibid;* Evaluation of the Brookline Schools by the New England Association of Colleges and Secondary Schools, 1972.

30. Altman, et al., *Brookline, Somerville, and Lexington;* New England Association of Colleges and Secondary School, Evaluation of Somerville Schools, 1970.

31. Altman, *et. al., ibid.*, p. 22.

32. *Ibid.*

33. Matthew Edel, *Property Taxes and Local Expenditures: A Hundred Year View*," Lynn: Massachusetts Public Finance Project Report 34, 1974.

34. Christopher Jencks, et al., *Inequality* (New York: Basic Books, 1974).

35. Rosina Becerra, *Does Equal Opportunity Mean Equal Access? A Study of the Relationship of a Student's Town of Residence and the Institution of Higher Education Attended.* Ph.D. diss., Brandeis University, Florence Heller Graduate School for Advanced Studies in Social Welfare, 1975.

36. *Ibid.*, p. 43–44.

37. *Ibid.*, pp. 73–93, explains method of grouping used.

38. *Ibid.* Data on students were gathered through a questionnaire, 24 of 30 public institutions and 44 of 50 members of the Association of Independent Colleges and Universities in Massachusetts responded.

39. *Ibid.*, p. 144.

40. *Ibid.*, p. 143.
41. *Ibid.*, p. 160.

6. BLAMING THE VICTIM

1. The concept of "blaming the victim" in social research was developed by William Ryan, *Blaming the Victim* (New York: Pantheon, 1971). See also William K. Tabb, "Blaming the Victim," in Roger E. Alcaly and David Mermelstein, eds., *The Fiscal Crisis of American Cities* (New York: Vintage Books, 1977), pp. 315–27.

2. National Housing Association, *Housing Problems in America: Proceedings of the Second National Conference on Housing, Philadelphia, Dec. 4, 5 and 6, 1912.* (Cambridge: Harvard University Press, 1913).

3. *Ibid.*, p. 279.
4. *Ibid.*, p. 272.
5. *Ibid.*, p. 283.
6. *Ibid.*, p. 279.

7. Frederick Engels, *The Housing Question* (New York: International Publishers, no date). Other examples include Carol Aronovici. *Housing the Masses* (New York: John Wiley, 1939); John McClaughry, et al., *Expanded Ownership* (Fond-du-Lac, Wisc., The Sabre Foundation, 1972); Blanche Halbert, ed., *The Better Homes Manual* (Chicago: University of Chicago Press, 1931), part 1; J. P. Dean, *Home Ownership: Is It Sound?* (New York: Harper and Bros., 1945); Charles Abrams, with Robert Kolodny, *Home Ownership for the Poor* (New York: Praeger, 1970).

8. Engels, *Housing Question*, p. 35, citing *La Emancipacion*, March 16, 1872.

9. Herbert Marcuse, *One-Dimensional Man* (Boston: Beacon Press, 1964), p. 9.

10. An additional argument against suburban development, involving its hidden ecological costs, can also be made. It is not considered here, but see Matthew Edel, *Economies and the Environment* (Englewood Cliffs: Prentice-Hall, 1973); Matthew Edel, "Pogo is Wrong," in David Mermelstein, ed., *Economics: Mainstream Readings and Radical Critiques* 3d ed. (New York: Random House, 1976), pp. 163–67; and K. H. Schaefer and E. Sclar, *Access for All* (New York: Columbia University Press, 1980).

11. Peter Marcuse, "Home Ownership for Low Income Families," *Land Economics* (May 1972); John P. Shelton, "The Cost of Renting vs. Owning a Home," *Land Economics* (February 1968).

12. Malvina Reynolds, "Little Boxes."

13. Paul Cowan, *The Making of an Un-American* (New York: Viking Press, 1970), p. 119.

14. Ibid, p. 120; cf. Paul Cowan, "Wallace in Yankeeland: The Invisible Revolution," *Village Voice* (July 18, 1968) 13(40):1, 17–19.

15. Oscar Handlin, *Boston's Immigrants* rev. ed. Cambridge: Harvard Uni-

versity Press, 1959); Sam Bass Warner, Jr., *Streetcar Suburbs* (Cambridge: Harvard University Press, 1960); Lloyd Rodwin, *Housing and Economic Progress* (Cambridge: Harvard University Press, 1961).

16. Frances Fox Piven and Richard A. Cloward, *Regulating the Poor* (New York: Random House, 1971); Samuel Bowles and Herbert Gintis, *Schooling in Capitalist America* (New York: Basic Books, 1976); Herbert Marcuse, *One-Dimensional Man.*

17. James M. Woodward, "U.S. Holds Record in Home Ownership," *Contra Costa Times,* August 5, 1973, p. 15.

18. Ely Chinoy, *Automobile Workers and the American Dream* (Boston: Beacon Press, 1955).

19. For critiques of this set of explanations, see William Ryan, *Blaming the Victim* (New York: Random House, 1971); Charles Valentine, *Culture and Poverty* (Chicago: University of Chicago Press, 1968).

20. For a critique of this position, which is implicit in many mathematical treatments of urban location, see David Harvey, *Social Justice and the City* (Baltimore: Johns Hopkins University Press, 1973), ch. 4.

21. Edel, *Economies and the Environment,* ch. 1.

22. Karl Marx, *Capital* (New York: International Publishers, 1967), 1:71–82.

23. Warner, *Streetcar Suburbs;* Rodwin, *Housing and Economic Progress.*

24. John Kain, "Postwar Metropolitan Development: Housing Preferences and Auto Ownership," *American Economic Review, Papers and Proceedings* (May 1967) 107(2):22–234.

25. Warner, *Streetcar Suburbs.*

26. Rodwin, *Housing and Economic Progress,* p. 2.

27. Warner, *Streetcar Suburbs.*

28. Sam Bass Warner, Jr., "The Discarded Suburbs" (Boston: Action for Boston Community Development, mimeo, n.d.).

29. Rodwin, *Housing and Economic Progress,* pp. 36–37.

30. John Kain, "Urban Form and the Costs of Urban Services," Harvard University, Department of Economics, discussion paper, 1967.

31. Homer Hoyt, *100 Years of Land Values in Chicago* (Chicago: University of Chicago Press, 1933), p. 442.

32. Stephan Thernstrom, *Poverty and Progress* (Cambridge: Harvard University Press, 1964).

33. Michael Lipton, "The Theory of the Optimizing Peasant," *Journal of Development Studies* (April 1968), vol. 4 discusses the case that risk aversion causes low returns in peasant agriculture. For a discussion of the immigrant as carrying over peasant familism, see D. P. Moynihan and N. Glazer, *Beyond the Melting Pot* (Cambridge: MIT Press, 1963).

34. Robert Park, "The City," in R. Sennett, ed. *Classic Essays on the Culture of Cities* (New York: Appleton-Century-Crofts, 1969, pp. 91–130); Sam Bass Warner, Jr., *The Private City* (Philadelphia: University of Pennsylvania Press, 1968).

35. Louis Wirth, "Urbanism as a Way of Life," in Sennett, ed., *Classic Essays.*

36. Richard Sennett, "Middle Class Families and Urban Violence," in S. Thernstrom and R. Sennett, eds., *Nineteenth Century Cities,* (New Haven: Yale University Press, 1969), p. 411.

37. William Muraskin, "The Social Control Theory in American History: A Critique," *Journal of Social History* (1976) 9(4):561.

38. John McClaughry, et. al, *Expanded Ownership* (Fond du Lac, Wisc.: Sabre Foundation, 1972), p. 1.

39. *Ibid.,* p. 2.

40. Hubert Humphrey, cited in the *Boston Globe,* Dec. 16, 1972.

41. Peter Lemos and Daniel Luria, "Worker Savings and Capital Investment: The Rise of Banking in Massachusetts," *Boston: Studies in Political Economy,* Working Paper #25.

42. *Ibid.*

43. Geoffrey Blodgett, *The Gentle Reformers* (Cambridge: Harvard University Press, 1966), pp. 125–26.

44. F. B. Sanborn, address to American Social Science Association, 1888, cited in Lemos and Luria, "Worker Savings."

45. S. M. Lipset and R. Bendix, *Social Mobility in Industrial Society* (Berkeley: University of California Press, 1967), p. 109. This view has been criticized within the empirical sociological tradition by Bennett Berger, *Working Class Suburb* (Berkeley: University of California Press, 1960).

46. Harvey Wasserman, *Harvey Wasserman's History of the United States* (New York: Harper and Row, 1972); Stanley Aronowitz, *False Promises* (New York: McGraw-Hill, 1974); Herbert Marcuse, *One-Dimensional Man;* Thomas Angotti, "The Housing Question: Engels and After," *Monthly* Review (Oct. 1977), pp. 39–61.

47. Eli Zaretsky, "Capitalism, the Family and Personal Life." *Socialist Revolution* (1973) 13(14):106–12.

48. Doris Lessing, "A Home for the Highland Cattle," *African Stories* (New York: Ballantine, 1966), p. 263.

49. John Kenneth Galbraith, *The Affluent Society* (Boston: Houghton Mifflin, 1967); Vance Packard, *The Hidden Persuaders* (New York: McKay, 1957); P. Baran and P. Sweezy, *Monopoly Capital* (New York: Monthly Review Press, 1966); Herbert Marcuse, *One-Dimensional Man.*

50. Muraskin, "Social Control Theory," p. 568.

51. *Ibid.,* p. 563.

52. Ellen Willis, "Consumerism and Women," *Socialist Revolution* (May–June, 1970) 1(3):76–82, criticizes the position of Marcuse and others about the manipulated consumer, arguing that "under present conditions, people are preoccupied with consumer goods not because they are brainwashed, but because buying is the one pleasurable activity not only permitted but actively encouraged by the power structure. . . . Although they have to cope with the gyppery inher-

ent in the profit system, people for the most part buy goods for practical, self-interested reasons. . . . Consumerism is the outgrowth of an aristocratic, European-oriented anti-materialism based on upper-class resentment against the rise of the vulgar bourgeois. Radical intellectuals have been attracted to this essentially reactionary position . . . because it appeals to both their dislike of capitalism and their feeling of superiority to the working class. This elitism is evident in radicals' conviction that they have seen through the system, while the average working slob is brainwashed by the media." See also Sherry Gorelick, "Undermining Hierarchy: Problems of Schooling in Capitalist America," *Monthly Review* (October, 1977), pp. 20–36.

53. Engels, *Housing Question.*
54. *Ibid.*
55. *Ibid.*, pp. 14–15. On rent theory, see Matthew Edel, "Marx's Theory of Rent: Urban Applications," *Kapitalistate* (1976) 4–5:100–124.
56. Engels, *Housing Question*, p. 35.
57. *Ibid.*, p. 28.
58. *Ibid.*, p. 53.
59. *Ibid.*, p. 35.
60. The clearest statement of this is Marx, *Value, Price and Profit* (New York: International Publishers, 1935). For urban applications, see Edel, "Marx's Theory of Rent."
61. Warner, *Streetcar Suburbs.*

7. LAND DEVELOPERS

1. Sam Bass Warner, Jr., *Streetcar Suburbs* (Cambridge: Harvard University Press, 1962).
2. *Ibid.*, p. 4.
3. *Ibid.*, p. 184.
4. Paul David Brophy, *Property Taxation Effects on Suburban Development.* Thesis for Bachelor of Science, Cambridge, Mass., MIT, 1970.
5. This section draws on Jane Goldstein Morris, *Harrison Gray Otis and the Development of Boston Real Estate.* Thesis for Master of Arts, Queens College, Flushing, New York, 1976.
6. Samuel Eliot Morison, *Harrison Gray Otis, 1765–1848: The Urbane Federalist* (Boston: Houghton Mifflin, 1969), pp. 29–41.
7. *Ibid.*, pp. 59–87.
8. *Ibid.*, p. 219.
9. Carl Seabury and Stanley Paterson, *Merchant Prince of Boston: Colonel T. H. Perkins, 1764–1854* (Cambridge: Harvard University Press, 1971), p. 212.
10. Walter Muir Whitehill, *Boston: A Topographical History* (Cambridge: Harvard University Press, 1968), p. 60. The Copley purchase, which was actually made by the artist's son-in-law, led to controversy when Copley disavowed the agreement. But Otis's purchase was sustined in court; cf Morison, *Otis*, p. 76.

11. Morison, *Otis*, p. 63.

12. Data in Suffolk County *Registry of Deeds* analyzed in Morris, *Otis and Real Estate.*

13. Alan Chamberlain, *Beacon Hill: Its Ancient Pastures and Early Mansions* (Boston: Houghton Mifflin, 1925), pp. 61–62.

14. Whitehill, *Topographical History*, p. 62.

15. Suffolk country Registry of Deeds, analyzed in Morris, *Otis and Real Estate.*

16. Whitehill, *Topographical History*, pp. 76–78; Morris, *Otis and Real Estate.*

17. Harold Kirker, *The Architecture of Charles Bulfinch* (Cambridge: MIT Press, 1969), pp. 188–90.

18. *Suffolk County Registry of Deeds*, cited in Morris, *Otis and Real Estate,* p. 46.

19. Morris, *ibid.*, p. 49.

20. *Ibid.*, p. 43.

21. Kirker, *Charles Bulfinch;* Morison, *Otis*, pp. 453–54.

22. Morris, *Otis and Real Estate.*

23. This section draws on Barbara J. Sproat, Henry Whitney's Streetcar Suburb: Beacon Street, Brookline, 1870–1910 (*Boston Studies in Urban Political Economy*, Working Paper #29).

24. Geoffrey Blodgett, *The Gentle Reformers: Massachusetts Democrats in the Cleveland Era* (Cambridge: Harvard University Press, 1966), p. 12; Edward S. Mason, *The Street Railway in Massachusetts* (Cambridge: Harvard University Press, 1932); K. H. Schaeffer and Elliott Sclar, *Access for All* (New York: Columbia University Press, 1980).

25. Warner, *Streetcar Suburbs*, p. 23.

26. Prentiss Cummings, "Street Railway System of Boston," in *Professional and Industrial History of Suffolk County, Massachusetts* (Boston: The Boston History Co., 1894), 3:294.

27. *Ibid.* See also Louis P. Hager, *History of the West End Street Railway* (Boston: Louis P. Hager, 1892), pp. 22–23.

28. Edwin M. Bacon, *The Book of Boston* (Boston: The Book of Boston Co., 1916), p. 112.

29. Warner, *Streetcar Suburbs*, pp. 22–26.

30. Mason, *Street Railway;* Schaefer and Sclar, *Access for All.*

31. Warner, *Streetcar Suburbs*, p. 26. As we shall show in chapter 9, Whitney did not, in fact, always follow this policy from his own desires.

32. Sproat, *Whitney's Streetcar Suburb*, pp. 4–5. Robert L. Miller, "The Development of Beacon Street in Brookline, Mass." Unpublished, MIT, 1971; D. G. Lacey, *Old Streets in Brookline* (1950).

33. Sproat, *Whitney's Streetcar Suburb;* Miller, *Beacon Street.*

34. Miller, *ibid.*

35. Sproat, *Whitney's Streetcar Suburb.* Of Whitney's maximum total holdings of 5.25 million square feet, 630,000, or 12 percent, were donated to the

town, and 4.4. million were sold. Hence the 1910 cutoff misses the disposition of only 4.2 percent of Whitney's land.

36. See Sproat, *Whitney's Streetcar Suburb* for further details by area.

37. This section is based in part on Richard Krushnic, Post-War Industrial Development on the Periphery of Metropolitan Boston, *Boston: Working Papers on Studies in Urban Political Economy*, Working Paper #13 and on Thomas Holzman, Post-War Land Speculation in Middlesex County: A Look Into the Activities of Cabot, Cabot and Forbes *ibid.*, #27.

38. Krushnic, *ibid.*; Christopher Rand, "Cambridge: Center of a New World," *The New Yorker* April 11, 18, 25, and May 2 (1963).

39. Schaefer and Sclar, *Access for All;* C. A. Maguire and Associates, *1948 Master Highway Plan for the Boston Metropolitan Area*, Mass. Dept. of Public Works, 1948, cited in Ralph Gakenheimer, *Transportation Planning as a Response to Controversy: The Boston Case* (Cambridge: MIT Press, 1976), p. 20.

40. On the industrial transformation of the area, see Barry Bluestone and Bennett Harrison, *The Deindustrialization of America* (New York: Basic Books, 1982). It should be noted that among the advantages of the older satellite town workforces is a complex mix of skill, ethnic "acceptability," economic entrapment, and increasingly over time, presence of female labor force with industrial experience.

41. Krushnic, *Post-War Industrial Development;* F. Lincoln, "After the Cabots—Jerry Blakely," *Fortune* (Nov. 1960), pp. 171–74.

42. Richard Dooley, "Communities on the Golden Semicircle," *Greater Boston Business*, Route 128 Supplement, 1959, p. 15.

43. Krushnic, *Post-War Industrial Development*, pp. 28–29, based on interviews with developers. Cabot, Cabot and Forbes Co., "New England Industrial Center," brochure (undated, late 1960s).

44. "The Manifest Destiny of Industrial Expansion," *Boston* magazine, 1971. Radelle Patterson, "Routes 495 and 128: Problems and Promise," *Boston Sunday Globe*, March 21, 1971.

45. Krushnic, *Post-War Industrial Development*, p. 17, based on interviews.

46. *MIT Economic Impact Study of Massachusetts Route 128* (1958).

47. Robert T. Killiam, Jr., "Boston's Golden Industrial Semicricle," *Greater Boston Business*, 1959, pp. 1, 48. Donald White, "CC & F Name Right for New Boston," *Boston Globe*, May 13, 1964.

48. Rand, "Cambridge."

49. Lincoln, "After the Cabots."

50. Cabot, Cabot and Forbes Land Trust, *Prospectus*, 1971.

51. *Fortune ibid.;* Holzman, *Post-War Land Speculation.*

52. Holzman, *Post-War Land Speculation.*

53. Holzman, *Post-War Land Speculation.* Although the confidence interval on the Waltham property indicates a possible return of from 55 percent per year to 1169 percent per year, the average of 612 percent should be cause for wonder. The main problem is the small sample size; unfortunately, one very important deal (Christine and Fred Viles to Blakely et al.) had a subordinate mortgage

trust indenture on it which did not specify the amount of the loan. Even if we assume there was a $300,000 mortgage loan taken on the property by CC & F, it still leaves the price paid for that land at slightly over $0.10 per square foot. If 0.10 is the correct figure (and this is a high estimate), the average return of 600 percent per year would be confirmed by matching the $0.10 with sales of portions of the parcel and the confidence interval would be narrowed.

54. Holzman, *Post-War Land Speculation*.

55. CC& F Land Trust *Prospectus*.

56. Gustavus Meyers, *Rise of the Great American Fortunes* (Chicago: Charles H. Kerr, 1907), 1:109–241; Robert Fogelson, *The Fragmented Metropolis* (Cambridge: Harvard University Press, 1967); Homer Hoyt, *100 Years of Land Values in Chicago* (Chicago: University of Chicago Press, 1933).

57. Michael Kramer and Sam Roberts, *"I Never Wanted To Be Vice President of Anything:" An Investigative Biography of Nelson Rockefeller* (New York: Basic Books, 1976); Samuel E. Bleecker, *The Politics of Architecture: A Perspective on Nelson A. Rockefeller* (New York: Rutledge Press, 1981).

58. Schaefer and Sclar, *Access for All*.

59. John Stuart Mill, *Principles of Political Economy* (London: Longmans Green, 1929; rpt. 1964); Henry George, *Progress and Poverty* (New York: Modern Library, 1929; originally published 1879).

60. Lester Thurow, *Generating Inequality* (New York: Basic Books, 1975).

61. Robert Fitch, "Planning New York," in R. Alcaly and D. Mermelstein, eds., *The Fiscal Crisis of American Cities* (New York: Vintage, 1977), pp. 246–84; John Mollenkopf, "The Postwar Politics of Urban Development," in W. Tabb and L. Sawers, *Marxism and the Metropolis* (New York: Oxford University Press, 1978), pp. 117–52.

8. FISCAL BALKANIZATION

1. John H. Mollenkopf, "The Postwar Politics of Urban Development," in W. Tabb and L. Sawers, *Marxism and the Metropolis* (New York: Oxford University Press, 1978), pp. 117–52.

2. Richard Muth, *Cities and Housing* (Chicago: University of Chicago Press, 1964).

3. Matthew Edel, "Capitalism, Accumulation and the Explanation of Urban Phenomena," in M. Dear and A. J. Scott, *Urbanization and Urban Planning in Capitalist Society* (London: Metheun, 1981), pp. 19–44.

4. For this "public choice" theory, see J. Buchanan and G. Tulloch, *The Calculus of Consent* (Ann Arbor: University of Michigan Press, 1963), J. Buchanan, *The Limits of Liberty* (Chicago: University of Chicago Press, 1975) and other works.

5. This account follows Walter Muir Whitehill, *Topographical History of Boston* (Cambridge: Harvard University Press, 1968) and Nathaniel Shurtleff, *Topographical and Historical Description of Boston* (Boston: Rockwell and Churchill, 1891).

6. Henry K. Rowe, *Tercentenary History of Newton, 1630–1930*, City of Newton, 1930, ch. 1.

7. Subdivisions in other towns at this time are discussed in Kenneth A. Lockridge, *A New England Town, the First Hundred Years:* Dedham, Masssachusetts, 1736–1836 (New York: W.W. Norton, 1970), and Sumner Chilton Powell, *Puritan Village: The Formation of a New England Town* (Middletown, Connecticut: Wesleyan University Press, 1963).

8. Michael J. Harran, "Entrapment and the Somerville Schools," unpublished thesis, Cambridge-Goddard School, 1973.

9. Eugene E. Oakes, *Studies in Massachusetts Town Finance* (Cambridge: Harvard University Press, 1937), ch. 5.

10. *Ibid.*

11. *Ibid.*

12. Charles Phillips Huse, *The Financial History of Boston from May 1, 1826 to January 31, 1905* (rpt., Russell and Russell, 1967), ch. 1.

13. *Ibid.*, ch. 2.

14. *Ibid.*, ch. 3.

15. The discussion here will be in current dollar terms. The available evidence indicates that the amount of inflation in the nineteenth century was minimal. The New York Federal Reserve cost of living index for the years 1820–1913 indicates that from 1820 to 1900, the rate of inflation was only .26% per annum. The data analysis presented here is derived from source material contained in the appendices to Huse, *Financial History*, unless otherwise specified.

16. Oscar Handlin, *Boston Immigrants* (Cambridge, Mass.: Harvard University Press, 1959).

17. Argument of Hon. M. E. Ingalls in favor of annexation to Boston of Brighton, Brookline and West Roxbury, before the Committee on Towns of the Massachusetts legislature, April 18, 1870.

18. Opening argument for the town of Brookline by Alfred Chandler, Esq., before the Committee on Towns of the Massachusetts legislature, March 11, 1880.

19. *Ibid.*

20. Derived from data contained in Royal S. Van de Woystyne, *State Control of Local Finance in Massachusetts* (Cambridge: Harvard University Press, 1934), and Huse, *Financial History*.

21. Van de Woystyne, *State Control*, chs. 2 and 3.

22. *Ibid.*

23. Harold Kirker, *The Architecture of Charles Bulfinch* (Cambridge, Mass.: Harvard Univ. Press, 1969).

24. J. H. Benton, Jr., "Inequality of Tax Valuation in Massachusetts," address delivered before the Beacon Society of Boston (Boston: Addison C. Gitchell, 1890).

25. Henry Whitmore, "Real Estate Values in Boston," *American Statistical Association, New Series*, 33 (March 1896), pp. 1–17.

26. Comparing Benton, "Inequality," with 1973 Commonwealth of Massachusetts documents.

27. See W. E. Oates, "The Effects of Property Taxes and Local Spending on Property Values: An Empirical Study of Tax Capitalization and the Tiebout Hypothesis," *Journal of Political Economy* (November–December 1969) 77(6):957–

71; and Matthew Edel, "Taxes, Spending and Property Values: Supply Adjustment in a Tiebout-Oates Model," *ibid.*, (September–October 1974) 82(5):941–54.

28. Oates, "Effects."

9. ORIGINS OF THE SUBURBAN COMPROMISE

1. On this period, see Jeremy Brecher, *Strike!* (Greenwich, Conn.: Fawcett, 1973), pp. 20–47, etc.

2. Karl Marx, "On the Question of Free Trade," in *The Poverty of Philosophy* (Moscow: Foreign Language Publishing House, 1956), appendix, p. 234.

3. Robert H. Wiebe, *The Search for Order, 1877–1920* (New York: Hill and Wang, 1967); Brecher, *Strike.*

4. Robert V. Bruce, *1877: Year of Violence* (Chicago: Quadrangle, 1970) pp. 37–36.

5. Brecher, *Strike.*

6. Geoffrey Blodgett, *The Gentle Reformers: Massachusetts Democrats in the Cleveland Era* (Cambridge: Harvard University Press), esp. pp. 63–66; Roger Lane, *Policing the City* (Cambridge: Harvard University Press, 1967); Steven E. Miller, "The Boston Irish Political Machine, 1830–1973," *Boston: Studies in Urban Political Economy* #15.

7. Peter Alexander Speek, *The Single Tax and the Labor Movement* (Madison: University of Wisconsin, 1977); Richard Sennett, "Middle Class Families and Urban Violence," in S. Thernstrom and R. Sennett, *Nineteenth Century Cities* (New Haven: Yale University Press, 1969), pp. 386–420.

8. Frederick Engels, "Preface," in *The Condition of the Working Class in England* (Moscow: Progress Publishers n.d.).

9. *Ibid.*, p. 16.

10. Henry George, *Progress and Poverty* (New York: Modern Library, 1938). Originally published in 1879.

11. *Ibid.*, pp. 70–254.

12. *Ibid.*, p. 328.

13. *Ibid.*, p. 405. See also, Matthew Edel, "Capital, Profit and Accumulation: the Perspectives of Karl Marx and Henry George Compared," in Richard Lindholm, ed., *Land Value Taxation: The Progress and Poverty Centenary* (Madison: University of Wisconsin Press, 1982), pp. 205–20.

14. David Hereshoff, *The Origins of American Marxism* (New York: Monad Press, 1973), pp. 110–11.

15. Cited in Eric F. Goldman, *Rendezvous with Destiny* (New York: Knopf, 1956), p. 20.

16. Speek, *Single Tax.*

17. *Ibid.*

18. Ira Kipnis, *The American Socialist Movement, 1897–1912* (New York: Columbia University Press, 1952); James Weinstein, *The Decline of Socialism in America* (New York: Monthly Review Press, 1967).

19. Bruce M. Stave, ed., *Socialism and the Cities* (Port Washington, N.Y.: Kennikat Press, 1975); James Weinstein, *The Corporate Ideal in the Liberal State* (Boston: Beacon Press, 1968), ch. 4; Speek, *Single Tax.*

20. Walter Lippman, Letter to Carl D. Thompson, 1913, reprinted in Stave, *Socialism,* pp. 184–96.

21. Herreshoff, *Origins,* pp. 150–51.

22. *Ibid.,* p. 150.

23. Patrick Renshaw, *The Wobblies* (Garden City: Doubleday, 1967), p. 26; Kipnis, *American Socialist.*

24. Stave, *Socialism;* Kipnis, *ibid.*

25. Henry F. Bedford, *Socialism and the Workers in Massachusetts, 1886– 1912* (Amherst: University of Massachusetts Press, 1966).

26. *Ibid.*

27. Gerald Friedberg, "Marxism in the United States," PhD. Diss. Harvard University, 1964, p. 24.

28. John Spargo, *Social Democracy Explained,* (New York: B. W. Huebsch, 1912), pp. 57–58.

29. Friedberg, "Marxism," p. 43.

30. Herreshoff, *Origins,* pp. 164–65.

31. Charles H. Trout *Boston, The Great Depression, and the New Deal* (New York: Oxford University Press, 1977); Miller, "Irish Political Machine."

32. Blodgett, *Gentle Reformers;* Arthur Mann, *Yankee Reformers in an Urban Age: Social Reform in Boston, 1880–1900* (New York: Harper, 1954).

33. Miller, "Political Machine," p. 68.

34. Albert Hart, *Commonwealth History of Massachusetts,* vol. 5, ch. 3 (New York: the States Publishing Co., 1930).

35. Richard M. Abrams, *Conservatism in a Progressive Era: Massachusetts Politics 1900–1912* (Cambridge: Harvard University Press, 1964), ch. 6.

36. Miller, "Political Machine"; James Michael Curley, *I'd Do It All Again: A Record of All My Uproarious Years* (Englewood Cliffs: Prentice Hall, 1947); Trout, *Boston, the Depression.*

37. Renshaw, *Wobblies,* p. 26; Nathan Fine, *Labor and Farmers Parties in the United States, 1828–1928* (New York: Russell & Russell, 1961).

38. Catherine Bauer, *Modern Housing* (Boston: Houghton Mifflin Co., 1934).

39. Don Parson, "The Development of Redevelopment," *International Journal of Urban and Regional Research* (Sept. 1983) 6(3): 393–413.

40. William Green, "Home Ownership and the Wage Earner," in Blanche Halbert, ed., *The Better Homes Manual* (Chicago: University of Chicago Press, published in cooperation with *Better Homes in America,* 1931), pp. 44–45.

41. *Ibid.,* pp. 43–49.

42. David M. Gordon, "Capitalist Development and the History of American Cities," in William V. Tabb and Larry Sawers, *Marxism and the Metropolis* (New York: Oxford University Press, 1978), pp. 25–63.

43. Sennett, "Middle-Class Families."

44. See, e.g., Sam Bass Warner, Jr., *Streetcar Suburbs* and *The Discarded*

Suburbs; unpublished manuscript, (Boston: Action for Boston Community Development, 1961).

45. On housing reform generally, see Roy Lubove, *The Progressives and the Slums* (Pittsburgh: Pittsburgh University Press, 1962), and Anthony Jackson, *A Place Called Home* (Cambridge: MIT Press, 1976).

46. This section follows Stephen A. Kersten, "Housing Regulation and Reform in Boston: 1822–1924: Antecedents of Zoning," Boston Studies in Urban Political Economy #7 (Waltham: Brandeis University, 1973); David M. Culver, "Tenement House Reform in Boston, 1846–1898," Ph.D. Dissertation, Boston: Boston University, 1972; Oscar Handlin, *Boston's Immigrants* (Cambridge: Harvard University Press, rev. ed., 1969); John Koren, *Boston 1822–1922* (City of Boston Printing Dept., 1923).

47. Robert T. Paine, Jr., "The Housing Conditions of Boston," *Annals of the American Academy of Political Science* (July 1902)3(124):128; Culver, "Tenement House Reform"; Kersten, "Housing Regulation."

48. Barbara Ehrenreich and Deirdre English, "The Manufacture of Housework," *Socialist Review* (Oct.–Dec. 1974)26:27; Galen Cranz, "Women in Urban Parks," *SIGNS* (Spring 1980)5(3), supplement, pp. 76–92.

49. Paine, "Housing Conditions," p. 125.

50. Dwight Porter, *Report Upon a Sanitary Inspection of Certain Tenement House Districts of Boston* (Boston: Rockwell and Churchill, 1889).

51. Benjamin Flower, *Progressive Men, Women and Movements of the Past 25 Years* (Boston: Arena Publishing Co., 1914); Benjamin Flower, *Civilization's Inferno* (Boston: Arena Publishing Co., 1893).

52. Culver, "Tenement House Reform," pp. 268–69.

53. F. Spencer Baldwin, *The Housing Problem* (Boston: 20th Century Club, 1900).

54. Culver, "Tenement House Reform," p. 278; Harold Kelsey Estabrook, *Some Slums in Boston* (Boston: 20th Century Club, 1898).

55. Edwin D. Mead, *Better Homes for the Boston Poor* (Boston, 1899).

56. Stuart D. Brandes, *American Welfare Capitalism* (Chicago: University of Chicago Press, 1976), pp. 38–39.

57. Brandes, *ibid.,* p. 48. Tamara K. Harevan and Randolph Lagenbach, *Amoskeag: Life and Work in an American Factory City* (New York: Pantheon, 1978).

58. Laurie Nisonoff, "Bread and Roses: The Proletarianization of Women Workers in New England Textile Mills: 1827–1848," *Historical Journal of Massachusetts* (Jan. 1981) 9(1):3–14.

59. Brandes, *Welfare Capitalism,* pp. 11–12.

60. Gordon, *Capitalist Development,* p. 48; Graham R. Taylor, *Satellite Cities: A Study of Industrial Suburbs* (New York: D. Appleton, 1915).

61. Brandes, *Welfare Capitalism,* p. 18; Ehrenreich and English, "Housework."

62. Edward E. Hale, *Workingmen's Homes* (Boston, 1879), p. 73.

63. Blodgett, *Gentle Reformers,* p. 124.

64. Paine, "Housing Conditions," p. 128.

65. Culver, "Tenement House Reform," p. 253; *Boston Evening Transcript,* June 28, 1893.

66. J. S. Hodgson, L. Southard and G. H. Walker, *Boston's Housing Problem, Preliminary Report of Committee Appointed by the Economic Club of Boston,* April 5, 1911, p. 3.

67. *Ibid.,* p. 15.

68. *Ibid.,* p. 13.

69. *Massachusetts Act and Resolves* 1911, Chapter 607; *Massachusetts Homestead Commission,* Bulletin 7, revised Oct. 18, 1917; *Massachusetts Homestead Commission,* report 1919, p. 12.

70. Roy Lubove, *Community Planning in the 1920s* (Pittsburgh: University of Pittsburgh Press, 1963), ch. 1.

71. Edward S. Mason, *The Street Railway in Massachusetts* (Cambridge: Harvard University Press, 1932).

72. Harold C. Passer, "Frank Julian Sprague: Father of Electric Traction 1857–1934" in William Miller, ed., *Men in Business* (Cambridge: Harvard University Press, 1952), pp. 212–38.

73. Glen E. Holt, "The Changing Perception of Urban Pathology," in Kenneth T. Jackson and Stanley K. Schultz, *Cities in American History* (New York: Knopf, 1972), p. 331; Gunther Barth, *Instant Cities* (New York: Oxford University Press, 1975).

74. Passer, "Sprague,"; Warner, *Streetcar Suburbs;* Dennen and Sproat, "Bedroom Communities in Transition."

75. Francis Walker, *Double Taxation in the United States* (New York: Arno Press, 1968).

76. Goldman, *Rendezvous With Destiny,* p. 129.

77. Weinstein, *Corporate Ideal,* Chapter 4.

78. Passer, "Sprague."

79. James Blaine Walker, *Fifty Years of Rapid Transit 1864–1917* (New York: Arno Press, 1970).

80. Ibid.; Adam Goodfarb, *History of Transportation Policy in the New York Region,* unpublished B.A. thesis, Brandeis University, 1973.

81. Gabriel Kolko, *Railroads and Regulation, 1877–1916* (Princeton: Princeton University Press, 1965).

82. Goodfarb, *History of Transportation Policy.*

83. Jackson, p. 71.

84. Lane, *op. cit.*

85. Blodgett, *Gentle Reformers.*

86. Nathan Matthews, Jr., *The City Government of Boston* (Boston: Rockwell and Churchill, 1895).

87. Bedford, *Social Workers.*

88. Blodgett, *Gentle Reformers.*

89. Peter Skerry, *The Massachusetts District Commission* (Lynn: Lynn Economic Opportunity, Massachusetts Public Finance Project Working Papers).

90. Blodgett, *Gentle Reformers;* Dennen and Sproat, "Bedroom Communities in Transition."

91. Blodgett, *ibid.*, p. 124.

92. Abrams, *Conservatism*, ch. 2.

93. Everett W. Burdett, *Argument for the Massachusetts Street Railway Association* (Boston: Rockwell and Churchill, 1897), p. 52.

94. *Ibid.*, and *Street Railway Laws of Massachusetts, 1882–1894* (pamphlet).

95. Burdett, *Argument;* Mason, *Street Railway.*

96. Massachusetts Commission on Relations Between Street Railways and Municipal Corporations, *Street Railways and Cities* (Boston: Wright and Potter, 1898).

97. Abrams, *Conservatism*, p. 202; cf Blodgett, *Gentle Reformers.*

98. Joel Schwartz, "Evolution of the Suburbs," in Philip Dolce, *Suburbia: The American Dream and Dilemma* (Garden City: Anchor Books, 1976), pp. 13–18.

99. Robert A. Woods and Albert J. Kennedy, *The Zone of Emergence: Observations of the Lower, Middle and Upper Working Class Communities of Boston, 1905–1919,* 2d ed. (Cambridge: MIT Press, 1969).

100. *Ibid.*, p. 69.

101. Sam Bass Warner, Jr., Preface to *ibid.*, p. 11.

10. THE COMPROMISE EVALUATED

1. Sam Bass Warner, Jr., *Streetcar Suburbs* (Cambridge: Harvard University Press, 1962).

2. John M. Gries and James S. Taylor, "Home Ownership and Home Financing," in Blanche Halbert, ed., *The Better Homes Manual* (Chicago: University of Chicago Press, 1931) p. 11.

3. *Ibid.*, U.S. Dept. of Housing and Urban Development, *1975 Annual Housing Survey, U.S. Censuses of Housing;* in M. Edel, P. Eilbott and A. M. Levenson, *The Future of Rental Housing and New Forms of Home-Ownership* (Flushing: Queens College, 1981).

4. Daniel Luria, trace of homeownership using subsample from Stephan Thernstrom's study of Boston families described in Thernstrom, *The Other Bostonians* (Cambridge: Harvard University Press, 1973) and Daniel Luria, "Suburbanization, Homeownership and Working Class Consciousness," Ph.D. dissertation, University of Massachusetts, 1976.

5. Daniel Luria, "Wealth, Capital and Power: The Social Meaning of Home Ownership," *Boston: Working Papers in Urban Political Economy* #5, p. 18.

6. David Harvey, "The Urban Process Under Capitalism" in M. Dear and A. J. Scott, *Urbanization and Urban Planning in Capitalist Society* (London: Methuen, 1981), pp. 91–121.

7. Brinley Thomas, *Migration and Economic Growth* (Cambridge: Cambridge University Press, 1973)

8. Antonio Gramsci, *Selections From the Prison Notebooks* (New York: International, 1972); Andre Gorz, *Strategy for Labor* (Boston: Beacon Press, 1962).

9. David Ricardo, *On the Principles of Political Economy and Taxation* (Cambridge: Cambridge University Press, 1951).

10. E.g., Paul A. Samuelson, *Foundations of Economic Analysis* (Cambridge: Harvard University Press, 1947), p. 35.

11. Henry George, *Progress and Poverty* (New York: Modern Library, 1938).

12. Frederick Engels, *The Housing Question* (New York: International Publishers, n.d.), pp. 51–52.

13. *Ibid.*, p. 52.

14. Karl Marx, *Capital* (New York: International Publishers, 1967), 1:33; E. G. Wakefield, *England and America* (London, 1899).

15. Marx, *Capital*, vol. 2, and Marx, *Theories of Surplus Value* (Moscow: Progress Publishers, 1963), vol. 2. For further commentary on the distinction, see Matthew Edel, "Marx's Theory of Rent: Urban Applications," *Kapitalistate* (1976) 4–5.

16. Edel, *Ibid.*; David Harvey, *Social Justice and the City* (Baltimore: Johns Hopkins University Press, 1973); Alain Lipietz, *Le Tribut Foncier Urbain* (Paris: Maspero, 1974); Michael Ball, "Differential Rent and the Role of Landed Property," *International Journal of Urban and Regional Research* (October 1977) 1(3):380–403.

17. Marx, *Capital* 3:657.

18. Marx, "On the Question of Free Trade," in *The Poverty of Philosophy* (Moscow: Foreign Language Publishing House, 1956), Appendix, p. 234.

19. Marx, *Capital*, 1:ch. 33.

20. Karl Marx, "Wages, Price and Profit," in K. Marx and F. Engels, *Selected Works* (New York: International Publishers, 1967).

21. Marx, *Capital*, chap. 33.

22. For formal models of this, see Matthew Edel, "Land Values and the Cost of Urban Congestion," *Social Science Information* 10(6):7–36.

23. Michael T. Roncich, "Land Value Change in an Area Undergoing Urbanization," *Land Economics* (February 1970), pp. 33–40; Marion Clawson, *Suburban Land Conversion in the United States* (Baltimore: Johns Hopkins University Press, 1971).

24. E. S. Mason, *The Street Railway in Massachusetts* (Cambridge: Harvard University Press, 1932).

25. Ibid.

26. Warner, *Streetcar Suburbs.*

27. *Ibid.*, and L. L. Elden, *The Boston Edison System* (Boston: Edison Electric Illuminating Co., 1900).

28. Marc Fried, *The World of the Urban Working Class* (Cambridge: Harvard University Press, 1973), pp. 49–50.

29. Leo F. Schnore and Peter R. Knight, "Residence and Social Structure," in S. Thernstrom and R. Sennett, *Nineteenth Century Cities* (New Haven: Yale University Press, 1969), pp. 247–57; U.S. *Censuses of Population.*

30. Robert A. Woods and Albert J. Kennedy, *The Zone of Emergence*, 2d ed. Cambridge: MIT Press, 1969); R. Woods, *The City Wilderness* (Boston: Houghton-Mifflin, 1898).

31. Lloyd Rodwin, Housing and Economic Progress (Cambridge: Harvard University Press, 1961); Daniel Luria, "Suburbanization, Homeownership and Working Class Consciousness."

32. For the various views, see Ira Kipnis, *The American Socialist Movement: 1897–1919* (New York: Columbia University Press, 1952); James Weinstein, *The Decline of Socialism in America* (New York: Monthly Review Press, 1967).

33. See Stave, *op. cit.*

34. Gwendolyn Wright, *Building the Dream: A Social History of Housing in America* (New York: Pantheon, 1981), pp. 198–99. See also Catherine Bauer, *Modern Housing* (Boston: Houghton-Mifflin, 1934).

35. Barbara Ehrenreich and Deirdre English, "The Manufacture of Housework," *Socialist Revolution* (Oct.-Dec. 1974), 26:25–26; Bruce Dancis, "Socialism and Women in the United States, 1900–1917" *Socialist Revolution* (Jan.-March 1976) 27:93–94; Dolores Hayden, *The Grand Domestic Revolution* (Cambridge: MIT Press, 1980).

36. John Spargo, in Dancis, "Socialism and Women."

37. Dancis, *ibid.*

38. Sally Miller, *Victor Berger and the Promise of Constructive Socialism, 1910–1920* (Westport, Conn.: Greenwood Press, 1973).

11. COMPROMISE LOST

1. See the discussion of these critiques in Bennett Burger, *Working Class Suburb* (Berkeley: University of California Press, 1960).

2. Raymond Vernon, *The Myth and Reality of Our Urban Problems* (Cambridge: Harvard University Press, 1964).

3. *Ibid.*

4. Herbert Gans, *The Urban Villagers* (New York: The Free Press, 1962).

6. Raymond Vernon, "The Changing Economic Function of the Central City," in *Metropolis 1985* (Cambridge: Harvard University Press, 1960).

6. For discussion of theories of the "slum" as incubator of poverty, see Lee Rainwater and Yancey, *The Moynihan Report and the Politics of Controversy* (New Brunswick, N.J.: Transaction Books, 1967); Daniel P. Moynihan, *Maximum Feasible Misunderstanding* (New York: Free Press, 1969); William Ryan, *Blaming the Victim.* On integration approaches, see Luigi Laurenti, *Property Values and Race* (Berkeley: University of California Pess, 1960): Linda and Paul Davidoff and Neil Gold, "The Suburbs Have to Open Their Gates," *New York Times Magazine*, November 7, 1971; Matthew Edel, "Development vs. Dispersal: Approaches to Ghetto Poverty," in M. Edel and J. Rothenberg, eds., *Readings in Urban Economics* (New York: Macmillan, 1972, pp. 307–24).

7. E. S. Mason, as quoted in the *Boston Globe*, August 9, 1970.

8. See Edel, "Development vs. Dispersal"; Thomas Vietorisz, *The Economic Development of Harlem* (New York: Praeger, 1970); Arthur Baustein and Geoffrey Faux, *Star Spangled Hustle* (Garden City: Doubleday, 1972).

9. Herbert Gans, *The New York Times,* February 12, 1977, p. 21.

10. K. N. Schaefer and Elliott Sclar, *Access for All* (New York: Columbia University Press, 1980).

11. See especially Fred Hirsch, *Social Limits to Growth* (Cambridge: Harvard University Press, 1976).

12. Richard Sennett and Jonathan Cobb, interviewing workers in the inner-ring neighborhoods of Boston, found that many people turned inward, accepting psychological blame for not doing better. Others turned their anger on their children or their parents, blaming them for the family's lack of economic mobility. Still others turned their anger on the groups slightly behind them in status and income, whose competition for jobs, education, or suburban land they felt to be a threat. However, the response was not always sullen or apathetic. In many cases, communities did organize to defend themselves, to defend the social and property values in which they felt they had an investment and against those they perceived as the rulers of the system. See Richard Sennett and Jonathan Cobb, *The Hidden Injuries of Class* (New York: Knopf, 1972); also, Gordon Fellman and Barbara Brandt, *The Deceived Majority* (New Brunswick, New Jersey: Transaction Books, 1973).

13. Karl E. Tauber and Alma F. Taeuber, *Negroes in Cities* (Chicago: Aldine, 1965).

14. James E. Teele, *Evaluating School Busing: A Case Study of Boston's Operation Exodus* (New York: Praeger, 1973).

15. Frank S. Levy, *The Racial Imbalance Act of Massachusetts*, Ph.D. thesis, Yale University, 1969.

16. Herman Thomas, *Education in the Black Community: A Study of the Boston Public Schools*. Master's Thesis, Queens College, 1974.

17. Langley C. Keyes, Jr., *The Rehabilitation Planning Game* (Cambridge: MIT Press, 1969).

18. Mel King, *Chain of Change* (Boston: South End Press, 1981).

19. Alan Lupo, Frank Colcord and Edmund P. Fowler, *Rites of Way* (Boston: Little, Brown and Co., 1971); Dorothy Nelkin, *Jetport: The Boston Airport Controversy* (New Brunswick: Transaction Books, 1974); Ralph Gakenheimer, *Transportation Planning as Response to Controversy: The Boston Case* (Cambridge: MIT Press, 1976); Fellman and Brandt, *Deceived Majority*. Another useful source is the film *Mission Hill and the Miracle of Boston*.

20. Gakenheimer, *Transportation Planning*.

21. Lupo et al., *Rites of Way*, p. 57.

22. Elliott D. Sclar, Ted Behr, Raymond Torto and Maralyn Edid, "Taxes, Taxpayers and Social Change," *Review of Radical Political Economies* (Spring 1974) 6(1):134–53.

23. Marya Levenson, "Comment on 'Racism and Busing in Boston,' " *Radical America* (May-June 1975) 9(3):71–74.

24. William J. Leary, School Superintendant of Boston, quoted in Robert Reinhold, "More Segregated Than Ever," *New York Times Magazine*, Sept. 30, 1973, pp. 35 *et seq*.

25. Jim Green and Allen Hunter, "Racism and Busing in Boston: An Editorial

Statement," *Radical America* (Nov.-Dec., 1974) 8(6):1–11; also in W. Tabb and C. Sawers, *Marxism and the Metropolitis* (New York: Oxford University Press, 1978), pp. 271–96.

26. Sclar, Edid et al., "Taxes."

27. *Ibid.*

28. *Ibid.*

29. First National Bank of Boston, *Look Out, Massachusetts* (pamphlet, 1972).

30. Bill Schecter, "Grassroots Report: Fighting Proposition 2½ in Massachusetts," *Dollars and Sense* (Dec. 1980) 62:15–17.

31. Diane B. Paul, *The Politics of the Property Tax* (Lexington, Mass.: D.C. Heath, 1975).

32. Gregory K. Palm, et al., "A Study of Rents in the Boston Metropolitan Area," unpublished report (Cambridge: MIT Dept. of Economics, 1969).

33. Urban Field Service and Urban Planning Aid, *Report on South End Urban Renewal Plan* prepared for Boston City Council Hearing, March 25, 1968.

34. Data were taken from Commonwealth of Massachusetts, Dept. of Corporations and Taxation, assessment statistics, and U.S. Census, 1970, 1980.

35. In the early 1980s, the value of single family homes rose less rapidly than such alternate assets as stocks, bonds, or gold, and only slightly exceeded the value increase for passbook savings accounts, *Fact* magazine, "Investment Report Card" March 1984.

36. Matthew Edel, "Home Ownership and Working Class Unity." *International Journal of Urban and Regional Research* (June 1982) 6(2):205–22.

37. The linkage between rent in different cities is treated theoretically in Andrew Broadbent, "An Attempt to Apply Marx's Theory of Ground Rent to Modern Urban Economy," unpublished paper, London: Center for Environment Studies, 1975.

38. Lester Thurow, *The Zero Sum Society* (New York: Basic Books, 1980).

39. David M. Gordon, "Up and Down the Long Roller Coaster," in Political Education Project, *U.S. Capitalism in Crisis* (New York: URPE, 1977); Robert Zevin, "The Political Economy of the American Empire, 1974," in U.R.P.E., *Radical Perspectives on the Economic Crisis of Monopoly Capitalism* (New York: U.R.P.E., 1975), pp. 131–37.

40. Frank Ackerman, *Reaganomics* (Boston: South End Press, 1981).

41. On the place of energy within possible economic restructuring, see Matthew Edel, "Energy and the Long Swing," *Review of Radical Political Economics* (1983).

42. David Harvey, "Class Monopoly Rent, Finance Capital, and the Urban Revolution," *Regional Studies* (1974) 8:252. See also Michael Stone, "The Housing Crisis, Mortgage Lending, and Class Struggle," *Antipode* (September, 1974) 7(2).

43. Michael Stone and Emily Achtenberg, *Hostage! Housing and the Massachusetts Fiscal Crisis* (Boston: Boston Community School, 1977).

44. Edel, "Rent Theory and Labor Strategy," *R.R.P.E.*, (Winter 1977) 9(4); Edel, "Home Ownership."

45. Nor can public service economies be considered a likely source of a new boom. See Edel, "Energy and the Long Swing."

46. Elliott Currie, Robert Dunn and David Fogarty, "The New Immiseration: Stagflation, Inequality, and the Working Class," *Socialist Review* Nov.-Dec. 1980) 10(6):8-9.

47. *Ibid.*

48. Peter Saunders, Domestic Property and Social Class, *International Journal of Urban and Regional Research* (June 1978), 2(2):242.

49. *Ibid.*

50. John Rex and Robert Moore, *Race, Community and Conflict* (London: Oxford University Press, 1967).

51. David Harvey, *Social Justice and the City* (Baltimore: Johns Hopkins University Press, 1973).

52. *Ibid.* See also David Harvey, "The Political Economy of Urbanization," in G. Gappert and Rose, *The Social Economy of Cities* (Beverly Hills: Sage, 1975).

53. Green and Hunter, "Rascism and Busing."

54. *Ibid.* The authors add: "The only hope for working-class unity in Boston and other segregated cities lies in a direct assault on segregation in all its forms and in an organized defense against racist attacks which segregation fosters. . . .

The implementation of busing, as one means of breaking down an important form of segregation, is a victory not only for the black struggle for equality but also for the working-class struggle for unity. . . . First of all, the breakdown of segregation raises the possibility of black-white cooperation for better education."

55. Levenson, "Comment on 'Racism and Busing.'"

APPENDIX B

1. The computations described here were performed by Alan Mathews who wrote the first draft of this appendix.

2. Martin J. Bailey, Richard F. Muth and Hugh Nourse, "A Regression Method for Real Estate Price Index Construction," in *American Statistical Association Journal* (December 1963); and Robert F. Engle, "De Facto Discrimination in Residential Assessments," in *National Tax Journal* (December 1975) 27(4):445-51.

3. This model is described by Robert Engle in "Construction of Property Indices," (MIT Department of Economics manuscript, April, 1970) and in Bailey, et al., *ibid.*

4. Robert E. Rebello, *Economic Software Package: User's Manual* (MIT Computer Center, November 1972).

5. For a mathematical explanation of the error problem, see Bailey, et al., "Regression Method."

APPENDIX C

1. This appendix is taken from a memorandum by Barbara Sproat which appears in its entirety in M. Edel and E. Sclar, "The Distribution of Real Estate Value Changes Measurement and Implications, Metropolitan Boston 1870–1970," *Boston: Studies in Urban Political Economy*, Working Paper #4.

2. The sample drawn for the city of Boston was larger so that we could break the data down by neighborhoods to differentiate assessment patterns in different areas of the city.

APPENDIX D

1. For a simple treatment of factor analysis, see Andrew L. Comrey, *A First Course in Factor Analysis* (New York: Wiley, 1973).

2. For example, the simple correlation between 1880 occupation and non-home wealth is 0.369. The first principal component gives weights on the two of .494 and .555, respectively. $.494 \times .555 = .272 = 74.2\%$ of .369. We say, then, that the first principal component captures nearly three-quarters of the common variance of occupation and wealth.

3. See Daniel Luria, "Trends in the Determinants Underlying the Process of Stratification: Boston, 1880–1930," *Review of Radical Economics* (1974) 6(2):174–193.

APPENDIX E

1. Stanley I. Kuntler, *Privilege and Creative Destruction: The Charles River Bridge Case* (Philadelphia: Lippincott, 1974).

2. Nathan Matthews, Jr. *The City Government of Boston* (Boston: Rockwell and Churchill, 1985) section 5.

3. Peter Skerry, *The Political Economy of the Metropolitan District Commission* (Lynn: Lynn Economic Opportunity, Massachusetts Public Finance Project).

4. Sclar, "The Public Financing of Transportation in the Greater Boston Area" unpublished Ph.D. dissertation, Tufts University, 1971.

5. *Ibid.*

6. Data are from *Transportation Facts for the Boston Area*, 1963, and from John Gardiner, *Traffic and the Police* (Cambridge: Harvard University Press, 1969).

7. Sclar, "Public Financing."

8. J. R. Meyer, J. Kain, and M. Wohl, *The Urban Transportation Problem* (Cambridge: Harvard University Press, 1965).

APPENDIX F

1. The cities are listed in Daniel Luria, *Suburbanization, Homeownership and Working Class Consciousness*, Ph.D. Dissertation, University of Massachusetts 1976.

2. Donald J. Bogue, *Population Growth in Standard Metropolitan Areas, 1900–*

1950 (Washington: Government Printing Office, 1953); Leo F. Schnore "The Growth of Metropolitan Suburbs" *American Sociological Review,* 22, (1957).

3. Ira Kipnis, *The American Socialist Movement, 1897–1912* (New York: Columbia University Press, 1952); Gerald Friedenberg, *Marxism in the United States,* Harvard University Ph.D. Dissertation 1964.

Select Bibliography

I. Publications of the Boston Suburbanization Project and Related Projects

A. Preliminary Published Materials

Chapman, Jere, Elliott Sclar and Raymond Torto. *The Rich Get Richer and the Rest Pay Taxes: A Massachusetts Tax Primer* Lynn: Massachusetts Public Finance Project, 1974.

Edel, Matthew. "Rent Theory and Labor Strategy: Marx, George and the Urban Crisis." *Review of Radical Political Economics* (Winter 1977) 9(4):1–15.

Edel, Matthew. "Home Ownership and Working Class Unity." *International Journal of Urban and Regional Research* (June 1982) 6(2):205–21.

Edel, Matthew, and Elliott Sclar, "The Distribution of Real Estate Value Changes: Metropolitan Boston, 1870–1970," *Journal of Urban Economics* (Fall 1975) 2(3):366–87.

Edel, Matthew, and Elliott Sclar. "Taxes, Spending and Property Values: Supply Adjustment in a Teibout-Oates Model." *Journal of Political Economy* (Sept.–Oct. 1974) 82(5):941–54.

Levenstein, Charles. "The Political Economy of Suburbanization: In Pursuit of a Class Analysis." *Review of Radical Political Economics* (Summer 1981) 13(2):23–31.

Luria, Daniel. "Trends in the Determinants Underlying the Process of Social Stratification: Boston 1880–1920." *Review of Radical Political Economics* (Winter 1974) 6(2):174–93.

Luria, Daniel. "Wealth, Capital and Power: The Social Meaning of Home Ownership." *Journal of Interdisciplinary History* (Autumn 1976) 7(2):261–82.

Luria, Daniel. "Suburbanization, Ethnicity and the Party Base: Spatial Aspects of the Decline of American Socialism." *Antipode* (1979) 11(3):76–80.

Schaeffer, K. H. and Elliott Sclar. *Access for All: Transportation and Urban Growth.* New York: Columbia University Press, 1980.

Sclar, Elliott, Ted Behr, Raymond Torto, and Maralyn Edid. "Taxes, Taxpayers and Social Change: The Political Economy of the State Sector." *Review of Radical Political Economics* (Spring 1974) 6(1):134–53.

B. Dissertations

Becerra, Rosina. "Does Equal Opportunity Mean Equal Access: A Study of the Relationship of a Student's Town of Residence and the Institution of Higher Education Attended." Ph.D. diss. Brandeis University, Florence Heller Graduate School for Advanced Studies in Social Welfare, 1975.

Brophy, Paul David. "Property Taxation Effects on Suburban Development." Masters. MIT, 1970.

Draisen, Marc D. "Regionalism versus Localism in Metropolitan Agencies: The Metropolitan District Commission as a Case Study." Masters, Brandies University, 1978.

Harran, Michael J. "Entrapment and the Somerville Schools." Cambridge-Goddard School, 1973.

Levenstein, Charles. "Class Suburbanization and Ethnic Homogenization: Towards a Theory of Social/Spatial Stratification." Ph.D. diss. MIT, 1975.

Luria, Daniel. "Suburbanization, Homeownership and Working Class Consciousness." Ph.D. diss. University of Massachusetts—Amherst, 1976.

Mathews, Alan. "A Study of Rehabilitated Homes in Cambridge." Masters, MIT, 1973.

Morris, Jane Goldstein. "Harrison Gray Otis and the Development of Boston Real Estate." Masters, Queens College, 1974.

Sclar, Elliott. "The Public Financing of Transportation in the Great Boston Area." Ph.D. diss. Tufts University, 1971.

Thomas, Herman K. "Education in the Black Community: A Study of the Boston Public Schools." Queens College, 1974.

C. *Boston: Studies in Urban Political Economy. Working Papers from NSF/NIMH Project*

Altman, Sandy, Steven Karp, Thomas Holzman, and Minna Strumpf. *Boston, Somerville and Lexington: A Study in Comparative Suburbanization.*

Dennen, Lisa. *Where the Other Half-Percent Lives.*

Dennen, Lisa and Barbara Sproat. *A Bedroom Community in Transition: Brookline, Massachusetts, 1870–1970.*

Edel, Matthew. *The Theory of Rent in Radical Economics.*

Edel, Matthew and Elliott Sclar. *Differential Taxation, Transportation, and Land Values in a Metropolitan Area: Boston, 1890–1970.*

Edel, Matthew and Elliott Sclar. *A Memorandum on the Entrapment Hypothesis.*

Edel, Matthew and Elliot Sclar. *Some Pitfalls of Suburbanization Policy.*

Edel, Matthew and Elliot Sclar. *Taxes, Spending and the Tiebout Hypothesis: What Did Oates Prove?*

Edel, Matthew and Elliot Sclar. *The Distribution of Real Estate Value Changes: Boston, 1870–1970.* Appendix by Barbara Sproat.

Edel, Matthew, Daniel Luria, and Elliott Sclar. *Bless Our (Mortgaged) Home.*

Goode, Dolores. *Intra-Urban Black Migration Patterns: Boston, 1638–1973.*

Holzman, Thomas. *Postwar Land Speculation in Middlesex County: A Look into the Activities of Cabot, Cabot, & Forbes.*

Huebsch, Sarah. *Women's Letters to the* Boston Globe, *1900–1970.*

Kersten, Stephen. *Housing Regulation and Reform in Boston, 1822–1924.*

Krushnic, Richard. *Post-War Industrial Development on Boston's Periphery.*

Lemos, Peter, with Daniel Luria. *Working Class Saving as Ruling Class Investment: The Rise of Massachusetts Banking.*

Levenstein, Charles. *Assimilation, Homogenization and Intermarriage.*

Levenstein, Charles. *Class, Assimilation and Suburbanization.*

Levenstein, Charles. *Homogenization of Ethnic Subcultures in a Working-Class Suburb.*

Levenstein, Charles. *A House Price Index for an Inner-Ring Suburb: Somerville, Massachusetts, 1870–1973.*

Levenstein, Charles. *Notes for a Theory of Social-Spatial Stratification.*

Levenstein, Charles. *Occupation, Home Ownership and Residential Persistance.*

Luria, Daniel. *All-America City as Inner-Ring Suburb: Somerville, 1870–1970.*

Luria, Daniel. *Stuck Inside of Boston with the Mobile Blues Again.*

Luria, Daniel. *Suburbanization, Ethnicity, and the Party Base: Spatial Aspects of the Decline of American Socialism.*

Luria, Daniel. *Toward an Analytic Measure of the Class Structure.*

Luria, Daniel. *Trends in the Determinants of the Stratification Process: Boston: 1880–1920.*

Luria, Daniel. *Wealth, Capital and Power: The Social Meaning of Home Ownership.*

Miller, Steven. *The Rise and Fall of the Boston Irish Political Machine.*

Sclar, Elliott, with the assistance of Donna Lind. *Age and Residential Location in Metropolitan Boston.*

Sproat, Barbara. *Henry Whitney's Streetcar Suburb: Brookline, 1870–1910.*

Zimmerman, Libby. *Economics, Child Care and the Family.*

D. Reports of the Massachusetts Public Finance Project

Attride, Anthony. "Property Tax Administration: A Case Study of Milton, Massachusetts."

Behr, Ted and Jere Chapman. "An Inquiry Into the Nature and Causes of Inequities in the System of Taxation in the Commonwealth of Massachusetts and Its Effect Upon the Economically Deprived."

Behr, Ted, Maralyn Edid, Raymond G. Torto, and Elliott Sclar. "The Graduated Income Tax Referendum in Massachusetts: League of Women Voters' Liberalism vs. Corporate Money."

Boelitz, Wendy. "Property Tax Administration in Quincy, Massachusetts."

Cater, Phyllis. "Property Tax Administration in Medford, Massachusetts,"

Chapman, Jere. "It's There! And It's Your Right!: An Introduction to Property Tax Research."

Chapman, Jere. "Let Them Eat Spaghetti!: An Inquiry Into the Political Ideology of Taxpayers' Perceptions."

Chapman, Jere. "The Political and Economic Implications of Property Tax Classification in Massachusetts."

Chapman, Jere. "Profile of the Lynn Municipal Research Group: A Political Analysis of Property Tax Research and Organizing."

Chapman, Jere. "Property Tax and Local Control: The Long Road to Reform."

Chapman, Jere. "Public Attitudes and Tax Reform: A Comparative Study of Massachusetts and Oregon Tax Referendum Experience."

Chapman, Jere and Ted Behr. "How To Do an Assessment-Sales Ratio Study: A Methodology Primer."

Chapman, Jere and Raymond G. Torto with Peter Stavros. "Property Tax Administration in Somerville, Massachusetts: How Fair Is It?"

Chester, Eric. "The Incidence of the Property Tax: Regressive or Progressive?"

Edel, Matthew. "Property Taxes and Local Expenditures: A Hundred Year View."

Edid, Maralyn. "Property Taxes and Property Tax Administration: A Case Study of Chelsea, Massachusetts.

Edid, Maralyn. "Revenue Sharing: Fact and Fiction."

Edid, Maralyn. "School Expenditure Inequalities: The Role of the Property Tax in Local Finance."

England, Richard. "Position Paper on Reform of School Finance in Massachusetts.

Eskowitz, Henry and Eileen Meeks. "Massachusetts' IDB Program: What Has It Accomplished?"

Greene, Timothy. "Revaluation of Real Property in Massachusetts Cities and Towns."

Greene, Timothy. "State Aid to Local Government in Massachusetts: An Historical and Statistical Study."

Greene, Timothy. "The Impact of Property Tax on Housing."

Harris, Anita. "Tax Reform in Massachusetts: Personalities, Pressures, and Politics."

Hellman, Daryl. "A Survey of Industrial Inducement Efforts and Their Application in Massachusetts."

Holzman, Thomas. "Municipal Employee Militance."

Lewis, J. Michael. "Property Tax Administration in Hingham, Massachusetts."

Moynihan, Francis X. Jr. "Property Tax Administration in Marblehead, Massachusetts."

Parlow, Robert. "Chelsea's Many Tanks: Property Tax Assessment of the Oil Storage Facilities in Chelsea, Massachusetts.

Paul, Diane. "Politics of the Property Tax."

Shirley, John and Raymond G. Torto. "Revolution in Waltham, Massachusetts: A Statistical Analysis."

Shirley, John M. "Property Assessment Revaluation and Property Tax Administration: A Case Study of Waltham, Massachusetts."

Silvia, John E. "State and Local Taxation of Financial Institutions."

Skerry, Peter. "The Metropolitan District Commission: A Historical Study of Metropolitan Government."

Slavin, Charles. "Profile and Analysis of the Massachusetts State Appellate Tax Board."

Stern, Hub. "Property Tax Appraisal Methods."

Sylvia, John E. "An Analysis of the Circuit-Breaker as Property Tax Relief in Massachusetts."

Torto, Raymond G. and Karl Wesolowski. "Property Tax Administration: How Fair Is It? A Case Study of Lynn, Massachusetts."

Vallely, Thomas. "Property Tax Administration in Lowell, Massachusetts."

II. Other Selected Works

A. References on Boston and Eastern New England

Abrams, Richard M. *Conservatism in a Progressive Era: Massachusetts Politics 1900–1912.* Cambridge: Harvard University Press, 1964.

Bacon, Edwin M. *The Book of Boston.* Boston: The Book of Boston Co., 1916, p. 112.

Bedford, Henry F. *Socialism and the Workers in Massachusetts, 1886–1912.* Amherst: University of Massachusetts Press, 1966.

Blodgett, Geoffrey. *The Gentle Reformers: Massachusetts Democrats in the Cleveland Era.* Cambridge: Harvard University Press, 1960.

Bushee, Frederick A. *Ethnic Factors in the Population of Boston.* New York: Arno Press, 1970.

Chamberlain, Allen. *Beacon Hill: Its Ancient Pastures and Early Mansions.* Boston: Houghton, Mifflin, 1925.

Culver, David M. "Tenement House Reform in Boston, 1846–1898." Ph.D. Diss. Boston: Boston University, 1972.

Curley, James Michael. *I'd Do It All Again: A Record of All My Uproarious Years*. Englewood Cliffs: Prentice Hall, 1947.

Curtis, J. G. *History of the Town of Brookline*. Boston: Houghton, Mifflin, 1933.

Elden, L. *The Boston Edison System*. Boston: Edison Electric Illuminating Co., 1900.

Engle, Robert F. "De Facto Discrimination in Residential Assessments." *National Tax Journal* (December, 1975), 27(4):445–51 ˙

Fellman, Gordon and Barbara Brandt. *The Deceived Majority*. New Brunswick, N.J.: Transaction Books, 1973.

Firey, Walter. *Land Use in Central Boston*. Reprint, New York: Greenwood Press, 1968.

Fried, Marc. *The World of the Urban Working Class*. Cambridge: Harvard University Press, 1973.

Gakenheimer, Ralph, *Transportation Planning as Response to Controversy: The Boston Case*. Cambridge: MIT Press, 1976.

Gans, Herbert. *The Urban Villagers*. New York: The Free Press, 1962.

Gardiner, John. *Traffic and the Police*. Cambridge: Harvard University Press, 1969.

Green, Jim and Allen Hunter. "Racism and Busing in Boston: An Editorial Statement." *Radical America* (Nov.–Dec., 1974), 8(6):1–11.

Hager, Louis P. *History of the West End Street Railway*. Boston: Louis P. Hager, 1892.

Handlin, Oscar. *Boston's Immigrants: A Study in Acculturation*. Rev. ed., Cambridge: Harvard University Press, 1959.

Harevan, Tamara K. and Randolph Langenbach. *Amoskeag: Life and Work in an American Factory City*. New York: Pantheon, 1978.

Hart, Albert. *Commonwealth History of Massachusetts*, New York: The States Publishing Co., 1930.

Huse, Charles Phillips. *The Financial History of Boston from May 1, 1826 to January 31, 1905*. Reprint, New York: Russell and Russell, 1967, ch. 1.

Keyes, Langley C. Jr. *The Rehabilitation Planning Game*. Cambridge: M. Press, 1969.

Kiley, John C. "Changes in Realty Values in the Nineteenth and Twentieth Centuries." *Bulletin of the Business Historical Society*, June 1941.

King, Mel. *Chain of Change*. Boston: South End Press, 1981.

Kirber, Harold. *The Architecture of Charles Bulfinch.* Cambridge: MIT Press, 1969.

Kuntler, Stanley I. *Privilege and Creative Destruction: The Charles River Bridge Case.* Philadelphia: Lippincott, 1974.

Lamb, Robert K. "The Entrepeneur and the Community." In William Miller, ed. *Men in Business.* Cambridge: Harvard University Press, 1952.

Lane, Roger. *Policing the City.* Cambridge: Harvard University Press, 1967.

Levenson, Marya. "Comment on 'Racism and Busing in Boston.'" *Radical America* (May–June 1975) 9(3):71–74.

Levy, Frank S. *The Racial Imbalance Act of Massachusetts.* Ph.D. diss. Yale University, 1969.

Lockridge, Kenneth A. *A New England Town, the First Hundred Years: Dedham, Massachusetts, 1736–1836* (New York: W. W. Norton, 1970.

Lupo, Alan. Frank Colcord, and Edmund P. Fowler. *Rites of Way.* Boston: Little, Brown, 1971.

Mann, Arthur. *Yankee Reformers in an Urban Age: Social Reform in Boston, 1880–1900.* New York: Harper and Row, 1954.

Mason, Edward S. *The Street Railway in Massachusetts: The Rise and Decline of an Industry.* Cambridge: Harvard University Press, 1932.

Matthews, Nathan Jr. *The City Government of Boston.* Boston: Rockwell and Churchill, 1895.

Morison, Samuel Eliot. *Harrison Gray Otis, 1765–1848: The Urbane Federalist.* Boston: Houghton Mifflin, 1969, pp. 29–41.

Nelkin, Dorothy. *Jetport: The Boston Airport Controversy.* New Brunswick: Transaction Books, 1974.

Oakes, Eugene E. *Studies in Massachusetts Town Finance.* Cambridge: Harvard University Press, 1937.

Paul, Diane B. *The Politics of the Property Tax.* Lexington, Mass.: D.C. Heath, 1975.

Porter, Alexander S. "Changes of Values in Real Estate in Boston." *Collections' of the Bostonian Society* (1888) 1(3):57–70.

Powell, Chilton. *Puritan Village: the Formation of a New England Summer Town.* Middletown, Connecticut: Wesleyan University Press, 1963.

Rodwin, Lloyd. *Housing and Economic Progress*. Cambridge: Harvard University Press, 1961.

Rowe, Henry K. *Tercentary History of Newton 1630–1930*. Newton: City of Newton, Government 1930.

Schnore, Leo F. and Peter R. Knights. "Residence and Social Structure: Boston in the Ante-Bellum Period." in S. Thernstrom and R. Sennett, *Nineteenth Century Cities*, pp. 247–57. New Haven: Yale University Press, 1971.

Seabury, Carl and Stanley Paterson. *Merchant Prince of Boston: Colonel T. H. Perkins, 1764–1854*. Cambridge: Harvard University Press, 1971.

Sennett, Richard and Jonathan Cobb. *The Hidden Injuries of Class*. New York: Knopf, 1972.

Shurtleff, Nathaniel B. *Topographical and Historical Description of Boston*. Boston: Rockwell and Churchill, 1891.

Stone, Michael and Emily Achtenberg. *Hostage! Housing and the Massachusetts Fiscal Crisis*. Boston: Boston Community School, 1977.

Teele, James E. *Evaluating School Busing: A Case Study of Boston's Operation Exodus*. New York: Praeger, 1973.

Thernstrom, Stephan. *Poverty and Progress*. New York: Atheneum, 1969.

Thernstrom, Stephan. *The Other Bostonians: Poverty and Progress in the American Metropolis, 1880–1970*. Cambridge: Harvard University Press, 1973.

Trout, Charles H. *Boston, The Great Depression and the New Deal*. New York: Oxford University Press, 1977.

Van de Woystyne, Royal S. *State Control of Local Finance in Massachusetts*. Cambridge: Harvard University Press, 1934.

Warner, Sam Bass Jr., *Streetcar Suburbs: The Process of Growth in Boston, 1870–1900*. Cambridge: Harvard University Press, 1960.

Whitehill, Walter Muir. *Boston: A Topographical History*, 2d ed, Cambridge: Harvard University Press, 1968.

Whitmore, Henry. "Real Estate Values in Boston." With comments by James R. Carrey and Dudley P. Bailey, *American Statistical Association* n. s. (March 1896) 37:1–17.

Wolfe, Albert B. *The Lodging House Problem in Boston*. Cambridge: Harvard University Press, 1906.

Woods, R. *The City Wilderness*. Boston: Houghton-Mifflin, 1898.

Woods, Robert A. and Albert J. Kennedy. *The Zone of Emergence: Ob-*

servations of the Lower, Middle and Upper Working Class Communities of Boston, 1905–1919, 2d ed. Cambridge, MIT Press, 1969.

B. References on Politics and Economics of Homeownership and of Inequality

Abrams, Charles. *Home Ownership for the Poor.* New York: Praeger, 1970, p. 197.

Alonso, William. *Location and Land Use.* Cambridge: Harvard University Press, 1964.

Angotti, Thomas. "The Housing Question: Engels and After." *Monthly Review* (Oct. 1977): 39–61.

Aronovici, Carol. *Housing the Masses.* New York: Wiley, 1939.

Bailey, Martin J., Richard F. Muth and Hugh Nourse. "A Regression Method for Real Estate Price Index Construction." In *American Statistical Association Journal* (December 1963).

Bauer, Catherine. *Modern Housing.* Boston: Houghton Mifflin, 1934.

Berg, Ivar. *Education and Jobs: The Great Training Robbery.* New York: Praeger, 1972.

Bluestone, Barry, and Bennett Harrison. *The Deindustrialization of America.* New York: Basic Books, 1982.

Blumberg, Paul. *Inequality in an Age of Decline.* New York: Oxford University Press, 1980.

Bowles, Samuel and Herbert Gintis. *Schooling in Capitalist America.* New York: Basic Books, 1976.

Brandes, Stuart D. *American Welfare Capitalism.* Chicago: University of Chicago Press, 1976, pp. 38–39.

Brecher, Jeremy. *Strike!* Greenwich, CT: Fawcett, 1973.

Burger, Bennett. *Working Class Suburb.* Berkeley: University of California Press, 1960.

Caminos, Horacio, John F. C. Turner, and John A. Steffian. *Urban Dwelling Environments.* Cambridge: MIT Press, 1969, pp. vi, ix.

Chinoy, Ely. *Automobile Workers and the American Dream.* Boston: Beacon Press, 1955.

Cowan, Paul. *The Making of an Un-American.* New York: Viking Press, 1970, p. 119.

Ibid. Cf. Paul Cowan, "Wallace in Yankeeland: The Invisible Revolution." *Village Voice* (July 18, 1968), 13(40):1, 17–19.

Currie, Elliott, Robert Dunn, and David Fogarty. "The New Immiseration Stagflation, Inequality, and the Working Class." *Socialist Review* (Nov.–Dec. 1980) 10(6):54.

Dancis, Bruce. "Socialism and Women in the United States, 1900–1917." *Socialist Revolution* 7 (Jan.–March 1976) 27:93–94.

Dean, J. P. *Home Ownership: Is It Sound?* New York: Harper, 1945.

Dear, Michael, and A. J. Scott. *Urbanization and Urban Planning in Capitalist Society.* London: Methuen, 1981.

Edel, Matthew. "Capital, Profit and Accumulation: The Perspectives of Karl Marx and Henry George Compared." In Richard Lindholm, ed. *Land Value Taxation: The Progress and Poverty Centenary.* Madison: University of Wisconsin Press, 1982, pp. 205–220.

Edel, Matthew and Jerome Rothenberg, eds., *Readings in Urban Economics.* New York: Macmillan, 1972.

Ehrenreich, Barbara and Deirdre English. "The Manufacture of Housework." *Socialist Review* (Oct.–Dec. 1974) 26:27.

Engels, Frederick. *The Condition of the Working Class in England.* Moscow: Progress Publishers, n.d.

Engels, Frederick. *The Housing Question.* New York: International Publishers, n.d.

Freeman, Richard B. *The Overeducated American.* New York: Academic Press, 1976.

Friedberg, Gerald. "Marxism in the United States." Ph.D. diss. Harvard University, 1964.

Gaffney, Mason. "Adequacy of Land as a Tax Base." In Daniel Holland, ed. *The Assessment of Land Value.* Madison, Wisc.: University of Wisconsin Press, 1970, pp. 157–212.

George, Henry. *Progress and Poverty.* New York: Modern Library, 1938.

Gordon, David M. *Theories of Poverty and Underemployment.* Lexington, Mass.: D. C. Heath, 1974.

Gorelick, Sherry. "Undermining Hierarchy: Problems of Schooling in Capitalist America," *Monthly Review* (October, 1977), pp. 20–36.

Gorz, Andre. *Strategy for Labor* (Boston: Beacon Press, 1964).

Haar, Charles M. ed. *An End to Innocence: A Suburban Anthology.* Glenview, Ill.: Scott Foresman and Co., 1972.

Halbert, Blanche ed. *The Better Homes Manual.* Chicago: University of Chicago Press, published in cooperation with *Better Homes in America,* 1931, pp. 44–45.

Harvey, David. *Social Justice and the City.* Baltimore: Johns Hopkins University Press, 1973.

Harvey, David. "The Political Economy of Urbanization in Advanced Capitalism." In Gappert and Rose. *The Social Economy of Cities.* Beverly Hills: Sage, 1975.

Hayden, Dolores. *The Grand Domestic Revolution.* Cambridge: MIT Press, 1980

Herreshoff, David. *The Origins of American Marxism.* New York: Monad Press, 1973.

Hirsch, Fred. *Social Limits to Growth.* Cambridge: Harvard University Press, 1976.

Hoyt, Homer. *100 Years of Land Values in Chicago.* Chicago: University of Chicago Press, 1963.

Jackson, Anthony. *A Place Called Home.* Cambridge: MIT Press, 1976.

Jencks, Christopher. *Inequality.* New York: Basic Books, 1974.

Kipnis, Ira. *The American Socialist Movement 1897–1912.* New York: Columbia University Press, 1952.

Kolko, Gabriel. *Railroads and Regulation, 1877–1916.* Princeton: Princeton University Press, 1965.

Lampman, Robert. *The Share of Top Wealth Holders in National Wealth 1922–1957.* Princeton: Princeton University Press, 1962.

Lipietz, Alain. *Le Tribut Foncier Urbain.* Paris: Maspero, 1974.

Lipset, S. M. and R. Bendix. *Social Mobility in Industrial Society.* Berkeley: University of California Press, 1967.

Lubove, Roy. *Community Planning the 1920s.* Pittsburgh: University of Pittsburgh Press, 1963, ch. 1.

Lubove, Roy. *The Progressives and the Slums.* Pittsburgh: Pittsburgh University Press, 1962.

Marcuse, Herbert. *One-Dimensional Man.* Boston: Beacon Press, 1964.

Marcuse, Peter. "Home Ownership for Low Income Families." *Land Economics* (May 1962).

Marglin, Stephen A. "What Do Bosses Do?—Part II." *Review of Radical Political Economics,* (1975), 7(1):22–23.

Marx, Karl. *Capital.* New York: International Publishers, 1967.

Marx, Karl. "On the Question of Free Trade." In *The Poverty of Philosophy*. Moscow: Foreign Language Publishing House, 1956.

Marx, Karl. *Theories of Surplus Value*. Moscow: Progress Publishers, 1963.

McKenzie, Roderick D. *The Metropolitan Community*. New York: McGraw Hill, 1933.

Miller, Sally. *Victor Berger and the Promise of Constructive Socialism, 1910–1920*. Westport, Conn.: Greenwood Press, 1973.

Muraskin, William. "The Social Control Theory in American History: A Critique," *Journal of Social History* (1976) 9(4).

Nisonoff, Laurie. "Bread and Roses: The Proletarianization of Women Workers in New England Textile Mills: 1827–1848." *Historical Journal of Massachusetts* (Jan. 1981) 9(1):3–14.

Parson, Don. "The Development of Redevelopment." *International Journal of Urban and Regional Research* (Sept. 1983) 6(3):393–413.

Perin, Constance. *Everything in Its Place*. Princeton: Princeton University Press, 1978, p. 32.

Piven, Frances Fox and Richard A. Cloward. *Regulating the Poor*. New York: Random House, 1971.

Rex, John, and Robert Moore. *Race, Community and Conflict*. London: Oxford University Press, 1967.

Ryan, William. *Blaming the Victim*. New York: Pantheon, 1971.

Saunders, Peter. Domestic Property and Social Class. *International Journal of Urban and Regional Research* (June 1978) 2(2):242.

Schwartz, Joel. "Evolution of the Suburbs." In Philip Dolce, *Suburbia: The American Dream and Dilemma*. Garden City: Anchor Books, 1976, pp. 13–18.

Sennett, Richard, ed. *Classic Essays on the Culture of Cities*. New York: Appleton-Century-Crofts, 1969, pp. 91–130.

Sennett, Richard. "Middle-Class Families and Urban Violence: The Experience of a Chicago Community in the 19th Century." In Stephan Thernstrom and Richard Sennett, eds. *Nineteenth Century Cities: Essays in the New Urban History*, New Haven: Yale University Press, 1969.

Shelton, John P. "The Cost of Renting vs. Owning a Home." *Land Economics* (February 1968).

Speek, Peter Alexander. *The Single Tax and the Labor Movement.* Madison: University of Wisconsin, 1977.

Stave, Bruce M. ed. *Socialism and the Cities.* Port Washington, N.Y.: Kennikat Press, 1975.

Sternlieb, George. *The Tenement Landlord.* New Brunswick, N.J.: Rutgers University Press, 1966.

Stimpson, Catherine R. et.al., eds. *Women and the American City.* Chicago: University of Chicago Press, 1980.

Stone, Michael. "The Housing Crisis, Mortgage Lending, and Class Struggle." *Antipode* (September, 1974) 7(2).

Szymanski, Albert. "Trends in the American Working Class." *Socialist Revolution* (July–August 1972) 10:116.

Tabb, William V. and Larry Sawers, eds. *Marxism and the Metropolis.* New York: Oxford University Press, 1978, pp. 25–63.

Tauber, Karl E. and Alma F. Taeuber. *Negroes in Cities.* Chicago: Aldine, 1965.

Thomas, Brinley. *Migration and Economic Growth.* Cambridge: Cambridge University Press, 1973.

Thurow, Lester. *Generating Inequality.* New York: Basic Books.

U.R.P.E. *Radical Perspectives on the Economic Crisis of Monopoly Capitalism.* New York: U.R.P.E., 1975.

U.S. Bureau of Labor Statistics. *Rent or Buy?* Bulletin 1823. Washington: G.P.O., 1974.

Valentine, Charles. *Culture and Poverty.* Chicago: University of Chicago Press, 1968.

Vernon, Raymond. *The Myth and Reality of Our Urban Problems.* Cambridge: Harvard University Press, 1964.

Weinstein, James. *The Corporate Ideal in the Liberal State.* Boston: Beacon Press, 1968.

Weinstein, James. *The Decline of Socialism in America.* New York: Monthly Review Press, 1967.

Wright, Gwendolyn. *Building the Dream: A Social History of Housing in America.* New York: Pantheon, 1981.

Willis, Ellen. "Consumerism and Women." *Socialist Revolution* (May–June, 1970) 1(3):76–82.

Zaretsky, Eli. "Capitalism, the Family and Personal Life." *Socialist Revolution* (1973) 13(14):106–112.

Index

The Columbia History of Urban Life

Kenneth T. Jackson, *General Editor*